Cave Biology

Biospeleology, the study of organisms that live in caves, has a tremendous potential to inform many aspects of modern biology; yet this area of knowledge remains largely anchored in neo-Lamarckian views of the natural world in both its approaches and jargon. Written for graduate students and academic researchers, this book provides a critical examination of current knowledge and ideas on cave biology, with emphasis on evolution, ecology, and conservation. Aldemaro Romero provides a historical analysis of ideas that have influenced biospeleology, discusses evolutionary phenomena in caves, from cave colonization to phenotypic and genotypic changes, and integrates concepts and knowledge from diverse biological viewpoints. He challenges the conventional wisdom regarding the biology of caves, and highlights urgent questions that should be addressed in order to get a better and more complete understanding of caves as ecosystems.

ALDEMARO ROMERO is Chair and Professor in the Department of Biological Sciences at Arkansas State University. He has authored more than 500 publications and his interests lie in questions in science that require an interdisciplinary approach.

Cave Biology
Life in Darkness

ALDEMARO ROMERO
Arkansas State University

Main Photography by DANTÉ FENOLIO, Ph.D.

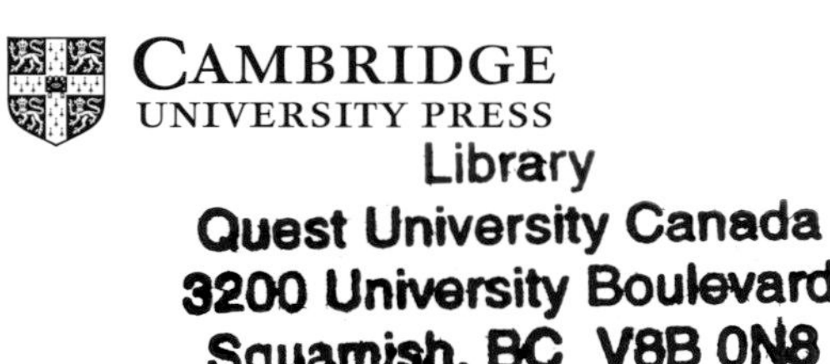

CAMBRIDGE
UNIVERSITY PRESS

CAMBRIDGE UNIVERSITY PRESS
Cambridge, New York, Melbourne, Madrid, Cape Town, Singapore, São Paulo, Delhi

Cambridge University Press
The Edinburgh Building, Cambridge CB2 8RU, UK

Published in the United States of America by Cambridge University Press, New York

www.cambridge.org
Information on this title: www.cambridge.org/9780521828468

First published 2009

Printed in the United Kingdom at the University Press, Cambridge

A catalog record for this publication is available from the British Library

Library of Congress Cataloging in Publication data
Romero Díaz, Aldemaro.
Cave biology : life in darkness / Aldemaro Romero ; main photography by Danté Fenolio.
p. cm.
Includes bibliographical references.
ISBN 978-0-521-82846-8 (hardback : alk. paper)
1. Biospeleology. I. Title.
QH89.R66 2009
578.75′84 – dc22 2009011364

ISBN 978-0-521-82846-8 hardback
ISBN 978-0-521-53553-3 paperback

To my wife Ana and my daughters Jessica and Andrea, who have accompanied me on so many trips to caves around the world.

Contents

The colour plates are between pages 178 and 179.

Preface

Let me say from the outset that this book will challenge much of the conventional wisdom regarding the biology of caves. There are several reasons for that. As the reader will perceive throughout the text, biospeleology has tremendous potential to inform many aspects of modern biology, yet this area of knowledge remains largely anchored in non-neo-Darwinian views of the natural world in both its approaches and its jargon. Therefore the ideas I present here are likely to create controversy in some quarters, but that is one of the approaches of science: to generate discussions that hopefully will illuminate many aspects of the workings of nature.

The reader should not expect an attempt to condense everything known about cave biology; this book is not written with an encyclopedic mindset. What this book is all about is a critical examination of our current knowledge and ideas regarding cave biology, with an emphasis on the areas of evolution, ecology, and conservation. To that end I have selected material for the discussion that is central to those topics while taking a critical thinking approach to what is considered conventional wisdom in this subject.

The book begins with a historical analysis of ideas that have influenced biospeleology and that have been generated by researchers working in that area. Thus the aim of Chapter 1 is to give the historical and philosophical background to why I think cave biology has yet to reach its full potential.

Chapter 2 deals with the biodiversity of hypogean organisms (both cave and phreatic). This chapter has three main objectives: (1) to show the enormous diversity of cave organisms, which goes well beyond the ones that have been categorized by many authors as 'true cavernicoles'; (2) to update the reader on the progress that has been made in the study of those groups; and (3) to highlight some of the most interesting biological phenomena among the hypogean biodiversity that will be discussed later in the book.

Chapter 3 deals with evolutionary phenomena in caves, from cave colonization to phenotypic and genotypic changes. Here, I advance ideas that, although well known in mainstream biology, have been, in my opinion, overlooked by many practitioners of biospeleology.

Chapter 4 has to do with the ecology of caves. My approach to this topic also aims to integrate concepts and knowledge from diverse biological viewpoints. I do not devote much space to aspects of the physical environment (autoecology) unless they are directly related to the discussion at hand. For that, the reader should refer him/herself to some of the literature cited in the book. Therefore the scope of the book is in the area of ecology defined as, "the biology of ecosystems" (*sensu* Margalef 1974). Because there have been so few modern ecological studies carried out in caves, a great deal of the discussion in this chapter is theoretical in nature while trying to point out the major areas in which we need more research.

Chapter 5 deals with conservation of the cave environment and its biota. Here, I present an integrated approach to the issue by using multiple examples from around the world with the underlying message that caves are both unique and fragile natural laboratories whose biota is being rapidly modified by humans.

I finish the book with an epilogue in which I try to point out some of the most urgent questions I think we should address in order to attain a better and more complete understanding of caves as ecosystems.

I have also added an appendix with a glossary of terms frequently employed in biospeleology. The reader not familiar with the biospeleology literature will find that cave biologists have developed a vocabulary that is hard to understand; in many ways, this reflects the typological and epistemological confusion that dominates biospeleology.

I hope you will enjoy the book. I certainly enjoyed researching for it and putting together the ideas presented here.

Acknowledgments

I want to thank a number of people who contributed to this book. First my most sincere thanks go to Dr Danté Fenolio, who donated the majority of the pictures used in this book. Ms Amy Awai-Barber drew the figure of a wingless cave cricket from a photograph of the original bone.

Several of my colleagues at Arkansas State University (ASU) read portions of the original manuscript and made valuable suggestions: Dr David F. Gilmore (bacteria), Dr Marty Huss (fungi), Dr Staria Vanderpool (plants), Dr Alan Christian (bivalves), Dr Tanja McKay (insects), and Dr Jim Bednarz (birds). Some graduate students at ASU also made similar contributions in their areas of work: David Hayes (gastropods) and Stephen Brandebura (mammals). Dr Joy Trauth, also from ASU, read many sections of the original manuscript and made valuable contributions in terms of style and clarity.

Special thanks to Professor Michael B. Usher, of the School of Biological and Environmental Sciences at the University of Stirling, who invited me to write this book and who, with a great deal of patience as editor of this series for Cambridge University Press, guided me with ideas and encouragement in what ended up being a very long but rewarding process.

Andrej Kranjc provided unpublished information about Luka Čeč.

I also thank my students in the two biospeleology courses I taught at Arkansas State University while writing this book. My interactions with them were highly useful and they provided me with some insights regarding many of the ideas I present in this book: Jane Anfinson, Stephen Brandebura, Michel Conner, Jason Craft, Josh Engelbert, Tiffany Hollinger, Kristen Irwin, Tracy L. Klotz, Raven Lawson, Kapil Mandrekar, Charles McDowell, Jacqueline McVey, Elizabeth Medlin, Robert Neal, Melanie Partin, Melissa Patrick, John Rains, Jacob Sawyer, Corey Shaffer, Jonathon Smith, Nathan Stephens, John Stewart, Granville Vaughan, Haley Widby, and Jarret Wright.

Thanks also to Dr Peter Luykx of the University of Miami for his thoughtful comments on my ideas about the evolution of cave fauna. Finally I want to thank my graduate adviser and colleague, Dr Steven M. Green, also of the University of Miami, for all the years of collaboration on this and other subjects.

1 · *A brief history of cave biology*

Some specialist books include a short introduction or brief chronology of the major historical events related to the branch of knowledge they cover. In this book there is an entire chapter on the history of biospeleological ideas. This is because it is essential to explain why biospeleology as a science in general, and our understanding of cave biology in particular, lags so far behind in mainstream organismal biology, particularly in terms of evolution and ecology. In fact, the author argues that this is so because many biospeleologists have failed to understand the historical framework in which this science has developed. This has led many to uncritically accept both concepts and lexicons that are inconsistent with current biological thought. Thus, this chapter provides a historical explanation of the ideological framework surrounding the majority of biospeleological research. This chapter also contains a number of illustrations (Figs. 1.1–1.5) related to the historical narrative presented here; more illustrations on this topic may be found in Romero (2001b).

1.1 Conceptual issues

An understanding of the history of any particular area of scientific inquiry is essential in order to really appreciate the significance of current knowledge and the voids that need to be filled. Most scientists are not particularly interested in pursuing such a task because the history of science is influenced by philosophy, politics, religion, and other expressions of human activities whose comprehension requires interdisciplinary approaches that go beyond what scientists have been normally trained for in universities. Yet, the history of science has demonstrated again and again that errors, fashion, and conceptual inertia have often delayed the development of certain areas of knowledge (Horder 1998). This chapter demonstrates that biospeleology is a perfect example of that.

There are two major ways to present the history of a particular branch of science: one is simply an uncritical chronological narrative, and the other is a critical examination of ideas that influenced the development of that area of study. Here, the second route is taken, because an appreciation of the historical background in which biospeleological ideas developed is necessary to understand why the full incorporation of modern biological thought in biospeleology has been delayed. As Ernst Mayr put it 'When scientists concentrate on the study of isolated objects and processes they seem to operate within an intellectual vacuum.' (Mayr 1982, pp. 66–7). Evidence is also provided that geography and religion played a major role in how this science evolved, first in the Protestant USA, and later in Catholic France.

To date there is still no comprehensive published history of biospeleology: Vandel (1964, pp. xxiii–xxiv) outlined a few historical facts; Barr (1966) wrote a brief history of biospeleology in the United States; Bellés (1991) wrote a largely chronological and anecdotal narrative on the subject; Shaw (1992) in his treatise on the history of speleology provided little information on biospeleology *per se*, and Romero's (2001b) article on hypogean fish research dealt mostly with the history of evolutionary ideas.

This chapter demonstrates that the most important issue regarding cave biology has been and continues to be the origin and evolution of cave fauna. Because of that, Darwinism is a central event in the development of biospeleology as a science but not for the reasons most people would assume. In fact, we can say that the history of biospeleology can hardly be depicted as another triumph of Darwinism as an idea. As will be shown, Charles Darwin, who was the first scientist who really tried to provide a scientific explanation about the origin of cave fauna and the phenomenon of what he called 'rudimentation' in the form of reduction and/or loss of the visual apparatus, espoused a rather neo-Lamarckian stance on the topic, to the point that his explanations were not fully Darwinian in the modern sense of the word. Furthermore, because of this and the fact that biospeleology developed mostly in France, where Lamarckism and its philosophical allies were very strong, not even the modern synthesis seriously changed the interpretation that most biospeleologists had of biological phenomena in caves.

Therefore, the following is a history of biospeleology focusing on five particular historic, intellectual, and/or geographic areas, each characterized by the dominance of a particular idea or set of ideas and mostly overlapping chronologically. These are: (1) pre-Darwinian thought (before 1859), (2) Darwinism and American neo-Lamarckism (1859–1919), (3) European selectionism and the death of the controversies

(1880–1921); (4) biospeleological ideas in France and elsewhere in continental Europe (1809–1950); and, (5) the impacts of the modern synthesis (1936–1947). There then follows a discussion of the roots of current intellectual inertia. This outline does not follow a strict chronological order but rather expresses the influence of culture on the development of ideas as delineated by geographic and intellectual boundaries. In order to make the narrative more fluid, this chapter contains a number of footnotes, which provide some biographical information on the major actors mentioned in the main text as well as explanations of philosophical terms so the reader can better appreciate the context in which many of these developments took place.

As the author explains the major ideas that have influenced biospeleology, he argues that many of those ideas by themselves do not represent paradigms in the Kuhnian sense of the word (Kuhn 1970, p. 10). They were never original ideas, but borrowed in both form and substance from neo-Lamarckism,and at the same time they ignored the pre-eminence of natural selection as an effective mechanism for the explanation of the evolution of cave organisms. Because of their restrictive nature and their incompatibility with the neo-Darwinian framework, these neo-Lamarckian ideas provide little opportunity for further elaboration and development.

1.2 Pre-Darwinian thought (before 1859)

1.2.1 From prehistory to mythology

Caves have been of human interest since prehistoric times, serving both as a shelter and as a source of artistic expression (Morgan 1943; Shaw 1992; Cigna 1993a; Romero 2001b). The earliest known human representation of cave fauna dates back to *c.* 22,000 YBP (years before the present) (Upper Paleolithic). It is a carved drawing of a wingless cave cricket, *Troglophilus* sp., on a bison (*Bison bonasus*) bone found in the Grotte des Trois Frères (Three Brothers Cave) in the central Pyrenees, France (Chopard 1928) (Fig. 1.1).

From the beginning of history humans have developed a close mythic–religious association among caves, the underworld, and death. Burials in caves have been common among many cultures (see, for example, Watson 1974; Stone 1995; Clottes 2003). The underworld or Hades (Άδης) in Greek mythology was believed to be the 'Kingdom of the Dead' to which one could gain access via caves (Mystakidou *et al.* 2004). Not surprisingly,

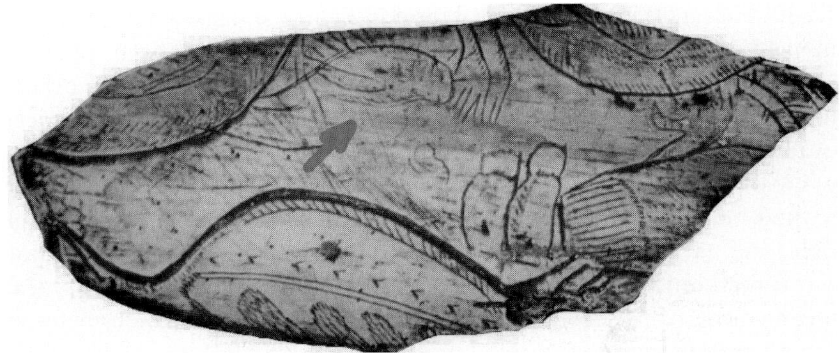

Figure 1.1 The earliest known human representation of cave fauna dates back to *c.* 22,000 YBP (years before the present) (Upper Paleolithic). It is a carved drawing of a wingless cave cricket, *Troglophilus* sp., on a bison (*Bison bonasus*) bone found in the Grotte des Trois Frères (Three Brothers Cave) in the central Pyrenees, France (Chopard 1928). Line drawing by Amy Awai-Barber from a photograph of the original. (See Plate 1.)

ideas about cave creatures were, from the beginning, a mixture of myth and reality. Dragons and other imaginary beasts had been described by many authors since before the invention of the printing press.

Such views of cave life survived up to the seventeenth century. For example, in 1665 a polymath Jesuit priest, Athanasius Kircher,[1] published what might be considered as the first book whose title gave the impression of being devoted solely to caves: *Mundus Subterraneus* (Kircher 1665). This was a gigantic, two-volume, folio-sized tome totaling 892 pages, whose second edition, published in Amsterdam in 1678, contained lengthy additions about caves in Switzerland, Austria, Italy, and the Greek Islands. This latter edition would be the one that achieved more popularity and became the standard geology text in the seventeenth century. Despite its title, Kircher dealt with many more topics than just caves, such as alchemy, chemistry, and metallurgy, among others.

Unfortunately, this was an extremely uncritical book full of inaccuracies and odd explanations of how water circulated underground (Fig. 1.2). It also contained descriptions of supposed cave fauna that included dragons, unicorns, and giants (he even provided illustrations of such alleged creatures). However, no blind and/or depigmented creature was included. Kircher was an uncritical repeater of other people's tales.

[1] *b.* Geisa, Germany, 2 May 1602; *d.* Rome, 28 November 1680.

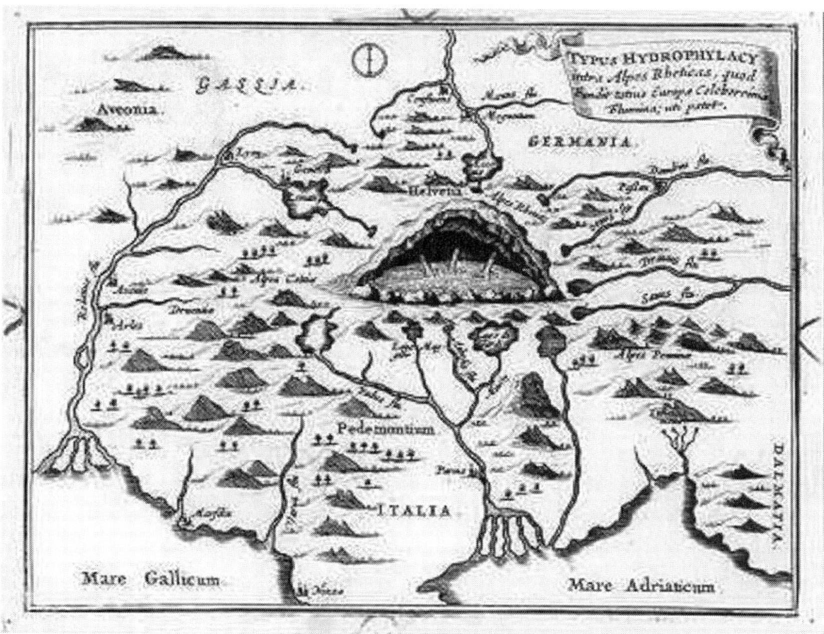

Figure 1.2 Illustration of 'hydrophylacy' from Kircher's *Mundus Subterraneus* (1665).

However, he was a very popular author because of his position as professor of the Collegio Romano (the Vatican's University), his reputation for being able to read 16 languages, having published 44 books (most of them huge in size, in large print and with impressive illustrations) on a great array of topics, and having written more than 2,000 manuscripts and letters (that have survived) (Romero 2000).

However, there is very little in Kircher's work of any value and his book is only a footnote in the history of biospeleology. The first real contributions would take place during the Renaissance in Europe and at the peak of ancient Chinese civilization.

1.2.2 European Renaissance and Ming Dynasty

Both the Renaissance (*c.* 1450–1650) in Europe and the Ming Dynasty (1368–1644) in China were characterized as eras of exploration. They provided the first significant contributions to our knowledge of the world fauna since antiquity. In Europe that was particularly true for animals that were new to the ones mentioned in the Bible or by ancient Greek and Roman authors.

The first written record of a true cave organism was in the form of a letter dated in 1537 written by the Venetian poet and philologist Giovanni Giorgio (GianGiorgio) Trissino.[2] In that letter he mentioned a cave amphipod ('*gamberetti picciolini*', probably *Niphargus costozzae*) from Monti Berici, Veneto, northern Italy. That letter was later reported by the Dominican friar and historian Leandro Alberti[3] in his most famous book, *Descrittione di Tutta Italia* (1550, pp. 471–2) in which he portrayed numerous Italian caves in detail (Hill 1974).

The first known written account of a cave fish came from China just three years after Trissino's letter. It was a travel report written in 1540 by Yi Jing Xie,[4] a local government official. This never published report was found in the records of Luxi County in 1905 by Ying Huang, the local governor, who had it engraved as an inscription on a stele (Y. Zhao, pers. comm.). In this document Xie referred to the hyaline fish(*Sinocyclocheilus hyalinus*) from the Alu caves, Yunnan, China. This fish was not collected for scientific purposes until 1991 and was not scientifically described until 1994 (Chen *et al.* 1994).

That these two discoveries took place almost simultaneously in Europe and China is not totally surprising since, as mentioned above, both cultures were experiencing their golden age of geographic discoveries. For China the sixteenth century, which coincided with the first half of the Ming Dynasty, was a century after the Chinese had embarked on impressive maritime explorations. However, by that time, the Yang Ming system of thought established by Shouren Wang[5] had replaced that of Xi Zhu.[6] Whereas Zhu, the most significant Confucian rationalist, insisted on the importance of observation and that learning should be based on reason and the 'investigation of things' (see his *Four Books*), Wang believed in the 'learning of the mind,' through intuition. This was, unfortunately, a reverse of the change in thought that occurred in Ancient Greece when the idealism of Plato,[7] based on the recognition

[2] *b*. Vicenza, Republic of Venice [today Italy], 8 July 1478; *d*. Rome, 8 December 1550.

[3] *b*. Bologna, Italy, 1479; *d*. Bologna, 1552? [4] Xie, Yi Jing (*b*. ?; *d*. ?).

[5] Wang, Shouren (Yangming) (*b*. Yuyao, Zhejian Province, China 1472; *d*. Nan'an, Jiangxi, China, 1528).

[6] Zhu, Xi (*b*. Yuxi, Fujian Province, China, 18 October 1130; *d*. China, 23 April 1200).

[7] *b*. Athens [?], 427 BC; *d*. Athens, 348/347 BC.

of tangible objects via individual perceptions was replaced by the logic based on observation by his student Aristotle.[8]

Aristotle's legacy would have a tremendous importance because it helped to establish one of the fundamental tenets of Western science (particularly in biology) after the Renaissance: knowledge via observation, not pure speculation. On the other hand, Chinese civilization declined owing to internal factors and invasions by Mongols and Westerners.

Thus, new scientific discoveries would continue to take place mostly in Europe instead of elsewhere, even when some of those discoveries represented unconfirmed findings and false starts. That was the case of the French engineer and inventor Jacques Besson,[9] who reported alleged underground little eels (*petites anguilles*) somewhere in Europe. In his book, Besson (1569) did not indicate the locality nor give a description of the fish in question. He did not mention the fish as being blind and/or depigmented (these would have been extraordinary characteristics to even the casual observer). Thus it is unclear whether Besson observed true hypogean fish, actual eels (*Anguilla anguilla*), or European freshwater fishes with eel-like bodies that are sympatric with the areas in which he traveled (France and Switzerland). Those possible fish families include Petromyzonidae, Cobitidae, Siluridae, and Clariidae (Blanc *et al.* 1971). Therefore, this description remains unconfirmed (Romero and Lomax 2000).

Another example of an unconfirmed report of underground fauna was that of Marc-René Marquis de Montalembert,[10] a French general and military engineer famous for devising simplified polygonal designs for fortresses that became the standard blueprint for European fortifications until the nineteenth century. Montalembert reported a blind, subterranean fish in a spring at Gabard, Angoumois, near one of his estates in southwestern France (Montalembert 1748). No specimen was preserved, and his description remains unconfirmed (Romero 1999a).

These casual reports (whether they were confirmed or not) were typical of the natural history of the Renaissance epitomized by 'bestiaries' and were later replaced by a more rigorous view of science.

[8] *b.* Stagira, Macedonia, [in today's northern Greece] 384 BC; *d.* Chalcis, Greece, 322 BC.

[9] *b.* Colombières, France, 1530?; *d.* Orléans, France, 1573.

[10] *b.* Angoulême, Charente, France, 16 July 1714; *d.* Paris, France, 29 March 1800.

1.2.3 Modern science (*c.* 1650–1800)

Unconfirmed reports and mythical tales typical of the Renaissance were followed in the seventeenth century by the flourishing of what has been termed 'modern science', characterized by direct observation and experimentation. During that time, in which precision in description and illustration of the natural world improved considerably, we see some good examples of new accounts of underground biota.

The first of those contributions was the earliest published reference to an underground fungus by the physician and naturalist Martin Lister,[11] (Lister 1674; Carr 1973). Lister received samples of this fungus from a Mr Jessops and called it '*Fungus subterraneus*'; it was found in a mine known as 'Old Man' in Castleton, Derbyshire, central England. Lister was part of the first generation of English naturalists extremely interested in describing and illustrating natural objects, particularly animals and rocks (Unwin 1995).

The next important contribution came from the Spanish Capuchin monk and missionary Francisco de Tauste.[12] He was the first to publish a reference to a cave bird, the oilbird (*Steatornis caripensis*). Tauste wrote his report based on his study of costumes and languages of the Chaimas, an ethnic group of Native Americans of northeastern Venezuela where these birds inhabit the Cueva del Guácharo (Oilbird Cave); (Tauste 1678; Longrás Otín 2002). This species, which had been exploited for many years by the Chaimas for its oil (Anonymous 1833), was not scientifically described until 1817 by the German polymath, explorer, and, above all, holistic naturalist Alexander von Humboldt,[13] based on a specimen he collected in 1799 (Humboldt 1817). Humboldt's other contributions to our knowledge of hypogean biota include the first description of underground plants in the mines of Freiberg (Humboldt 1793) and a description of a freshwater species of catfish, which he claimed originated from an underground volcano in Ecuador (Humboldt 1805) (Fig. 1.3), yet this claim remains unsubstantiated (Romero 2001a; Romero and Paulson 2001d).

The earliest species of cave animal that underwent intense and continuous scientific study was the first species of cave salamander ever described:

[11] *b.* Radclive, Buckinghamshire, England, April 1639; *d.* Epsom, Surrey, England, 2 February 1712.

[12] *né* Miguel Torralba de Rada; *b.* Tauste, Zaragoza, Spain, 1626; *d.* Santa María de Los Ángeles del Guácharo, Venezuela, 11 April 1685.

[13] *b.* Berlin, Germany, 14 September 1769; *d.* Berlin, 6 May 1859.

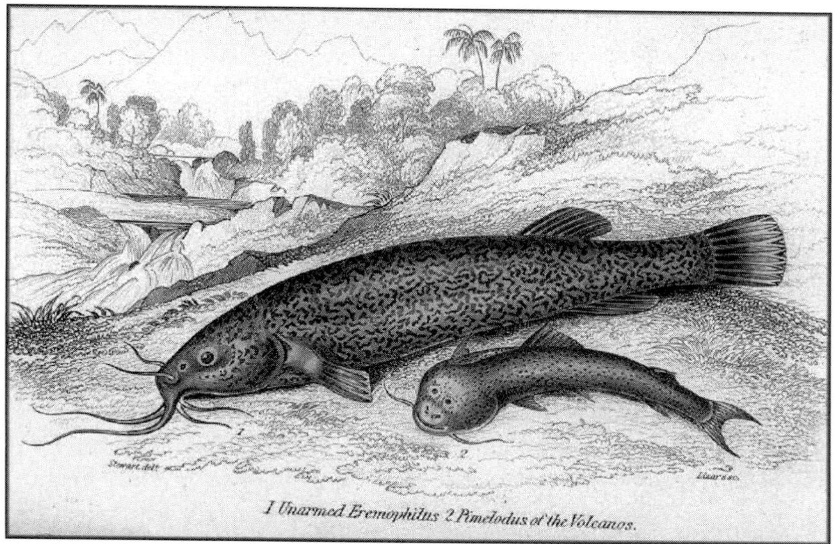

Figure 1.3 Illustration of the alleged subterranean fishes from a volcano in Ecuador by Humboldt (1805). (See Plate 2.)

Proteus anguinus from a region known then as Carniola, in today's Slovenia. This blind amphibian was originally identified as a 'dragon's larva' by the traveler and naturalist Janez Vajkard Valvasor[14] (Valvasor 1689). *P. anguinus* was later described scientifically by the Austrian naturalist Josephi Nicolai Laurenti[15] (Laurenti 1768) in the first post-Linnean description of a cave organism.

1.2.4 First professional studies before Darwin (1800–59)

The period between 1800 and 1859 is characterized by three major events. The first two were circumstantial in nature. One was the beginning of biology as a formal discipline and gave rise to the first generation of professional biologists; in fact, the term 'biology' began to be used around 1800 (McLaughlin 2002). The second was the discussions on evolution including the loss or rudimentation of organs such as eyes and pigmentation, a phenomenon common (but not unique) among many

[14] *b.* Ljubljana, Carniola (today Slovenia), 28 May 1641; *d.* Ljubljana, 19 September 1693.

[15] *b.* Vienna, Austria, 4 December 1735; *d.* Austria, 17 February 1805.

cave organisms. The third event was the scientific exploration of two of the most important cave systems in the world: the one occupying the southeastern regions of the United States epitomized by Mammoth Cave, and the other in what is now known as Slovenia. These factors combined to make the discussion on the biology of cave organisms an important aspect of the biological dialectic from Darwin until the end of the nineteenth century.

All this began with the first scientific description of the cave salamander, *Eurycea lucifuga* (Rafinesque 1822). This description was made by the French–American Constantine Samuel Rafinesque[16] (Fig. 1.4) when he was professor of botany and natural history at Transylvania University in Lexington, Kentucky, between 1819 and 1826. Rafinesque had been exploring the caves of that state since 1818 (Rafinesque 1832) and so was probably the first professional scientist to study them. He encountered a salamander that the locals called 'cave puppet' in 1821 in caves near Lexington. Kentucky encompasses a great deal of karst formations including large and complex cave systems. Although he did not provide too many details about the exact location, not only of the cave but in what portion of it he found this amphibian, this is one of the cave organisms most frequently encountered because it is usually seen near cave entrances. Thus, finding this salamander does not require in-depth exploration of cave systems. This discovery in itself was not particularly striking to the scientific community at that time for two reasons: first, the cave salamander is neither blind nor depigmented, so it was not particularly remarkable to the casual observer; second, Rafinesque had a poor reputation as a scientist due to his lack of critical thinking and his almost compulsive behavior in naming species (more than 6,700), many of them previously described by others or just varieties of the same one. Yet, his discovery of the cave salamander was the first indication that the biota of caves in that part of the United States was worth looking at (Ewan 1975; Warren 2004).

Rafinesque's explorations included Mammoth Cave, which since the 1830s had rapidly become a great tourist attraction. Used by Native Americans for about 4,000 YBP, this cave was first reported by people of European descent in 1797 (Goode 1986). Mammoth Cave and its fauna became famous thanks, mainly, to the exploratory work performed by

[16] *b.* Galata, near Constantinople, Turkey, 22 October 1783; *d.* Philadelphia, Pennsylvania, USA, 18 September 1840.

Figure 1.4 Contemporary portrait of Constantine Samuel Rafinesque from the frontispiece of his *Analyse de la Nature* (1815).

Stephen Bishop.[17] Bishop was born and died in slavery. He was acquired by the lawyer Franklin Gorin[18] when Stephen was about 13 years old. Gorin purchased Mammoth Cave in 1838; Bishop soon became a guide

[17] *b.* Kentucky, USA?, 1821?; *d.* Kentucky, 1857.

[18] *b.* Barren County, Kentucky, USA, 3 May 1798, *d.* Glasgow, Kentucky, 10 December 1877.

Figure 1.5 Nineteenth-century illustration on a postcard of Bottomless Pit at Mammoth Cave by an anonymous artist. (See Plate 3.)

and explorer of the cave. Although by that time the most accessible parts of Mammoth Cave had been visited, explored, and mapped, a major obstacle remained for the expansion of its exploration: Bottomless Pit (Fig. 1.5). Bishop is consistently credited with having suspended either a pole or a log pole ladder across Bottomless Pit, and thus was able to significantly expand the known area of the cave (Anonymous 1981; Barr 1986; Anonymous 1992) and collect its fauna, which were given as curiosities to visitors (mostly tourists from the northeastern United States) who, in turn, took those specimens to the museums in New England where they were studied by local biologists (Romero and Woodward 2005).

About the same time the Postojna Cave in Carniola (today Slovenia) was being explored. This and other caves in the area had been known for a long time. Ancient Greek and Roman authors such as Strabo, Virgil, and Pliny had mentioned them, and so did Kircher (1665) and Valvasor (1687). In 1818 Luka Čeč[19] (Lukas Tschesch in the German spelling), an assistant to a lamplighter, discovered new passages, which notably expanded the known area of the cave (which, with about 20 km of passages, is the largest in Europe). This was a feat similar to that of Bishop in Mammoth Cave. Just as Bishop did, Čeč was able to collect new species of cave fauna in the newly discovered areas and in September 1831 found the first species of blind cave beetle ever reported. Čeč donated the specimen to the Earl Franz Josef Hannibal Graf von Hohenwart,[20] the district governor, who in turn presented it for study to the Austrian businessman and amateur entomologist Ferdinand Jožef Schmidt.[21] In 1832 Schmidt published its description as a new genus and species, *Leptodirus hohenwarti*, with the Carniolian name *drobnovratnik* (the 'narrow-necked-one'). Since the holotype had been damaged, Schmidt offered 25 florins for a new one; it took many years until other explorers found more specimens, as well as other fauna, which included springtails, pseudoscorpions, and crustaceans (Mader 2003; Novak *et al.* 2003; Južnič 2006).

The crustacean *Gammarus puteanus* (today *Niphargus puteanus*) was described by C. L. Koch in either 1835 or 1836 (the publication was not dated so we are not sure) from wells in Regensburg, Germany. The description of 'Gammarus puteanus Koch' published by Panzer in *Faunae Insectorum Germanicae Initia* in 1836 is the first unambiguous record of a *Niphargus*. A year later Koch (the author of the species) published the identical description and drawings in *Deutschlands Crustaceen, Myriapoden und Arachniden*. The genus *Niphargus* was established 13 years later when Schiödte re-examined his own description of *Gammarus stygius* from the Postojnska jama (Postojnska Cave) in Slovenia.

Another example of a species discovery in the region was that of the science teacher and political activist Emil Adolf Rossmässler.[22] He described the first species of cave mollusk: a cave snail, *Carychium spelaeum*, (today *Zospeum spelaeum*), from the Postojnska Cave (Rossmässler 1838–1844). Rossmässler, a great admirer of Humboldt and who believed in the importance of popularizing science, discovered the cave mollusk in one of his many scientific trips in the 1830s.

[19] *b.* Postojna, Carniola (today Slovenia), 11 October 1785; *d.* Postojna, 31 July 1836.

[20] *b.* Laibach (today Ljubljana, Slovenia), 24 May 1771, *d.* Laibach, 2 August 1844.

[21] *b.* Ödenburg, Sorpon, Hungary 20 February 1791, *d.* Ljubljana, Carniola (today Slovenia), 16 February 1878.

[22] *b.* Leipzig, Germany, 3 March 1806; *d.* Leipzig, 9 April 1867.

These discoveries elicited a great deal of interest for cave fauna and the caves of the karst system of Carniola. Although initially most of the published works from both Carniola and the USA were descriptions of new species, European and American scientists had divergent interests beyond purely taxonomic ones. Whereas the European researchers showed more consideration in grouping cave organisms based on ecology and habits, their American counterparts (some of whom were European-born) tried to explain the archetypical or unique morphology (blindness and depigmentation) of many cave organisms via the influence of environmental factors on development.

In Europe, besides Schmidt, other pioneer researchers of the cave system in Carniola included the Danish entomologist Jørgen Matthias Christian Schiödte[23] and the Austrian entomologist Ignaz Rudolph Schiner.[24] Schiödte was particularly interested in the correlations between anatomical characters and the biological conditions under which organisms live; however, he went further by providing the first classification of cave animals (shade animals, twilight animals, animals in the dark zone, and animals living on stalactites) (Schiödte 1849). This categorization, however, was abandoned and replaced by the one proposed by Schiner (1854), who classified cave organisms according to their degree of dependence toward the underground environment as troglobites, troglophiles, and 'occasional cavernicoles' (trogloxenes), terms still in use today. See Table 1.1 for a summary of historical events.

In pre-Darwinian times American researchers were not only involved in species descriptions, like their European counterparts, but seemed to be fixated on issues of functional morphology and how that morphology could be used to explain the 'types' and development of those organisms. Virtually all of the research was being conducted in Mammoth Cave and began in the 1840s. Of all the organisms discovered in that cave none attracted more attention than the first description of a blind cave fish, *Amblyopsis spelaea*, by James DeKay[25] (DeKay 1842).

Dekay, originally trained as a physician, was an amateur natural historian and friend of writers that represented the American Romantic Movement. He was hired by the Geological Survey of New York and put in charge of the 'zoological productions.' Applying his own Romantic

[23] *b.* Slaegt, Denmark, 20 April 1815; *d.* Copenhagen, Denmark, 12 January 1884.

[24] *b.* Fronsburg, Horn, Austria, 1813; *d.* Vienna, Austria, 6 July 1873.

[25] *b.* Lisbon, Portugal, 12 October 1792; *d.* Oyster Bay, Long Island, New York, USA, 21 November 1851.

Table 1.1 *A summary of major events in the development of biospeleology before Darwin's publication of the first edition of the* Origin of Species by Means of Natural Selection (1859)

This shows that the development of biospeleology was characterized by chance or random discoveries, false starts, and uncritical tales about cave fauna, and ultimately most of these early events were largely inconsequential to the development of later ideas on cave biology.

Date	Fact	Source(s)
20,000 YBP	Knowledge of the cave cricket, *Troglophilus* sp.	Chopard (1928)
AD 1537	First written report of a cave organism: a cave amphipod (probably *Niphargus*)	Trissino (1537)
1540	First written (but unpublished) reference to a hypogean fish, *Sinocyclocheilus hyalinus*. This species was not scientifically described until 1994	Xie (1540); Chen *et al.* (1994)
1550	The first confirmed published record of a cave creature: a cave amphipod (probably *Niphargus*) in northern Italy	Alberti (1550)
1569	Obscure mention of underground little eels (*petites anguilles*) somewhere in Europe	Besson (1569); Romero and Lomax (2000)
1665	Publication of *Mundus Subterraneus*, the first speleological treatise	Kircher (1665); Romero (2000)
1674	First published reference to underground fungi	Lister (1674)
1678	First published reference to a cave bird	Tauste (1678); Humboldt (1817)
1689	First published reference to a cave salamander, *Proteus anguinus*	Valvasor (1689); Laurenti (1768)
1748	An unconfirmed report of a hypogean fish (a 'pike') in France	Montalembert (1748); Romero (1999a)
1793	First description of underground plants in the mines of Freiberg	Humboldt (1793)
1805	Description of a freshwater species of catfish allegedly originating from an underground volcano in Ecuador	Humboldt (1805)
1817	Scientific description of the guacharo or oil-bird, *Steatornis capipensis*	Humboldt (1817)
1822	First scientific description of a cave salamander, *Eurycea lucifuga*, for the American continent	Rafinesque (1822)

(cont.)

Table 1.1 *(cont.)*

Date	Fact	Source(s)
1832	First scientific description in print of a cave insect, *Leptodirus hohenwarti*, a blind beetle	Schmidt (1832)
1835–1836	First scientific description of a hypogean crustacean: *Niphargus puteanus*	Koch (1835–6)
1839	Published mention of a second cave fish for China	Zheng (1839)
1839	First description of a cave mollusk, *Zospeum spelaeum* from Slovenia	Rossmässler (1838–44)
1842	First scientific description of a blind cave fish, *Amblyopsis spelaeus*, from Mammoth Cave, Kentucky	DeKay (1842); Romero (2002b)
1849	First cave species survey for an entire region (Slovenia) in *Specimen Faunae subterraneae.* The author provides first ecological classification of cave organisms (shade animals, twilight animals, animals in the dark zone, and animals living on stalactites)	Schiödte (1849)
1854	The terms troglobites, troglophiles, and accidentals are introduced	Schiner (1854)

ideas, he included in his relation of the fauna of New York species of fauna that were far away from that state, such as the northern cavefish from Mammoth Cave (*Amblyopsis spelaea*), which became the first blind cave fish to be described in the scientific literature in the post-Linnean era. Although his scientific work was criticized by many of his fellow naturalists as being shallow, his description of this cave fish attracted a great deal of attention and generated a lot of research and speculation until the American Civil War interrupted the efforts from scientists in the North to visit and collect at Mammoth Cave, which was in the South (Romero 2002a).

Unlike papers describing species being found elsewhere, the reports on species from Mammoth Cave generated a lot of speculation about the origin of such fauna. That is surprising because the authors of those papers published before Darwin's *Origin* were still creationists and not inclined to believe in evolution, or 'transformism' as it was then called. Most of the discussions concerned the question of why these animals were blind and depigmented in the first place. The first to engage in this type of debate was Jeffries Wyman.[26] Wyman studied under George Cuvier[27] and Richard Owen[28] (Gifford 1967), both staunch creationists. Because of that influence and also because he was a very modest man who, like Cuvier, avoided sweeping generalizations, Wyman essentially stuck to purely anatomical studies. For example, in his first paper on the blind cave fish *A. spelaea*, he reported, 'On the most careful dissection no traces of eyes were found' (Wyman 1843, p. 96). Later he wrote that

> The optic lobes existed (sic); according to the general rules of physiology these should not exist; as they bare strict relation to the sense of sight, which receives its nerve from them (. . .) Here the optic lobes were not so large as the allied fishes, but yet they were of good size, and nearly as large as the cerebral lobes. (*Wyman 1851, p. 349*)

He later re-examined three specimens of this fish species and found imperfect eyes covered by tissue, which explained to him why the fish were unable to see. He proposed that this imperfection of the eyes 'might be owing to a want of stimulus through a series of generations', and though the organ of vision was imperfect, 'it is more like the eyes of other vertebrates' (Wyman 1854a, p. 19). The phrase 'want of stimulus' is a Lamarckian term (see below) that probably had a developmental meaning for Wyman, i.e. the organ did not develop because the environmental stimulus was not there. In any case, he wondered about numerous structures without obvious functions, organs that were of morphological rather than physiological value (Wyman 1854b). He later produced very detailed drawings of the internal anatomy of *A. spelaea* (Wyman 1872), but by that time he had embraced evolution as a natural phenomenon (see below) (Romero 2001a).

[26] *b.* Chelmsford, Middlesex, Massachusetts, 11 August 1814; *d.* Bethlehem, New Hampshire, 4 September 1874.

[27] *b.* Montbéliard, France, 23 August 1769; *d.* Paris, France, 13 May 1832. He was one of the most influential biologists of his time, a brilliant comparative anatomist who believed in the Great Chain of Being and that the only changes that had occurred on earth were due to natural catastrophes after all species had been created by God (Coleman 1964; Bourdier 1971; Rudwick 1997).

[28] *b.* Lancaster, England, 20 July 1804; *d.* Richmond Park, London, England, 18 December 1892. He was a comparative anatomist and one of the early critics of Darwin's evolutionary ideas. He criticized Putnam's interpretation of the optic lobes in blind cave fishes in that their optic lobes are not reduced because they serve other functions beyond sight (based on Wyman's ideas). Owen believed that the lobes were atrophied owing to lack of light.

Another example of a naturalist interested in taxonomy and morphology of the Mammoth Cave fauna was the German physician August Otto Theodor Tellkampf[29] (Romero 2001b). He apparently developed an interest in cave fauna from visiting Mammoth Cave in October 1842 (Tellkampf 1844a,b), after which he described several species of invertebrate. He also made contributions to the study of the cave fish *A. spelaea* and concluded that its eyes and those of blind cave crayfishes had become rudimentary as a result of disuse:

> While it is true, in general, that all animals retain their essential form, and that no species passes over into another by transformation, we know that less material changes of form are produced by external influences such as changes in climate or food, lasting through many generations of the same species.

In other words, he had the idea that disuse led to rudimentation while negating the possibility of evolution above the species level, despite the fact that he could not find the unmodified form that gave rise to the blind and depigmented one. For him, the relationship of the blind fauna to unmodified species could not be settled until 'such species, corresponding with them in all essential points, are found' (Tellkampf 1844b, p. 393).

To elucidate this issue, Jean Louis Rodolphe Agassiz,[30] America's most famous naturalist of his time, intervened. The son of a minister, Agassiz studied medicine in universities of Switzerland and Germany. His teachers included Lorenz Oken,[31] Ignaz von Döllinger,[32] and Georges Cuvier. The first two were followers of *Naturphilosophie*. This was a German Romantic philosophy that sought metaphysical correspondences and interconnections within the world of living things. This philosophy was developed in early-nineteenth-century Germany by Friedrich Schelling

[29] *b*. Heinde, Germany, 27 April 1812; *d*. Hanover, Germany, 7 September 1883.

[30] *b*. Motier-en-Vuly, Switzerland, 28 May 1807; *d*. Cambridge, Massachusetts, USA, 14 December 1873.

[31] *b*. Bohlsbach bei Offenburg, Baden, Germany, 1 August 1779; *d*. Zurich, Switzerland, 11 August 1851. Although a physician by training, Oken championed *Naturphilosophie* with metaphysical abstractions and mystical speculations about science (particularly biology) and Romanticism, despite his scientific background and his rigor as a comparative anatomist. He believed that imagination and feeling should play a part in scientific understanding and in progressive complexity, with humans at the zenith.

[32] *b*. Bamberg, Germany, 27 May 1770; *d*. Munich, Germany, 14 January 1841. A professor of physiology and general pathology; one of his students was Lorenz Oken. He went beyond the typical *Naturphilosophie* approach to natural sciences by insisting on the importance of observation and experimentation (Risse 1971).

and G. W. F. Hegel, who followed Plato's idealism. Despite its apparent scientific mantra, *Naturphilosophie* ideals inundated philosophical postures and the literary movement while opposing the materialistic and mechanist views of modern science. *Naturphilosophie* viewed both mind and body as designed by God and as equally important. Many naturalists that opposed Darwin were followers of *Naturphilosophie*.

Agassiz studied comparative anatomy under Cuvier and developed his ideas along the lines of natural theology, that is, to prove the existence of God through the study of nature. Agassiz became professor of natural history at Harvard (1847–73), where he established the Museum of Comparative Zoology in 1859, combining research, teaching, and public outreach while securing large amounts of funds both public and private to support such endeavors.

During the 5 October 1847 meeting of the American Academy of Arts and Sciences, Agassiz proposed a 'Plan for an investigation of the embryology, anatomy and effect of light on the blind-fish of the Mammoth Cave, *Amblyopsis spelaeus*' (Agassiz 1847, p. 180). In this plan he suggested that by studying this fish 'there was an opportunity to settle, by actual experiment, the extent of physical influences in causing organized beings to assume their peculiar and distinctive characteristics in relation to the media in which they live.' Agassiz, the unrepentant creationist, was not proposing to study the effects of the environment on evolution, but rather the effects of the environment on development. He proposed to raise individuals of *A. spelaea* under different light conditions (darkness, moderate, and intense light) and see whether 'there is an eye formed in the dark to ascertain when and how (the pigmentation) disappears, as it is entirely wanting in the full-grown individuals, and again notice the differences in this respect between specimens growing under the influence of light' (Agassiz 1847, p. 180).

Although Agassiz never carried out those experiments, he kept insisting on the importance of *A. spelaea* in biological research:

> You asked me to give my opinion, respecting the primitive state of the eyeless animals of the Mammoth Cave. This is one of the most important questions to settle in natural history, and I have several years ago, proposed a plan for its investigation which, if well conducted would lead to as important results, for it might settle, once for ever, the question, in what condition and where the animals now living on the earth, were first called into existence. But the investigation would involve such long and laborious researches, that I doubt it will ever be undertaken. (. . .) If physical circumstances ever modified organized beings, it should be easily ascertained here. (. . .) Whoever would settle the

question by direct experiment might be sure to earn the everlasting gratitude of men of science, and here is a great aim for the young American naturalist who would not shrink from the idea of devoting his life to the solution of one great question'. (*Agassiz 1851, p. 255*)

Agassiz' words leave no doubt about that since he considered *A. spelaea* to be an 'aberrant cyprinodont (. . .) created under the circumstances in which they now live' (Agassiz 1851, p. 256) while 'The (rudimentary) organ remains, not for the performance of a function, but with reference to a plan' (Agassiz 1859, p. 11). The latter statement shows that Agassiz (together with Wyman) embraced so-called philosophical or transcendental anatomy, i.e. the search for ideal patterns of structure in nature (Appel 1988). That is why, for both Wyman and Agassiz, *A. spelaea* was an excellent subject of study in their quest for evidence of a common plan underlying the differences caused by immediate adaptation through modifications during the developmental process.

Despite these challenging ideas, Agassiz' proposals were not undertaken because of a variety of reasons. One was the scientists' inability then and now to breed amblyopsid fishes in captivity. The second was Agassiz' personality: his refusal to accept ideas other than his own diminished his status among his colleagues as time went by. Agassiz never acknowledged the transmutability of species and fiercely opposed Darwin's theory of evolution. Several of his students, including his son Alexander,showed a great deal of interest in cave fauna, but left Harvard, and accepted the idea of evolution (see below) (L. Agassiz 1847; E. C. Agassiz 1890; Dexter 1965, 1979; Lurie 1960, 1970; Morris 1997; Smith and Brown 2000; Romero 2001b).

In many ways, Agassiz' interpretation of *Naturphilosophie* was a derivation of the idea of the *Scala Naturae*, also known as the ladder of life or 'Great Chain of Being' with man at the top of the pyramid. This is a concept that originated with Aristotle and the Stoics and was closely tied to Plato's essentialism, i.e. the idea that objects (in this case individuals, organisms, or species) have an ideal, eternal, unchanging 'essence' (*eidos*). These ideas in turn gave rise to the typological notion that all 'true' cave animals must be blind and depigmented. Agassiz passed these ideas on to his students at Harvard.

This was pretty much the state of things among American scientists at the time of Darwin's publication of the first edition of the *Origin* in 1859: a mixture of creationist views, intriguing questions about environmental effects on development, and an explicit endorsement of the typological (essentialist) view of life.

1.3 Darwinism and American neo-Lamarckism (1859–1919)

It may be surprising that Darwin is mentioned before Lamarck in this analysis of biospeleological ideas, since the latter preceded him by more than half a century. The reasons are two-fold: first, Lamarck never mentioned cave fauna in his evolutionary writings; second, Lamarckism or neo-Lamarckian ideas for explaining biological phenomena in caves did not become popular until after Darwin's publication of his *Origin of Species*. Furthermore, it is here argued that Darwin was largely responsible for some (but not all) of the neo-Lamarckian views on cave biota that have survived in both perception and substance to this day.

Although Charles Darwin[33] never studied cave fauna himself, he was interested in the topic, particularly as it related to two issues. The first concerned cave colonization and the similarities between cave fauna and their presumed ancestors in the surrounding areas. The second issue, and the more attractive to him, was the cause of the phenomenon of rudimentation or the loss of organs, i.e. the eyes. He saw this trend as part of a larger compensatory-process issue, i.e. the enlargement of other sensory organs, regardless of whether compensation occurred among cave fauna or not. An analysis of Darwin's writings, including his notebooks and correspondence, provides insight on how intrigued he was by these topics and how, also, he changed his opinions on these matters, sometimes as a response to criticism and sometimes as he received new information.

The first written documentation of Darwin's interest in these topics is in his notebook and is dated 8 December 1844. He wrote a few notes after a conversation he had with Joseph Dalton Hooker,[34] a distinguished botanist and a close friend of his. Darwin wrote that 'I see our cow, which

[33] *b.* The Mount, Shrewsbury, England, 12 February 1809; *d.* Downe, Kent, England, 19 April 1882.

[34] *b.* Halesworth, Suffolk, England, 30 June 1817; *d.* Sunningdale, Berkshire, England, 10 December 1911. Hooker's initial reaction to Darwin's theory of transmutation of species was not very enthusiastic, but he would later change his mind. He provided Darwin with many botanical facts, particularly in the areas of taxonomy and biogeography (Desmond 1972; Colp 1986; Bellon 2001).

has two abortive mammae, then these two are uniquely developed', adding later

Believe part, which is normally in a species abortive appears often as a rudiment– [Hooker] Has lately seen and describe this in case of pistil of dioecious *Umbellieferous plant*: does not know anything on Bentham's law of variability of abortive parts.

George Bentham's[35] 'law of abortive parts' was worded by Darwin himself as follows: 'where parts of flower are reduced from normal number, they are apt to vary in number in individuals of same species' (Burkhardt and Smith 1987, pp. 400–3).

However, Darwin did not develop an interest in cave fauna until early 1852, shortly after he read an article on Mammoth Cave. Beginning in the early 1840s a number of blind and depigmented species of both vertebrates and invertebrates were described for that locality and in 1851 Benjamin Silliman Jr.[36] published an article summarizing the current knowledge about those cave creatures (Silliman 1851). In that article, Silliman made a number of statements that, without question, intrigued Darwin. Silliman described several cave species of animal that were not only blind and depigmented but that also displayed elongated antennae. He made a special mention of the 'cave rat,' of which he had heard that it had large but apparently non-functional eyes, and according to Silliman, 'By keeping them however in captivity and diffuse light they gradually appeared to attain some power of vision.' These presumed facts defied the basic explanation Darwin had already formulated in his mind regarding natural selection's role in determining morphological features of cave organisms. After all, if the alleged cave rat had larger non-functional eyes, that would defy the logic of natural selection.

Part of the problem was that Silliman had given a faulty account of this organism. First of all the alleged 'cave rat' (*Neotoma* sp.) was not an obligatory cave organism but rather a nocturnal creature found both in and outside caves. The reason it had such large eyes was that, like those of many other nocturnal vertebrates, its eyes were enlarged for better

35 *b.* Stoke, Devon, England, 22 September 1800; *d.* London, England, 10 September 1884. A polyglot and polymath very interested in botany who was a friend and supporter of Darwin's (Taylor 1970).

36 *b.* New Haven, Connecticut, USA, 4 December 1816; *d.* New Haven, 14 January 1885. Silliman taught at Yale and helped his father, the founder in 1818 and first editor of the *American Journal of Science and Arts*, to edit that journal, in which a number of articles on cave animals were published in the nineteenth century.

night vision. No wonder Darwin had problems trying to understand the phenomenon.

Yet, intrigued by all this, Darwin, in a letter dated 8 May 1852, asked his friend and colleague the American naturalist James Dwight Dana[37] whether he could receive a specimen of the 'cave rat' (Burkhardt and Smith 1989, p. 92). The reason that Darwin wrote to Dana (one of the most notable American naturalists of the time) and not Silliman was two-fold: Darwin was acquainted with Dana, not Silliman, and Dana was Silliman's brother-in-law, so Darwin probably figured this was the best way to obtain information on the subject.

In another letter to Dana, dated 14 July 1856, Darwin wrote that he was 'extremely much interested in regard to the blind cave animals, described one time since in your Journal by Prof. Silliman Jun$^{r.}$ as the subject is connected with a work of somewhat general nature, which I am endevouring to draw up on variation & the origin of species, classification & c.' (Burkhardt and Smith 1990, p. 180). In another letter to Dana, dated 8 September 1856, he confirms that most of the species found in Mammoth Cave are 'American in type' (Burkhardt and Smith 1990, pp. 215–17), meaning that they must be related to other fauna found in adjacent areas. This was an important point for Darwin since he had by then developed the idea that all species were derived from those found in neighboring ecosystems. Darwin makes this point again in a letter to Hooker dated 23 November 1856 (Burkhardt and Smith 1990, pp. 281–4).

Apparently Darwin never obtained the 'cave rat' but that did not deter him from asking more questions. Darwin received a letter from Dana dated 8 December 1856 in which the American naturalist told Darwin that he had confirmed with Agassiz that the blind rat of Mammoth Cave is 'American in type'. For Darwin this confirmed his own hypothesis that cave animals were derived from species of the surrounding areas. In the same letter Dana goes into a long discourse about the idea of progress. He described progress as 'a law which involves the expression of a type-idea in forms or groups of increasing diversity, and generally of higher

[37] *b.* Utica, New York, USA, 12 February 1813; *d.* New Haven, Connecticut, USA, 14 April 1895. Dana studied at Yale under his future father-in-law Benjamin Silliman. Dana believed that the earth was a changing place through catastrophes (volcanism, erosion, and subsidence) which, in turn, generated changes in forms of life toward higher levels of complexity, an explanation he tried to reconcile with his strong religious beliefs by saying that this was the result of God's design (Sanford 1965; Stanton 1971).

elevation; always resulting in a purer & fuller exhibition of the type' and that 'it is the simple before the complex' (Burkhardt and Smith 1990, pp. 299–300). Here we can see how strong the idea of progressionism was in the minds of naturalists even before evolutionary ideas became a matter of discussion and as Bowler (2005) wrote, Darwin's 'theory was sucked into a wave of enthusiasm for progressionist evolutionism (. . .) which reached its climax in later nineteenth century.' Also, Darwin is reading in this account a message of order in nature, not necessarily an evolutionary one, but one confirming the idea of the Great Chain of Being already present in Plato's and Aristotle's writings. According to this account, nature is characterized by richness in forms, which show continuity in the form of gradation. Therefore the universe is filled with everything that is possible that shares characteristics between the neighboring forms, and because of this they can be arranged in hierarchical order from the smallest, simplest type of existence to God himself.

Correspondence between Darwin and Dana on the subject of the cave fauna continued; in a letter dated 14 July 1856, Darwin asked Dana for more anatomical information about North American cave fauna, particularly arthropods (Burkhardt and Smith 1990, p. 180). Dana replied on 8 September 1856 with mostly systematic information (Burkhardt and Smith 1990, pp. 215–17). On 29 September 1856, Darwin wrote back to Dana thanking him for the information and asking for additional facts about the 'blind rat' (Burkhardt and Smith 1990, pp. 235–7).

Darwin was evidently unsatisfied by the mostly taxonomic and philosophical answers from Dana and wrote to one other scientist for more information on the subject. This was John Obadiah Westwood,[38] a British entomologist, who replied to Darwin in a letter dated 23 November 1856, giving him some taxonomical and distributional information about cave insects from both North America and Europe (Burkhardt and Smith 1990, pp. 283–4). By 1856 Darwin was already keeping a portfolio on abortive organs (Burkhardt and Smith 1990, pp. 253–4).

Darwin's information about cave fauna, however, came not only from what he read about Mammoth Cave and from his correspondence with Dana and Westwood, but also from an article written by the Danish naturalist Schiödte. As mentioned earlier, Schiödte was particularly

[38] *b.* Sheffield, England, 22 December 1805; *d.* Oxford, England, 1 January 1893. Entomologist, archaeologist and a superb illustrator with strong religious beliefs, who disagreed with Darwin regarding his theory of evolution while respecting him as a scientist.

interested in the correlations between anatomical characters and the biological conditions under which organisms live, and also provided the first classification of cave animals (shade animals, twilight animals, animals in the dark zone, and animals living on stalactites) (Schiödte 1849). Although Schiödte's article was originally written in Danish, Darwin (who always struggled with foreign languages, which is the reason he almost exclusively referred to literature that was originally written in or translated into English) had access to the paper because it had been translated and published in English by the Danish naturalist Nathaniel Wallich,[39] who read it at the meeting of the Entomological Society of London on 6 January 1851 (Wallich 1851; Burkhardt and Smith 1990, pp. 283–4).

Armed with this information, Darwin speculated in the first edition of his *Origin* (1859, pp. 137–8) that 'in the case of the cave-rat natural selection seems to have struggled with the loss of light and to have increased the size of the eyes; whereas with all the other inhabitants of the caves, disuse by itself seems to have done its work.' Darwin cited Schiödte's paper as a reference (p. 138). At first Darwin considered the mechanisms of both natural selection and disuse to explain blindness and depigmentation as well as the enlargement of some sensory systems and appendages. To Darwin, this meant a 'contest (. . .) between selection enlarging and disuse alone reducing these organs' (Darwin 1859, p. 296). Later Darwin noted that cave fauna were more closely related to the fauna of the surrounding regions than elsewhere, as is the case for fauna of other more or less isolated habitats such as islands. Thus, he argued that the cave fauna descended from the fauna of the surrounding region, 'the colonists having been subsequently modified and better fitted to their new homes' (Darwin 1859, p. 403).

Although the second edition (1860) of the *Origin* contains very few substantial changes from the first, beginning with the third edition (1861), Darwin makes major changes not only in the book as a whole but on the explanation of the phenomenon of rudimentation of organs among cave animals in particular. Darwin's critics, who had a hard time accepting the role of natural selection in general and its effect on cave animals in particular, found in the latter ammunition for their anti-selectionist criticisms; after all, it seemed that on the surface that Darwin himself was providing the best argument favoring disuse over random selection to explain the reduction and/or disappearance of organs.

[39] *b.* Copenhagen, Denmark, 28 January 1786, *d.* England, 28 April 1854.

Thus, by the third edition of the *Origin* Darwin de-emphasized the importance of natural selection by eliminating his discussion of a 'contest' between selection and disuse. In fact, in the first two editions, in the paragraphs relative to cave animals and rudimentation, he used the words *disuse* and *selection* seven times each; by the third edition, it was five and two, respectively.

Yet, criticism mounted. In 1865 Carl Wilhelm von Nägeli,[40] a botanist and one of the rediscoverers of Mendel's work, made the point that characters considered useless could not have arisen via natural selection or even Lamarckism for that matter. Darwin respected von Nägeli's opinions very much and, thus, by the sixth edition, he responded to this criticism by significantly expanding his discussion on morphological reductions and natural selection, although suggesting that there were mechanisms yet to be discovered to explain this phenomenon.

Another criticism was expressed by George John Douglas Campbell, Duke of Argyll.[41] With a sort of finalistic ideology, this politician and prolific writer attacked Darwin's explanation of rudimentation by saying that rudimentary organs were not remnants of useful structures but rather incipient structures being prepared for some future use (Argyll 1867, p. 213). Campbell's expression may foreshadow the concept of 'preadaptation', so popular among classical biospeleologists (see Chapter 3 of this book). Further, the Duke of Argyll did not understand how Charles Darwin could have proposed natural selection without a 'selector', just as animal breeders make selective choices. The Duke of Argyll and Richard Owen were staunch creationists, who tried to prevent the influence of Darwin's ideas on British society.

Finally, in 1871 George Mivart[42] (who studied under Owen among others) published his *Genesis of Species*, a work heralded by an article in the *Quarterly Review* of the same year. Mivart articulated many criticisms of Darwin's ideas, criticisms to which Darwin responded in full in the sixth edition (1872) of his *Origin*. One of these criticisms was that 'Natural selection utterly fails to account for the conservation and development

[40] *b*. Kilchberg, Switzerland, 27 March 1817; *d*. Munich, Germany, 10 May 1891.

[41] *b*. Ardencaple Castle, Dunbartonshire, Scotland, 30 April 1823, *d*. Inveraray Castle, Scotland, 24 April 1900.

[42] *b*. London, England, 30 November 1827; *d*. London, 1 April 1900. A morphologist with a finalistic argument for design by a higher intelligence and a believer of neo-Lamarckism. His book *On the Genesis of Species* (1871) was a sour and personal criticism of Darwin's ideas on natural selection and human evolution while disparaging the 'bad' influence of Darwinism on British society (Artigas *et al.* 2006).

of the minute and rudimentary beginnings, the slight and infinitesimal commencements of structures, however useful those structures may afterwards become' (Mivart 1871, p. 23).

By the *Origin*'s sixth edition (the first of his famous book to use the word 'evolution') Darwin remained cautious about the role that natural selection might have played in the reduction of morphological characters by saying that this process may have been 'aided perhaps by natural selection.' By now the number of times he uses the word *disuse* (when discussing cave organisms and rudimentation) has risen to nine, and *selection* to ten. He also added the idea that animals subjected to darkness may develop 'inflammations of the eyes' and that the covering of those organs by tissue can 'be an advantage' (that is, where selection may play a role). He then made the statement that rudimentary organs are very common among many organisms (a fact usually overlooked by the practitioners of the 'regressive evolution' concept today). He supported the statement by providing numerous examples from plants to whales. Yet he remained fixed in his idea that 'It appears probable that disuse has been the main agent in rendering organs rudimentary.' Although he mentioned the benefit derived by an organism in reducing organs that are no longer utilized for the sake of 'economy,' he had no explanation for why some organs totally disappear whereas others are retained (for a word-by-word comparison of these texts, see http://www.clt.astate.edu/aromero/new_page_29.htm).

So, which one is the real Darwin when it comes to the evolution of cave faunas and the phenomenon of rudimentation? Was he a selectionist or a Lamarckian? Essentially, Darwin's views were neo-Lamarckian in relation to loss or rudimentation of organs; therefore, to say that later neo-Lamarckism was 'anti-Darwinian' concerning cave fauna is a misinterpretation of the facts since Darwin himself held neo-Lamarckian ideas. This despite the fact that Darwin wrote to Lyell on 11 October 1859, that 'I do not know what you think about it [Lamarck's work], but it appeared to me extremely poor; I got not a fact or idea from it' (F. Darwin 1896, vol. 2, p. 10).

The present author's proposition that Darwin held neo-Lamarckian ideas when dealing with cave fauna is consistent with the interpretation that in many ways Darwin held a modified version of the Great Chain of Being (Bowler 1983, pp. 55–9). This was a position also championed by the Swiss entomologist Charles Bonnet[43] and the French

[43] *b.* Geneva, Switzerland, 13 March 1720; *d.* Geneva, 20 May 1793.

philosopher–naturalist Jean-Baptiste-René Robinet.[44] They both endorsed the idea of organic progress (Burkhardt 1977, pp. 83–4).

For Bonnet God had a plan, but His divine role only took place at the beginning of the universe. For Bonnet there were always intermediate forms between species. He was a proponent of the theory of preformation, i.e. that all organisms have a preformed 'germ' in the female germ cell. For him, all these preformed germs were there at the time of the beginning of the universe. He believed that the Earth had been affected by cataclysms (similar to Cuvier's catastrophes) that had destroyed life several times over but then every time the 'germs' were reborn into better and more perfect (and complex) forms of life, culminating in a 'paligenesis' or resurrection as interpreted by the Christian gospel. Bonnet's beliefs were very popular, particularly in France (Pilet 1973; Anderson 1976; Rigotti 1986). Thus, Bonnet equated the idea of progressive development with the term 'evolution' meaning the unfolding of a providential plan to replenish the earth with life (Richards 1992, 2002).

Both Bonnet and Robinet were strict Lamarckians. Lamarck argued that organisms experience 'needs' (*besoins*) that are brought about by the environment and that trigger fluids (including electricity) which, when circulated in the body, enlarge or develop the appropriate organ. According to Lamarck, a crucial causal factor in 'higher' animals is the 'inner consciousness' (*sentiment interieur*), which causes body parts to respond and develop. This line of thought resulted in the idea of the inheritance of acquired characters. Although Darwin was less inclined to metaphysical interpretations than his French-speaking colleagues, he favored the idea of inheritance of acquired characters, and his selectionist explanations regarding cave animals were at best weak and at worst confusing.

Given this muddled state of science, the void created by Darwin himself by his lack of a rational explanation for the phenomenon of rudimentation was filled by orthogenesis and its related conceptions, first in the United States and later in continental Europe.

The publication of Darwin's *Origin* in 1859 stimulated American naturalists not only intellectually but also sociologically. On the one hand Louis Agassiz completely dismissed the idea of transmutation of species and Darwin's book as a whole, which he attacked unrelentingly, particularly in academic circles (he qualified Darwin's books as 'poor, very poor'; F. Darwin 1896, vol. 2, p. 63); on the other Wyman (Agassiz' colleague at Harvard) and the students of Agassiz himself (including his son Alexander) eventually embraced the idea of evolution though they

[44] *b*. Rennes, France, 23 June 1735; *d*. Rennes, 24 March 1820.

dismissed natural selection as its main mechanism. These, together with Alpheus Hyatt[45] and Edward Drinker Cope,[46] were the founders of the American neo-Lamarckian school, and they saw cave fauna as the perfect example to support their ideas. Since Darwin himself adhered to the explanation of disuse as a mechanism for change and had not articulated a strong argument in favor of selection acting on cave organisms, they did not feel they were contradicting in any significant measure the tenets of the later editions of the *Origin* on this matter.

Three historical factors influenced biospeleological research in the United States after the appearance of Darwin's *Origin*: (1) the American Civil War (1861–1865), (2) the emergence of the Hyatt–Cope Progressionist School (from 1864 on), and (3) the 'Salem Secession' of 1864.

1.3.1 The American Civil War

The onset of this conflict meant, essentially, that any field and laboratory study of Mammoth Cave fauna stalled. The reason was very simple: the scientists interested in the topic were in the North whereas the Mammoth Cave was in the South. In fact, there would not be a renewal of interest in these fauna until 1871, when, after the Indianapolis meeting of the American Association for the Advancement of Science, many of the participants visited Mammoth Cave and collected new specimens. Thus for more than a decade American naturalists had to be content to engage in speculation about the cave fauna and their origin without the benefit of direct observation. In at least one instance, a person most interested in the issue was kept away forever. This was Charles Frédéric Girard.[47] He had been brought to the United States by Louis Agassiz in 1847 and had worked at the Smithsonian Institution until 1860. While there, he was given some specimens collected by a J. E. Younglove 'from a well near Bowling Green, Ky'. He bestowed on those specimens a new species status, *Typhlichthys subterraneus*, which he included in the family Amblyopsidae (Girard 1859). This new species seemed to have 'characters apparently transitory' between *A. spelaea* and the other species of the amblyopsid family known at that time: *Chologaster cornutus*, an

[45] *b.* Washington, D.C., USA, 5 April 1838; *d.* Cambridge, Massachusetts, USA, 15 January 1902.

[46] *b.* Philadelphia, Pennsylvania, USA, 28 July 1840; *d.* Philadelphia, 12 April 1897.

[47] *b.* Mulhouse, France, 8 March 1822; *d.* Neuilly-sur-Seine, France, 29 March 1895.

epigean species. *A. spelaea* lacked eyes but had ventral fins; *T. subterraneus* lacked both eyes and ventral fins, whereas *C. cornutus* had eyes and lacked ventral fins. Obviously, the discovery of this sort of 'intermediate' species should have fueled much further discussion on the issue of evolution. However, its discovery occurred right before the beginning of the Civil War, so no more information could be obtained. It is quite possible that Girard would have continued working on it, but hostilities broke out while Girard was in Paris, and he spent most of the rest of his life there practicing medicine. His support for the Confederate cause (by sending drugs, medical supplies, and arms) and the animosity that Agassiz had developed toward him (Jackson and Kimler 1999) probably led Girard to believe that he would not be welcome back in the United States, especially since the vast majority of his colleagues had supported the Union. Yet, he must have maintained some interest in cave fishes because later in life he published a number of popular articles on this topic (e.g. Girard 1888) (Romero 2001a).

1.3.2 The emergence of the Hyatt–Cope Progressionist School

Alpheus Hyatt, a former student of Agassiz with whom he broke up, after the 'Salem Secession,' (see below) and who embraced evolution (to the dismay of Agassiz), visited Mammoth Cave in September 1859, much earlier than his contemporary colleagues, and collected specimens of its fauna (Bocking 1988; Romero 2001a). Hyatt's evolutionary ideas were based on three tenets: (1) species have, as do individuals, an inevitable life cycle that includes decline as age advances; (2) for a species the preceding step before extinction is 'degeneration' of the species (cave creatures with their lack of eyes and pigmentation epitomized to him this degeneration); and (3) species 'transmutation' is the result of the speeding ('acceleration') or slowing ('retardation') of development, which, in turn, is caused by use and disuse (for a summary of Hyatt's ideas see Brooks 1909).

Hyatt's ideas were influenced by two currents of thought: (1) the Americanized version of *Naturphilosophie* that was based on Oken's German idealism and transcendentalism, which Agassiz had championed and passed on to his students including Hyatt himself; and (2) progressionist ideas popularized by Ernst Haeckel's[48] 'Principle of

[48] *b.* Potsdam, Prussia, Germany, 16 February 1834; *d.* Jena, Germany, 9 August 1919. Haeckel studied medicine and was still practicing when he read Darwin's *Origin of Species* in 1859. That made him abandon his medical profession to study natural history

Recapitulation' which Hyatt used to formulate his 'Law of Acceleration.' The best compendium of Haeckel's philosophy of progressive evolution can be found in his 1891 *Evolution of Man* (*Anthropogenie*), which was based on an analytical comparison of embryonic development and evolution, better known today as the 'Biogenic or Biogenetic Law' (i.e. 'ontogeny recapitulates phylogeny') or the recapitulation theory.

Interestingly enough, although Haeckel was very impressed with Darwin's *Origin*, he was not very enthusiastic about natural selection as the primordial mechanism and tended instead to emphasize Lamarckian mechanisms. This may explain, at least in part, why Haeckel did not like Darwin's natural selection explanation: he was a German idealist and transcendentalist whereas Darwin represented the best of the British natural theology.

In other words, since Darwin himself advocated disuse as the mechanism to explain the loss of phenotypic features among cave animals, for the American neo-Lamarckians that point was not in dispute. What they disputed was the impression of randomness and lack of direction implied in Darwin's ideas; therefore their point of contention with Darwin was not a disagreement over evolution as a fact or disuse as a mechanism, but their philosophical view of directionality in nature. This is still the major philosophical contention that creationists have today. No wonder the triumph of Darwinism has been called 'The triumph of chance and change' (Greene 1959).

The other proponent of progressionism in the USA was Edward Drinker Cope. He was a highly prolific naturalist who became a very influential, although controversial, figure in his time. His first dealing with alleged cave fauna took place with the description of what he thought to be a new genus and species of troglomorphic fish, '*Gronias nigrilabris*', from Pennsylvania (Cope 1864, p. 231). Although he did not present any evidence that such fish had been captured in the hypogean

at the University of Jena, where he later became a professor of comparative anatomy and the leading German Darwinist. For him all living organisms were plasmatic bodies differing only in degrees of organization. This was a metaphysical view, according to which all living matter is made of the same essence. Another notable influence on him was the vitalist and comparative anatomist and physiologist, Johannes Müller. Haeckel was also influenced by *Naturphilosophie* and he ultimately developed pantheistic ideas. He was also a progressionist who believed that advances in science would allow humankind to reach new heights in rationality and morality, while civilizations that did not adhere to these concepts were considered 'degenerate.' He inspired many students, among them Anton Dohrn (Uschmann 1972; Oppenheimer 1982).

environment, he was quick to suggest that such fish 'is supposed to issue from a subterranean stream, said to traverse the Silurian limestone in that part of the (sic) Lancaster county, and discharge into the Conestoga'. Cope was known for his hasty conclusions and the superficiality of some of his work (Romero and Romero 1999). Further studies have shown that the specimens on which he based this description were specimens of *Ictalurus nebulosus* that had eyes present that were asymmetrically developed, probably as a result of a teratological condition. Unfortunately his assertion concerning this fish continued to be repeated in the literature until recently (see Romero 1999b for a full history of this misconception).

But more important than this alleged discovery was the position that Cope himself took about evolution in general and how that influenced biospeleological thinking. Cope and Hyatt developed what was to be known as the Hyatt–Cope position or school, which was based on parallels drawn between embryology and phylogeny. Early in his career Cope took a stand against natural selection, never acknowledging it as an important evolutionary force (see, for example, Cope 1864); like the rest of his contemporaries, he became a strong supporter of Lamarckism. However, he extended Lamarck's ideas by representing evolution as a phenomenon governed by trends: 'The method of evolution has apparently been one of successional increment or decrement of parts along definite lines' (Cope 1896, p. 24). This is what was later called orthogenesis, the view that evolution has a life of its own that can take it in certain directions. As Hyatt had also done, Cope proposed evolutionary principles such as the 'Law of the Unspecialized' which when applied to cave organisms meant that these cave creatures without eyes and pigmentation were at the end of their phylogenetic life because they were too specialized to evolve into something else; therefore, the next step had to be extinction (see Cope 1896, pp. 172–4). As we shall see, these ideas became the distinguishing feature of American neo-Lamarckism, and much of the discussion on the evolution of cave species (even today) was heavily influenced by such views as those epitomized by the use of terminology such as 'regressive evolution' (Cope 1864, 1872, 1896; Davidson 1997; Romero and Romero 1999; Wallace 1999).

1.3.3 The 'Salem Secession'

This was the breakup of professional relationships between Agassiz and many of his students at Harvard because of a combination of disputes over labor issues, the ownership of collected material, the freedom of the students to publish, economic issues created by the Civil War, and philosophical differences. Since most of these students went to the Peabody Academy of Sciences in Salem, Massachusetts, their departure from Agassiz was termed the 'Salem Secession' by Dexter (1965). The fact that most, if not all, of the most notable of Agassiz' students used cave organisms as either the subjects of their research or for purposes of philosophical disquisitions shows how influential Agassiz was in planting interesting questions in his students' minds. Yet, because Agassiz was an unrepentant creationist, they distanced themselves from their former master, sometimes more in form than in substance. Wyman, for example, quickly converted to evolutionism (but without accepting natural selection as its mechanism) and regarded Agassiz as backward for his refusal to accept evolution (Appel 1988); other students of his (Hyatt, Alpheus Packard,[49] Edward Morse,[50] and to a lesser extent Frederic Putnam[51] and Nathaniel Shaler[52]) went on to contribute to the popularity of neo-Lamarckism in America.

Packard, after breaking with Agassiz in the Salem Secession, went on to become a leading figure of American neo-Lamarckism, which he championed from his positions at the Boston Society of Natural History, the Peabody Academy of Sciences at Salem, Massachusetts, and at Brown University (Dexter 1965; Bocking 1988). It was Packard who coined the term 'neo-Lamarckism' and called Lamarck 'the real founder of organic evolution' (Packard 1901, p. v). In 1867, together with Morse and Hyatt, Packard founded *The American Naturalist*, the journal that published the most articles on American cave fauna during the nineteenth century. He first examined Mammoth Cave specimens after the Indianapolis meeting of the American Association for the Advancement of Science in 1871,

49 *b.* Brunswick, Maine, USA, 19 February 1839; *d.* Providence, Rhode Island, USA, 14 February 1905.

50 *b.* Portland, Maine, USA, 18 June 1838; *d.* Salem, Massachusetts, USA, 20 December 1925). A naturalist, writer, and later director of the Peabody Museum of Archaeology and Ethnology (1880–1914).

51 *b.* Salem, Massachusetts, USA, 16 April 1839; *d.* Cambridge, Massachusetts, USA, 14 August 1915.

52 *b.* Newport, Kentucky, USA, 22 February 1841; *d.* Cambridge, Massachusetts, USA, 10 April 1906. A geologist and paleontologist initially opposed to evolution out of deference to his teacher Agassiz, but once he secured his position as Dean at Harvard he accepted Darwin's theory, although maintaining a neo-Lamarckian interpretation of it.

and published an account of the fauna that same year. Just as his former teacher had been, he was enthusiastic about the possibilities that cave animals offered to scientists interested in evolutionary studies: 'We trust naturalists the world over will be led to explore caves with new zeal'. Packard saw the study of Mammoth Cave fauna as the means of fulfilling his higher interest in the issue of evolution, i.e. the knowledge derived from their study could impact broader evolutionary issues (Packard 1871, p. 761). The Mammoth Cave fauna convinced him of their usefulness as a demonstration of evolution (Packard 1871). For him and Putnam 'The comparatively sudden creation of these cave animals affords, it seems to us, a very strong argument for the theory of Cope and Hyatt of creation by acceleration and retardation which has been fully set forth in this journal' [*American Naturalist*] (Packard and Putnam 1872). He thought that cave fauna was of very recent origin and that the loss of certain organs was compensated by the hypertrophy of others.

In 1874, after Packard became associated with the Kentucky Geological Survey, his interest in the fauna of Mammoth Cave and other caverns in the midsouth USA intensified, although he never abandoned his neo-Lamarckian views concerning cave faunas (see, for example, Packard 1888).

The other leading figure of this time was Frederic Ward Putnam. Like Packard, Putnam studied under Agassiz and was his assistant until the Salem Secession of 1864. He worked either as an ichthyologist or as a vertebrate biologist for the Boston Society of Natural History, the Essex Institute, the Peabody Academy of Science, and Harvard's Museum of Comparative Zoology. He was the one out of all of Agassiz' students who took the longest to accept evolution as a fact, and when he did (between 1872 and 1874) he appeared to do so reluctantly (Dexter 1979). In fact, there is no clear indication that he expressively espoused the neo-Lamarckian ideas of the Hyatt–Cope school, but there is no proof to the contrary either, and he worked very closely with both Packard and Shaler, whose sympathies for the American neo-Lamarckian school are indisputable.

Of all of Putnam's experiences, it was his position in 1874 as assistant of the Kentucky Geological Survey that brought him into direct contact with hypogean fauna, particularly fishes. Putnam also first visited Mammoth Cave to collect fishes, crayfish, leeches, beetles, and crickets in 1871 after the meeting of the American Association for the Advancement of Science. He returned in 1874 following an invitation from Nathaniel Southgate Shaler, another of Agassiz's students, who, as director of the

Kentucky State Geological Survey, appointed Putnam as special assistant to the Survey that year. Although less well known than Packard because he was not very much inclined to provide grandiose generalizations or engage in much speculation, Putnam was very critical of hasty conclusions by others, particularly Cope.

Putnam carried out experiments that suggested that blind cave crayfishes would not take food, unlike the eyed ones, and did not acquire pigmentation in subsequent molts even when kept in sunlight (Putnam 1875). He also described a new species of amblyopsid, *Chologaster agassizi* (Putnam 1872). He always had problems in accepting evolution as an idea:

> I think that we have as good reasons for the belief in the immutability and early origin of the species (. . .) as we have for their mutability and late development, and, to one of my, perhaps, too deeply rooted ideas, a far more satisfactory theory; for, with our present knowledge, it is but theory on either side'. (*Packard and Putnam 1872, p. 52*)

However, when dealing with specifics Putnam's arguments always seemed to be to the point. For example, he criticized Cope's interpretation that *A. spelaea* was able to survive in hypogean waters because its

> projecting under jaw and upward direction of the mouth renders it easy for the fish to feed at the surface of the water (. . .) This structure also probably explains the fact of its being the sole representative of the fishes of subterranean waters. No doubt many other forms were carried into the caverns since the waters first found their way there, but most of them were like those of our present rivers, deep waters or bottom feeders. Such fishes would starve in a cave river, where much of the food is carried to them on the surface of the stream . . .

Putnam then asked: where are the surface forms of the 'surface feeders'? Why are other surface feeders not found in caves? He did not understand how Cope could justify the above statement when he himself had described an alleged 'subterranean' fish ('*Gronias nigrilabris*') from Pennsylvania that was a bottom feeder, and the blind cave fishes from Cuba (discovered by Felipe Poey[53] in 1858) were bottom feeders as well. Putnam noted that studies of stomach contents in *A. spelaea* had

[53] *b.* La Habana, Cuba, 26 May 1799; *d.* La Habana, 28 January 1891. A lawyer by training, he became the foremost Cuban naturalist and discovered two species of cave fishes in that island, the first ones scientifically recognized outside the United States (Romero 2007).

shown that they eat mostly crayfish and other fishes. He asked, if blindness is the direct result of darkness, as some contended, 'how is it that *Chologaster* from the well in Tennessee or the 'mud fish' at Mammoth Cave are found with eyes?' (Putnam 1872, p. 24).

Putnam (1872, p. 6) also stated that

> the blind fish of the Mammoth Cave has from its discovery been regarded with curiosity by all who have heard of its existence, while anatomists and physiologists have considered it as one of those singular animals whose special anatomy must be studied in order to understand correctly facts that have been demonstrated from other sources; and, in these days of the Darwinian and development theories, the little blind fish is called forth to give its testimony, pro or con.

He viewed the amblyopsids as former marine and saltwater estuary fishes that were slowly trapped in that geographical area. He substantiated this hypothesis by pointing out that the eyed amblyopsid *C. cornuta* was

> now living in the ditches of the rice fields of South Carolina, under very similar conditions to those under which others of the family may have lived in long preceding geological time; and to prove that the development of the family was not brought about by the subterranean conditions under which some of the species now live, we have the ones with eyes living with the one without, and the South Carolina species to show that a subterranean life is not essential to the development of the singular characters which the family possess.

He further supported this hypothesis by mentioning that the Cuban blind cave fishes belonged to the genera 'with their nearest representative in the family a marine form, and with the whole family of cods and their allies, to which group they belong, essentially marine'.

How can we summarize, thus, the views of this generation of American naturalists regarding the evolution and ecology of cave fauna? Although generalizations are always dangerous (particularly when dealing with the ideas of people like Cope, who kept modifying his), here are some of their views of which we are certain:

1. Disuse, not natural selection, was the major (if not the only) evolutionary force behind the morphological 'oddities' (blindness and depigmentation) of cave fauna. Thus, cave fauna provided excellent evidence of the effect of the environment on the evolution of organisms (Packard attributed more evolutionary importance to the direct effect of the environment than to the effect of changes in habits).

2. The maintenance of rudimentary (but useless) organs among the cave fauna was explained within the concepts of *Bauplane* (blueprints or archetypes), homologies, and parallelisms between embryology and phylogeny. These ideas originated from Agassiz as a result of his own *Naturphilosophie*.
3. Hypertrophy of certain organs appears as compensation for the rudimentation of others.
4. Cave fauna represented one of the best examples of progressionism or orthogenetic ideas. With orthogenesis comes the idea of progress; with loss of characters, the idea of regression. Bowler (1983, p. 57) suggested that Lamarckism and orthogenesis were allies in their war against Darwinism. That was particularly true among American naturalists.
5. All cave fauna were of recent origin.

1.4 European selectionism and the death of the controversies (1880–1921)

Despite the tremendous popularity of American neo-Lamarckism, some European researchers were not satisfied with the metaphysical explanations for the evolution of cave fauna in particular and the general dismissal of natural selection as the major driving force of evolution. The main opposition came from August Weismann[54] and Edward Ray Lankester.[55] Although the first did not specifically study cave organisms, he adopted a pro-selectionist position in part because his teacher Jacob Henle[56] (a very keen observer) had encouraged him to be suspicious of any ideas based on the idealistic *Naturphilosophie*. More explicit regarding cave fauna was Lankester, a comparative anatomist influenced by the German biologist Anton Dohrn[57] (a student of Haeckel's). Lankester wrote that a special kind of natural selection was responsible for blindness

[54] *b.* Frankfurt am Main, Germany, 17 January 1834; *d.* Freiburg im Breisgau, Germany, 5 November 1914. He conducted a series of experiments in which he cut off the tails of mice for 22 generations, disproving the notion that acquired characteristics could be inherited since the mice kept being born with tails.

[55] *b.* London, England, 15 May 1847; *d.* London, 15 August 1929.

[56] *b.* Fürth, near Nuremberg, Bavaria, Germany, 19 July 1809; *d.* Göttingen, Germany, 13 May 1885. Henle was originally trained in medicine, studied under Johannes Müller, and taught biology to August Weismann (Hintzsche 1972).

[57] *b.* Stettin, Germany [now Szczecin, Poland], 29 September 1840; *d.* Munich, Germany, 26 September 1909. Dohrn became very enthusiastic about natural history after reading Darwin's *Origin*. His major area of interest was comparative anatomy and

among cave animals. His ideas can be summarized as follows: (1) within any population some animal individuals are, by chance, born with defective eyes, and occasionally a sample of both those born with normal eyes and some born with defective eyes fall or are swept into caves; (2) in each generation, those that have good eyes are able to see the light and escape, so eventually only those that are blind will remain in the cave (Lankester 1893); (3) one can find organisms degenerating ontogenetically and phylogenetically; 'degeneration' or 'a loss of organization making the descendent far simpler or lower in structure than its ancestor,' is a widespread phenomenon (Lankester 1880; De Beer 1973). He did not synonymize evolution with progress.

Any new set of conditions occurring to an animal which render its food and safety very easily attained, seem to lead as a Rule of Degeneration; just as an active healthy man sometimes degenerates when he becomes suddenly possessed of a fortune. (. . .) Let the parasitic life once be secured, and away go legs, jaws, eyes, and ears'. (*Lankester 1880, p. 33*)

Note here the influence of the 'Hyatt–Cope school' and the fact that he was trying to draw a parallelism between parasitology and the complacency of the British Empire at its zenith.

Despite these controversies and the rediscovery of Mendel's work, little more than speculation was added to the discussion. Hugo De Vries,[58] for example, one of the rediscoverers of Mendel's laws, believed that there were two types of mutation: retrogressive (leading toward the loss of characters) and progressive (leading toward complexity). But these were theoretical considerations without a solid experimental backing. Notice that De Vries, despite his distaste for orthogenesis and teleological explanations, was using the jargon of progressionists when referring to these mutations. Lankester had also proposed that each useless character was correlated with a useful one, an idea that found tangential support from Thomas Hunt Morgan,[59] who discovered that one gene may have

the use of embryos to establish phylogenetic relationships. He maintained an active correspondence with Darwin (Heuss 1991).

[58] *b*. Haarlem, The Netherlands, 16 February 1848; *d*. Lunteren, The Netherlands, 21 May 1935.

[59] *b*. Lexington, Kentucky, USA, 25 September 1866; *d*. Pasadena, California, USA, 4 December 1945. A leading twentieth-century geneticist who established the fact that genes were located in the chromosomes and made the use of fruit flies a common feature in experimental genetics.

multiple effects (pleiotropism). Morgan, the experimentalist, was also speculative about cave fauna: when observing the appearance of eyeless *Drosophila* in the laboratory, he proposed that blind cave animals could be the result of a single mutation, an assertion he never tested.

The last major biologist working on cave fauna who operated more or less under the influence of the American neo-Lamarckian school was Carl H. Eigenmann.[60] Influenced by David Starr Jordan[61] (a student of Louis Agassiz' son, Alexander), Eigenmann became a biologist particularly interested in fishes. His first experience with blind cave fishes took place in 1886 while at Indiana University, when he received a living blind fish taken from a well in Corydon, Indiana. The next year he married Rosa Smith,[62] an ichthyologist in her own right, and who introduced him to the blind goby *Othonops eos* (formerly *Typhologobius californiensis*) found among the rocks of the California coast (see Eigenmann (1890) for a historical account of this encounter and how much it impressed him). In 1891 he was appointed Professor of Zoology at Indiana University, a perfect location from which to study the blind vertebrates of the caves in the nearby areas. This motivated him to devote a substantial part of his scientific career to the study of blind vertebrates, most of them from caves (Romero 1986b).

Between 1887 and 1909, much of his work was devoted to understanding the process by which cave vertebrates lost their visual structures. He also described two new species of cave fish: *Amblyopsis rosae* from Missouri (Eigenmann 1898) and *Trogloglanis pattersoni* (Eigenmann 1919) from the artesian waters of Texas. Eigenmann frequently visited the caves of Indiana, Kentucky, Texas, and Missouri in search of specimens for his work; in March 1902 he visited Cuba for the first time and secured cave specimens for his comparative studies. He had previously been working on fish reproduction and quickly recognized that the two species of Cuban hypogean fish known at that time were viviparous.

[60] *b.* Flehingen, Beden, Germany, 9 March 1863; *d.* Chula Vista, California, USA, 24 April 1927. He arrived in the United States at the age of 16.

[61] *b.* Gainesville, New York, USA, 19 January 1851; *d.* Stanford, California, USA, 19 September 1931. Inspired by Louis Agassiz, Jordan devoted his academic research to the study of fishes and accepted Darwinism. He believed that extreme specialization would be followed by 'degeneration' as in the case of cave fishes. He taught Carl H. Eigenmann and indirectly influenced Carl L. Hubbs (Hubbs 1964; Shor 1973).

[62] *b.* Monmouth, Illinois, USA, 7 October 1858; *d.* San Diego, California, USA, 12 January 1947.

Eigenmann found the localities for the Cuban blind fish to be 'monotonous' (Eigenmann 1903), unlike Mammoth Cave, which exhibited great diversity, not surprising given the enormous size of the latter. From 1906 to 1907 he conducted laboratory studies in Europe, mostly in Germany, with the Cuban specimens he had collected. From 1898 to 1905 Eigenmann published at least 39 papers and abstracts on cave vertebrates, dealing mostly with developmental and anatomical aspects of vision loss in fishes, salamanders, lizards, and mammals in an attempt to understand the basic process that results in blindness among hypogean vertebrates. He summarized all this research in his *Cave Vertebrates of North America* (Eigenmann 1909).

Although a taxonomist by training, Eigenmann diligently sought explanations for the origin and evolution of the cave fauna. Originally a neo-Lamarckian, Eigenmann thought that the reduction or disappearance of organs among many cave animals was an example of convergent evolution. In other words, the well-defined conditions of the subterranean environment facilitate the evolutionary changes that result in blindness and depigmentation in a variety of animals. He pointed out that lack of pigmentation had to be understood as the result of a combination of genetically fixed and epigenetically (environmentally influenced) determined characters; in other words, even though a character may be genetically determined, its degree of development can vary when exposed to different amounts of light. For Eigenmann, cave evolution was essentially 'degenerative', and all successful cave-invaders had to be somehow 'pre-adapted' to that milieu. The origin of caves and that of the blind fauna in them were to him two distinct questions because of his experience with the blind fish found among the rocks of California's coast. He insisted on a strong link between ontogeny and phylogeny; his constant use of terms such as 'phyletic degeneration' indicates that he held orthogenetic views. He followed Herbert Spencer's idea that cave fauna are not the result of 'accidents' but rather the product of an active process of colonization (Eigenmann 1909; Romero 1986b).

At the same time Eigenmann was at the peak of his work on blind vertebrates, his student Arthur Mangun Banta[63] proposed some variations to the popular explanation of the origin of reduction/loss of phenotypic characters. For Banta 'degeneration' of eyes and pigmentation was due

[63] *b.* near Greenwood, Indiana, USA, 31 December 1877; *d.* 2 January 1946.

to the influence of the environment, and such phenomena had to occur at the embryonic level before cave colonization could take place (Banta 1921). Because such animals have already suffered 'degeneration' they go 'voluntarily' into caves and do not return to the surface because they are 'unfit' to survive in epigean conditions (Banta 1909, p. 99). Banta, thus, was not a neo-Lamarckian in the sense that he did not believe in disuse as the cause of rudimentation; he even acknowledged that natural selection was the explanatory mechanism for the increased sensory organs of some cave creatures (Banta 1909, p. 104). Although Banta's hypothesis as to why cave animals had colonized the hypogean environment (and why they were blind and depigmented) never acquired much credence, his emphasis on the notion of preadaptations became very popular when four years later Cuénot coined the term (see Chapter 2).

In summary, by the beginning of the twentieth century, with genetics gaining importance, no new ideas about cave biology were proposed even though the neo-Lamarckian explanations based on use and disuse had been discredited. This is not surprising: even the topic of evolution in general languished at this time, primarily because it was obvious that no progress was being made, and 'Morphology having been explored in its minutest corners, we turned elsewhere' (Bateson 1922, p. 1412). Lankester, for example, left his professorship at Oxford to become Director of the British Museum of Natural History (Ruse 1996, p. 239) and Eigenmann began a general study of freshwater fish fauna of the Western hemisphere.

Now that biospeleology was essentially dead in English-speaking countries, this science would experience a revival in continental Europe, particularly in France, where they had their own brand of neo-Lamarckism and orthogenesis. How was this possible?

1.5 Biospeleological ideas in France and elsewhere in continental Europe (1809–1950)

French and French-based researchers from Lamarck to the biospeleologists of the 1950s have had and continue to have a tremendous intellectual influence on biospeleological ideas. Their way of thinking and their terminology have been pervasive in cave biology. To understand why this is so, we must (1) review the political and intellectual environment in France previous to the publication of Darwin's *Origin*;

(2) examine how Darwin's book was received; and (3) investigate how and particularly why the French developed an evolutionary ideology of their own, particularly when it came to interpreting the nature of cave fauna.

Ideas on evolution (biological and otherwise) in pre-*Origin* France abound, but all have something in common: a strong philosophical rather than an empiric basis. Jean Baptiste Lamarck,[64] a physician by training, became first an assistant botanist at the French Royal Botanical Gardens, an active participant of the *Société d'Histoire naturelle*, and was then given a position of professor of 'insects and worms' at the newly created *Muséum National d'Histoire Naturelle*.

Lamarck considered himself a 'naturalist–philosopher', and therefore much of his narrative was colored with speculations and metaphysics rather than facts. In addition, his evolutionary views (mostly expressed in his 1809 *Philosophie Zoologique* and the 1815 supplement to the *Histoire Naturelle*) were never very well formulated and even sometimes contradictory. To make things worse, Lamarck's writings were translated into numerous languages, but such translations were not always accurate and some of his statements were reproduced out of context; this contributed to the general confusion as to what Lamarck really said (Corsi 2005). However, one thing is certain: he was an early organicist and progressionist who viewed nature as being linearly organized and saw today's organisms as the result of increasing complexity (Burkhardt 1977, pp. 58ff.).

Lamarck was the main (although not the first) advocate of the idea of the inheritance of acquired traits and of evolution as a goal-oriented process striving towards progressive complexity and perfection. He did not believe in the extinction of species but rather on the constant transformation into new ones. He described a metaphysical 'power of life' leading this process of increasing complexity. That, together with the modifying power of the environment, was responsible for the life forms we see on Earth. Although he never wrote about cave fauna, the case of parasites with simplified organization amused him. For this, he had a perfect explanation: they appeared primitive because they had been the recent product of spontaneous generation. External circumstances were responsible for deviations from the rule of progression,

[64] *b*. Bazentin-le- Petit, Picardy, France, 1 August 1744; *d*. Paris, France, 28 December 1829.

and some contingency (e.g. the disuse of an organ) could alter the path to complexity, generating lateral ramifications in his linear view of progression. For him the lack of teeth in whales and of eyes in (subterranean) moles were perfect examples. Lamarck had a great influence on many scientists, not only during his own time but through the twentieth century. The progressionist ideas of Lamarck also had a great influence not only in Europe but also in America, where a vigorous neo-Lamarckian school developed. That school followed Lamarck's tenets, with the exception of those that were more mystical in nature (Burkhardt 1977).

Two of Lamarck's contemporaries would also make their own contributions to the notion of increasing complexity in nature. Cuvier, for example, although a creationist, noticed some 'progression' in the succession of the geologic record. Cuvier admitted the existence of anatomical vestiges but did not seek explanations for them. He considered vestigial organs 'one of the remarkable peculiarities of natural history' (Coleman 1964, p. 154) and that is as far as he went. Geoffroy Saint-Hillaire,[65] a curator of vertebrates at the *Muséum National d'Histoire Naturelle*, was a believer in evolution, progressionism, and the Great Chain of Being, always looking for transitional forms (Bourdier 1972b; Appel 1988). He discussed the issue of the origin of vestigial organs from a mystic–religious viewpoint and interpreted them as 'disgraces' of natural beauty. Saint-Hillaire, a protégé of Lamarck, was even less materialistic than his mentor and added an aura of mysticism to evolutionary ideas, which in turn were influenced largely by the Oken's *Naturphilosophie*.

At this same time French philosophers were thinking along the same lines. For example, Marie-Jean-Antoine-Nicolas de Caritat, Marquis de Condorcet,[66] a brilliant mathematician, philosopher, and political activist, infused the idea of progress into virtually all of his historical interpretations. He adopted the concept of inheritance of acquired characters in constructing his vision for the social and organic progressive improvement of humankind, an idea also espoused by other philosophers such as

[65] *b.* Etampes, France, 15 April 1772; *d.* Paris, France, 19 June 1844.

[66] *b.* Ribemont, Picardy, France, 17 September 1743; *d.* Bourg-la-Reine, France, 28 March 1794. His book *Esquisse d'un Tableau Historique des Progrès de l'Esprit Humain*, published posthumously in 1795 and translated in 1802, analyzed human history under the view of progressiveness. For him humanity was destined to achieve an evolutionary apex through the education of the masses. His ideas were mirrored later by Teilhard de Chardin (Granger 1971; Leith 1989; Baker 2004).

Herbert Spencer,[67] Friedrich Engels,[68] and Lester Ward[69] (see Condorcet 1793–4). These ideas strongly influenced the positivist school founded by the French philosopher Auguste Comte[70] and the ideas of another French philosopher, Marcel de Serres.[71] The latter proposed the view that life was a manifestation of progressive perfection.

Thus, the intellectual environment in pre-*Origin* France was not anti-evolution as in other parts of Europe and the United States; actually one can say that no well-educated French person at that time harbored any predisposition against evolution (*transformisme*). In fact, in France, the idea of progression could be traced as far back as the development of the Modern Science period (1650–1800) at the time of the Enlightenment and the French Encyclopedism. Lamarck's contemporaries, with

[67] *b.* Derby, England, 27 April 1820; *d.* Brighton, England, 8 December 1903. He was a Lamarckian who tried to apply evolutionary ideas to support free market ideologies; he also believed that humans were on a natural progressionist route and that the state might create obstacles to economic progress by trying to regulate free society. He rejected the notion of special creation and believed that species were the result of modification of pre-existing ones. For him evolution (a term he introduced in the biological lexicon) was change from the homogenous to the heterogeneous. He was an agnostic who believed that science and religion were trying to answer different questions and that even if you believed in God that was not necessarily incompatible with the idea of evolution. He later embraced Darwinism but still believed in Lamarckian mechanisms to explain the transformation from simple to complex structures in nature. He believed that individuals also evolved as a consequence of learning from good and bad experiences and that at the end the good learner survived. He introduced the concept of 'survival of the fittest', and the roots of social Darwinism can be traced to him.

[68] *b.* Barmen [now part of Wuppertal], Prussian Rhineland, Germany, 28 November 1820; *d.* London, England, 5 August 1895. Engels' writings gave the philosophical background to Marxism. His philosophy was based on a materialism that was in accordance with the views of the sciences of the nineteenth century.

[69] *b.* Joliet, Illinois, USA, 18 June 1841; *d.* Washington, D.C., USA, 18 April 1913. One of the founders of American sociology, he advocated the intervention of the state to humanize society by eliminating poverty. He also advocated the regulation of competition, the establishment of equal opportunities, and cooperation. Ward attacked the very notion of social Darwinism, the *laissez-faire* doctrine and determinism. By doing so he turned against Herbert Spencer, whom he had admired earlier in his career.

[70] *b.* Montpellier, France, 17 January 1798; *d.* Paris, France, 5 September 1857. He is considered the father of positivism in philosophy.

[71] *b.* Montpellier, France, 3 November 1780; *d.* Montpellier, 22 July 1862. He was a paleontologist and zoologist who believed that the pursuit of truth required the violation of artificial disciplinary boundaries.

the exception of Cuvier, embraced some sort of transformism, although they were not sympathetic to (and even ridiculed to a certain extent) Lamarck's unfounded speculations, particularly the idea that a new organ could be produced by the 'desire' of an organism to create it. However, the French were unprepared to view evolution as a materialistic, random process that excluded any metaphysical explanation. And the way in which Darwin's *Origin* was translated into French made matters worse.

The *Origin* was translated into French by Clémence-Augustine Royer.[72] This polymath and feminist writer was not only a great believer in science, but also thought that women should transform it into 'female science.' Royer probably first heard of Darwin's new work on evolution through a review of the *Origin* by the Geneva-based Swiss entomologist and paleontologist Françoise Jules Pictet de la Rive[73] while lecturing on Lamarck in Geneva in 1860. Pictet was one of the first to receive a copy of *The Origin of Species* directly from Darwin. As soon as Royer read the *Origin*, she convinced her publisher, Guillaumin, to print the first translation of Darwin's work into French. According to Royer

> It was then [after lecturing in Geneva] that I translated the *Origin of Species* of Ch. Darwin, which had appeared in England, during the same winter in which I had affirmed in my course the doctrine of Lamarck. If I translated Darwin, it was because he had brought new proofs to the support of my thesis. (*Harvey 1999*)

In other words, her interest in translating Darwin was not so much to spread the Briton's gospel, but rather to prove how important Lamarck was as the father of evolution as an idea. And it showed.

With the advice of the French zoologist and early Darwinian enthusiast René-Edouard Claparède,[74] who had also enthusiastically reviewed Darwin's book, she translated the third edition of *The Origin* (which was, in terms of explanations on rudimentation, more Lamarckian than the first two editions), adding not only numerous footnotes, but also a lengthy prologue in which she espoused eugenics, being probably the first author to do so by applying Darwin's ideas. Darwin, who had authorized the move to have his book translated into French, was not happy with Royer's preface and footnotes. She not only changed the title of the book, but more significantly, Royer used the word 'election' instead of

[72] *b*. Nantes, Brittany, France, 21 April 1830; *d*. Paris, France; 6 February 1902.

[73] *b*. Geneva, Switzerland, 27 September 1809; *d*. Geneva, 15 March 1872.

[74] *b*. Chancy, Geneva Canton, Switzerland, 24 April 1832; *d*. Sienna, Tuscany, Italy, 31 May 1871.

'selection', thus giving the impression that nature had a mind of its own, directing evolutionary events in a purposeful manner.

The title of Darwin's book in French was *De l'Origine des Espèces, ou Des Lois de Progrès chez les Êtres Organizés* (*The Origin of Species, or the Laws of Progress among Organized Beings*), giving the impression that Darwin emphasized the idea of progress, a principle on which he was ambiguous at best. Darwin himself, in his correspondence to several of his colleagues such as Jean Louis Armand de Quatrefages,[75] Charles Lyell,[76] and Asa Gray,[77] made it known that he was extremely unhappy with the French translation. Despite this version of the *Origin* being closer to the French state of mind, Darwin sensed that the book had a cold reception in France. In a letter to Quatrefages, a French naturalist who opposed Darwin's ideas on evolution but yet respected him, Darwin wrote

A week hardly passes without my hearing of some naturalist in Germany who supports my view, & often puts an exaggerated value on my works; whilst in France I have not heard of a single zoologist except M. Gaudry [Albert Jean Gaudry[78]] (and he only partially) who supports my views'. (*F. Darwin 1896, vol. 2, p. 299*)

[75] *b.* Berthezène, near Valleraugue (Gard), France, 12 February 1810; *d.* Paris, France, 1892. He specialized in invertebrates and was particularly interested in the degeneration (*dégradation*) of structures among organisms, although most of his ideas in this matter were wrong. He opposed Darwin's evolutionary ideas (he believed in the fixity of species) but maintained very cordial relations with him.

[76] *b.* Kinnordy, Angus, Scotland, 14 November 1797; *d.* London, England, 22 February 1875. The most influential geologist of the nineteenth century. His ideas set the stage for Darwin's thinking that life must have been evolving on Earth as the geology of the planet had also been changing over long periods of time. He was a close friend of Darwin and accepted Darwin's evolutionary ideas, one of the few who immediately accepted the notion of natural selection as a major force of evolution (Wilson 1973).

[77] *b.* Sauquoit (Paris), Oneida County, New York, USA, 18 November 1810; *d.* Cambridge, Massachusetts, USA, 30 January 1888. A physician who became the leading American botanist of the nineteenth century. He embraced Darwinian evolution, corresponding extensively with Darwin, but was not enthusiastic about natural selection as its mechanism, to say the least. He tried to reconcile Darwinism with religion through a sort of theistic evolutionism.

[78] *b.* St.-Germain-en-Laye, France, 15 September 1827; *d.* Paris, France, 27 November 1908. Affected by the death of his mother when he was very young, he developed a strong mysticism during his entire life. He worked at the *Muséum National d'Histoire Naturelle* in Paris and was a great believer in the Great Chain of Being. For him humans were the ultimate example of perfection. He later became a defender of the idea of evolution. Yet his explanation for evolution was mystical: that it was designed by God and that God rejoiced in his own continuous creation, in which God was the only fixed and untransmutable being (Bourdier 1972a).

Darwin may have not been happy with this translation; however, he might not have any other alternatives since he had trouble finding a publisher in France for his book anyway (Herbert 2005).

For years to come, Royer continued publishing and lecturing about Lamarck, her personal hero. She, who was probably the first European woman recognized as a professional anthropologist, had also been an enthusiastic caver.

Royer's translation of *Origin* was very much celebrated by Étienne Rabaud.[79] Rabaud had been a student of Alfred Girard, the first holder of the Chair of Evolution at the Sorbonne and a rabid Lamarckian. Rabaud became such a fanatical supporter of Lamarck's ideas that by the 1930s he was even questioning the value of Darwinism (see, for example, Rabaud 1941). When commenting on Royer's preface, Rabaud was enthusiastic because she had restored Lamarck to public attention.

Were this inaccurate translation and the current intellectual climate the only reasons for the poor reception of Darwin's ideas in France? Not really. Just before the publication of the *Origin*, France had witnessed one of the most public and passionate scientific controversies in history. Between 1858 and 1859 French society was inundated with the tales of the dispute between Félix Archimède Pouchet[80] and Louis Pasteur,[81] that is, between the belief in spontaneous generation and the belief that the ability to beget life is an exclusive and continual property of living beings. Although Pasteur won the argument and his was a triumph for science as a method of inquiry, Pouchet's sympathizers also supported agnosticism whereas Pasteur's were more comfortable with religious and metaphysical ideas. Thus, despite the fact that the French were not opposed to evolution as an idea per se, the mechanism championed by Darwin, natural selection, reminded them of the agnosticism and materialism attached to spontaneous generation. Thus, the land that had given birth to precursors of evolutionary ideas such as Georges-Louis Buffon,[82] Lamarck, and

[79] *b.* 1868; *d.* 1956. An anti-Darwinian who taught Pierre-Paul Grassé.

[80] *b.* Rouen, France, 26 August 1800; *d.* Rouen, 6 December 1872. A physician who became the Director of the *Muséum d'Histoire Naturelle* in Rouen. He was a prolific author who gained notoriety because of his dispute with Pasteur over spontaneous generation.

[81] *b.* Dole, Jura, France, 27 December 1822, *d.* Chateau Villeneuve-l'Étang, near Paris, France, 28 September 1895. One of the world's most important scientists, he was a chemist by training. Recognized microbes as transmitters of diseases, invented vaccines, and disproved spontaneous generation.

[82] *b.* Montbard, Bourgogne [Burgundy], France, 7 September 1707; *d.* Paris, France, 16 April 1788. Well known for his 36-volume *Histoire Naturelle (Natural History)*

Geoffroy Saint-Hillaire, gave Darwin the cold shoulder, and little public controversy of the book took place.

Other political and social events further cemented the French view of evolution as a mystical idea. One experience that generated a nationwide feeling of disgrace was the political and military humiliation of the French by the Prussians during the 1870–1871 War (Howard 1981). As in any nation that has been defeated, their people found consolation in mystical nationalistic ideas. The ideas of national destiny and historical progress became strongly rooted in the French psyche and were reinforced through revisions of school curricula. The Spencerian interpretation of 'survival of the fittest' became very unpopular: Prussia had developed into an imperialistic and invincible neighbor and looked like 'the fittest' to the French psyche. Now French intellectuals threw themselves fully into the arms of mysticism to explain their grand views of nature, and evolution was at the center of all this.

It was in this intellectual atmosphere that the seeds for French neo-Lamarckism were planted, and these seeds were sown in abundance by French biospeleologists. The father of these neo-Lamarckian ideas in France was Henri Louis Bergson.[83] Bergson was a philosopher and a mathematician whose ideas on evolution were largely anti-materialistic and maintained that organic evolution was just part of a larger, universal cosmic evolution. He was a Lamarckian follower regarding the canon of use and disuse and the principle that evolution was directed by an internal force, which he called *élan vital*. He was fiercely patriotic and opposed Darwinism because he did not accept the notion of an undirected mechanism such as natural selection as the major force of evolution. Part of his popularity was due to the fact that by using the notion of an *élan vital*, he was allowing for a role to be played by religion in evolutionary processes (Goudge 1973).

Bergson was familiar with the ideas of Cope and Theodor Gustav Heinrich Eimer,[84] a disciple of Rudolf Albert Kölliker,[85] who

(1749–88). He maintained very advanced evolutionary ideas for his time (Roger 1973, 1997; Farber 1975; Sloan 1975; Eddy 1994).

[83] *b*. Paris, France, 18 October 1859; *d*. Paris, 4 January 1941.

[84] *b*. Stäfa, near Zurich, Switzerland, 22 September 1843; *d*. Tübingen, Germany, 29 May 1898. In 1875, he became a professor of zoology and comparative anatomy at the University of Tübingen. He described orthogenesis as an intrinsic drive in life towards perfection, a form of directed evolution. He dismissed natural selection as a major force in evolution while rejecting vitalism.

[85] *b*. Zurich, Switzerland, 6 July 1817; *d*. Würzburg, Germany, 2 November 1905. He studied under Lorenz Oken, Johannes Müller, and F. G. J. Henle and was greatly

championed the idea of and popularized the term *orthogenesis* (Eimer 1887–8). This term was first proposed by the zoologist Johann Wilhelm Haacke[86] (1893). Others used different terms for essentially the same concept: orthoevolution (Plate 1913), nomogenesis (Berg 1926), aristogenesis (H. F. Osborn 1934), and the omega principle (T. de Chardin 1955). Bergson, an intense French patriot, proposed in 1907 the idea of the *élan vital* or vital impetus (the term is so obscure that it is usually left untranslated, but is reminiscent of Lamarck's expression of the 'power of life'). He used this term to refer to a characteristic of life that, according to him, always pushes life in the direction of complexity; this, for Bergson, was the mechanism of orthogenesis, which moved evolution from the domain of the divine into the natural world. Given that Bergson did not like natural selection as an idea because of its materialistic implications, but at the same time he could not find strong evidence supporting the inheritance of acquired characters, *élan vital* was for him the answer. Of course, and unlike natural selection or the inheritance of acquired characters, since this idea could not be tested, it could not be disproved either.

According to Bergson, both Darwinian evolution and finalism (the idea that evolution has a sense of directedness toward an end and that such a path has already been laid) could coexist. And what is the unifying force behind such a possibility? It cannot be natural selection, of course, since that is based on apparent randomness, but rather it must be a mystical force, *élan vital*. These ideas may have been interpreted as Lamarckian with a religious twist, but that is also unclear. Bergson, a man profoundly concerned about the fate of his fellow Jews, almost became a Catholic; it is evident therefore that his religious views were also complex.

Bergson's ideas became extremely popular, and other philosophers such as the French Lucien Cuénot[87] expanded them by arguing that species succeed in a particular environment because they were

influenced by *Naturphilosophie*, being a close associate of Nägeli. He embraced evolution but opposed the role of natural selection (Hintzsche 1973).

86 *b.* Clenze, Germany, 23 August 1855; *d.* Luneburg, Germany, 6 December 1912.

87 *b.* Paris, France, 21 October 1866; *d.* Nancy, France, 7 January 1951. Cuénot was a brilliant scientist and the first French biologist to accept Darwinist ideas in Lamarckian France, although he was not fully convinced of the all-powerful role played by natural selection. He also pioneered genetic studies in France, which aimed to prove Mendelian inheritance. However, he refused to completely accept neo-Darwinism because he maintained a finalistic view of evolution. One of his most lasting influences in biospeleology was the development of his notion of preadaptation, according to which new ecological niches were occupied by mutants that already had some characteristics that favored them to colonize such environments (Tétry 1971b).

'preadapted.' The term he coined was *préadaptation* (Cuénot 1911, vol. IV, p. 306), and it became an extremely popular idea among biospeleologists, many of whom still firmly believe in it today. Needless to say, Cuénot espoused linear evolution, except that, in the new era of experimental genetics of the early twentieth century, he believed that mutation (*sensu stricto*) was the cause of it.

In summary, Bergson was a progressionist but he did not believe that there was a necessarily pre-designed goal; rather, that final progression would lead to a less predictable result. He was thus attempting to taint Darwinism with the very popular idea of progression.

All of these new philosophies of life were developed at the time when speleology in general and biospeleology in particular were becoming sciences in their own right, and all their foundations were being laid by French or France-based naturalists. One such was the French jurist Édouard-Alfred Martel,[88] a lawyer and a geographer by training. He was known for his pioneer work in 1894 on the physiography and accessibility of caves, and he coined the term speleology (in both French and English) in the 1890s. He explored the limestone caves of Cévennes and, with others, made descents into previously unknown caves of Europe, Asia, and America. In 1895 he founded the *Société de Spéléologie* in France. Martel was the judge of the Tribunal of Commerce in Paris from 1886 until 1899, when he became a professor of subterranean geography at the Sorbonne (the first speleological academic post in the world); he was appointed a member of the staff of the Department of Geological Maps of France in 1901. He is often called 'the father of modern speleology' and his publication record includes more than 1,000 articles and books on the subject. In 1904 Armand Viré,[89] another Frenchman, coined the term biospeleology (*biospeleologie*). Viré had written his doctoral thesis on cave fauna in 1899 and thereafter established an underground laboratory in the catacombs of Paris.

However, the two figures that would ultimately consolidate biospeleology as a science and give it many of the distinctive features that it has today were Emil G. Racovitza[90] and René Gabriel Jeannel.[91] Racovitza,

[88] *b.* Pontoise, France, 1 July 1859; *d.* Château de la Garde, near de Montbrison, France, 3 June 1938.

[89] *b.* Lorrez-le-Bocage-Préaux, Saine-et-Marne, France, 28 January 1869; d. Moissac, France, 15 July 1951.

[90] *b.* Iasi, Romania, 15 November 1868; *d.* Bucharest, Romania, 17 November 1947.

[91] *b.* Toulouse, France, 22 March 1879; *d.* Paris, France, 20 February 1965.

a Romanian-born, French-educated naturalist, started exploring caves in the Pyrenees in 1905 together with his protégé Jeannel. Racovitza initiated an extensive international research program under the umbrella of *Biospéologica* (a supplement to the scientific French publication *Archives de Zoologie Experimentale et Generale*), primarily intending to document and collect cave fauna. In 1920 he founded in Cluj, Romania, the world's first speleological institute. He explored 1,200 caves in Europe and Africa, collected about 50,000 specimens of cave animals, and published 66 papers on subterranean fauna totaling almost 6,000 pages (Motas 1962). He read, and was greatly influenced by, Eimer and Cope (on orthogenesis), Packard (on neo-Lamarckism), and Louis Dollo[92] (on general evolutionary ideas). He had a great deal of distaste for the selectionist Weisman (Motas 1962).

Racovitza's two main publications dealing with biospeleological theory were his 1907 *Essai sur les Problemes Biospeologiques* (*Essays on Biospeleological Problems*, published at the same time that Bergson was proposing his *élan vital* and considered to be the birth certificate of biospeleology as a science) and his little known 1929 book *Evolutia si Problemele ei* (*Evolution and its Problems*). In these publications he clearly delineated his evolutionary thought about cave organisms, which can be summarized as follows.

1. All cave organisms were 'preadapted' to the cave environment.
2. Function (or lack thereof) creates the organ (or generates its disappearance). He was a strong supported of the use vs. disuse concept.
3. Natural selection is of little importance because natural variation is virtually non-existent (he was a staunch typologist).
4. Evolution is directional as evidenced by 'phyletic lines.'

Similar views were endorsed by his student Jeannel (Jeannel 1950, p. 7) who studied subterranean beetles from Europe and Africa. With Racovitza he founded in 1907 the journal *Biospeleologica* and in 1926 published *Faune Cavernicole de la France*. He considered many of the organisms found in caves as 'living fossils', and these ideas continue to have a tremendous impact on biospeleologists all over the world.

[92] *b*. Lille, France, 7 December 1857; *d*. Bruxelles, Belgium, 19 April 1931. An engineer turned biologist, Dollo became famous for the reconstruction of *Iguanodon* fossils in Belgium and for stating 'Dollo's Law of Irreversibility' according to which organisms never return to their original state, particularly when losing complex structures.

Although all this can be presented as a great accomplishment for the French in terms of initiating and developing the systematic study of caves, none of these figures ever embraced any form of Darwinism, but rather different shades of neo-Lamarckism first and different forms of finalism such as orthogenesis and organicism later. Thus, the French biologists who embraced transformism beginning in 1880 did so via neo-Lamarckism while strongly opposing the idea of natural selection (Grimoult 1998, p. 150). This philosophy extended well into the twentieth century with Lucien Cuénot, Maurice Caullery,[93] and Jean Rostand.[94]

Therefore, the utilization of cave organisms as perfect examples for demonstrating the legitimacy of the French version of neo-Lamarckism seemed to be inevitable, and this is exactly what happened. The main points in common of these French intellectuals were:

1. Acceptance of evolution as a linear phenomenon (orthogenesis) leading to a perfecting complexity in nature
2. Rejection of natural selection as a phenomenon of any relevance
3. Development of finalism, vitalism, organicism, and other expressions of essentialism in biology
4. Utilization of cave organisms as 'perfect' examples of these views of life
5. Mutual reinforcement of ideas concerning biospeleological paradigms (blind, depigmented animals) and philosophical notions of progress within the same country: France.

1.6 The impact of the modern synthesis (1936–47)

The modern synthesis was, without question, the major philosophical and scientific revolution that established evolution as the central idea in biology in the twentieth century. It meant that the non-Lamarckian Darwin was rescued; also that metaphysical ideas in biology were abandoned, and that the typological (essentialist) views of life were replaced by populational ones. Of all the major architects of this

[93] *b*. Bergues, France, 5 September 1868; *d*. Paris, France, 13 July 1958. He lectured at the University of Paris (1903) where he taught evolution from a neo-Lamarckian perspective (Tétry 1971a).

[94] *b*. Paris, France, 30 October 1894; *d*. Ville d'Avray, France, 4 September 1977. A biologist and philosopher who worked on developmental biology and maintained neo-Lamarckian views of evolution.

movement, only one specifically approached the issue of evolution of cave organisms.

Theodosius Dobzhansky[95] (1970, pp. 405–7) put the issue of evolution in caves in its right perspective, and his ideas can be summarized as follows.

1. Evolution is opportunistic
2. Adaptation to a new environment may decrease the importance of some organs/functions which may become vestigial and disappear
3. There are numerous examples of rudimentation and/or loss of organs among both animals and plants
4. Acquisition/enlargement of organs can occur among organisms that otherwise show 'regression' of other organs and/or functions
5. Cave animals provide some of the best examples of the phenomenon of 'regression' but it is not unique or exclusive to them: some cave organisms do not display regression, and regressions may be found among non-cave animals
6. A great deal of variation exists for these characters even within the same species and/or population
7. Both genes and phenotypic plasticity are responsible for troglomorphic characters
8. Neo-Lamarckian explanation aside, two major hypotheses for explaining the genetic mechanisms of rudimentation can be considered: (a) mutation pressure (neutral mutation) if not opposed to natural selection (relaxation of selection); and (b) natural selection directly favoring rudimentation via energy economy or 'struggle of the parts.' Evidence seems to support the latter, not the former.

The scientific evidence accumulated during the second half of the twentieth century supports all these statements (except for 8, or the 'struggle of the parts').

The major contributions of Dobzhansky to our understanding of the evolution of cave biota were numerous. The first one was to stress the role played by opportunism in evolution. Opportunism is probably much more important in natural systems than is generally appreciated (Berry

[95] *b.* Nemirov, Ukraine, Russia, 25 January 1900; *d.* Sacramento, California, USA, 18 December 1975. In 1927 Dobzhansky moved to the United States, where he worked with Thomas Hunt Morgan. Although a religious person, he rejected the idea of a god directing the course of nature or a direction in evolution (Hecht and Steere 1970; Ayala 1971).

1989). As proven again and again, evolution is a by-product of disrupted communities in which brief opportunities for divergence are created (Dimichele *et al.* 1987). Opportunistic organisms can take advantage of previous conditions (Andersson 1990) to fill empty adaptive zones (Bronson 1979; Benton 1983; Harries *et al.* 1996) for feeding (Jaksĭć & Braker 1983), breeding (Tindle 1984), and social behavior (McKenna 1979). Opportunism has also been proven to lead to mutualism (Fiedler 2001), intraspecific parasitism (Tinsley 1990; Field 1992), and reproduction (Kasyanov *et al.* 1997). Opportunism has been described even at the molecular level (Doolittle 1988; Meléndez-Hevia *et al.* 1996; Green 2001) and has also been identified as a major factor for colonizing species (Martin and Braga 1994) particularly when colonizing extreme environments (Tunnicliffe 1991). As discussed in Chapter 3 of this book, these very same statements can be made about cave organisms.

As a matter of fact, opportunism is the reason behind life being so ubiquitous on earth: life on earth can be found at naturally extremely low and high temperatures (from polar regions to geothermal environments), in both high and low pH and high salinity, including but not limited to hydrothermal vents, freshwater alkaline hot springs, acidic solfatara fields, anaerobic geothermal mud and soils, acidic sulfur and pyrite areas, carbonate springs and alkaline soils, the cold pressurized depths of the ocean, and soda and highly alkaline lakes (Kristjánsson and Hreggvidsson 1995; Horikoshi and Grant 1998). In fact, there is now an entire branch of biology dealing with what are called extremophiles (a term coined by MacElroy in 1974). The discovery of hydrothermal vents in 1977 opened the door to an entirely new set of habitats that did not need light to be self-sustaining. In other words, life has shown an incredible ability to succeed in such a diversity of environments, leading some to predict the occurrence of life on other planets, including some in our solar system (Nealson and Conrad 1999). Today, life forms in caves do not seem so 'extreme', nor do we need to use metaphysical explanations to understand their origin and evolution. As George Gaylord Simpson,[96] another of the architects of the modern synthesis, put it, 'The course of evolution follows opportunity rather than plan' (Simpson 1949, p. 160).

The second major contribution of Dobzhansky to this issue was to remind biospeleologists that the phenomenon of reduction and/or

[96] *b.* Chicago, Illinois, USA, 16 June 1902; *d.* Tucson, Arizona, USA, 6 October 1984. Simpson was one of the most prominent paleontologists of the twentieth century.

loss of phenotypic features is not unique to cave organisms and is actually ubiquitous throughout all animal and plant taxa. Other typical animal examples include parasites, deep-sea creatures, and inhabitants of murky waters. Even some parasitic plants have lost chlorophyll. In addition, limblessness and flightlessness are common among animals living on small islands and high mountains (Darlington 1943; Byers 1969; Livezey and Humphrey 1986; Roff 1990; Finston and Peck 1995). The loss of limbs among cetaceans and snakes is an example of a major evolutionary novelty by default. Even humans have lost or reduced a number of ancestral characters (Diamond and Stermer 1999). Thus, troglomorphisms can be explained by using well-known evolutionary mechanisms without the need to resort to neo-Lamarckian explanations or terminology such as 'regressive evolution.' The problem is that, despite Dobzhansky's pointed comments on this issue, the study of this phenomenon has been largely neglected by mainstream evolutionary biologists for at least two reasons: (a) the prevailing idea that evolutionary novelties should result from addition, not subtraction, of characters and (b) the use of this biological phenomenon by neo-Lamarckians to advance their own cause of either inheritance of acquired characters or the notion that evolution has some sort of directionality, which has made this field less attractive to modern evolutionary biologists (Romero 2001b).

The third major contribution by Dobzhansky was to point out that variability of reduced phenotypic characters is widespread. As shown in Chapter 3, that is clearly the case, but more importantly, Dobzhansky's statement was a serious blow to typological or essentialist beliefs among biospeleologists: in other words, there is not such a thing as a characteristic 'archetype' for cave animals. Not all of them are blind and depigmented; when they are, the degree to which such features (and others) are expressed varies greatly.

The final and perhaps most important contribution by Dobzhansky, especially from the mechanistic viewpoint, was his statement that the loss and/or reduction of characters had a genetic basis but was also influenced by phenotypic plasticity. This should not be surprising: there is a correlation between behavioral plasticity and opportunism (Brown 1990; Werdelin and Asa Fortelius 1999; Johnson 2000). Lefebvre and colleagues (1997) found links between opportunism and phenotypic evolution; they also proposed that innovation rate in the field may be a useful measure of behavioral plasticity. These are issues that are fully explored later in this book.

Ernst Mayr[97] also acknowledged that '(the) evolutionary phenomena dealing with regression and the loss of structures (. . .) are entirely consistent with the synthetic theory of evolution' (Mayr 1960, p. 351). One might think that this line of reasoning would have had a major impact on biospeleologists as a whole, but the fact of the matter is that it did not.

For one thing, biospeleology continued to flourish in France and struggled elsewhere. A major speleological journal, *Annales de Speleologie*, was founded in France in 1946, and the first international Speleological Congress took place in France in 1952. More importantly than that, French evolutionists in general and biospeleologists in particular, rather than softening their neo-Lamarckian and orthogenetic stances, hardened them. We see this rigidity in the writings not only of Lucien Cuénot but also of Jeannel, Maurice Caullery, Jean Rostand, and Pierre-Paul Grassé.[98] They kept espousing neo-Lamarckian explanations on heredity despite all of the evidence to the contrary, and their firm belief in orthogenetic ideas had now reached an uncompromising finalism: the belief that natural processes, especially evolution, are directed towards some predetermined end or goal by some sort of unexplained or untested force.

This was taken to an extreme by one of the most influential twentieth-century biospeleologists, Albert Vandel.[99] Vandel championed the idea of organicism and orthogenesis in his writings (duly summarized in his influential book, which was made available in both French and English; see Vandel (1965, pp. 471ff. of the English translation). According to him, all phyletic lines pass through successive stages: the stage of creation, the stage of expansion and diversification, and finally the stage of specialization and senescence. The last stage of this cycle was 'regressive or gerontocratic' evolution. He considered cavernicoles good examples of regressive evolution. The title of another influential biospeleological

[97] *b.* Kempten, Germany, 5 July 1904; *d.* Bedford, Massachusetts, USA, 3 February 2005. He was a leading evolutionary biologist of the twentieth century and one of the architects of the modern synthesis. He was a severe critic of typological thinking and finalistic interpretations of evolution.

[98] *b.* Périgueux, France, 27 November 1895; *d.* Paris, France, 9 July 1985. He was mostly known as the editor of the 35-volume *Traité de Zoologie*. He did not believe in natural selection and/or mutation as the causes of evolution but rather on an 'internal factor' as the engine of evolutionary change. He claimed that such an 'internal factor' was real, not mystical, and that was different from the mystical vitalism espoused by some of his predecessors.

[99] *b.* Besançon, Jura, France, 26 December 1894; *d.* Toulouse, France, 11 October 1980.

book, *L'Evolution Regressive des Poissons Cavernicoles et Abyssaux* (*The Regressive Evolution of the Cave and Abyssal Fishes*) by Georges Thinès[100] (1969) leaves little doubt of the orthogenetic state of mind of this and most other biospeleologists at the time. Probably the most famous orthogenecist of this time was the Jesuit French paleontologist Pierre Teilhard de Chardin,[101] who believed that evolution was constantly marching toward some sort of point of perfection (the 'Omega point').

How did all these distinguished French intellectuals and naturalists remain blind to the evidence being accumulated by biologists elsewhere? Bowler (1983, p. 108) has argued that, unlike their British, American, and German counterparts, French biologists of the Darwinian and neo-Darwinian eras were rather isolated from their colleagues elsewhere and also seemed to be content with Cuvier's legacy, and since Cuvier had beaten Lamarck in the argument about evolution, why bother to discuss the ideas of a Briton in this regard? In addition, French biologists had remained closely tied to the morphological–systematic tradition of Cuvier and Geoffroy Saint-Hillaire, were totally uninterested in other areas such as ecology or developmental biology, and maintained a fixed, descriptive view of life. However, two other factors should be mentioned (discussed earlier) that also contributed to the French view of life: their feelings of nationalism and Catholic mysticism. After all, no one prevented them from reading Dobzhansky, Mayr, Simpson, or any other major contributor to the modern synthesis.

[100] *b.* Liège, Belgium, 10 February 1923. An experimental psychologist, poet, and essayist.

[101] *b.* Sarcenat, France, 1 May 1881; *d.* New York City, New York, 10 April 1955. Chardin was heavily influenced by Henri Louis Bergson and the Bergsonian scholar Eduard Le Roy. His opinions carried some weight since he distinguished himself as a paleoanthropologist. His evolutionary views, better articulated in his posthumously published *Le Phénomène Humaine* (*The Phenomenon of Man*) (1955) contended that cosmic evolution is the process by which God brings into being a 'fullness of Christ' that includes a morally and spiritually mature humanity and a fully developed natural world. For Chardin the evolutionary process is governed by a 'law of complexification' according to which inorganic matter will reach ever more complex forms, resulting in inorganic matter being followed by organic matter and organic matter being followed by conscious life forms. He expected that at some point this 'complexification' in humans would enable them to attain an 'Omega Point' at which Christ's fullness would include as his 'body' a unified humanity that was at peace. Chardin epitomized the mixture of mystic Catholicism and progressionist/positivist views that have dominated many evolutionary concepts in biospeleology (Olivier 1967; Dobzhansky 1968; Gentner 1968; Potter 1968).

It is interesting to note that the only French scientists who embraced the new populational view of evolution were not biologists but mathematicians: these rare exceptions were the population geneticists Georges Téissier[102] and Philippe L'Heritier,[103] who, because they worked entirely outside the realms of biology and in a field (mathematics) that did not need metaphysics to achieve its goals, were free to pursue the mathematical population ideas of Ronald Fisher[104] and Sewall Wright[105] who so greatly contributed to our current ideas in evolution.

How did the non-French thinkers and biospeleologists respond when faced with the clear contrast of ideas between the modern synthesis on one side and neo-Lamarckism and orthogenesis on the other? Not particularly well. First of all, many philosophers of the 1920s and 1930s, such as Samuel Alexander,[106] a British realist metaphysician, and Jan Smuts,[107] the South African statesman, continued to support orthogenetic theories. The same can be said of later philosophers such as Alfred North Whitehead[108] with his theory of organisms and Mihály Polanyi[109] with his theory of personal knowledge.

[102] *b.* Paris, France, 19 February 1900; *d.* Roscoff, France, 7 January 1972. He profoundly influenced many French scientists including Jacques Monod.

[103] *b.* Ambert (Puy de Dôme), France, 1906; *d.* 1990.

[104] *b.* East Finchley, London, UK, 17 February 1890; *d.* Adelaide, Australia, 29 July 1962.

[105] *b.* Melrose, Massachusetts, USA, 21 December 1889; *d.* Madison, Wisconsin, USA, 3 March 1988.

[106] *b.* Sydney, New South Wales, Australia, 6 January 1859; *d.* Manchester, England, 13 September 1938. He was a philosopher that proposed the idea of 'emergent evolution' according to which evolution allows for the appearance of certain features such as consciousness due to some reorganization of pre-existing features. These ideas were an extension of Henri Bergson's *Créative Evolution* (1907).

[107] *b.* Bovenplaats, near Malmesbury, Cape Colony, South Africa, 24 May 1870; *d.* Doornkloof, Irene, near Pretoria, South Africa, 11 September 1950. He was a soldier, statement, and scholar who in 1926 published a book, *Holism and Evolution*, in which he proposed that nature had the tendency of creating wholes that were greater than the parts through the process of 'creative evolution' by which he was espousing an orthogenetic view of evolutions.

[108] *b.* Ramsgate, Kent, England, 15 February 1861; *d.* Cambridge, Massachusetts, USA, 30 December 1947. A mathematician by training, he became very interested in speculative metaphysics dealing with the issue of the role played by constructions of mathematics, science, and philosophy in the nature or things.

[109] *b.* Budapest, Hungary, 12 March 1891; *d.* Northampton, England, 22 February 1976. He was trained as a physician but worked on philosophy and social sciences. His philosophical work was full of examples from natural sciences.

Biospeleology in other countries was delayed and anemic and therefore leaned heavily on French ideas and concepts in its development. In the United States, for example, very little had been done since the early twentieth century when Eigenmann published his 1909 book on the cave vertebrates of America. In fact what was accomplished in the remainder of the first half of the twentieth century was by foreign researchers such as the Spaniard Ignacio Bolívar[110] and the French Jeannel, who extensively explored US caves in 1928 (the results were published in 1931). After that, a few taxonomists showed sparse interest in some cave groups (see Barr 1966) but without contributing anything to biospeleological theory. In fact, the National Speleological Society (NSS) was not founded until 1941, i.e. 47 years after the founding of its French counterpart, and as Barr (1966, p. 16) himself put it, 'for the first 15 years of its existence, the society had little effect on cave biology.'

The first American scientist who started to look at cave organisms from a non-orthogenetic stance was Charles Marcus Breder,[111] whose behavioral, physiological, and ecological studies on cave fishes are still cited in the literature. However, since he was not a cave explorer, his contributions have been largely ignored by 'hard core' speleologists (Barr (1966) does not even mention him in his history of cave biology of the USA). This is an interesting phenomenon that permeates biospeleology to this date: on one side of the fence are the cave explorers/scientists still strongly influenced by orthogenetic ideas on cave fauna; on the other side we find the 'outside' scientists who just happen to study cave organisms because they find them interesting, not because these scientists happen to be spelunkers.

In fact, it was not until the 1960s that the first modern generation of American biologists began making contributions to biospeleology beyond a purely taxonomic level. Names such as Thomas Poulson, David Culver, Thomas Barr, John Holsinger, and Kenneth Christiansen are the first to come to mind, but they are not the only ones. Yet, although they did not subscribe to Vandel's extreme orthogenetic interpretation of cave fauna, they were certainly ambiguous about the importance

[110] *b.* Madrid, Spain, 9 November 1850; *d.* Mexico City, Mexico, 19 November 1944. He was an entomologist who described more than 1,000 species of insect, some of them from caves.

[111] *b.* Jersey City, New Jersey, USA, 25 June 1897; *d.* Englewood, Florida, USA, 28 October 1983. Breder led the renaissance of the study of cave fishes by using *Astyanax fasciatus* as a prime research subject. He was the dominant figure in hypogean fish research in the 1940s and 1950s (Romero 1984b, 1986a, 2001a).

of natural selection, heavily utilized orthogenetic concepts and jargon such as preadaptation and 'regressive evolution,' and rarely (if ever) mentioned opportunism or phenotypic plasticity as mechanisms directly involved in the evolution of cave fauna. Unfortunately, it seems that even today biospeleology has not recovered from the distractions of its slow, stumbling beginning and still fails to fully embrace modern evolutionary and ecological theory.

1.7 The roots of current intellectual inertia

The effects of this intellectual inertia continue to be pervasive. In France, natural selection has yet to become central to evolutionary discussions; French evolutionary biologists seem to have jumped from neo-Lamarckism right into molecular evolution. Fortunately, the French molecular biologist and Nobel Prize winner Jacques Monod,[112] one of the best spokespeople for the latter, wrote a very strong argument against finalism and other forms of teleology in his 1970 *Le Hasard et la Necessité* (*Chance and Necessity*). But somehow these and other strong arguments against metaphysical biology have yet to fully impact biospeleology, even in Anglo-Saxon countries. As Mayr (1982, p. 516) put it: 'To convince someone who is not familiar with the evolutionary mechanisms that the world is not predetermined and – so to speak – programmed seems hopelessly difficult.'

Even current American biospeleologists have not escaped the shadow of neo-Lamarckism and orthogenesis, as shown by their uncritical use of concepts and terms such as preadaptation and 'regressive evolution'. Not only have such intellectual schools of thought been created in the United States, but they also used cave organisms to epitomize these ideas. What the French did, as true developers of biospeleology as a science, was to color their explanations with additional metaphysical auras.

Unfortunately the belief that evolution has a direction, such as toward complexity, is deeply rooted, although no one has proven that such is the case (see, for example, Maynard Smith 1970 for a discussion). Biospeleology is a science characterized by confusion in both terminology and

[112] *b*. Paris, France, 9 February 1910; *d*. Paris, 31 May 1976. He read Darwin at an early age and this motivated him to become a biologist. He was influenced by George Teissier, among others. He was extraordinary in comparison to his fellow French biologists in that he viewed evolution as the result of chance, not as a predetermined phenomenon in the best of the neo-Darwinian tradition.

concepts. In the present author's view, this confusion is the result of biospeleology being a science whose pioneers and major practitioners, having been very resistant to any neo-Darwinian ideas, espoused, rather, neo-Lamarckian views in conjunction with the related concepts of orthogenesis, organicism, and other forms of finalism.

Later in this book, convincing evidence is provided that although cave organisms are extremely interesting and deserve much more attention, biospeleological phenomena can be explained by using current biological ideas without the need to invoke metaphysical explanations of any kind. Does that mean that biospeleology requires a new paradigm? Not really. All that we need to do is find explanations for the phenomena that occur in caves via the scientific body of information available in modern biology. The loss or simplification of phenotypic characters is neither unique nor exclusive to hypogean organisms; many cave organisms represent excellent examples of natural selection by means of phenotypic plasticity, and those hypogean organisms and their habitats represent excellent subjects in natural laboratories for the test and expansion of current and new ideas in modern biology.

2 · *Cave biodiversity*

It has been conventional wisdom for many years to consider caves as depauperate ecosystems in terms of both biodiversity and biomass. Such a notion derives from a confluence of factors: the lack of primary producers for the most part, the limitations of space, and the fact that most studies have been done in temperate latitudes, in which caves are rather poor in terms of biodiversity when compared with their tropical counterparts. This chapter surveys the biodiversity in caves to demonstrate (a) that there is a large array of taxa represented in these ecosystems and (b) that the role played by many of these organisms is much more important than previously acknowledged. Some of the biological phenomena that occur throughout hypogean biodiversity, and that will be synthesized later on in the other chapters of this book when dealing with issues related to evolution, ecology, and conservation, are also highlighted.

This survey follows the conventional list of major taxa found in most general biodiversity sources. Although the systematics of all major living groups is always changing and subject to discussion, it is preferable to follow a list of names that are familiar to the general reader, since phylogenetic discussions are beyond the scope of this book.

2.1 Bacteria (Archaeobacteria and Eubacteria)

2.1.1 Introduction

In the past all bacteria were classified under a single umbrella (prokaryotes) but better understanding of their relationships through new molecular techniques has split them into two major groups: Archaeobacteria and Eubacteria. The former represent a distinct domain of living things, which are chemically and genetically different from Eubacteria and can be found in extreme environments. Eubacteria are more commonly encountered in most environments and are better studied, owing to the relative ease of providing suitable growth conditions and to the association of some Eubacteria with plant and animal diseases. For practical reasons, both groups are discussed together in this section.

Bacterial systematics has always been a difficult issue to tackle, for several reasons. In addition to their asexual mode of reproduction, bacteria come in relatively few sizes and shapes, and nuances in these morphological features vary with environmental conditions. Morphology may be quite unrelated to true phylogenetic relationships. Originally, classifications were based on whether or not these organisms could be stained with a particular substance (Gram-positive, Gram-negative), on their shape or morphotype (rod, filament, etc.) and most importantly, what ecological role they played (photosynthetic, organotrophic, nitrogen fixer). Furthermore, these approaches can be highly deceptive: what appears to be a patch of uniform bacterial filaments may in fact be a variety of filamentous species. A study done in Lower Kane Cave, Wyoming, found four morphotypes: gray filaments, white filament bundles, yellow and white feathery mats, and thin white web-like structures. The filamentous structures consisted of two or three different phylotypes; the feather- and web-like structures had much higher species richness (Engel *et al.* 2001).

Despite the fact that the study of bacteria in caves is very recent and rather limited, what has been learned so far emphasizes the importance of these organisms in the ecology of caves. There are two main ways in which bacteria are studied: cultivation and molecular phylogenetic analysis (Barton *et al.* 2001). Because it has been estimated that as many as 99% of bacterial species in an environment are viable but non-culturable, molecular phylogenetic analysis is the preferred method for surveys of cave microbiota. The few surveys for bacteria in caves have yielded a large number and abundance of them (see, for example, Northup *et al.* 2003; Chelius and Moore 2004).

In many ways, the diversity of bacterial taxa in caves mirrors that of the epigean environment. Thus, the phylum Proteobacteria is also the one with the most representatives in caves, with members of all five of its subdivisions found in the hypogean environment. Epsilon proteobacteria appear to dominate most of the microbial ecosystems. Other groups found in caves include Actinobacteria, Bacteroidetes/Chlorobi, Flavobacteria/Bacteroides, Firmicutus, Planctomycetes, and Nitrospira. These bacteria can be found in all geological types of cave: limestone, lava, or granitic.

This phylogenetic diversity is accompanied by complex associations of these microorganisms. For example, a microbial mat may consist of sulfur oxidizers, nitrite oxidizers, and organotrophic bacteria, all working as a community of organisms. Furthermore, two particular species will not necessarily always be associated with each other, and variation can be found not only among caves but also within the same cave (Holmes *et al.* 2001; Engel *et al.* 2001, 2004a; Barton and Luiszer 2005).

Engel *et al.* (2004b) found that bacterial species diversity increased with the distance downstream in Lower Cane Cave, with colonies upstream dominated by single species. They hypothesized that this was due to a single group, epsilon Proteobacteria, taking advantage of the dissolved sulfide produced by the upstream spring, and an increased diversity of organisms taking advantage of the multiple compounds created by these bacteria as they wash downstream.

2.1.2 Bacterial physiological types in caves

Heterotrophic bacteria (associated formation: carbonate)

There are two different types of heterotrophic bacterium in the cave environment: typical epigean bacteria that are accidentally transported into the cave either by flowing water or by the activity of animals and humans that move in and out (see, for example, Schabereiter-Gurtner *et al.* 2002) and bacteria that spend their entire life cycle in the cave (see, for example, Simon *et al.* 2003).

Sulfur-oxidizing bacteria (associated formations: gypsum and carbonate)

Hydrogen sulfide is an energy-yielding substrate, so it is not surprising that there are high densities of microbial communities associated with its presence (Engel *et al.* 2004b). Sulfur-oxidizing bacteria occur most frequently at the redox boundary, that is, at the boundary at which conditions change from oxic to anoxic. This is typically in areas with sulfidic springs. Chemolithotrophic bacteria are able to gain energy by using many sulfur molecules as electron donors. Sulfur-oxidizing bacteria are the most commonly studied and possibly the most commonly found type of bacteria in caves. Examples are the phototrophic sulfur reducers: purple sulfur bacteria present at the reduction/oxidation boundary. They are phototrophic and occur along the furthest edges of the twilight zone, utilizing the smallest amounts of solar radiation.

Ammonia and nitrite oxidizers (associated formation: saltpeter)

Saltpeter caves are rich in nitrogen in the form of ammonium and nitrite. Ammonia-oxidizing bacteria are able to convert ammonia into nitrite.

The nitrite oxidizers are then able to convert this into nitrate, which is deposited in the useful chemical form of saltpeter (Northup and Lavoie 2001).

Iron and manganese oxidation bacteria (associated formation: corrosion residue)
These bacteria have been found in marine associated caves. Three caves sampled off the Mediterranean coast of France contain a group of chemolithoautotrophic bacteria that oxidize iron and manganese (Allouc and Harmelin 2001). The result is either black crusts or, in larger passages, three-dimensional structures composed of manganese and iron oxides.

2.1.3 The ecological role of bacteria in caves

One of the most important contributions of the study of bacteria in caves has been the recognition that they play an ecological role well beyond what was imagined just a few years ago. Two major findings have been responsible for this change in the perception of bacteria in caves: bacteria as primary producers, and bacteria as responsible for modifying the shapes of caves.

Although it was not surprising to find heterotrophic bacteria acting as decomposers in caves, and a few autotrophic ones in areas of twilight, the discovery of chemolithoautotrophic bacteria in 1986 in Movile Cave, Romania, was a major breakthrough. Although chemotrophic bacteria had been reported in caves before, the discovery of these microorganisms in Movile Cave really showed how important they can be for the ecology of these habitats. Chemolithoautotrophic bacteria are able to gain energy through the conversion of inorganic compounds and act as primary producers, debunking the old myth that all caves must be energetically very poor because of the lack of primary producers. Lechuguilla Cave, New Mexico, has been shown to have very little allochthonous input, but continues to support a large microbial web based on chemolithoautotrophic bacteria (Cunningham *et al.* 1995). Movile Cave has even been shown to support larger organisms such as arthropods on chemolithotrophic production (Sarbu *et al.* 1996). Chemolithoautotrophic bacteria carry out many metabolic processes, including sulfur oxidation, ammonia and nitrite oxidation, iron and manganese reduction, etc.

Bacteria can play a major role in shaping the interiors of caves, a process known as speleogenesis. Bacteria and other microorganisms have been found to contribute to the dissolution of cave walls (Northup and Lavoie

2001). This can be caused by many processes, including physical attack, acid production, salt stress, and exoenzymes (Sand 1997). Microbial life, including not only bacteria but also fungi and algae, has been increasingly found to be associated with all sorts of cave formations.

Geological formations that have been found associated with bacteria include:

1. **Gypsum** Gypsum is formed from the reaction between hydrogen sulfide, oxygen, and limestone. It occurs when hydrogen sulfide seeping up through a cave meets with an oxygenated zone. The resulting reaction traps the sulfur in gypsum formations while releasing CO_2. This process, like many others, can be the result of bacterial metabolism of the hydrogen sulfide. Different bacteria present in this zone may in fact be oxidizing and reducing at the same time, increasing the amount of acid available for reaction (Barton and Luiszer 2005). The result is a large amount of speleogenesis, creating gypsum formations in the form of crystals or structures resembling snowballs on a cave wall.
2. **Granite and opal** Microorganisms have been found to form a number of silicate-based geological precipitates such as quartz, clay, and opal. Biogenic quartz is fungal in origin, biogenic clays are detrital, but biogenic opals have been observed to be bacterially formed. In particular, opals have been found in the twilight zones, growing towards the light (Northup and Lavoie 2001). Willems *et al.* (2002) also found filamentous bacteria associated with granitic speleothems in south Cameroon.
3. **Corrosion residue** Corrosion residues are soft deposits, on the floor or ceiling of a passage, that are rich in iron and manganese. These patches will develop in the natural environment but may form at a rate up to five times faster with the help of biological oxidation (Northup and Lavoie 2001). In particular, they are present in the cave system of Carlsbad Caverns National Park, New Mexico. Originally these residues were thought to be abiogenic in origin, being left over after acid dissolution of the bedrock, but they have been found to be associated with bacteria and fungi. It has been hypothesized that the residue is actually being created by these microorganisms (Cunningham *et al.* 2000).
4. **Saltpeter** There have been multiple hypotheses as to the origins of saltpeter, including leaching of nitrates and accumulation of bat guano. The problem with both of these is that, historically, saltpeter leached of its nitrogen could be returned to its original location and regenerated

in 3–5 years (Fliermans and Schmidt 1977). The first scientist to suggest a bacterial origin for saltpeter was Faust (1967). Fliermans and Schmidt (1977) cultured the saltpeter earth and found *Nitrobacter* in all but two of the caves. They also found that the nitrates were easy to remove but the bacteria were not, providing an explanation for saltpeter regeneration.

5. **Carbonate dripstone and biokarst** Calcium carbonate is the most common material for speleological formations, since most caves are formed in limestone. Precipitation of calcium carbonate was historically thought to be a natural process in all caves, but has been increasingly found to have a biogenic origin. In particular, some cultured heterotrophic microorganisms have been shown to precipitate calcium carbonate during respiration in the laboratory (Danielli and Edington 1983). Within the cave environment, bacteria have been found to be associated with pool finger formations (Melim *et al.* 2001).
6. **Moonmilk** Calcium carbonate precipitation can also result in the formation of a moonmilk (cave clay). Although not all moonmilk is associated with bacteria, many examples are. Northup *et al.* (2000) found multiple bacterial morphotypes (coccoid, ovoid, rod-shaped) associated with a single occurrence of moonmilk.

In summary, cave bacteria remain poorly studied, yet they represent a tremendous potential from many viewpoints: phylogenetic, ecological, and pharmaceutical. From the phylogenetic viewpoint, scientists need to understand the origin of cave species and their evolutionary relationship with epigean ones. It is now known that bacteria can play a major role in speleogenesis and cave ecology, but that does not mean that there is a good general understanding of those roles. From the pharmaceutical viewpoint, cave bacteria often grow in rather nutrient-poor environments. In such environments, production of antibiotics may assist competition between bacteria occupying similar niches, and some of these antibiotics may be novel. Finally, the presence of certain types of bacterium can indicate pollution from epigean sources that threaten the natural conditions in cave habitats (Schabereiter-Gurtner *et al.* 2002; Hunter *et al.* 2004; Barton and Pace 2005).

2.2 Algae (including Cyanobacteria)

The broadest definition of algae is that of a common lifestyle: algae include photosynthetic organisms that are typically found in moist to wet habitats. The organisms commonly recognized as algae are in fact a diverse, non-monophyletic assemblage of organisms that includes both eukaryotes and prokaryotes. Their body form ranges from unicellular to multicellular, their body size from microscopic to some several meters in length, and 'algae' are found in areas of high humidity and in all kinds of waters, from marine to freshwater. Some are floating (e.g. phytoplankton); others are anchored to a substrate (e.g. seaweeds). All of them contain chlorophyll *a*. Different algal groups are characterized on the basis of additional associated photosynthetic pigments, including carotenes and phycobiliproteins.

Of the different groups that are informally called 'algae', three have been found in freshwater hypogean environments: Cyanobacteria (blue-green algae), Bacillariophyta (diatoms), and Chlorophyta (green algae). In some marine caves communities of Phaeophyta (brown algae) and Rhodophyta (red algae) have been reported (see, for example, Baldock and Womersley 2005).

Although most of these photosynthetic organisms are found in cave entrances, some have been found deep in the caves and even in phreatic waters. Up to 21 species of alga have been reported in totally aphotic environments, as is the case for the Edwards Aquifer in central Texas. The majority of them are typical edaphic algae that probably penetrated the aquifer by percolation. These algae seem to be able to survive under these conditions for at least several days, and hence contribute to the biomass of these hypogean waters (Kuehn *et al.* 1992). Their persistence may be enhanced by the known ability of some algal groups (dinoflagellates, euglenoids and others) to switch from a photosynthetic lifestyle to a heterotrophic one. They are able to absorb organic compounds from their environment and metabolize those to provide organic energy. Other algae in caves show a remarkable ability to survive under extreme conditions. Some algae can be found as far as 25 m into a cave and living in highly alkaline conditions with pH as high as 9.2 (Budel *et al.* 1993). Algae have been found in cave entrances at high altitude (6,000 m) in the Andes (Halloy 1991).

In addition to being found in aphotic areas it is also remarkable that these photosynthetic organisms can be found in great diversity. More than 40 species of Cyanobacteria have been reported for a single cave (Vinogradova *et al.* 1998). Diatoms are the dominant algae in cave communities large enough to sustain them, as is the case in the waters of cenotes (sinkholes) and anchialine caves in northeastern Quintana Roo, Mexico. The composition of the flora in these hypogean environments is related to the distance to the ocean and influenced by the tidal movement, with the diatoms constituting up to 75% of species diversity.

Biofilm communities in a particular area may contain up to 57 species of alga together with lichens, bacteria, and fungi. Caves in sedimentary rock, such as some limestone cavities near Barcelona, Spain, contain expansive biofilm communities (Roldan *et al.* 2004). In these cavities the distribution of biofilms shows a gradient in abundance and composition largely influenced by light intensity. All these organisms show a great deal of phenotypic plasticity in terms of coloration and shape.

A similar phenomenon has been reported for marine caves. Secord and Muller-Parker (2005) found that algal performance influences the distribution of cnidarians in marine caves because sea anemones tend to live in symbiosis with the algae. Further, they also found that these host–symbiont associations can respond plastically to environmental change. One of the ways in which algae adapt to low light intensity is by having an increased number of thylakoids, the internal membranes in the chloroplasts where photosynthesis takes place (Dove *et al.* 2006).

Algae play many roles in the cave environment. For example, in many cases they are part of the processes that lead to speleothem formation, as well as being involved in rock erosion. Biofilms have a role in the processes of precipitation of calcite, dolomite, gypsum, halite, and sylvite (Jones 1995). They are also part of the food chain; for example, cave isopods in Slovenia have been found to consume algae (Sustr *et al.* 2005). If algae are very abundant they can also contribute to nitrification (Pohlman *et al.* 1997).

Cyanobacteria are found in artificially illuminated areas of caves, constituting what is known as lamp-flora. Sometimes these algae are found together with ferns and mosses (Grobbelaar 2000). The removal of these organisms is commonly achieved by using a sodium hypochlorite solution. Because chlorine and other deleterious compounds are released into a cave environment during lamp-flora cleansing, hydrogen peroxide has been tested as an alternative agent (Faimon *et al.* 2003). Biofilms with algae may damage more than the cave itself: the Altamira caves in northeast Spain, famous for their Paleolithic paintings, have had these paintings damaged by biofilms (Canaveras *et al.* 2001). Cyanobacteria can also destroy bone tissue in caves, in a phenomenon known as bioerosion (Davis 1997).

2.3 Fungi

More than 100,000 species of fungus have been described so far (Moore-Landecker 1996). Of these, astonishingly few (about 100) have been reported for caves. This is surprising because fungi are heterotrophic, thus the lack of light is not a limiting factor for them in the cave environment. Some fungi found in caves cause a number of health-related problems among humans; this in itself is of interest, if not for innately biological reasons, then to those people who are frequent visitors to the darker regions located below ground. Many of the cave fungi are saprobic, i.e. feeding on the remains of dead organisms or other organic sources such as guano and plant debris carried into caverns by water sources. Other fungi glean a living not as decomposers but as parasites, relying on living organisms for food (Moore-Landecker 1996). The only limiting factors for fungi in caves are lack or organic material on which to grow, low relative humidity and moisture, and little or no air flow (important for spore dispersal).

The inherent characteristics of some caves, particularly the stable temperature and high relative humidity, are factors that have been used since the nineteenth century for growing edible fungi, particularly in France. One species that was cultivated in great extent was the 'snowball' or 'horse' mushroom, *Agaricus arvensis*. A cave at Mery, in 1867, contained about 34 km of cultivating beds and produced no less than 1,300 kg of mushrooms a day (Anonymous 1889). In the late 1800s the French began cultivating *Agaricus bisporus*, the common white button mushroom. Although cave cultivation is less common today, it is still practiced in the United States, particularly in caves created by the mining of limestone, to grow *A. bisporus* (Kerrigan *et al.* 1995, M. Huss, pers. comm.).

The fungal species that have been found in caves are representatives of all three major phyla of this Kingdom: Ascomycota, Basidiomycota, and Zygomycota (Kajihiro 1965; Went 1969; Cunningham *et al.* 1995; Groth and Saiz-Jimenez 1999; Reeves 2000; Northup and Lavoie 2001). Within these three phyla certain species are known to form symbiotic associations with the roots of plants to form various forms of mycorrhiza, a name that literally means, 'fungus roots'. A Mycorrhizal fungus has been reported in lava tubes in Hawaii (Gemma *et al.* 1992) (see below).

At one time, the mycetozoans or 'fungus animals', a group of social amoebae, which include the true, cellular, and protostelid slime molds, were placed taxonomically in the Kingdom Fungi, but are now located within the Kingdom Protista. These have also been recorded in caves (Raper 1984; Reeves 2000). One species of dictyostelid slime mold, *Dicytostelium caveatum*, found in caves, is predatory on other species of amoebae and is considered to be cannibalistic (Waddell and Duffy 1986).

2.3.1 Zygomycota

Although relatively low in number of species (about 900 worldwide) this is the most ecologically diverse group of fungi. The typical examples are the molds that grow on food. *Enterobryus oxidi* and other species of the same genus have been found in the hind gut of the cave millipede *Oxidus gracilis* and other invertebrates in caves in Georgia, USA (Reeves 2000). Spores of *Conidiobolus coronatus*, *Mucor ramannianus*, *Phycomyces nitens,* and *Rhizopus stolonifer* have been reported in the air of a cave in Toirano, Italy (Fiorina *et al.* 2000).

2.3.2 Ascomycota

Eight species of fungus that are human pathogens have been reported in Carlsbad Caverns, New Mexico (Cunningham *et al.* 1995). Probably the most famous cave fungus is *Histoplasma capsulatum*. This fungus causes human pulmonary infections and is responsible for many of the 'cave illnesses' that have been reported among people who visit caves and are later diagnosed with histoplasmosis. *H. capsulatum* has been reported in caves in tropical and subtropical areas of the American, European, African and Asian continents as well as Australia. They affect people in varying degrees depending upon the immune response (Lewis 1989; Erkens *et al.* 2002) eliciting symptoms that range from influenza-like to life-threatening respiratory ailments (Rippon 1988). Interestingly enough, the bats that produce the guano on which *H. capsulatum* grows have not tested positive for histoplasmosis (McMurray and Russell 1982).

Geophilic dermatophytic fungi such as *Microsporum gypseum* and *Trichophyton terrestre* have been found in bat guano and cause ringworm (Kajihiro 1965). Zoophilic species of dermatophyte, such as *Trichophyton mentagrophytes* and *T. rubrum*, have been found in caves and are also responsible for certain forms of ringworm skin infection among animals and humans (Moore-Landecker 1996; Rippon 1988).

The genera *Penicillium* spp. and *Fusarium* spp., which are diverse in species and distributed worldwide, have been reported in the Milos catacombs in Greece (Groth and Saiz-Jimenez 1999). *Cephalosporium lamellaecola* has been found associated with stalactite growth in Lehman Cave in Nevada (Went 1969).

2.3.3 Basidiomycota

Members of the phylum Basidiomycota are represented by such organisms as puffballs, the polypores, gilled mushrooms, boletes, and a variety of less visible fungi, including some types of yeast. Despite their relative size, many gilled mushrooms have been found in caves but in most cases they have not been identified at the species level (see, for example, Northup and Lavoie 2001).

2.3.4 Mycorrhiza

A study by Gemma (1992) recorded only one mycorrhizal fungus in the lava tubes of Hawaii. The species was not identified but it was recorded that is was associated with the roots of the maidenhair fern of the islands. The absence of light in caves limits the intrusion of plants into this environment, although plant root systems occasionally penetrate the walls of caves or survive in the shadows of cave entrances. Such plants are worth additional study to see how fungi interact, although perhaps such interactions are not always as symbionts but sometimes rather as pathogens (Agrios 2004).

2.3.5 Mycetozoa

Mycetozoans, collectively referred to as the slime molds, were until recently considered members of the Kingdom Fungi. Nine species were identified in a survey of 23 caves in West Virginia; in many cases there were more than one species and colonies were found in great abundance in the same cave (Landoldt *et al.* 1992). Most of them belong to the genus *Dictyostelium* (Landoldt *et al.* 1992; Reeves 2000).

Based on the discussion so far it is clear that there is much research to be done regarding fungi in caves. A single survey in a cave in Israel yielded 68 species from 28 genera of fungi (Grishkan *et al.* 2004). Similar spectacular results have been obtained in caves in Texas (Kuehn and Koehn 1991), West Virginia (e.g. Landoldt *et al.* 1992), India (Koilraj *et al.* 1999), and Taiwan (Hsu and Agoramoorthy 2001). This shows that even simple surveys can yield a great number of species. The ecological role of fungi in caves also needs to be studied, not only as decomposers of organic material but also as potential food sources for other organisms (Sustr *et al.* 2005). Fungi also appear as part of the internal and external mycoflora of many cave animals (see, for example, Benoit *et al.* 2004) and there is no question that they help to shape the geology of the cave itself (Jones 2001) although the precise way in which this manifests itself is the fodder for future research.

2.4 Lichens

Lichens are communal associations or organisms composed of fungal filaments and either green algae or Cyanobacteria (blue-green algae). The identification of these organisms is very difficult in the field and usually requires microscopic and/or chemical analysis. There are between 15,000 and 30,000 species known so far, including a number found in caves. Their habitat can be extremely variable, ranging from ice caves in New York State (Dirig 1994) to geothermal hotspots at about 6,000 m above sea level (m asl) in the Andes (Halloy 1991).

Sometimes several species of lichen can be found in a single cave. Lichens (usually of the crustose body form) are generally found in the areas of the cave that receive some light. In deeper parts of the caves crustose lichens are replaced by others with a leprose thallus, such as *Botryolepraria lesdainii* and *Macentina stigonemoides* (Garbacki *et al.* 1999; Roldan *et al.* 2004). Sometimes lichens constitute the main nesting material for cave birds such as the mountain swiftlet, *Aerodramus hirundinaceus* (Tarburton 2003).

2.5 Plants (liverworts, mosses, ferns, and seed plants)

This section includes all the members of the Kingdom Plantae found in caves, from liverworts, mosses, and ferns to seed-producing plants, primarily flowering plants. These organisms can be found in areas where some light penetrates the cave. They typically demonstrate zonal distribution, with seed plants found in areas of higher light intensity, followed by ferns, mosses and liverworts. In some karstic caves overlain by soil, the roots of epigean trees in the immediate area of the cave may penetrate into the cave itself through the crevices and sometimes even reach underground waters. Access to water may be particularly significant during drought periods (Penuelas and Filella 2003).

The leaves of many species found in caves show a number of adaptations to low light intensity such as an increase in leaf surface area, reduction in leaf thickness, fewer stomata (in caves with high humidity), elongated stems, and reduced branching. Some cave mosses (*Mittenia* spp.

and *Schistostega* spp.) have specialized cells that act as lenses to focus light on the chloroplasts.

In addition to plants adapted to, or persisting in, cave environments, plants may be transported from terrestrial surfaces to the interior of caves. Significant amounts of plant biomass may be regularly deposited in caves by flood events from the surrounding watershed. Humans and other animals are also responsible for the deposition of plant materials in caves. In many cases these provide carbon sources for heterotrophs. In other cases, dry sheltered areas preserve plant material, providing an archeological record of human plant use through time. In the North American southwest, packrat middens in caves preserve plant materials from the surrounding areas, allowing paleoclimatologists to reconstruct the vegetation history of the region.

2.5.1 Liverworts or hepatics (Hepatophyta or Marchantiophyta)

These are small, primitive plants usually found in the same microhabitats that support mosses, covering large areas of the ground as well as rocks and trees. They prefer shaded, humid areas. They comprise two classes: the leafy liverworts, which are similar to leafy mosses, and the thalloid liverworts, which are flattened and ribbon-like, adhering to the substrate by numerous rhizoids. There are more than 8,000 species of liverwort, of which a few are found in caves.

One of the species of liverwort found in caves is *Frullania tamarisci*, from Terceira Island in the Azores. This species has been shown to have the highest maximum photosynthetic rate in the world, compared with mosses and other plants, meaning that it is highly efficient in capturing and converting light into chemical energy (Gabriel and Bates 2003). Liverworts have also been found in geothermal hotspots at 6,000 m asl in the Andes (Halloy 1991).

2.5.2 Mosses (Bryophyta)

These plants clearly illustrate the characteristic alternation of generations typical of the plant kingdom. The first generation, the gametophyte, constitutes the plant body we usually identify as a moss. The gametophytes produce gametes, which fuse in fertilization to produce a zygote that grows into the next generation: the sporophyte. The sporophyte produces little or no chlorophyll, and relies on the gametophyte plant for supplemental chemical energy. In many species the sporophyte is wholly parasitic on the gametophyte plant. As the sporophyte matures, the capsule releases spores that will grow into a new generation of gametophyte plants. There are approximately 13,500 described species of moss worldwide, of which a few have been found in caves.

Mosses serve as habitat for tardigrates (Bartels and Nelson 2006) and copepods (Brancelj 2006), and as food for the Brazilian cave harvestman (an opilionid) *Goniosoma spelaeum* (Santos and Gnaspini 2002). Mosses have also been found in geothermal hotspots at 6,000 m asl in the Andes (Halloy 1991).

One species of moss is known as the cave or luminous moss: *Schistostega pennata*. This species constitutes the monotypic family Schistostegaceae. It is found in sandstone and limestone formations in the north temperate regions of the world: Europe, Japan, Canada, and the northern United States, from Minnesota to Rhode Island. Although *Schistostega* is found in caves it has also been recorded under old barns and on upturned roots. Though rather rare it is fairly widely distributed throughout its range. This species has a loosely tufted, leafy structure reaching only 7 mm in height. The cave moss sporophytes frequently have stomata, but it is unusual for gametophytes to have stomata, and the plant grows from a threadlike, luminous protonema. Chlorophyll-containing cells are oriented with their chloroplasts grouped within the cytoplasm in the plane on the plant that faces the light that penetrates the cave. When light enters the cave and falls on the plant the rays are refracted to form a cone of light. When the refracted light hits the green spot, photosynthetically active wavelengths of light are absorbed and the rest is reflected, producing a luminous appearance (Crum 1983; Ignatov and Ignatova 2001).

2.5.3 Ferns (Pteridophyta or Filicophyta)

Ferns are vascular plants with true leaves that do not produce seeds. Like all vascular plants they show alternation of generations, with a diploid sporophytic and a haploid gametophytic phase. Unlike that of flowering plants, the gametophyte phase in ferns is in the form of a free-living organism. There are about 9,000 known species of fern of which a few, such as the Venus maidenhair (*Adiantum* sp.), are found in cave entrances. In many caves the moist shaded area around the cave entrance supports such extensive colonies of ferns that they are known as 'fern falls'.

2.5.4 Flowering plants (Magnoliophyta)

This group includes the vascular plant species with seeds. There are about 260,000 known species, of which a few are found in caves in the twilight zone or interacting with the hypogean environment by penetrating the soil with their roots in order to obtain water.

2.6 Protozoans

The name 'protozoan' is a colloquial term for unicellular heterotrophs of the Kingdom Protista or Protoctista, which includes eukaryotes that have not developed specialized tissues. This grouping contains not only protozoans, but also algae and myxomycetes (slime molds, described on p. 70). This is therefore a paraphyletic kingdom. Protozoans are unicellular organisms that can sometimes be found forming colonies. The kingdom comprises five protist phyla: Mastigophora or Flagellata, Sarcodina, Ciliophora, Opalinida, and Sporozoa. The 26,000 living species of protozoan that have been described so far can be found in fresh, estuarine, and marine waters as well as in soils all around the world. Most are heterotrophs and some are parasites.

Gittleson and Hoover (1969) identified 350 species from caves, most of them species that can be found in the surrounding epigean soils although some are parasites of obligate cavernicoles. The distribution of some of them is remarkable. Foissner (2003) found *Spathidium faurefremieti*, originally described from Romanian cave water in 1962, in savannah soil from the Shimba Hills National Reserve in Kenya, Africa, and in floodplain soils of Brazil and Australia.

Carey *et al.* (2001) found nine species of ciliate in an anchihaline lagoon in Mallorca, Spain, that were stratified not only in the water column mostly near the surface but also in mid-water as well. These authors hypothesized that floating calcite crystals may form a distinct biotope for ciliate populations.

2.7 Porifera (sponges)

One of the most surprising sources of information on cave ecology comes from an unsuspected group of animals: sponges. Sponges are classified by the composition and shape of their spicules in three classes: (a) Calcarea, with calcareous spicules; (b) Hexatinellida, with six-rayed siliceous spicules; and (c) Demospongiae, with skeleton of siliceous spicules, spongin (collagen), or both. Some 5,000 species of Porifera have been described so far. Most of these sponges are marine but about 150, all in the class Demospongiae, are found in freshwaters.

Several dozens of species of sponge have been found in (mostly marine) caves and almost all cave-dwelling sponges belong to the class Demospongiae, with the notable exception of one glass sponge (class Hexatinellida). The only freshwater sponge found in caves is *Euanapis subterraneus*, also in the Demospongiae, in Croatia.

The importance of sponges in caves can be divided into three areas: (a) their evolutionary origin, (b) their phenotypic plasticity; and (c) their ecology.

2.7.1 The origin of cave sponges

The study of sponges in caves has yielded some interesting contributions to the understanding of the phylogeny of this phylum. Rowland (2001) reported the discovery of living calcareous sponges in caves that resolved the phylogenetic placement of an enigmatic group of fossils known as the archaeocyaths as a new class of fossil sponges, Archaeocyatha.

Another cave sponge, *Oopsacas minuta*, has provided important clues about the origin of multicellular metazoans. Leys *et al.* (2006) studied the development of this glass sponge and found support for the hypothesis that the original metazoans were cellular, not syncytial, (made of a multinucleated mass of cytoplasm).

Because there is an unusual abundance of sponges in marine temperate caves, it is worth while to ask about their origin. Most researchers believe that sponges were more widespread when the oceans were warmer and that many have survived in temperate oceans only because they were able to find refuge in microenvironments such as caves. It is interesting that two species of the same genus of sponge, *Gastrophanella phoemciensis* from Lebanon and *G. cavernicola* from Brazil and Belize, have been found in caves in such distant geographic places from each other, suggesting that they represent a relict of a much more widespread genus (Perez *et al.* 2004).

Some species that are known from deep waters are only found in shallow waters when inhabiting caves. An example is *Thrombus jancai* from a cave at 30 m depth in Jamaica. Other species of this genus are known only from depths exceeding 100 m (Lehnert 1998). *Higginsia ciccaresei*, found living in a cave in the eastern Mediterranean at 250 m from the cave entrance, is also considered a Tethyan relict (Pansini and Pesce 1998).

However, the relictual hypothesis has recently been challenged. Könnecker and Freiwald (2005) found a new species of pharetronid sponge off northern Norway to be very common in those waters; this defies the conventional wisdom of sponges being found only in tropical and temperate zones, with the latter being just relict species living in cryptic habitats such as caves.

The explanation for finding the same or closely related species of sponges in deep waters and caves only has been attributed to several factors: (1) the fact that shallow-water caves retain a cold water mass that results in stable temperature conditions throughout the year; (2) lack of light; and (3) limited food resources (Vacelet *et al.* 1994).

Until recently, the model assumed to explain the colonization of marine caves in shallow areas by deep water species was a saltatory dispersal model through stepping-stone habitats. However, direct colonization has been advocated, at least for the French Mediterranean coast, which is characterized by a cold homothermal regime below a within-cave thermocline. Harmelin (1997) suggested that the successful colonization of the cold homothermal cave by allochthonous larvae is likely to be dependent on rare pulse fluxes.

2.7.2 Phenotypic plasticity

As will be seen in Chapter 3, one of the major arguments made in this book is that phenotypic plasticity plays a major role in the evolution of hypogean fauna; sponges are notable for their phenotypic plasticity (Barnes and Bell 2002). Meroz-Fine *et al.* (2005) discovered a Mediterranean cave sponge in calm, shallow water, which they hypothesized, influenced the sponge's morphology and physiology: the specimens in the cave were smaller and had shorter spicules and earlier gamete release than their open-water conspecifics. A reproductive advantage of earlier gamete release may be influenced by the energetic trade-off of having shorter spicules.

Another sponge with spicules seemingly affected by its environment is *Higginsia ciccaresei*. Silica spicules are formed with an irregular shape and surface, perhaps because of the mixed water of the anchialine cave which they inhabit (Pansini and Pesce 1998).

Teilla spp., a common sponge in the eastern Mediterranean, can be found in four different habitats (shallow caves and deep waters with calm waters, and shallow exposed sites and tide pools with turbulent waters). The ones found in caves and deep waters are smaller and have a lower proportion of structural silica and fewer and shorter spicules (Meroz-Fine *et al.* 2005).

Astrosclera willeyana is a predominantly bright orange, coralline sponge found mainly in reef caves of the Indo-Pacific, whose habitat is generally restricted to cryptic and light-reduced environments. This species sometimes also occurs in the dim-light areas of cave entrances, where it is colored green on the side that faces the light (Worheide 1998).

2.7.3 Ecology

Sponges may dominate benthic communities in caves (Marti *et al*; 2004; Preciado and Maldonado 2005) and are therefore of tremendous ecological importance. Uriz *et al.* (1992) found that different species of sponge are distributed according to the available light, with some in twilight areas and others in areas of total darkness. They also found that sponge abundance in caves was inversely correlated with the intensity of light, a result also found in marine caves in Ireland (Bell 2002).

It is interesting that, although sponges are highly dependent upon water circulation for their filter-feeding needs, some of them can be found in caves with very little, if any, water circulation. That is the case of *Tethya omanensis*, an endemic species from a sinkhole in Oman (Sara and Bavestrello 1995).

Some of the most remarkable cave sponges are the *Asbestopluma* spp. found in a Mediterranean cave at a depth of 20m (Vacelet *et al.* 1994). Instead of filter-feeding, this species captures invertebrates (mostly crustaceans) of up to 8 mm in length in its spiky filaments, grows more filaments around its captured prey, and then absorbs the prey in a process that lasts up to 10 days, making it a truly carnivorous sponge. These sponges belong to the deep-sea family Cladorhizidae but live in littoral environments. In an analogy with carnivorous plants, these sponges have a lifestyle adapted to oligotrophic environments, in this case deep sea waters or caves (Vacelet and Duport 2004).

Another hexactinellid sponge, *Oopsacas minuta*, from the Mediterranean, shows a great deal of retention of suspended particles. This has been interpreted as an adaptation to the scarcity of such particles in both caves and deep waters (Perez 1996).

2.8 Cnidarians (anemones, jellyfish)

Cnidarians are animals with radial or near-radial symmetry that adopt a great variety of forms, including colonial sinophonophores, medusae, jellyfishes, corals, and hydroids. They all have stinging cells called nematocysts. There are more than 10,000 species in all the oceans of the world from tropical to polar waters, floating, free-living, attached to substrates, and even burrowing in the sand. Some species have been found in fresh water. A few marine species have been reported in caves.

Most cave species are of burrowing habits (e.g. *Halcampoides purpurea*) (Boero *et al.* 1991) and many species of cave cnidarian are therefore quite cryptic. An example is *Codonorchis octaedrus*, which was recorded in 1997 for the first time since its discovery by Haeckel in 1879. A hydroid colony of this species was collected in a cave on the Apulian coast (between the Ionian and the Adriatic Seas) (Boero *et al.* 1991). Other species have been found in the Spanish Atlantic (Camacho *et al.* 2006) but most described species come from the Mediterranean (see, for example Marti *et al.* 2005). *Velkovrhia enigmatica* (Bougainvilliidae) is believed to be endemic to Dinaric Caves (Matjašič and Sket 1971).

One unusual species of cave cnidarian is the scyphozoan *Thecoscyphus zibrowii*. Among the remarkable characteristics of this polyp are a translucent periderm tube, a great deal of phenotypic plasticity, and a suppression of the medusa phase. In this species only females exist; they reproduce via parthenogenesis. This shortened life cycle has been hypothesized to be adaptation to the cave environment (Sötje and Jarms 1999).

Secord and Muller-Parker (2005) found that in an association between an abundant temperate sea anemone and its two endosymbiont algae, the densities and ratios of the anemones' symbionts changed along a light gradient generated by intertidal caves in Washington State, USA. They showed that caves are divided into three distinct regions based on anemones' algal complements: a brown region of zooxanthellate anemones near the mouth of the cave, a green region of zoochlorellate anemones in the middle of the cave, and a white region of alga-free anemones near the back of the cave. Their results were consistent with the idea that temperate, as well as tropical, host–symbiont associations can respond plastically to environmental change.

Similar distributional patterns have been found in sublittoral marine cave with sulfur-water springs in Italy. Benedetti-Cecchi *et al.* (1998)

observed that the abundance of the stony coral *Astroides calycularis* decreased from the outer to the inner part of a cave, whereas the reverse was observed for the sunset cup coral *Leptopsammia pruvoti*. The abundance of *L. pruvoti* decreased close to the sulfur boundary, whereas the percentage cover of *A. calycularis* increased, but only at locations near the cave mouth. This suggests a case of resource partitioning by two species of coral in the same cave, and may be related to distribution of bacterial mats around the sulfur sources (Southward *et al.* 1996).

2.9 Platyhelminthes (flatworms)

The phylum Platyhelminthes or flatworms is composed of very simple animals characterized by a lack of segmentation. There are about 25,000 described species of both free-living and parasitic flatworm, of which nearly 200 (mostly planarians) have been found in caves (Dumnicka 2005). They include both marine and freshwater species. Some of them are detritivores (Ferreira and Martins 1999) but many are necrophagous and some are parasitic (Dumnicka 2005). Most of them are blind and depigmented and can occupy more than one cave allopatrically (e.g. *Dendrocoelum beauchamoi*; Sluys and Benazzi 1992).

Cave planarians serve as food sources for cave fish, crayfish, and salamanders; they can be infected by protozoan parasites (Carpenter 1970). In turn they feed on drowned cave crickets and amphipods (Mitchell 1970).

A blind and depigmented planarian, *Sphalloplana percaeca*, was first described from Mammoth Cave, KY, in 1876 (Fig. 2.1). In an attempt to determine the relatedness of this species to epigean flatworms, by means of experiments that involved changes in gravity, water pressure, light exposure, temperature, water acidity, and regeneration, Buchanan (1936) recorded the responses of each and compared the two groups. He found that changes in water pressure, temperature, and gravity did not cause responses in the cave flatworms, but disturbed the epigean worms. His light tests on the blind cave flatworms were interesting but fatal to these creatures: they writhed dramatically when exposed to direct sunlight but did not move to shaded areas when given the chance. Finally, the flatworms disintegrated within 12 hours of exposure. Because of some similar responses to changes in environment, that author concluded that the cave flatworm was more closely related to epigean worms from a different family. Unfortunately, the time at which he did his research was

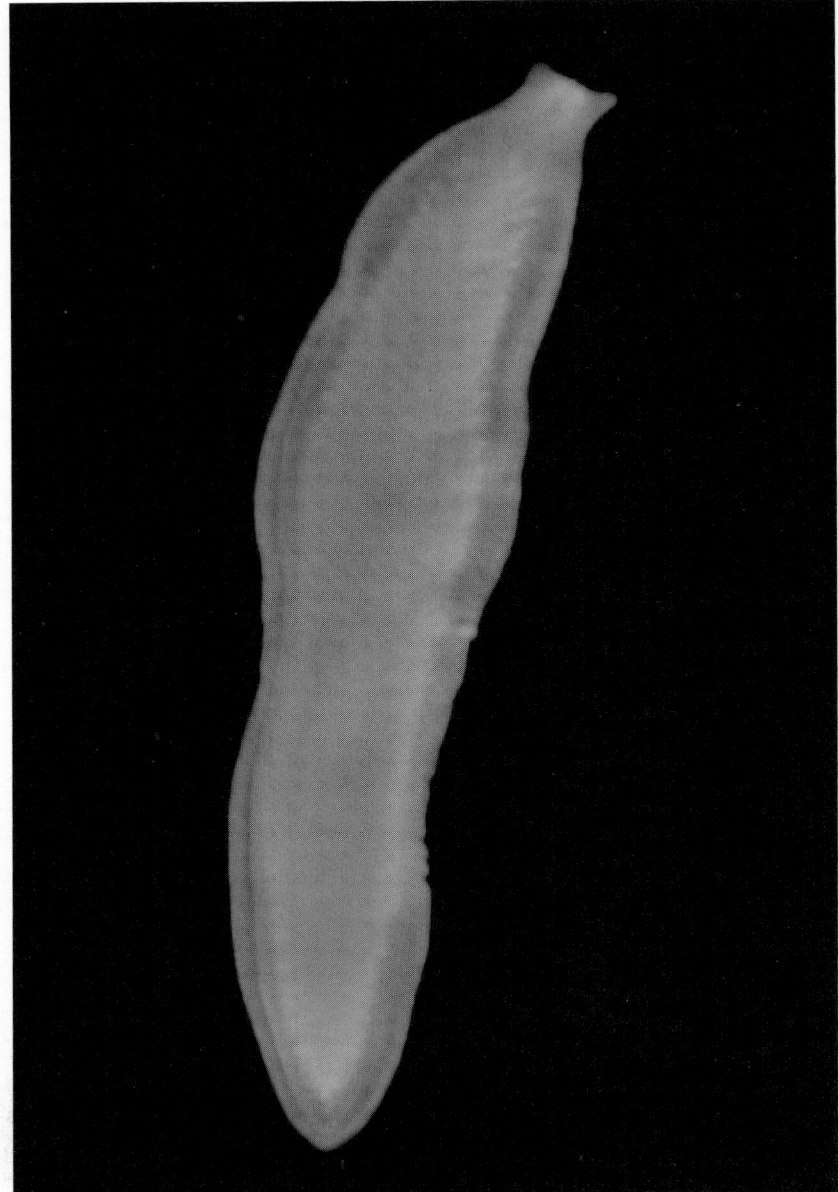

Figure 2.1 Sphalloplana percaeca from Big Mouth Cave, Grundy County, Tennessee. Photo by Danté Fenolio. (See Plate 4.)

too early for the genetic analysis needed to accurately map the phylogeny of these flatworms.

In a study of West Virginia karst caves, Culver (1970) suggested that the cave ecosystems, which included planarians, were island-like in their species distribution and isolation from each other. His evidence to support this hypothesis was that caves without the connectivity of spring flooding had higher species diversity, at least among the four crustacean species on which he focused his study. He did, however, find members of the family Planariidae in most of these caves, suggesting that the caves are not so completely isolated even without connective flooding. Culver acknowledged the differences between island and cave environments, such as lack of area effect on species diversity in caves, difference in nutrient energy sources in each type of system, and cases of species' immigration among caves.

A high-profile cave flatworm is *Macrocotyla glandulosa*, the federally listed endangered pink planarian of the Devil's Icebox Cave in the Missouri Ozarks (Missouri State Parks 2006). The rarity of the pink planarian was used successfully as an argument to stop a shopping mall from being built on the border of Rock Bridge Memorial State Park, where the Devil's Icebox is located. This troglobite is monitored by the US Department of Agriculture as part of a watershed-wide water quality project (United States Department of Agriculture 2002).

2.10 Nemertina (ribbon worms)

Also known as Nemertea, Nemertida, Rhynchocaela, or ribbon worms, these are vermiform carnivorous animals characterized by having an eversible proboscis. Most of them are marine but a few species are fresh-water and even terrestrial. Of the 900 or so known species, three or four have been described in caves in Europe and New Zealand (Dumnicka 2005).

2.11 Gastrotricha (gastrotrichs)

This is a group of small, free-living vermiform aquatic animals with about 450 species known. Most of these animals are interstitial and therefore little studied, particularly in caves. In fact it was not until 2006 that the first species of this group were reported in a cave (Todaro *et al.* 2006). They surveyed a cave along the Ionian coast of Apulia (southern Italy) and found 16 different species of gastrotrich.

2.12 Kinorhyncha (kinorhynchs)

The Kinorhyncha are extremely small worms, less than 1 mm in length, that burrow into muddy marine substrates by forcing body fluids into the head, everting the body, anchoring the head in the substrate by using spines, and then moving forward as the head retracts (Harris 2006). There are about 150 species described for this phylum, all of them living in sediments. Two kinorhynch species have been found in sea caves: *Echinoderes dujardini* in 1966 in two Mediterranean locations, and *Echinoderes cavernus* in 2000 (Boesgaard and Kristensen 2001). *E. cavernus*, from Australia, was the first kinorhynch described in the southern hemisphere (Sorensen *et al.* 2000). The cave community in which it was found is thought to be related to similar assemblages found in the Caribbean Sea. Both areas could have been on the coastline of the ancient Tethys Sea and then became refugia.

2.13 Nematoda (roundworms)

Nematodes, commonly called roundworms, constitute a group of about 20,000 described species, although some researchers predict that the group may have up to 500,000 species (Hickman *et al.* 2000). The systematics of this group is complex and constantly changing. They are found as both free-living (terrestrial and aquatic) and parasitic (even in humans). About 20 species have been described from caves.

Nematodes can be an important part of the food chain in caves. Welbourn (1999) found nematodes feeding on bacteria in bat guano at Kartchner Cavern, Arizona. These very same nematodes were consumed by cave mites and other arthropods. Up to 50% of the diet of the young of the cave spring fish (*Forbesichthys agassizi*) from caves in Kentucky, Tennessee, and Illinois was composed of nematodes (Hill 1969).

Nematodes can be found as parasites of cave animals and as saprotrophs. Nematodes in terrestrial caves are associated with troglophilic host fauna, which, when infected, bring the nematodes into the cave. For example, several species of nematode have been found in the digestive and urinary tracts of cave fish (Moravec *et al.* 1996), cave salamanders (McAllister and Bursey 2004; Yildirimhan *et al.* 2005), and bats (Ubelaker & Dailey 1969; Guerrero *et al.* 2003).

Humans in caves have interacted with nematodes for thousands of years, either by hosting them or by affecting their environments. Anasazi communities living in Western US caves as long ago as 10,000 years

BP have been shown to have had multiple species infestations, as determined by inspection of archaeologically recovered feces (Reinhart *et al.* 1985). Modern cave visitors, specifically those to Wind and Jewel Caves in South Dakota, may have influenced the measurably increased nematode colonization at cave entrances and along tour routes and traveled corridors, due to increased carbon inputs into these areas of the caves (Moore 1996).

2.14 Annelida (segmented worms)

The Annelida or segmented worms include earthworms, leeches, and a variety of marine worms. They can be found worldwide in terrestrial, freshwater, and marine environments. Although most are free-living, some species are parasitic and even mutualistic. There are about 15,000 species of annelid, of which nearly 200 have been described for the hypogean environment.

Living Annelida have been traditionally classified into three classes: Polychaeta (mostly marine), Oligochaeta (earthworms), and Hirudinea (leeches). All of them have representatives in the hypogean environment.

2.14.1 Class Polychaeta

Although most polychaetes are marine and some of the cave species are anchialine (see, for example, Worsaae *et al.* 2004), the majority of the few that are freshwater are found in hypogean environments, particularly in the tropics. An exception is *Marifugia cavatica*, a freshwater species from Slovenia and Croatia (Dumnicka 2005). Hypogean polychaetes have been recorded in marine and anchialine caves as well as in caves at high altitudes (*c.* 1,600 m asl) and many are considered to be relicts of ancient marine species. Some cave polychaetes have been found associated with sulfur-based spring ecosystems (Southward *et al.* 1996; Airoldi *et al.* 1997).

2.14.2 Class Oligochaeta

Among the oligochaetes we find aquatic, semiaquatic, and terrestrial representatives in caves. More than 140 species of oligochaete have been described in caves, with many of the same genera being found in Europe and North America (Cook 1975). Many of these species are located in both the epigean and the hypogean environment (see, for example, Dumnicka and Wojtan 1990) but some genera are endemic to caves (see, for example, Juget 2006). Many of these species are interstitial or live anchored to the sediments and can form cysts during extreme environmental conditions. Although they are mostly detrivorous, some feed on algae and a few are even predators of small invertebrates. Although oligochaetes are mostly terrestrial and freshwater, one cave species has been described from anchialine waters (Erseus 1986).

2.14.3 Class Hirudinea

There are few species of hirudinean in caves. Many of the hypogean leeches are actually cave populations of epigean ones showing different degrees of depigmentation and eye reduction. Many leeches are hematophagous, feeding on the blood of mollusks, earthworms, and bats. Some epigean species have cave populations that are partly depigmented; some cave species are totally blind. Interestingly, many of these species have lost their pigmentation but not their eyes. Cave leeches have been found in a chemoautotrophically based groundwater ecosystem (Manoleli *et al.* 1998).

2.15 Mollusca (mollusks)

Mollusks represent a large and highly diverse phylum that has been very successful from the ecological viewpoint for hundreds of millions of years. There are approximately 200,000 described and undescribed species of mollusk (Lydeard *et al.* 2004) and many have been found in caves. Of the seven classes of living mollusk (Ponder and Lindberg 2008), the two most diverse (gastropods and bivalves) are also the ones represented in the hypogean environment.

2.15.1 Class Bivalvia

A literature review (references cited in this section) shows that more than 60 species of hypogean bivalve have been reported so far, most of them in marine caves below sea level. Most, if not all, of these caves were at sea level during the last glaciation. All the reported marine cave bivalves have been found in the northwestern Pacific Ocean, near such islands as Ryukyu Island and Okinawa, but their overall dispersal is unknown. Because the areas around the caves have been little studied, it is not known whether these species are indigenous to the caves or just opportunistic invaders; several species have also been found in sunken ships. Many marine cave bivalvesreach an average adult length of less than 6 mm; this is much smaller than their non-cave-dwelling relatives (Hayami and Kase 1996).

Adult hypogean bivalves usually have a translucent shell and a white, depigmented body. Juveniles of non-cavernicolous bivalves also have translucent, thin shells and depigmented bodies, but adults exhibit a wide range of shell thicknesses and colors as well as having colored body parts. This suggests that cave bivalves may be paedomorphic (Hayami and Kase 1996).

All bivalves (including epigean species) are suspension feeders and dioecious, and most are long-lived. One distinct difference between epigean and hypogean bivalves is their fecundity. Most epigean bivalves (both brooding and non-brooding species) have a high fecundity owing to the nature of their fertilization, the early release of offspring in non-brooders, and their larger adult size (allowing a larger clutch size in brooders). Hypogean species, however, exhibit lower fecundity because most species are brooders: the female holds her offspring within her body until they transform into a juvenile state, at which time the juveniles 'crawl' away from their parent (Hayami and Kase 1996; Morton *et al.* 1998). Because a female holds her offspring throughout this development and most species in caves have an extremely reduced adult size, hypogean females cannot brood as many juveniles as epigean females.

Of all reported hypogean bivalves, only one species, the Dinaric Cave clam, *Congeria kusceri*, is reported as non-submarine and may represent the only true 'cave-limited' bivalve species. This unique bivalve is related to the zebra mussel, in the genus *Dreissena.* Its morphological features are the same as described for the submarine bivalves, including being depigmented and possessing few sensory organs, i.e. no statocysts or light receptors, but it can reach a maximum adult length of over 12 mm. This species can live up to 25 years, compared with 1–2 years for non-cave forms in the same family (Morton *et al.* 1998).

This Dinaric Cave clam is limited to caves in Herzegovina and Croatia, but relict shells have been reported in Slovenia. This species was once an inhabitant of the Mediterranean Sea before it dried up during the late Miocene near the Balkans, Hungary, and Romania. At the time of these falling water levels, this bivalve escaped extinction by colonizing the caves fed by subterranean waters of the Mediterranean Sea. Current evidence suggests that the species is being affected by pollution within its habitat (Morton *et al.* 1998; Stepien *et al.* 2001).

2.15.2 Class Gastropoda

Based on the author's literature review, more than 600 species of gastropod have been reported for caves and aquifers from around the world (for phreatic ones, see Hershler and Longley 1986). Gastropods inhabiting caves are mostly freshwater and terrestrial. Approximately 97% belong to the freshwater family Hydrobiidae (Hershler and Holsinger 1990). Many hypogean gastropods are characterized by having a thin, subhyaline shell and a depigmented body. They can also have depigmented, reduced, or totally absent eyes (e.g. *Potamolithus karsticus*; Desimone and Moracchiolin 1994). In addition, cave snails differ in their internal anatomy from their epigean relatives by having complex coiling of the intestines, loss or reduction of the ctenidium, a simplification of gonadal morphology, and a loss of sperm sacs, all largely as a result of their smaller body size. They also have a specialized radula that allows them to feed on organic matter and animal secretions (Hershler and Holsinger 1990). Smaller body size seems to be a common feature among cave snails (Graening 2003).

Gastropods may colonize caves that are episodically flooded (Bernasconi 1999). They can be found in large densities in tropical caves, particularly in the wetter and warmer parts of them in both the neotropics and New Zealand (Emberton *et al.* 1997, Bichuette and Trajano 2003b).

Ponder *et al.* (2005) described a radiation of 10 species belonging to two genera of hydrobiid snail from caves in southern Tasmania. This comprises two closely related genera, *Pseudotricula*, endemic to the Precipitous Bluff caves, and *Nanocochlea*, found in these caves and surface streams and seepages, but also known from elsewhere in southern Tasmania.

Schilthuizen *et al.* (2005) described a new species of the snail genus *Georissa* in a limestone cave in Borneo; molecular phylogenetic analysis showed that this species is descended from a local epigean species, *G. saulae*, living in the rainforest directly at the cave entrances. Their work showed that although the troglobitic form had diverged morphologically from its epigean ancestor, there was still gene flow going on between the two of them, with one population showing an intermediate morph in between the two, suggesting that speciation had occurred without complete isolation.

Bodon *et al.* (1999) found two distinct coexisting shell morphs, almost without intermediates, for the same population of *Litthabitella chilodia* living in a small brook in the Grotta del Tasso cave, Apulia, Italy. However, that does not mean that there are necessarily different species since a great deal of variation within morphs of the same species has been found in caves (see discussion on *Astyanax fasciatus* in Chapter 3).

Unlike conventional wisdom in biospeleology, where cave species are generally considered 'dead ends' from a phylogenetic viewpoint, some species inhabiting submarine caves have been the source of further radiation since as far back as the Paleocene (*c.* 65–55 mya), as in some species of the family Neritiliidae (Kano and Kase 2002; Kano *et al.* 2002; Lozouet 2004).

2.16 Brachiopoda (lamp shells)

Brachiopods or lamp shells are bivalve animals that despite their resemblance to clams are not really related to mollusks. They are all marine, most commonly found in cold or deep waters. There are about 300 living species known so far; a few have been described from caves.

Species of hypogean brachiopod have been found in submarine caves from the Mediterranean to the Indian Ocean to Australia (see, for example, Logan and Zibrowius 1994; Grobe and Luter 1999; Luter *et al.* 2003; Logan 2005). Some hypogean species inhabiting warmer waters in submarine caves have been documented as far back as the Paleocene (*c.* 65 mya) (Lozouet 2004). Some species are neotenic (Logan and Zibrowius 1994).

2.17 Bryozoa (moss animals)

Bryozoans, also known as moss animals or sea mats, are small, mostly colonial animals that generally grow on hard surfaces. They are found mostly in warm, tropical marine waters worldwide (even at great depths) with a few species also found in freshwater. There are about 5,000 known living species and a few have been reported from caves. So far all hypogean species have been found either in the Mediterranean (see, for example, Harmelin 1990; Dhondt and Harmelin 1993; Mariani 2003; Mariani *et al.* 2005; Marti *et al.* 2005) or in Bermuda (Thomas *et al.* 1992). This is most likely the result of two factors: one is that, owing to their size and habits, bryozoans are rather cryptic species, and the other is that those two regions are the ones in which marine caves have been most intensively studied.

Despite this paucity of studies, some findings on the biology of these organisms have been interesting: Harmelin (1997) found that colonization of caves by bryozoan larvae was the result of rare pulse fluxes and that the source of those organisms was not deep-water bryozoans. This represents a big contrast when compared with coastal cave sponges, whose original source seems to be deep-water species that colonize those aphotic environments via saltatory dispersal through stepping-stone habitats.

2.18 Crustacea (crustaceans)

The subphylum Crustacea has about 52,000 known living marine, freshwater, and terrestrial species with worldwide distribution (Martin and Davis 2006). Although the phylogeny of this group is still a matter of controversy (Giribet and Ribera 2000; Martin and Davis 2006), six classes of crustacean are generally recognized, of which at least five are represented in the hypogean environment. A literature search yielded more than 4,800 species of cave, phreatic, and anchialine crustacean from all over the world, including marine, freshwater, and terrestrial ones (see, for example, Dumont and Negrea 1996; Sket 1999, 2004) (Table 2.1). Most of them show reduction and/or loss of the visual apparatus and/or pigmentation as well as elongation of appendages (e.g., Sket 1999).

This group appears to be the most widely represented in the hypogean environment among the aquatic macrofauna. The classification of Crustacea here follows that of Martin and Davis (2006).

2.18.1 Class Branchiopoda

This is the most primitive crustacean group. They are small (up to 2 mm in length) and display a great diversity of morphology; they are found

Table 2.1 *Approximate number of described hypogean species of crustacean by class*

Class	Total no. of species	No. of hypogean species
Branchiopoda	>900	*c.* 100
Cephalocarida	9	0
Remipedia	12	12
Maxillopoda	>14,000	>1,200
Ostracoda	>5,700	*c.* 1,000
Malacostraca	>31,500	>2,200
Total	*c.* 52,000	*c.* 4,862

Sources: cited in text.

worldwide. About 100 species have been reported from the hypogean environment, most of them belonging to the suborder Cladocera. Most species show some degree of depigmentation; some have lost their eyes and in many cases their ocelli. Most of them are benthic 'scrapers.' Dumont (1995) pointed out the fact that most cladocerans are most common in the underflow of rivers and that many epigean species colonize hypogean waters, particularly members of the family Eurycercidae. At least three lineages of the genus *Alona* evolved exclusively as groundwater species. All hypogean Cladocera are freshwater, belonging to genera of epigean species. Most species are located in a single locality and few display any troglomorphic characteristics at all (Dumont and Negrea 1996).

2.18.2 Class Remipedia

This is another primitive group of crustaceans, small in size (up to 45 mm in total length) that were not discovered until 1979 in waters of the Lucayan Cavern of the Grand Bahama. Twelve species have been found in oxygen-poor waters of anchialine environments of the Caribbean, the Yucatán Peninsula, the Canary Islands, and Australia. They are all characterized by being blind and depigmented and prey on other invertebrates, which they find via chemosensory organs.

2.18.3 Class Maxillopoda

All the hypogean representatives of this class belong to the subclass Copepoda. This is a very diverse group of crustaceans with more than 14,000 species. Most members of this subclass are between 1 and 2 mm in length. They seem to be very common in African caves (Messana 2004). Within this subclass there are seven orders with cave representatives. Of the approximately 14,000 species, more than 1,000 have been described for the hypogean environment from around the world. Information about this class and its hypogean representatives is summarized in Table 2.2.

The Order Platycopioida has two hypogean species, found in the same anchialine cave in Bermuda (Worsaae *et al.* 2004). The Order Calanoida is composed of filter-feeding species that are part of the zooplankton. This taxon contains 43 families and approximately 2000 species (Boltovskoy *et al.* 1999). Two of these families contain hypogean representatives worldwide, including Madagascar. The family Ridgewayiidae is represented by one cave genus, *Exumella*, containing four species, two of which have

Table 2.2 *Orders of the class Maxillopoda and their hypogean representatives*

Order	Total no. of species	No. of hypogean species	Distribution
Platycopioida	12	2	Bermuda
Calanoida	*c.* 2,000	>20	Worldwide
Misophrioida	37	18	Atlantic, Mediterranean, and Pacific
Cyclopoida	>1,000	*c.* 180	Circumglobal?
Gelyelloida	2	2	Europe
Harpacticoidea	*c.* 3,000	*c.* 500	Circumglobal
Total	>14,051	>1,022	

Sources: cited in text.

been described as cave organisms from the Caribbean (Suarez-Morales and Iliffe 2005). The family Pseudocyclopiidae contains one hypogean species, *Stygocyclopia australis*, from an Australian sinkhole (Jaume *et al.* 2001).

Three families of the Order Misophrioida have cave representatives: Palpophriidae, Speleophriidae, and Misophriidae. They are marine and anchialine and found in Bermuda, the Bahamas, the Canary Islands, the Mediterranean, northwestern Australia, and the Pacific. The family Palpophriidae was described in 2000 (Boxshall and Jaume 2000). The family Speleophriidae contains a single cave species from northwestern Australia, *Speleophria bunderae* (Jaume *et al.* 2001). The family Misophriidae has several genera represented in the Bahamas including *Spelaeomysis, Stygiomysis, Antromysis*, and *Heteromysis*, and a new species, *Palaumysis bahamensis* (Pesce and Iliffe 2002).

There are about 180 hypogean species of the order Cyclopoda found in karstic caves, phreatic waters, and anchialine environments of the American continent, Africa (including Madagascar), Europe, and Asia. They are all blind and depigmented.

The Order Gelyelloida contains only two species, both of them in caves of France and Switzerland, respectively.

The Order Harpacticoida has cave and phreatic representatives from southern Mexico, Texas, Bermuda, the Canary Islands, the central and eastern Mediterranean Sea, and the Korean peninsula. These vermiform crustaceans scrape food from the sediments. The species found in the Canary Islands (*Stygotantulus stocki*) is actually a parasite on copepods (Brancelj 2000; Fiers and Iliffe 2000).

2.18.4 Class Ostracoda

Members of the Class Ostracoda are usually around 1 mm in length with a chitinous hinged shell similar to that of a bivalve. Of the approximately 5,700 species, more than 1,000 have been described from the hypogean environment, including cave, phreatic, and anchialine environments from all over the world. The Cuban representative of this order, *Spelaeoecia saturno*, belongs to the family Halocyprididae and is the only known cave representative of this family; it is found along the northeast coast of Cuba (Kornicker and Yager 2002). Another cave representative of this class is *Danielopolina kornickeri*, of the family Thaumatocypridoidea, found in an anchialine cave in Western Australia (Danielopol *et al.* 2000). In general they show reduction of their visual apparatus and pigmentation, as well as enhancement of chemosensory organs and reduction in size. Some appear to be relicts of more ancient fauna; others appear to have invaded the hypogean environment in recent times.

2.18.5 Class Malacostraca

The Class Malacostraca, with approximately 25,000 species, is the largest subgroup of crustaceans and contains what most people consider the more widely recognizable crustaceans such as lobsters, crabs, shrimps, pill bugs, and crawfishes. This class is complex in its systematics. Hypogean representatives by taxa, number and distribution are summarized in Table 2.3.

The Order Leptostraca is represented by a single hypogean species: *Speonebalia cannoni* from two caves in the Caicos Islands. It is depigmented and the eye stalks lack visual apparatus (Bowman *et al.* 1985).

The Order Bathynellacea is composed of about 250 freshwater species, of which its 200 hypogean species can be found in phreatic and cave environments from all over the world.

The Order Anaspidacea is a freshwater group endemic to Australia, where hypogean representatives are found in springs and caves.

The Order Bochusacea has one species (*Thetispelecaris remix*) of anchialine crustacean from the Bahamas.

The Order Spelaeogriphacea represents an old clade from the southern hemisphere (Brazil, South Africa, and Western Australia) which reveals its Gondwanan origin. They are small, blind, and depigmented, able to swim fast, and apparently feed on detritus.

All species of the Order Thermosbaenacea are hypogean (including phreatic and interstitial) and found in a great range of salinities and even

Table 2.3 *The orders of the class Malacostraca and their hypogean representation*

Order	Total no. of species	No. of hypogean species	Distribution of hypogean species
Leptostraca	*c.* 20	1	Caicos Islands
Bathynellacea	*c.* 200	150	Circumglobal
Anaspidacea	17	13	Southern hemisphere
Bochusacea	3	1	Bahamas
Spelaeogriphacea	4	4	Southern hemisphere
Thermosbaenacea	34	34	Circumglobal
Mysidacea	>1,000	45	Circumglobal
Mictacea	5	2	North Atlantic and southwestern Pacific
Amphipoda	*c.* 7,000	>850	Circumglobal
Isopoda	>11,000	*c.* 1,000	Circumglobal
Tanaidacea	>900	6	Atlantic, Pacific
Cumacea	>1,400	12	North Atlantic
Decapoda	*c.* 10,000	>400	Circumglobal
Total	>31,581	>2,521	

Sources: cited in text.

in thermal springs. They are small in size (4 mm or less) and show varying degrees of eye reduction, including total loss of the visual apparatus.

The Order Mysidacea contains a number of hypogean species derived from marine ancestors with a varying degree of depigmentation and loss of eyes (but not the eye stalks). Some examples of this group are *Palaumysis bahamensis, P. pilifera,* and *P. simonae*. *P. bahamensis* is from the Bahamas (Pesce and Iliffe 2002); *P. pilifera* and *P. simonae* are both from Japan (Hanamura and Kase 2003).

The Order Mictacea is represented by two anchialine species from Bermuda and Australia.

The Order Amphipoda is a group of small (up to 50 mm in length) shrimp-like crustaceans that live primarily in marine environments, but some species are found in freshwater. Although many species of this order are hypogean, most of them are found in freshwater habitats and belong to the families Hadziidae, Niphargidae, Bogidiellidae, and Crangonyctidae, all of them belonging to the suborder Gammaridae. Hypogean representatives have been found around the world and have both a marine and a freshwater origin, with some species apparently being relicts whereas others represent more recent invasions of the hypogean environment

(Sawicki *et al.* 2003; Ozbek and Guloglu 2005; Karaman and Matocec 2006). Reduction and loss of eyes and pigmentation are common, as is elongation of appendages. Members of other families of amphipod have been found in caves but tend to be species that move in and out of the hypogean environment; these sometimes show a certain amount of reduction in eyes and pigmentation. They feed mostly on detritus.

The Order Isopoda has hypogean representatives in freshwater and marine caves as well as in phreatic waters (including hot springs) and anchialine environments from all over the world. Some (the Oniscidea) are terrestrial and live in caves with high relative humidity. Most of them are blind and depigmented and some are microphthalmic, with elongated bodies and appendages, and with slow metabolism and long life cycles. Their feeding habits include scavenging and predation. The family Asellidae contains several cave representatives from North America, including the troglobitic *Caecidotea cumberlandensis* (Fig. 2.2.). This species can be found in caves in southwestern Virginia along with others in the genus, including *C. teresae*, *C. paurotrigonus*, *C. barri*, *C. jordani*, and *C. incurva*, all of them with some degree of eye reduction (Lewis 2000). The family Calabozoidae contains only a single troglomorphic species, *Calabozoa pellucida*, which is found in Brazil (Messana *et al.* 2002). A lone Japanese member of the family Mesoniscidae, *Mesoniscus graniger*, has been documented in caves (Sustr *et al.* 2005). There is not much information available on troglomorphic species of the family Philosciidae, but there are anecdotal references of both epigean and cave forms within this family even though there is no confirmation (Rivera *et al.* 2002). The Indonesian cave representative of this order, *Stenasellus strinatii*, belongs to the family Stenasellidae (Magniez 2001).

All the hypogean species of the Order Tanaidacea are marine or anchialine and found on islands.

The Order Cumacea are all marine/anchialine and from Bermuda and other islands in the North Atlantic (Corbera 2002).

The Order Decapoda (shrimps, crabs, lobsters, prawns, crayfish, and scampi) is subdivided into six infraorders, with four of these containing hypogean representatives in marine, anchialine, freshwater, and terrestrial environments. Most of them show different degrees of blindness and depigmentation as well lower metabolism, elongated appendages, and long life cycles when compared with their epigean relatives (Okuno 1999; Yeo and Ng 1999; Anker and Iliffe 2000; Yeo 2001; Ng 2002a,b; Osawa and Takeda 2004; Von Sternberg and Schotte 2004; Osawa *et al.* 2006). Many other decapods have been found in caves but they appear

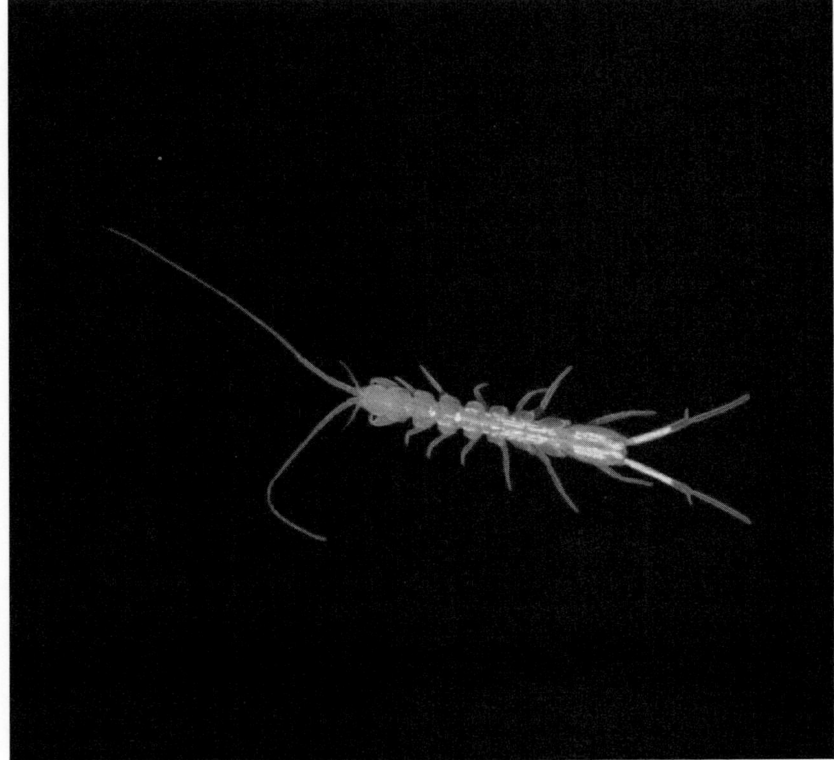

Figure 2.2 Caecidotea sp. Photo by Danté Fenolio. (See Plate 5.)

to be casual visitors with no evident troglomorphisms. The infraorder Palinura is one of the most easily recognizable groups of cave crustaceans. There is at least one family and 11 species in two genera found in the hypogean environment. This is largely a North American group of species of the genus *Orconectes* (Rhodes 1962; Mejia-Ortiz *et al.* 2003). A number of decapods have been classified by the International Union for the Conservation of Nature in various threat categories. One of those is *Procambarus lucifugus* from Florida, USA (Fig. 2.3).

2.19 Chelicerata (arachnids and their relatives)

The arthropod subphylum Chelicerata is composed of five classes, two of which are extinct: Eurypterida, or sea scorpions, and Chasmataspidida. The other three are Pycnogonida or sea spiders, Xiphosura or horseshoe

Figure 2.3 Procambarus lucifugus. Photo by Danté Fenolio. (See Plate 6.)

crabs, and Arachnida, which includes spiders, scorpions, and mites. Only the last has hypogean representatives.

2.19.1 Class Arachnida

The Class Arachnida is a very diverse group of more than 93,000 species but it is widely believed that there must be hundreds of thousands of undescribed species (Coddington 2005). Of the 11 orders of Arachnida, nine have hypogean representatives (Table 2.4). The phylogeny of this group is very complex and controversial. Here the phylogeny follows that of Giribet *et al.* (2002) but is simplified by grouping all the Opiliones together as a single order, as has been done traditionally. With the exception of many members of the Suborder Acari, all arachnids are terrestrial, with worldwide distribution. Hypogean Arachnida are found in a wide range of latitudes; in some cases their relationships with epigean species are clear and in other cases less so, with most being terrestrial but many cave mites being aquatic. Some belong to ancient lineages whereas others seem to be recent invaders of the hypogean environment. Among the characteristics of many troglobitic arachnids are the reduction and/or total loss of the visual apparatus and pigmentation, elongation of appendages, lower metabolic rates, production of fewer and larger eggs,

Table 2.4 *The orders of the Class Arachnida and their hypogean representation*

Order	Total no. of species	No. of hypogean species	Distribution
Acari	*c.* 45,000	>1,000	Circumglobal
Palpigradi	*c.* 85	30	Tropical
Ricinulei	*c.* 60	11	Tropics and subtropics of America and Western Africa
Araneae	*c.* 40,000	>1,000	Circumglobal
Amblipygi	*c.* 140	>40	Circumglobal: tropical and subtropical
Uropygi (=Thelyphonida)	>100	0	
Schizomida	*c.* 240	*c.* 80	Circumglobal: tropical and subtropical areas
Scorpionida	>1,300		
Pseudoscorpionida	*c.* 3,000	>400	Circumglobal
Solifugae (=Solpugida)	>1,000	0	
Opilionida	*c.* 6,400	*c.* 130	Cosmopolitan

Sources: cited in text.

and longer life spans. Feeding habits include predation, consumption of detritus, and parasitism. Because many species of hypogean arachnid are endemic to restricted areas and may depend upon resources outside the cave, such as leaf litter, they are threatened by environmental modifications of their habitat and introduction of exotic species, such as red ants.

Order Acari

The Order Acari, Acarina or Acarimorpha (ticks and mites) is the most diverse and abundant group of living arachnids, with probably more than 45,000 described species and very complex systematics. There are more than 1,000 described species reported from caves with some, being troglomorphic or troglophiles to some degree, generally showing reduction or loss of eyes and pigmentation as well as elongation of appendages and well-developed sensory setae. Among the aquatic species (Suborder Prostigmata) it is common to find not only species with reduction or loss of eyes and pigmentation but also those with elongated bodies and shorter legs, which contrasts with the pattern of longer appendages for other cave arthropods. This is probably due to the interstitial nature of many of them. Some cave guanophile Acari are so abundant that their populations have been estimated to be of up to several million individuals per square meter.

Most of the cave species have been found as parasites of bats and other cave mammals as well as salamanders. There is not much specificity in the relationships between Acari parasites and their hosts, with many single species parasitizing several species of cave vertebrate and the same host being parasitized by two or more species of Acari. Most of them do not show typical troglomorphisms regarding their visual apparatus or pigmentation, but some do show elongated appendages. A number of cave Acari prey on small invertebrates (including invertebrate eggs and larvae) found as part of guano communities. Others feed on fungi, detritus, and dead animals.

Sources of information on cave Acari were Ryckman (1956), Nicholas (1962), Peck (1974), Moraz and Lindquist (1998), Welbourn (1999), Culver *et al.* (2000), Zacharda (2000), Mahunka (2001), Halliday (2001), Reeves (2001), Fain and Bochkov (2002), Harvey (2002), Andre and Ducarme (2003), Guzman-Cornejo *et al.* (2003), Husband and O'Conner (2003), Ducarme *et al.* (2004a,b), Reeves *et al.* (2004), Makol and Gabrys (2005), Sendra *et al.* (2006), and Kurta *et al.* (2007).

Order Palpigradi

The Order Palpigradi (microwhip scorpions) is a small group in both number of species (*c.* 85) and individual size (no more than 3 mm in length) (Harvey 2002). About 85 species have been described so far, of which about 30 have been described from caves. All members of this order, whether they are epigean or hypogean, are blind and have a very thin cuticle. Almost nothing is known about their natural history but it is believed that they are predators of smaller invertebrates and lay only a few eggs. They are usually found in damp soil underneath rocks (Welbourn 1999; Christian 2005; Barranco and Mayoral 2007).

Order Ricinulei

The Order Ricinulei (hooded tickspiders) is a small group of arachnids with about 60 species and of sizes ranging between 5 and 10 mm. They are all blind; the hypogean species tend to have elongated appendages. Little is known about their natural history. They live in damp habitats in tropical and subtropical areas of the American and Western African continents. All of the 11 species of this group that have been reported from caves are from Mexico, Guatemala, Venezuela, Brazil, and Cuba.

They are predators on smaller vertebrates (Talarico *et al.* 2006; Pinto da Rocha and Bonaldo 2007).

Order Araneae

The Order Araneae (spiders) with nearly 40,000 described species, contains almost 40% of all arachnids (Harvey 2002). About 1,000 species of arachnid show troglomorphisms; many more species normally found in the epigean environment are found at the entrances of caves. Like many other species of cave arthropod, many cave spiders are blind and depigmented, have elongated appendages, simplified respiratory systems, lower metabolism and activities, and longer life spans, and lay fewer and larger eggs (see, for example, Kuntner *et al.* 1999; Jager 2005; Miller 2005). Despite being top predators, they tend to be abundant.

Independent colonization by the same genus (*Dysdera*) of nearby hypogean habitats in the Canary Islands has been suggested based on molecular and morphological studies, with each cave population somewhat different from the others as a result of different environmental conditions (Arnedo *et al.* 2007). In at least some cases invasions have been recent and evolution of cave species very rapid (see, for example, Hedin 1997). Cave spiders prey on almost anything as big as they are, including worms, slugs, and flying insects, but mostly soil or litter fauna (Smithers 2005). It seems that the lack of light in the hypogean environment does not necessarily affect the mating behavior of at least some of the cave spider species. *Hickmania troglodytes*, the Tasmanian cave spider, for example, shows ritualized courtship and mating behavior, as well as complex egg-sac construction, brooding, emergence, and molting activities (Doran *et al.* 2001).

Order Amblypygi

The Order Amblypygi (tailless whipscorpions) comprises about 140 nocturnal species, of which almost one third are hypogean. These rather large (up to 4.5 cm in body length) and predatory animals are very conspicuous when present in caves, owing not only to their size but also to the fact that they do not seem to fear other animals, including humans (Weygoldt 1994; Harvey 2002). Some show normal eye development and pigmentation, but most do not (Pinto da Rocha *et al.* 2002). One of the largest species, *Tarantula fuscimana*, feeds on cave crickets and also on dead bats (Peck 1974).

Order Schizomida

The Order Schizomida (short-tailed whipscorpions) comprises about 240 species, of which about one third have been recorded from caves. They are of rather small size although the largest is a cave species: *Agastoschizomus lucifer*, from Mexico, with a length of 12.4 mm. They are found in tropical and subtropical areas, particularly in leaf litter, where they feed on invertebrates (Harvey 2002). Peck (1974) mentioned *Schizomus portoricensis* as being 'heavily associated with guano'. Many show a great deal of variation in terms of eye development and pigmentation (Nicholas 1962; Culver *et al.* 1973; Rowland and Reddell 1979; Humphreys 1991; Harvey, cited in BESPL 2005[1]).

Order Scorpionida

The Order Scorpionida (scorpions) comprises more than 1,300 species of worldwide distribution; all are predators. They are well known for their large claws and venomous 'sting' (telson) (Harvey 2002). There are at least 16 species inhabiting caves that show troglomorphisms. Twelve of these are from Mexico and the other four are found in Ecuador, the Pyrenees, India, and Laos (Lourenco 1995, 2007). Several other species not showing troglomorphisms and also inhabiting the epigean environment have been found underground (Mitchell and Peck 1977). In caves they are usually associated with guano communities, in which they prey on guanophiles (see, for example, Ferreira and Martins 1999).

Order Pseudoscorpionida

The Order Pseudoscorpionida is composed of species of rather small size, only up to 1 cm in length (Harvey 2002). Although similar to scorpions, the pseudoscorpions are different because they lack the metasoma and telson. They are predators, with cave species showing either reduction or total loss of eyes and pigmentation as well as elongation of appendages and slender bodies. Although most cave species have been recorded from temperate areas, it is possible that there are many undescribed ones in tropical caves. According to Chamberlin and Malcolm (1960) there are about 293 cave-dwelling pseudoscorpion species; Culver *et al.* (2000) claim 130 species of cave-dwelling pseudoscorpion from 28 genera in the USA alone. Most of the cave dwelling pseudoscorpions (*c.* 92%) are

[1] Harvey, M. *Schizomids.* [cited April 18, 2006]; about 2 pp. Available from: http://www.australasian-arachnology.org/arachnology/schizomida/

in the superfamilies Chthonoidea and Neobisioidea (Chamberlin and Malcolm 1960). The most likely number of cave species is somewhat bigger than 400. In North America Pseudoscorpionida has a higher rate of cave endemism than any other order, with 69% of the order being made up of obligately cave-dwelling species. In general, pseudoscorpions tend to be among the most abundant and diverse taxa of cave invertebrates (Christman *et al.* 2005).

Albiorix anophthalmus from Arizona is a blind species about 3 mm long, which feeds on psocids (booklice or barklice, *c.* 1 mm), which in turn feed on cave cricket guano (Muchmore and Pape 1999). In general bat guano in caves provides the appropriate environment for many of the species on which pseudoscorpions prey (Ferreira *et al.* 2007). *Tuberochernes aalbui* and *T. ubicki*, also blind, are known from localities at 2,200 m and 1,600 m asl, respectively (Muchmore 1997). *Mundochthonius singularis* has reduced eyes and is found in Colorado; it is derived from the local epigean species *M. montanus* (Muchmore 2001).

Order Opilionida

The Order Opilionida (Opiliones or harvestmen), with about 6,400 species, accounts for about 6.1% of all known arachnids (Harvey 2002). According to Rambla and Juberthie (1994), 115 species of harvestman live in caves, 82 being obligatory cave-dwellers; however, based on the present author's own literature search there are at least 130 species found in caves (Fig. 2.4). Harvestmen are usually long-legged predators but can also be opportunist feeders on animal and plant matter. They, in turn, serve as nutrient sources for other harvestmen (including those of the same species), spiders, cave crickets, and fungi, particularly their eggs, of which they produce sometimes more than 200. Even some marsupials, amphibians, and reptiles feed on them, but outside the cave (Gnaspini 1996; Machado and Oliveira 1998). Many species leave the cave at night to forage, mostly on flying insects in the forest canopy, capturing them with a pseudoweb. They then consume their prey at the same spot where they captured them (Hoenen and Gnaspini 1999; Santos and Gnaspini 2002) and return to the cave before dawn, when they are usually found resting on the walls and ceilings (see, for example, Machado *et al.* 2002). This behavior is triggered by the day–night cycle based on light intensity (Gnaspini *et al.* 2003). Once in the cave the harvestmen defecate, bringing in energy to the hypogean environment, although they can also feed on dead matter in the cave (Machado *et al.* 2000). For example, the Brazilian cave harvestman *Goniosoma albiscriptum* regularly uses caves

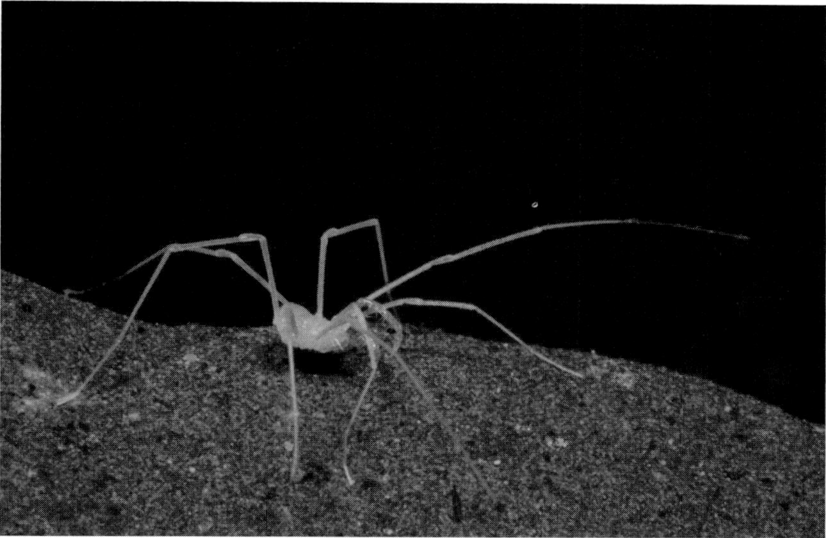

Figure 2.4 A cave opilionid showing the typical blindness and depigmentation of troglomorphic species. Photo by Danté Fenolio. (See Plate 7.)

during the day, leaving them to forage on the vegetation after dusk. Willemart and Gnaspini (2004a,b) observed that these opilionids segregated into nine groups within a single cave, all of them with females and males. However, only males moved from one group to another, although rarely, suggesting that they do so to maintain genetic diversity. Not all the individuals move in and out of the cave through the same openings. Further, this species showed a variety of mechanical defensive behaviors, particularly by females toward their eggs (Gnaspini and Cavalheiro 1998; Machado 2003), and also produce a repellent liquid that individuals collectively discharge towards an aggressor before fleeing under attack (Machado *et al.* 2000).

The troglomorphic species show the expected features of reduction or loss of eyes and pigmentation and even more elongated appendages (see, for example, Goodnight and Goodnight 1960). *Stylocellus globosus* from Malaysia is a mite predator with eyes but no cornea (Schwendinger *et al.* 2004). It is known from six caves that are thought not to be interconnected but may in fact be connected through a system of small crevices, given the dispersal abilities of this species. *Fangensis* species, from Thailand, are eyeless (Schwendinger and Giribet 2005). The one epigean form has eyes but no cornea; this species is a leaf-litter dweller. *Fangensis spelaeus* tends to remain in a larger area of the cave and is usually found on wet loam. It is suspected that it needs the humid environment to survive. *F. leclerci* prefers dark areas of caves and was found on wet loam next to a river within the cave. These species were observed in captivity to burrow into loose, moist soil for shelter. *F. cavernarus* is found around 300–600 m deep inside the cave where it occurs, and was found on both sides of the underground river on wet loam. This species is much less abundant than the previous two. In addition, it is apparently very sensitive to ground vibrations and has acute olfactory abilities.

In New Zealand there are two species of harvestman, *Hendea myersi cavernicola* and *Megalopsalis tumida,* which inhabit a system of caves with one species of glowworm, *Arachnocampa luminosa* (Meyer-Rochow and Liddle 1988). The glowworm is a bioluminescent invertebrate that is believed to use its bioluminescence to attract prey and mates. The two harvestmen have eyes that are degenerate but have maximized photon capture. The harvestmen respond negatively to UV light but positively to glowworm light. They not only navigate by using this light but also predate the glowworm. *H. m. cavernicola* prefers to predate the eggs and early instars of the glowworm, whereas *M. tumida* prefers to predate the last three instars, the pupae, and the adults. *A. luminosa* also predates chironomids as well as the younger life stages of the harvestmen (see also Culver *et al.* 2000; Gnaspini *et al.* 2003; Pinto da Rocha and Kury 2003).

2.20 Onychophora (velvet worms)

Onychophora (velvet worms) is a phylum of very interesting organisms considered ancestral to the arthropods. With about 200 described living species, found mostly in tropical and subtropical regions, this group has a few cave representatives, almost all of them in the Southern Hemisphere with the exception of the eyeless and depigmented Jamaican species *Speleoperipatus speleus* (Peck 1975). *Opisthopatus herbertorum* from South Africa has reduced eyes and lacks pigmentation (Ruhberg and Hamer 2005); the depigmented *Peripatopsis alba* is also from a South African cave (Sharratt *et al.* 2000).

2.21 Tardigrada (water bears)

The Phylum Tardigrada (water bears) is represented by about 1,000 species found worldwide, from the Himalayas to the deep seas, and from the Equator to the polar regions. They are found in freshwater, in terrestrial environments associated with terrestrial mosses and lichens, and in marine environments (Hickman *et al.* 2000). They are microscopic (usually less than 1 mm in length), segmented creatures; despite being aquatic they do not swim, but rather creep along while clinging to surfaces with their claws. Their body is covered by a non-chitinous cuticle and several species have eyespots. They feed on nematodes, rotifers, and plant cell cytoplasm, which they gather by using piercing stylets and then suck through their pharynx.

Several species of tardigrade have been identified from marine caves. Boesgaard and Kristensen (2001), for example, electroshocked sediment samples from two sea caves in Australia to inspect interstitial fauna and found a high diversity of tardigrades despite a low number of individuals overall. They found nine genera, one of which, *Actinarctus*, had not been described for the South Pacific before. As with the kinorhynchs found in the same study, these researchers suggested that the caves are refugia left from a shifting shoreline of the ancient Tethys Sea, as *Actinarctus* has been found in Mediterranean Sea caves. These authors hypothesized that tardigrades, kinorhynchs and other interstitial cave fauna from Australia that are the same species as marine cave fauna in Italy may not have evolved and become separate species because of the caves' stable environments, where selective pressure has been low for long periods of time.

The large number of primitive tardigrades in Mediterranean caves suggests that this group originated in the old Tethys Sea from which the basin of the Mediterranean Sea was formed (Boesgaard and Kristensen 2001; Grimaldi and D'Addabbo 2001). Others seem to be closely related to deep-sea taxa (Villoria Moreno 1996).

2.22 Myriapoda (millipedes and centipedes)

The Subphylum Myriapoda is made up of worm-like arthropods with multiple pairs of legs. This group has about 13,000 living species described so far, most of which are found associated with decaying material in a great variety of habitats. Some of them are nocturnal predators. Almost 300 cave species have been described so far (Fig. 2.5). This subphylum is divided into four classes: Chilopoda (centipedes), Diplopoda (millipedes), Pauropoda (centipede-like arthropods), and Symphyla (garden centipedes or glasshouse symphylans) (Table 2.5).

Table 2.5 *The classes of the Subphyllum Myriapoda and their hypogean representation*

Class	Total no. of species	No. of hypogean species	Distribution
Chilopoda	*c*. 2,500	*c*. 60	Circumglobal
Diplopoda	*c*. 10,000	*c*. 200	Circumglobal
Pauropoda	*c*. 500	2 or more	Circumglobal
Symphyla	*c*. 200	4	Circumglobal

Sources: cited in text.

Figure 2.5 A cave millipede from Blevins Cave, Arkansas. Photo by Danté Fenolio. (See Plate 8.)

2.22.1 Class Chilopoda

The Class Chilopoda or centipedes is composed of flattened, highly segmented arthropods up to 30 cm in length. They are known for their predatory habits. There are about 2,500 species described and they are distributed worldwide. About 60 species have been found in caves on all continents except Antarctica (see, for example, Murakami 1975; Zapparoli 1984; Peck 1998; Bulhmann 2001; Stoev 2001; Edgecombe 2006). Cave species are usually depigmented and have very elongated appendages (up to 15 cm in length) including legs, antennae and abundant sensory setae (see, for example, Foddai and Minelli 1999).

Cave centipedes show a great deal of adaptation to a wide range of temperatures (Grgic and Kos 2001). They are generalist predators with prey ranging from mosquitoes (Taguchi and Makiya 1982) to bats (Molinari *et al.* 2005). The centipede *Scolopendra gigantea* has been reported preying on three species of bat in a limestone cave in northwestern Venezuela. These centipedes were able to climb the walls and ceilings of the cave where they preyed upon the bats, which were several times larger in terms of body mass.

2.22.2 Class Diplopoda

The Class Diplopoda or millipedes are cylindrical arthropods with up to 100 segments. This group is camprises about 10,000 known herbivorous and detritivorous species. About 200 species in five orders of millipede have been reported from caves. Most of these have reduced pigmentation and ocelli, a less calcified cuticle, and longer legs and antennae compared with epigean species (Shear 1969; Golovatch and Wytwer 2004; Lewis 2005; Golovatch *et al.* 2006).

The Order Chordeumida makes up about 80% of cave millipedes, and species of the Order Polydesmida become depigmented after several molts. There is no overall size differentiation between epigean and hypogean millipedes. Cave Diplopoda usually depended on food resources brought into the cave via guano or rotting wood (Shear 1969). The cave representatives of the order Julida have a unique morphological modification for feeding on bacterial films. Their comb-like mouthparts also allow them to filter food particles from water (Culver and White 2005).

Although most of the species known until the 1990s were from Europe and North America, a number of new species have been discovered in the past few years not only in those regions but also elsewhere in the world. Many of these new findings are providing not only a much more diverse picture of millipedes in caves but also some with unusual characteristics.

Millipedes of the genus *Motyxia* in Crystal Cave of Sequoia and King's Canyon National Park, California, are bioluminescent and depigmented, feeding on mold- and guano-eating millipedes (Causey and Tiemann 1969; National Park Service 2005). Arkansas and other Ozark Range states are home to two depigmented cave millipede species from the Family Trichopelatidae (Shear 2003). These species were discovered as part of the Ozark Subterranean Biodiversity Project, a study conducted for over 20 years by government, conservation, and academic institutions. A great number of new cave species have been discovered in the past few years in Europe (see, for example, Makarov *et al.* 2002, 2003a,b,c, 2006), China (see, for example, Stoev 2004; Stoev and Enghoff 2005; Golovatch *et al.* 2006), South America (see, for example, Golovatch and Wytwer 2004), the United States (see, for example, Lewis 2005), and Australia (see, for example, Mesibov 2005).

In addition to the discovery of new species of cave millipede, a number of studies have included diverse aspects of their ecology and behavior. Using electrophoresis techniques, Laing *et al.* (1976a,b) studied two Kentucky populations of blind cave millipedes, *Scoterpes copei*, to see whether the river that separated their two localities presented a geographic barrier to gene flow. The two populations had a genetic similarity of 22%, and each population had very low genetic variability. Because of their results, the authors suggested that the two populations were actually sibling species, externally resembling each other but having reproductive isolation.

Changing the water and organic matter regimes of a cave in semi-arid and tropical Western Australia caused immigration of millipedes and other taxa to the cave, providing evidence of pulse-driven colonization of caves (Humphreys 1991). In this study, the addition of either water or organic matter did not cause colonization, but the combination of the two did.

A study to determine the presence of circadian rhythms in the cave-dwelling millipede *Glyphiulus cavernicolus* was conducted among individuals that had never been exposed to light; most of them showed circadian rhythms in their locomotory periods that lasted about 26 h. After a light–dark cycle, 66% of subjects took on the activity cycle. A constant light setting induced arrhythmia in 80% of the millipedes (Koilraj *et al.* 2000).

2.22.3 Class Pauropoda

The Class Pauropoda is made up of about 500 species with worldwide distribution. They are small (generally no more than 2 mm in length), centipede-like arthropods that lack eyes and are generally depigmented (whether they are found in caves or not), being encountered in soils and decaying plant material. A few species have been found in caves and mines in Europe and Japan. One example is *Pauropus furcifer*, from a cave in Serbia (Scheller *et al.* 1997).

2.22.4 Class Symphyla

The Class Symphyla or garden centipedes is made up of about 200 species of soil-dwelling animals with worldwide distribution. These small creatures (rarely more than 10 mm in length) are all eyeless and generally depigmented, regardless of where they are found. Two cave species have been reported for Postojna Cave in Slovenia, one in Mexico, and another one in Tasmania (Australia) (Scheller 1996). The latter shows an elongated body and appendages.

2.23 Insecta (insects)

With more than one million living species so far described (and millions more yet to be discovered), insects represent more than half of all the described biodiversity of living organisms on Earth. It is not surprising, therefore, that they are also well represented in the hypogean environment. With such large numbers, the systematics of insects is still far from being agreed. Most sources identify more than 30 orders and nearly 700 families of these organisms. What follows is a brief survey of the most important orders of insects represented in the cave environment. The classification is based on that of Triplehorn and Johnson (2005).

2.23.1 Order Collembola (springtails)

These small (up to 8 mm in length), primitive insects are found worldwide, including in Antarctica. There are about 7,000 species, of which more than 400 are hypogean. Out of the 15 springtail families, at least nine have been documented for the hypogean environment. They are: Cyphoderidae, Hypogastruridae and Isotomidae (Trajano 2000), Entomobryidae (Christiansen and Culver 1987), Neelidae, Oncopoduridae, Onychiuridae, Sminthuridae, and Tomoceridae (Nicholas 1960). Many more are expected to be discovered, particularly in the tropics. They usually constitute a large portion of the biomass in the hypogean environment. Hypogean species tend to display characteristics typical of other underground arthropods, such as a reduction and/or total loss of

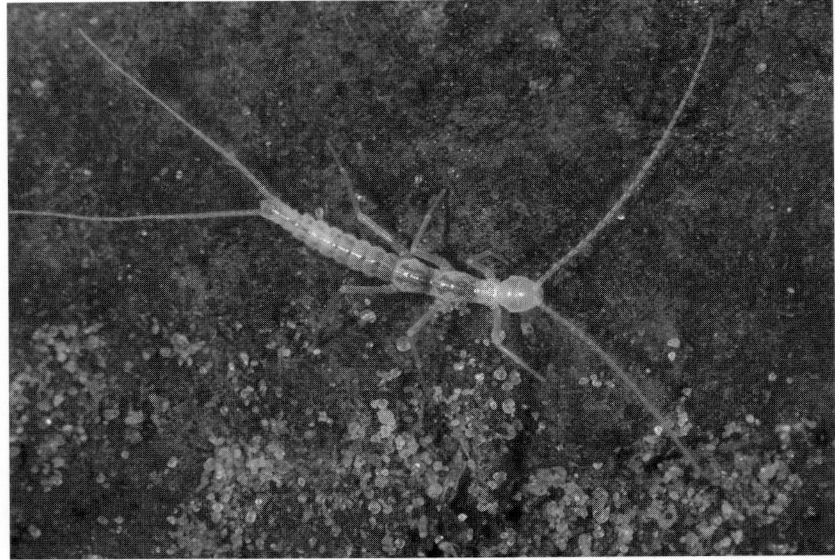

Figure 2.6 A Campodeidae dipluran from the Ozarks in Oklahoma. Photo by Danté Fenolio. (See Plate 9.)

eyes and pigmentation, elongated appendages, larger body size, lower fecundity, and slower development and metabolism (see, for example, Christiansen 1965). Many of the cave species are guanobitic (Ferreira *et al.* 2007).

2.23.2 Order Diplura (two-pronged bristletails)

With about 800 species, these elongated insects are represented by about 100 species in the hypogean environment, where they always lack eyes. Representatives of at least two of the six families occur in caves: Campodeidae (Fig. 2.6) and Japygidae. Some troglomorphic species show a remarkable degree of convergent evolution in their cave-related characters (Ferguson 1996).

2.23.3 Order Microcoryphia (bristletails)

Some species of this group have been found at the entrances of caves (Graening *et al.* 2006a).

2.23.4 Order Thysanura (Zygentoma or silverfish)

These organisms are decomposers and myrmecophilous. Two of the five families occur in caves: Lepismatidae and Nicoletiidae. About 20 species are hypogean (see, for example, Espinasa and Fisher 2006).

2.23.5 Order Ephemeroptera (mayflies)

At least one of the 26 families of mayfly has been found in caves: the Leptophlebiidae (Trajano 2000).

2.23.6 Order Orthoptera (crickets, grasshoppers, and members of the family Tettigoniidae)

Representatives of three of the 20 families (about 250 species) of this order have been found in caves: Gryllacrididae, Gryllidae, and Tettigoniidae. They have been found not only in traditional caves but also in lava tubes of Hawaii. Some of them, such as the Hawaiian species, have reduced eyes, and are depigmented and flightless. When present, they may represent a very large portion of the total biomass in caves. This is so in many temperate caves, particularly in North America (Lavoie *et al.* 2007), where they usually interact with the epigean environment either daily or seasonally. Examples are the cave crickets (Family Gryllacrididae) of Mammoth Cave in Kentucky. They forage outside the cave and then contribute to the cave ecology through the cricket guano they deposit when they come into the cave at night (Poulson *et al.* 1995).

2.23.7 Order Dermaptera (earwigs)

About 15 hypogean species of this order have been documented so far. They seem to be associated with guano; in tropical parts of the world, such as Thailand, they may represent a large portion of the cave biomass. They display a varying degree of troglomorphism. A couple of earwigs in caves are worth mentioning. One is *Carcinophora americana*, which has been found in three caves in Puerto Rico and is widespread in the American tropics (Peck 1974). The other is the Hawaiian species *Anisolabis howarthi*, which is omnivorous, seeking both live prey and organic material that it might scavenge (Brindle 1980).

2.23.8 Order Isoptera (termites)

Termites have been documented in guano communities of caves (see, for example, Ferreira *et al.* 2007).

2.23.9 Order Blattodea (cockroaches)

Four of the six families of this order have been found to be represented in caves: Blaberidae and Blattellidae (Trajano 2000), Blattidae (Roth 1988), and Nocticolidae (Vidlicka *et al.* 2003). Most of the hypogean species are from tropical areas and show reduction and/or loss of eyes, depigmentation, reduced wings, and lengthened legs (Vidlicka *et al.* 2003).

2.23.10 Order Hemiptera (including Heteroptera and Homoptera or true bugs, cicadas, hoppers, psyllids, whiteflies, aphids, and scale insects)

Six of the 98 hemipteran families have been reported to be represented in caves: Cimicidae, Cixiidae, Mesoveliidae, Nepidae, Psylloidae, and Veliidae. They can be predators or consumers of fluids from rotting organic material. They are also found in association with guano. Sometimes they are seen penetrating caves through the cracks created by roots. About 80 species have been reported from caves all over the world, particularly on islands, with most of them showing the troglomorphisms typical of other insects (see Lee and Kim 2006).

2.23.11 Order Thysanoptera (thrips)

Members of at least one of the nine thysanopteran families occur in caves: Phlaeothripidae. They are part of guano communities (e.g. Ferreira *et al.* 2007).

2.23.12 Order Psocoptera (book- and barklice)

Representatives of five of the 37 psocopteran families occur in caves: Ectopsocidae, Liposcelidae, Psocidae, Psyllipsocidae, and Trigiidae (Ashmole and Ashmole 1997). At least a dozen species of this order show troglomorphisms, with some cave species showing instances of parthenogenesis. They tend to be associated with guano communities (see, for example, Ferreira *et al.* 2007).

2.23.13 Order Phthiraptera (lice)

At least one of the 18 louse families is represented in caves: the Menoponidae. The lice found in caves occur on swiftlets (see below) (Clayton *et al.* 1996).

2.23.14 Order Coleoptera (beetles)

With more than 300,000 living species described so far the Coleoptera is the most diverse order of living organisms (Brusca and Brusca 1990). More than 100 families of beetle have been described, of which at least 18 have representatives in the subterranean environment.

Hypogean beetles are found in all kinds of hypogean environments with a great range of temperature and humidity. Some of them are even aquatic, living in the phreatic environment. They show a wide variety of feeding habits in caves, including predation, guanophilia, mycophilia, rhizophilia, xylophilia, scavenging, and saprophytic opportunism. Some have a generalist diet whereas others have a highly specialized one. Phenotypic characteristics of hypogean Coleoptera are typical of other cave arthropods, such as reduction and/or loss of eyes and ocelli, depigmentation, thinning of the cuticle, reduction of wings, elongation of the body and appendages (both sensory and mechanical), reduction in the number of eggs (sometimes to only one) while producing larger eggs, reduction of the number of larval stages, higher lipid storage, and reduction or total loss of circadian rhythms.

The most important coleopteran families represented in the hypogean environment are the following.

Carabidae (ground beetles)

Carabids are typically long-legged beetles with striate elytra. Their antennae insert between the eye and mandible and are threadlike or, more rarely, beadlike. The body is usually shiny and black in epigean forms. The Carabidae is one of the largest beetle families, with 150 genera and around 2,000 species, of which more than half are troglomorphic. Many are predators of other invertebrates, sometimes attacking almost any potential prey; there are even those that specialize on feeding exclusively on the eggs or larvae of a particular insect species. Hypogean carabids are found on all continents except Antarctica (see, for example, Nicholas 1960; Barr 1967; White 1983; Peck 1990, 1974; Griffith and Poulson 1993; Culver *et al.* 2000).

Cholevidae/Leptodiridae (small carrion beetles)

Small carrion beetles have an elongated, oval body that tapers posteriorly. The head is barely visible from above. The antennae have a gradually enlarging club of five segments. Cross striations are present on the elytra. They feed on decomposed organic material and 'moonmilk' or cave clay that contains algae, fungi, and bacteria. More than 700 species have been described for the hypogean environment on the American continent and in Eurasia (Nicholas 1960; Barr 1962a; Peck 1968, 1970; White 1983; Casale *et al.* 2004).

Curculionidae (snout beetles or weevils)

These have an elongated, narrow snout. The antennae are usually elbowed, with a three-segmented club. Most of these beetles are less than 10 mm long, but sizes range from 0.6 to 35 mm. Most of them feed on roots, whether dead or alive. Hypogean forms often have elongated legs and rostra; some have rudimentary or absent eyes. About 30 species have been described from caves (White 1983; Reddell and Veni 1996; Peck *et al.* 1998; Osella and Zuppa 2006).

Dryopidae (long-toed water beetles)

Dryopids have somewhat cylindrical elytra. The pronotum is narrower than the head. The legs and claws are large, whereas the antennae are short and often hidden altogether. Long-toed water beetles range in size from 4 to 8 mm. Aquatic coleopterans, in general, are found mainly in springs and wells between 45° north and south in the Eastern and Western hemispheres. There are three genera and 15 species of dryopid. Culver *et al.* (2000) reported *Stygoporus* and *Stygoparuns* as stygobitic dryopids from the continental United States. Each of these genera has one representative species (White 1983; Larson and Labonte 1994).

Dytiscidae (predatory diving beetles)

These beetles have legs with abundant marginal hairs that are specialized for swimming. The antennae are threadlike. Dytiscids range in length between 1.2 and 40 mm. Stygobitic dytiscids such as *Haideporus texensis* can be found within the continental United States (Culver *et al.* 2000). In Cuba, Peck (1998) found many accidental dytiscids within caves: *Copelatus, Derovatellus, Laccophilus*, and *Dinetus.* These, however, do not exhibit troglomorphisms. Epigean adults of this family are voracious carnivores, adept at swimming and flying (White 1983). *H. texensis*, a stygobite, is thought to retain the predatory nature of its family (Peck 1998).

Elmidae (riffle beetles)

Oval to cylindrical in shape, riffle beetles are about 1–8 millimeters in length. They possess long legs with large claws. They are found mainly in springs and wells between 45° latitude north and south in the Eastern and

Western hemispheres. Epigean elmids feed on algae, moss, and other plant material in small, clear, cool streams that have a high concentration of dissolved oxygen. There is a lack of information on the habits of hypogean forms (White 1983). *Limnius stygius*, from a karstic river in Morocco, is weakly pigmented, microphthalmic, and brachypterous (Hernando *et al.* 2001).

Histeridae (hister beetles)
The elytra are short, commonly exposing the abdomen. The antennae are short and elbowed with three distinct segments comprising the club (White 1983). The *c.* 12 species that have been described for caves show diverse degrees of troglomorphisms and they feed on guano (White 1983; Peck 1998; Peck *et al.* 1998; Trajano 2000).

Hydrophilidae (water scavenger beetles)
Hydrophilids range from 1 mm to 40 mm long. They possess long maxillary palps and short antennae that have a three- or four-segmented club. They are found throughout the American continent. About 275 species make up this family. In Cuba, the troglophilic beetle *Oosternum* can be found scavenging in moist guano. This is a widespread species, occurring throughout Central and South America. Although cave associations are frequent, this species is not confined to caves. Although epigean examples are aquatic, hypogean inhabitants often occur in guano-rich areas far from standing water (Peck *et al.* 1998).

Leiodidae (round fungus beetles)
The body of leiodid beetles is almost spherical and measures from 1 to 6.5 mm in diameter. They have striated elytra and the antennae end with a 3- to 5-segmented club. Most of them are guano scavengers (White 1983; Peck *et al.* 1998).

Merophysidae/Lathridiidae (minute scavenger beetles)
Lathriids have elongated elytra that are often striated. The head is prominent, because the pronotum is narrowed. The antennae have a club of 2–3 segments. Hypogean species show marked eye reduction. Subterranean merophysid beetles can be found on Fiji. There are 16 genera and 108 species of minute scavenger beetle (White 1983; Ruecker 1988; Peck 1990).

Pselaphidae (short-winged mold beetles)

Pselaphids generally possess a short, tight pair of elytra. The antennae are beadlike with a 1- to 4-segmented club. Epigean forms are usually red or orange. They feed on fungi and prey upon some small invertebrates. The nearly 150 hypogean species of this taxon have been found all around the world except for Antarctica (White 1983; Peck 1998; Trajano 2000; Reddell and Veni 1996; Culver *et al.* 2000).

Ptilidae (feather-winged beetles)

These are the smallest of all beetles, at a length of only 0.4–1.5 mm. The hindwings are feather-like and the antennae are relatively long and hairy. A club of 2–3 segments exists on the terminal portion of each antenna. The hypogean species feed on guano and can also be scavengers; they tend to be eyeless, depigmented and apteric (lacking wings). They have been found on the American and African continents (White 1983; Peck *et al.* 1998).

Scarabeidae (scarab beetles)

These beetles typically range in length from 2 to 20 mm. They have distinct antennae with lamellate segments forming the club. Scarab beetles are usually stout-bodied. Cave scarab beetles occur in the Greater Antilles; accidental cave inhabitants occur in karst regions throughout the world. Some troglophilic scarabeids make dung balls of guano and lay their eggs within these balls (White 1983; Peck *et al.* 1998).

Scydmaenidae (antlike stone beetles)

This is another group of small beetles, 0.6–2.5 mm long. The elytra are oval and widest near the middle; the pronotum is somewhat wider than the head. The antennae are long and hairy, with a 3–4-segmented club. *Scydmaenus aelleni*, from New Caledonia in the Southwest Pacific, is depigmented, anophthalmic, and apteric (Besuchet 1981; White 1983).

Staphylinidae (rove beetles)

These beetles are from 1 to 10 mm in length. They have short elytra and threadlike or clubbed antennae. They feed upon decaying plant and animal matter; some are scavengers. The nearly 30 hypogean species in this family are found in the Canary Islands, Madeira, Northern Africa, southern Europe, the Galapagos, and Ascension Island (White 1983; Peck 1990, 1998; Ashmole and Ashmole 1997).

Tenebrionidae (darkling beetles)

The sizes of epigean darkling beetles vary considerably, ranging from 2 to 35 mm. The antennae are 11-segmented and are threadlike, beadlike, or clubbed. Hypogean species of this family have been described from Mexico, Puerto Rico, Cuba, Venezuela, Ascension Island, and the Galapagos, most of them anophthalmic. Typically, hypogean and epigean tenebrionids are scavengers on decaying organic matter (White 1983; Peck *et al.* 1974; Peck 1990, 1998; Ashmole and Ashmole 1997; Trajano 2000).

2.23.15 Order Hymenoptera (ants, bees, and wasps)

One of the 38 hymenopteran families, Formicidae, has been documented to occur in caves. *Cyphomyrmex rimosus* is a small fungus ant that is usually found with cow dung. It is classified as a troglophile and guano scavenger (Peck 1974). Many others are associated with guano communities (Ferreira *et al.* 2007). Exotic fire ants, *Solenopsis invicta*, have invaded caves in Texas, seriously disturbing the ecological balance of caves (Roberts 2000).

2.23.16 Order Trichoptera (caddisflies)

Three of the 34 families of these aquatic insects have been found in caves: Hydropsychidae, Leptoceridae, and Philopotamidae, in both running and stagnant waters (Trajano 2000; Cianficconi *et al.* 2001).

2.23.17 Order Lepidoptera (moths and butterflies)

At least three of the 90 families in this order occur in caves. These are the Lyonetiidae (Peck 1974), Nocturidae, and Tineidae (Trajano 2000). Tineids are moths that are usually associated with bat guano. Others feed on roots penetrating the cave (Peck 1974; Ferreira *et al.* 2007).

2.23.18 Order Siphonaptera (fleas)

At least one of the 21 families has been documented in caves: Ischnopsyllidae. They are found among mammals that carry them into the caves, as well as being associated with guano communities (Ferreira *et al.* 2007).

2.23.19 Order Diptera (flies, mosquitoes, and midges)

At least 13 of the more than 110 dipteran families occur in caves. These families are: Chironomidae, Culcidae, Drosophilidae, Keroplatidae,

Milichiidae, Muscidae, Mycetophilidae, Phoridae, Psychodidae, Sciaridae, Sphaeroceridae, Streblidae, and Tipulidae (Trajano 2000). The Keroplatidae contains by far one of the more interesting species, *Arachnocampa luminosa* or the New Zealand fungus gnat. The larvae of this species use bioluminescence when feeding. They climb to a horizontal ceiling, make a nest area with silk, and then lower several threads of silk covered with beads of sticky mucus. Once the threads have been lowered, the larvae, or glowworms as they are known, will begin to glow. The glow attracts insects, which become ensnared in the strands. Once captured, the insects are pulled up by the larva and eaten. This behavior is restricted to the larvae; the sole purpose of the adults is to mate. All three stages (larvae, pupae, and adults) can glow. The adults use the glow to attract mates.

2.24 Pisces (fishes)

There are about 28,000 species of fish in the world (Nelson 2006, p. 5). Of all the world species of fish, 299 have been reported from the hypogean environment (Romero *et al.* 2009). Some regions of the planet are very rich in cave species whereas others are not. For example, 92 species of hypogean fish belonging to three families have been reported for China (Romero *et al.* 2009), whereas not a single species of troglomorphic fish has been reported from Europe. Some hypogean fishes are found in caves but a few are found in phreatic waters (Fig. 2.7). Most species of hypogean fish are freshwater but a few are found in anchialine and marine environments. Some are even able to move in and out of caves regularly (Romero 1985c).

Romero and Green (2005) listed characters considered as troglomorphisms in fishes; these include reduction or total loss of eyes, depigmentation, reduced number and size of scales, and a smaller gas (swim) bladder. Recently, Romero *et al.* (2009) added new features that could be considered troglomorphic among cave fishes, such as the horn-like structure found among some species of hypogean fishes of China. Although the function of this structure is still unknown, it is found only among some hypogean species of the genus *Sinocyclocheilus*. An analogous structure has been reported for the epigean *Kustus gulliveri* (Perciformes: Kurtidae). In this species this structure, called a 'hook', is found only among males and is used to nurse eggs (Berra and Humphrey 2002). The horn reported for some species of *Sinocyclocheilus* is found in both sexes. Li *et al.* (1997) hypothesized that this structure could function as a protective organ

Figure 2.7 Pritella phreatophila from the Edwards Aquifer in Texas. Photo by Danté Fenolio. (See Plate 10.)

but no confirmation one way or another has been offered so far. The humpbacked profile also found among some species of hypogean *Sinocyclocheilus* has an unknown function. However, it is interesting to note that both characters may have a similar function, because some species present a horn-like organ formed by the humpback (Romero *et al.* 2009).

Although the most striking hypogean fishes are totally blind and depigmented (troglomorphic), most of the species reported for the hypogean environment so far are not identical in terms of eye and pigmentation development. In fact many show different degrees of reduction of eyes, pigmentation, and scales, with a vast array of intermediate forms even within the same biological species (Romero and Paulson 2001a). Even the intermediate forms (which may or may not be the result of hybridization between the epigean and the troglomorphic forms) display unpredictable combinations of features; some are totally depigmented but have functional eyes, or vice versa. Some have shown remarkable changes in their morphology in time periods as short as 100 years or less (e.g. *Rhamdia quelen* in Trinidad) (Romero *et al.* 2002a).

A great deal of phenotypic plasticity (the ability to rapidly respond to environmental influences, such as increasing pigmentation under higher light intensities) has been reported within individuals of the same species. Thus, many cave fish populations defy conventional taxonomic approaches. With very few exceptions (e.g. some populations of the Mexican cave tetra *Astyanax fasciatus*), those populations are totally isolated and contain only a small number of individuals. That is why each one of those populations must be considered not only unique from the ecological viewpoint but also as evolutionary experiments that can help us answer major questions in science about the underlying causes and mechanisms in the reduction/loss of phenotypic features or the nature of convergent evolution (i.e. why so many cave organisms are blind and depigmented) (Romero and Green 2005).

Like most other cave fauna, hypogean fishes show their greatest diversity in the tropics; very few have yet been studied in any depth. Even the North American cave fishes of the family Amblyopsidae, which contains the first species described in the scientific literature, are not well known, from their systematics to their reproductive modes. This directly affects our understanding of their conservation status. Their ecological role is also poorly understood: we know that some are top predators, whereas others are detritivores; there are even several cases of two or more cave fish species occupying the same confined waters.

Although many species have been placed within several of the protection categories by IUCN, most have not. Protection is particularly important given that most hypogean species discovered in the past few years have been found in developing countries with poor environmental legislation and even weaker law enforcement. However, that does not mean that species located in developed countries are safe; most of them are threatened by water pollution and overcollecting. In fact *Speoplatyrhynus poulsoni*, from Alabama, USA, has a population of less than 100 individuals, making it probably the most endangered fish species in the world.

2.25 Amphibians (salamanders, frogs, toads)

Although frogs can occasionally be seen in caves, no frog species has been found displaying troglomorphic characters (e.g. blindness and depigmentation). On the other hand, there are at least 11 species or subspecies of salamander that are obligate cavernicoles showing troglomorphisms. Many more species are known to frequent the hypogean environment and show some level of troglomorphisms as well (mostly reduction and/or absence of eyes and depigmentation). They usually have elongated and flattened bodies. Two obligate cave salamander species attain sexual maturity without reaching full morphological development; in other words, they retain larval characters, such as external gills, to the end of their lives, a phenomenon known as neoteny. Like many other cave vertebrates, sexual maturity is reached late in life: 11–14 years for males and 15–18 for females in *Proteus anguinus*. Cave salamanders feed mostly on aquatic invertebrates and occasionally other salamanders as well as guano. They have mechano- and chemoreceptors that allow them to detect pressure waves and chemicals, respectively. They use these receptors for finding both food and members of the same species. Cave salamanders usually have very low population numbers and a very restricted range; they are all considered to have threatened status.

The 11 species and subspecies of troglomorphic salamander belong to two families: Proteidae and Plethodontidae.

2.25.1 Family Proteidae

The family Proteidae is represented by a single troglomorphic species: *Proteus anguinus*, with variable depigmentation, found only in the Dinaric Karst of Slovenia, Bosnia, and Croatia. They can reach up to 40 cm in length. This species can actually live for up to 80 years.

2.25.2 Family Plethodontidae

The family Plethodontidae contains 10 troglobitic species in five genera. Of these five genera four are found only in the USA; the fifth, *Hydromantes*, is found in California and the caves of Sardinia, Italy, where it utilizes buccal and cutaneous respiration as it lacks gills and lungs. The exclusively American genera can be found in central Texas, the Ozarks, the Cumberland Plateau of Tennessee and Alabama, the Virginias, and the Dougherty Plain of Georgia and Florida.

The genus *Eurycea* is one of complicated systematics (Larson *et al.* 2003) (Fig. 2.8). The blind and depigmented species *E. tridentifera* is found in the Edward's Plateau region of central Texas.

The genus *Gyrinophilus* contains three species that are hypogean; all can be found in eastern Tennessee, western West Virginia, and Alabama. The species *G. p.* is subdivided into two subspecies: *G. p. necturoides* and *G. p. palleucus*. The primary distinguishing feature between these two subspecies is that the former (Big Mouth Cave salamander) has a pinkish

Figure 2.8 A still undescribed species of *Eurycea* from a cave in southern Texas. Photo by Danté Fenolio. (See Plate 11.)

coloration, whereas the latter (pale salamander) is whitish and exhibits a darker back. All *Gyrinophilus* lack a dorsal fin but have caudal fins.

Haideotriton wallacei is found in Georgia and northern Florida. This species has external gills and, like *Gyrinophilus*, does not have a dorsal fin but does have a caudal fin.

Typhlomolge rathbuni and *T. robusta* are from the Balcones Aquifer in Texas.

Eurycea spelaea (the grotto salamander) is particularly interesting because it is the only hypogean salamander that undergoes metamorphosis in the wild. After its aquatic cycle is completed its eyelids cover the eyes, causing it to lose its sight, and the gills regress, making this organism dependent on cutaneous and buccal respiration. This dependency on moist conditions for respiration makes it understandable that the species is found in hypogean environments (Wiens *et al.* 2003).

2.26 Reptilia (reptiles)

No known reptile has been found to display any sort of troglomorphism. However, several species of snake (e.g. western ratsnakes, *Pantherophis obsoleta*) have been reported in caves, which they enter usually in search of food or to better regulate their body temperature. Some aquatic turtles and the American alligator (*Alligator mississippiensis*) have been reported entering caves for short distances.

2.27 Aves (birds)

There are approximately 10,000 species of bird (Class Aves). They occur on all continents and have been able to exploit almost every environment, including the hypogean one. Excluding species that nest in cliffs, crevices, and cracks (e.g. swallows, the Canyon wren, flycatchers, owls, vultures, and some falcons), two bird families are known to use caves extensively: the oilbirds and the swiftlets.

2.27.1 Family Steatornidae (oilbirds)

The oilbird or guácharo (*Steatornis caripensis)* is the only member of the family Steatornidae. This species is a large bird with long slim wings. It is mostly reddish-brown with small white spots on the wings and the back of the neck. Oilbirds are subtropical; their distribution ranges from Trinidad and northeastern South America, south along the Andes as far as Bolivia.

Oilbirds are colonial nesters that roost in caves during the day. Their nest is made of fecal matter and placed on a ledge within the cave. At night oilbirds will leave their roosting sites in search of food. They eat aromatic fruits such as those of the oil palm (Arecaceae), tropical laurels (Lauraceae), and coffee-like plants (Rubiaceae). They may use olfaction to help them locate fruit at night. Oilbirds are the only birds known to feed their young on fruit pulp (Bosque and De Parra 1992). Colonies can be as large as 19,000 birds, playing an important ecological role as seed dispersers. A female can lay 2–4 eggs. Little else is known about their reproduction.

The vision of oilbirds is very sensitive. They possess highly concentrated, small, dense retinal rods (a million per square millimeter, is the highest known rod density of any vertebrate) (Martin *et al.* 2004a; Rojas *et al.* 2004). They possess very few cones. This leads to vision that is very sensitive to light, but of low resolution (Martin *et al.* 2004a). In addition, they have binocular vision similar to that of diurnal birds (Martin *et al.* 2004b) and a visual cortex larger than that of other birds (Iwaniuk *et al.* 2008). This suggests that the oilbird's vision is geared towards avoiding obstacles while flying in very low light conditions.

These visual abilities are complemented with echolocation. The oilbird is one of two bird groups to exhibit echolocation (Griffin 1953). The echolocation used by oilbirds is of a low frequency, and thus low sensitivity. When obstacles are placed in the flight corridor or the birds are in a dark passage in a cave, oilbirds can successfully avoid obstacles 20 cm in diameter. The oilbirds will dodge or momentarily hover in front of the obstacle. Smaller obstacles the oilbirds will either not notice or notice too late, and collide with them (Konishi and Knudsen 1979).

2.27.2 Family Apodidae (swiftlets)

The Apodidae is a family with about 100 species, of which 30 species in four genera have been reported in caves. These are small birds with narrow wings for fast flight, and a small beak with bristles to aid in catching insects. They are found from southeastern Asia (India and Sri Lanka) and the Malay Peninsula through the Philippines, and eastward to the islands of the South Pacific.

Swiftlets nest in very large colonies, some of which occur on cliffs in caves. The nest is made of various materials glued together by the bird's saliva (Tarburton 2003) and can be converted by humans into bird's-nest soup. This has generated high levels of exploitation and conservation concerns (Tompkins 1999; Sankaran 2001). Tarburton (2003) found that the mountain swiftlet had a clutch size of one, and a fledging rate of 61%.

Swiftlets, like other apodids, are insectivores (Lourie and Tompkins 2000; Voisin *et al.* 2005). In the early morning, they leave their roost sites to feed, which they do on the wing. Swiftlets primarily prey upon hymenopterans and dipterans. At dusk they return to their roost.

Swiftlets that have the ability to echolocate have been placed in the genus *Aerodramus*. However, echolocation has recently been described in *Collocalia*, and this has generated a lot of discussions about the systematics of the swiftlets (Lee *et al.* 1996; Price *et al.* 2004, 2005; Thomassen *et al.* 2005). Two hypotheses have been proposed to explain the acquisition of echolocation in swiftlets. The first is that a common ancestor developed echolocation and some members of the group lost it. The second is that echolocation evolved independently in different groups of swiftlets (Price *et al.* 2004).

Swiftlets use a series of clicks to echolocate (Fullard *et al.* 1993). The acuity of swiftlet echolocation has been tested by placing rods of varying sizes within a mine shaft that the swiftlets were using; and it was found that the swiftlets could avoid 10 mm rods better than 4 mm and 1 mm rods (Fenton 1975).

The differences between oilbirds and swiftlets are that the latter are a relatively young group from an evolutionary viewpoint, whereas oilbirds have a fossil history that dates back 50 million years. Echolocation appears to be a recent evolutionary development among swiftlets. Swiftlets are insectivorous, as opposed to the fruit-eating oilbirds. Oilbirds feed nocturnally, whereas swiftlets fly in search of insects during the day. Their similarities are that they are both colonial nesters, and they seek refuge in caves. In addition, their echolocation has a low resolution and appears to have developed for navigation purposes only.

2.28 Mammalia (mammals)

There are about 5,400 species of mammal, divided into 29 orders. From an ecological viewpoint, the mammals that have invaded the hypogean environment can be divided into two major groups: flying mammals (chiropterans or bats) and non-flying ones; all of them are nocturnal. The latter can, in turn, be divided into two ecological subgroups: (1) non-insectivorous, epitomized by rodents and (2) insectivorous, epitomized by marsupials (Nevo 1979). Of these groups the most diversified and abundant are the bats.

2.28.1 Chiroptera (bats)

With more than 1,000 species in about 17 families, the Order Chiroptera (bats) is the second most diversified order of mammals, surpassed only by the rodents (Order Rodentia). More than 200 species of bat regularly roost in caves, which they utilize for hibernation and as nurseries to take care of their young. Several caves have populations of more than a million bats; Bracken Cave near San Antonio, Texas, has about 20 million.

Bats are unique among mammals because of their capacity for powered flight. In addition, most species of bat are able to echolocate. This ability occurs in every species within 16 bat families. The exceptions are in the Family Pteropodidae (flying foxes), which is composed of large bats, but in which only three species of the genus *Rousettus* echolocate. The bats' abilities to echolocate and fly allow them to exploit a nocturnal life. At night, bats are relatively free from predatory birds and are hidden from their prey by the darkness. Then, when it comes to seeking a daytime refuge, they look for a stable and protective niche. Sometimes these daytime roosts are trees, but many species of bat roost in caves where available. Thus, bats are better able to exploit this environment than any other mammal. An echolocating bat can quickly fly deep within a cave and roost on the ceiling, protected from the outside elements and predators. For this reason, the majority of bat species can utilize caves as roosts although the bats' dependence on roosts is somewhat variable. Wide-ranging surveys have shown that many species of bat roost in caves: 10 out of the 13 species in Puerto Rico (Rodriguez-Duran 1998), 18 out of 39 species in the USA (McCracken 1989), 60 out of 134 species in Mexico (Arita 1993), 15 out of 21 species in Jamaica (McFarlane 1986), and 7 out of 19 species in Taiwan (Hsu 1997).

In temperate areas all over the world bats utilize caves for hibernation. In some cases bats migrate hundreds of kilometers to hibernate in caves. Caves are also used as maternity grounds by bats.

Bats play a central role in much of the ecology of caves and their surrounding environments. Because the cave environment generally lacks primary producers, food webs in caves are influenced by bat guano. Although cave cricket and wood rat guano can be found in large accumulations in temperate caves, in almost every cave at any latitude (but particularly in the tropics) bats are the dominant producers of guano. Piles of guano provide the basic nutritional requirements of cave flora and fauna, predominantly invertebrates (Ferreira and Martins 1999). Caves with large numbers of bats also receive organic material via decomposing bat cadavers (Fig. 2.9).

Bats and caves are also linked in the predator–prey relationships of cave ecosystems. Most of these interactions occur near the entrances of caves. There, snakes, birds, and other mammals are all known to prey on bats as they enter and leave the cave. The bat *Tadarida brasiliensis* is preyed upon by six species of hawk, Mississippi kites, sparrowhawks (falcons), and great horned and barred owls regularly in the evening as bats leave the caves in dense flocks (Baker 1962; Taylor 1964). On the other hand, some caves in Brazil are used exclusively as feeding shelters by the bat *Tonatia bidens*, where it brings birds it has captured (Martuscelli 1995). Snakes also feed on cave bats. Congregations of Cuban and Puerto Rican boas gather at cave entrances and are often successful in capturing bats (Hardy 1957; Rodriguez and Reagan 1984). In the Malay Peninsula the snake *Elaphe taeniura* preys on flying bats (Price 1996). In a Venezuelan cave, the giant centipede (*Scolopendra gigantea*) actively hunts for bats inside the cave (Molinari *et al.* 2005).

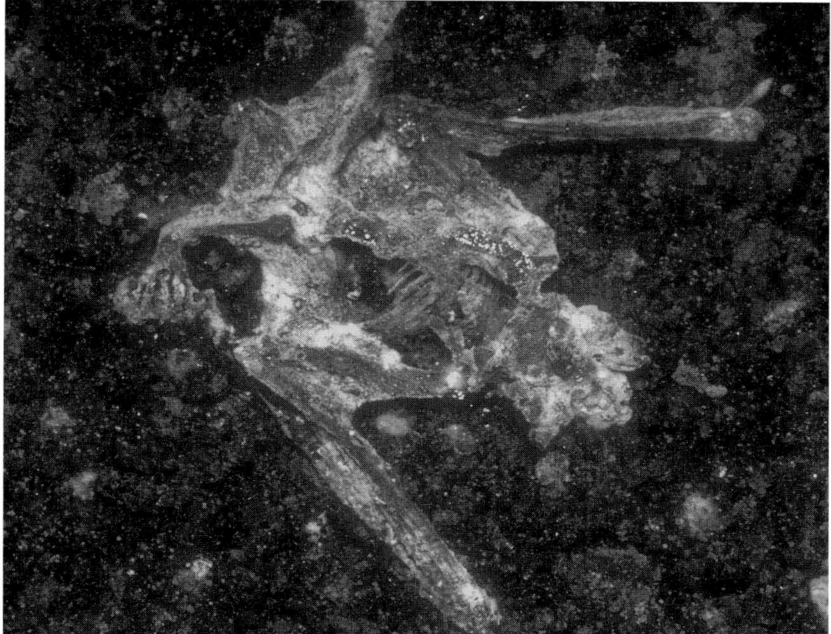

Figure 2.9 A decomposing bat from the Ozarks of Arkansas. Photo by Danté Fenolio. (See Plate 12.)

2.28.2 Non-flying mammals

The occurrence of non-flying mammals in caves is not uncommon; however, it does not appear that any cave-related, non-flying mammal has any specific adaptation for the cave environment. Some fossorial mammal species have traits such as blindness, specialized olfactory perception, and other adaptations that might be considered to be related to their hypogean existence (Cooper *et al.* 1993; Buffenstein 1996; Heth *et al.* 1996; Todrank and Heth 1996; Burda *et al.* 1999), yet there are no examples of these taxa in caves.

Most cave-associated non-flying mammals spend part of their life history in the epigean environment (Resetarits 1986). They primarily utilize cave entrances for shelter, for scavenging on bats, and for creating middens. Most of them stay near the entrance of the caves, although some species of rodent, as well as raccoons and skunks, have been reported much deeper into caves (Winkler and Adams 1972).

Although bears are associated with caves in the popular imagination, studies of bear denning ecology and den site selection reveal that bears do not commonly select natural caves. Ciarniello *et al.* (2005) reported that grizzly bears (*Ursus arctos*) in a region of British Columbia, Canada, use caves only 26% of the time. In all other cases, these bears excavate their own dens in sloping, rocky hillsides or under trees. Seryodkin *et al.* (2003) noted that, of 27 Asiatic black bears (*U. thibetanus*), only 3 used caves or rock outcropps. Grizzly bears in this study ($n = 12$) did not use caves at all. This may have been a function of availability, but neither study reported the density of caves in the study area. Cave use by bears may be more common in regions where these habitats are available. However, their contribution to the cave ecosystem has not been documented. Instances of bear remains and fossils in caves indicated that bears have sometimes entered caves and perished (Richards 1982, 1983).

Rodents are also known to use caves. Woodrats (*Neotoma* spp.) are closely associated with rocky outcrops and occur in regions where caves are common (Richards 1972, 1980; Clark and Clark 1994; Castleberry *et al.* 2001).

The critically endangered Mediterranean monk seal (*Monachus monachus*) uses sea caves for resting and pupping (Gucu *et al.* 2004; Karamanlidis *et al.* 2004). These seals show a preference for caves with beaches and cryptic entrances during the pupping season but have no specific preferences regarding cave characteristics when resting. Gray seals (*Halichoerus grypus*) are also known to use sea caves during a certain period of their breeding cycle (Lidgard *et al.* 2001).

Ancient humans are popularly associated with caves; however, there are also contemporary studies of primates using caves (Barrett *et al.* 2004; McGrew *et al.* 2003). For the most part, baboons (*Papio* spp.) use caves for shelter, but other features such as salt-rich rock and water have been hypothesized to be reasons for primates entering caves. The caves used by primates are described in the papers that report the phenomenon, but there are no systematic studies of cave selection. Among the factors that may induce cave utilization by primates are thermoregulation, shelter, and predator avoidance. Barrett *et al.* (2003) described video evidence of baboon behavior within the cave and the interaction of baboons with other organisms in the cave, but not troglobitic organisms. These baboons were seen grooming each other and defecating in the cave; such activities would deposit organisms (parasitic insects, etc.) and nutrients (waste) in the cave. Interestingly, this was done in total darkness because the entrance to the cave was a vertical shaft and the caverns used by the baboons were well away from any light source. It is well known that ancient humans, and other animals, regularly brought food into caves and this may have affected the cave ecosystem; however, this information is known only from fossils recovered in caves.

Cave environments are well suited for the fossilization of bones and other biological artifacts such as coprolites and rodent middens (Thompson *et al.* 1980; Van Dyck 1982; Erdbrink 1983; Simms 1994; Grayson 2000; Plug 2004; McFarlane and Lundberg 2005). The high rate of deposition, relatively mild conditions, and low rate of erosion provide good conditions for the preservation of biotic remains.

Mammalian fossils in caves include those of ungulates, marsupials, rodents, felids, ursids, primates, and humans, among others. They date from the early Cenozoic (65.5 mya) to recent times (Plug 2004; McFarlane and Lundberg 2005). Studies of mammal fossils from caves have utilized faunal assemblages to estimate the effects of climate change (Grayson 2000).

2.29 Conclusions

Despite the fact that most caves are small in size, representatives of virtually all major taxa of living beings are found in caves. From the above survey it is clear that, in addition to the tens of thousands of species that have been described from caves, many more have yet to be discovered, particularly at lower latitudes. A number of patterns also emerge: although some troglomorphisms are common, such as reduction or loss of pigmentation and visual apparatus, that is not necessarily the case for all of organisms; there is a multitude of intermediate forms. Phenotypic plasticity is also a common phenomenon, as is the commonality of organisms that move in and out of caves on a regular basis. Other characteristics such as echolocation by birds and bats that use caves seem rather common, yet it is unclear whether their development occurred prior to cave colonization or during that process. Ecological opportunism also seems common, as is the existence of relictual taxa, particularly in marine caves. These and many other evolutionary and ecological questions will be addressed in the next two chapters.

3 · *The evolutionary biology of cave organisms*

This chapter offers a summary of current knowledge of the major adaptations that characterize cave organisms, with special emphasis on their origin and evolution. Fauna that do not show typical 'cave' adaptations (blindness and depigmentation) are included, with an explanation of why they are so important for understanding cave biology.

3.1 What is a hypogean/cave organism?

Although some of the terminology commonly used in biospeleology is worthy of criticism, because it furthers typological thinking about nature, it is imperative to begin by clarifying some of the nomenclature frequently used in cave science. Appendix 1 contains a more or less complete list of terms commonly used in biospeleology.

In general, biospeleologists divide the world into two environments: the epigean and the hypogean ones. The former refers to the environment outside caves, which is exposed to light directly or indirectly on a regular basis; the latter represents any part of the biosphere that is found underground. The hypogean (sometimes called endogean) environment includes the following ecosystems: soil or interstitial (both are sometimes used interchangeably, and the latter term is often used by aquatic biologists only when dealing with spaces filled with water), phreatic or artesian, and cave. Phreatic waters are those water deposits in compact rocks that can be studied only indirectly through wells. These are extremely important: 97% of the world's freshwater is underground (Marmonier *et al.* 1993). The term 'cave' refers to an underground habitat that can be directly explored by humans (for further subdivisions, see Appendix 1). This book explores in depth only cave and phreatic habitats, and for the sake of simplicity and because of the scope of this book, whenever the term 'hypogean' is used, it is referring to organisms found in either caves or phreatic habitats or both.

Although many species are found exclusively in one of these habitats, sometimes there are congeneric species that show transitional characteristics. Peck and Gnaspini (1997), for example, described *Ptomaphagus inyoensis* as a new species of microphthalmic beetle from California, and found that this species represented a morphological 'intermediate' between *P. fisus*, a species widespread in animal nests and burrows, and *P. manzano*, a montane litter species from New Mexico, on the one hand, and *P. cocytus*, a cave species from the Grand Canyon of Arizona, on the other.

Despite the fact that the terms mentioned above seem to clearly subdivide different ecosystems, the truth of the matter is that this is a more or less artificial classification. Many species, particularly some bats, birds, and invertebrates, alternate between epigean and hypogean environments during their life cycle; some soil and interstitial organisms also move between that milieu and other hypogean and epigean ones; some phreatic organisms are found in springs, i.e. in what is supposedly the epigean environment, and so on. This clarification is important since some biospeleologists tend to be very rigid in their typological approach to classifying cave organisms according to the environment where they live.

Furthermore, discontinuities in terms of exposure to light are also present throughout the hypogean world. One of the most interesting phenomena in biospeleology is the existence of caves with openings that allow the passage of light. In those areas of caves where light interrupts what is otherwise total darkness, there occur eyed, pigmented organisms normally found outside caves. Sometimes those organisms belong to typical epigean species; sometimes they are eyed, pigmented forms of hypogean ones. An example of the former is found in a cave at Torre Castiglione on the Ionian coast of Apulia, southeastern Italy. There, two species of mysidacean crustacean have been found: one was previously reported only from hypogean waters (*Spelaeomysis bottazzii*, which is blind), and the other was previously reported only for epigean brackish to marine waters (*Diamysis* sp., which has eyes) (Ariani *et al.* 1999). An example of the morphological differentiation among individuals of the same species occurs in the characid fish *Astyanax fasciatus*, which inhabits the Sótano del Caballo Moro cave in Mexico. Part of the ceiling of this cave has collapsed, allowing light to illuminate part of one of its underground lakes. Espinasa and Borowsky (2000) reported that the lake contains fish exhibiting a distributional bias, i.e. blind, depigmented individuals are found preferentially in the dark side, whereas eyed, pigmented fish are found in the illuminated side. Genetic analysis revealed that the cave eyed fish is closer to the blind fish than to the surface one; this suggests that the cave eyed fish were originally members of the cave population and re-acquired eyes and pigmentation following the collapse of the cave ceiling and exposure to the light.

Just as there is a classification system for the different types of hypogean environment, hypogean organisms are also grouped on the basis of their morphology and behavior. Terms abound, but the most popular classification terminology defines (a) troglobites, which always show characters such as total blindness and depigmentation; (b) troglophiles,which show some degree of reduction in those characters; (c) trogloxenes, organisms without such reductions but still spending significant portions of their lives in caves (e.g. some bat species); and (d) accidentals, organisms allegedly found in caves 'by chance' and not because they normally live there. Notice that this is a very ad hoc definition: in theory, when an individual of a species that later may become a permanent inhabitant of caves first enters a cave, it could also be called an 'accidental.' Furthermore, as we will see later, there are many species of animal that spend their entire life cycle in the hypogean environment and do not show any apparent morphological feature associated with their underground habitat. These characters, such as blindness and depigmentation, are commonly referred to as troglomorphisms (Christiansen 1962).

To start understanding the biology of these organisms, it is necessary to question whether or not these (and other) classifications based mostly on morphology (and to a lesser degree, habits) really have a biological significance.

3.2 Character concept in biospeleology

One of the conclusions from Chapter 1 is that most biospeleologists have been obsessed with troglomorphic (blind and depigmented) organisms. This has been integral to their research program regarding the construction of the cave archetype. Given that most biospeleologists tend to be involved in systematics, it is not surprising that the development of the idea of a character concept has played a major role in their views of cave organisms. Systematists usually employ a definition of the character concept that is more or less as follows: any observable difference between two groups of organisms that can be used to distinguish these groups (Wagner 2001b). However, in the past few years a more evolutionarily

Table 3.1 *Characters usually associated with cave organisms and called troglomorphisms (*sensu *Christiansen 1962)*

Morphological	Physiological	Behavioral
Reduced or lost		
Eyes, ocelli	Metabolism	Photoresponses
Visual brain centers	Circadian rhythms	Aggregation
Pigmentation	Fecundity	Response to alarm substances
Pineal organ	Egg volume	Aggression
Body size		
Cuticles (terrestrial arthropods)		
Scales (fishes)		
Swimbladder (fishes)		
Enlarged		
Chemo- and mechanosensors	Life span	
Appendages	Lipid storage	
Body size	Metabolism	

oriented character concept has emerged: that of a character whose presence and/or absence has a real evolutionary meaning, i.e. via adaptation (see Wagner 2001a for a comprehensive discussion of this issue).

This section will address two questions. (1) Is there anything resembling a 'hypogean archetype' that fits most if not all hypogean organisms? (2) What is the evolutionary meaning of the phenotypic characters that have been used to epitomize hypogean organisms, if any?

In most of the biospeleological literature, one can see how a set of troglomorphic characters has been proposed that distinguish cave organisms. Table 3.1 summarizes such a set of characters.

The first challenge to accepting a hypogean archetype is that phenotypic characters may be enlarged as well as reduced among these organisms, and the rules are not always consistent. As is evident from Table 3.1, most changes in morphological characters are associated with absence of light. Reduction of the visual apparatus, whether eyes or ocelli, is considered a rule for troglomorphic organisms; however, there are exceptions. One is the cyprinid fish *Sinocyclocheilus macrophthalmus* (Zhang and Zhao 2001). Although other species of the same genus found in caves in China are blind (or have highly reduced eye size) and depigmented, this particular cave species has eyes larger than those of any other species in the genus, including the epigean species, despite the fact that the species in

Table 3.2 *A quantitative comparison of the development of troglomorphisms among hypogean fishes*

Absent, none of the characters is expressed; Slight pigmentation, a few (>50% than normal) melanophores with pigment; Mostly pigmented, most (but not all, (between 50% and 90% of normal number) melanophores with pigment; Microphthalmic, eyes greatly reduced in size; Sunken, eyes more or less of normal size but covered by epidermal tissue. Embedded scales, some scales are present, but they are embedded in or covered by skin; Reduced scales, scales are in normal position (covering the skin) but are reduced in size. The term 'fully expressed' is used to indicate correspondence with their epigean counterparts in the same family.

Quantitative rank	Pigmentation	Eyes	Scales
1	Absent	Absent	Absent
2	Slight	Microphthalmic	Embedded
3	Mostly	Sunken	Reduced
4	Fully expressed	Fully expressed	Fully expressed

question is depigmented. Regarding the eyes, thus, this species shows an adaptation that is unusual for fishes, but one that is common among nocturnal vertebrates.

However, the enlargement of the size of sensory organs is not necessarily the rule for other troglomorphic organisms. One example is the phreatic Texas blind catfish *Trogloglanis pattersoni*, which has minute barbels, whereas most hypogean catfishes tend to have barbels larger than those of their epigean ancestors (Langecker and Longley 1993). The same can be said about metabolism: the cave form of the characid fish *Astyanax fasciatus* has nearly twice the resting metabolic rate of its epigean form (Schlagel and Breder 1947).

In addition, troglomorphisms can be highly variable. For example, character development for blindness and depigmentation does not occur in parallel among most species. Based on the data presented by Romero and Green (2005), quantitative levels for blindness, depigmentation, and scale development can be established among troglomorphic fishes (Table 3.2). From this, it is found that only seven out of 86 species of troglomorphic fish have the same level of troglomorphism for each one of those characters (Fig. 3.1). Furthermore, when all the characters were combined in a phenotypic landscape (Fig. 3.2), the results

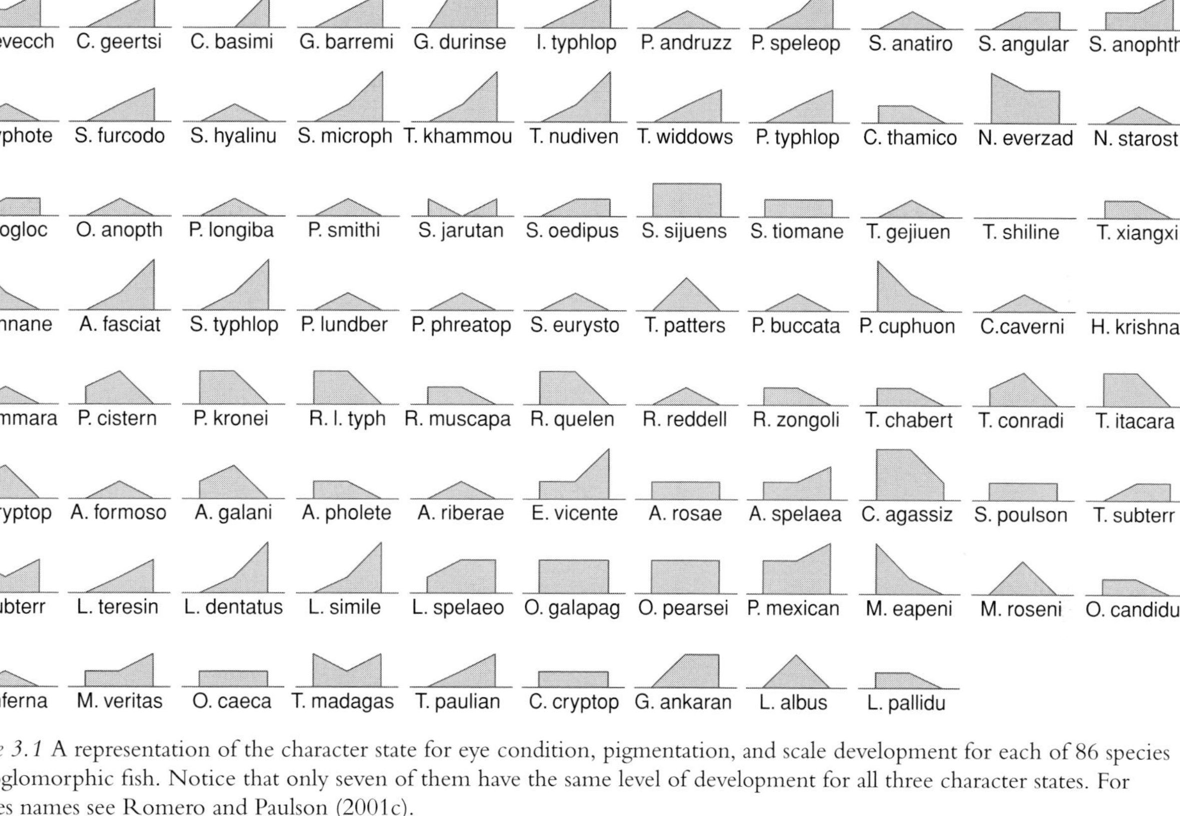

Figure 3.1 A representation of the character state for eye condition, pigmentation, and scale development for each of 86 species of troglomorphic fish. Notice that only seven of them have the same level of development for all three character states. For species names see Romero and Paulson (2001c).

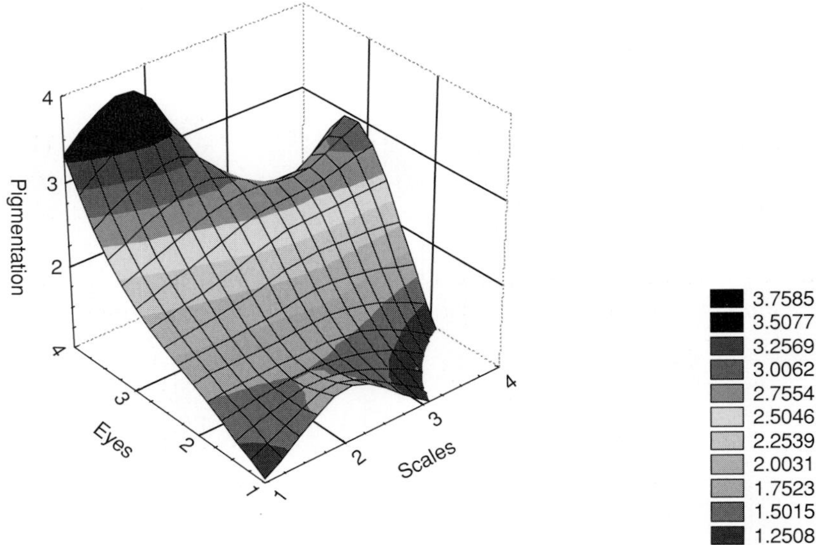

Figure 3.2 A landscape representation of the character state for all troglomorphic fish species. The irregular landscape illustrates the lack of complete (or even partial) convergence in character development for all these fish species. (See Plate 13.)

showed a highly diverse mixture of character development, thus rejecting the hypothesis that troglomorphic characters developed in parallel. This disparity in character development among species suggests that both the evolutionary history of the species involved and the peculiar characteristics of the environment in which they live must be taken into consideration to explain such a mosaic of character development.

To make things even more complicated, a large number of species that are found in the hypogean environment never show any kind of troglomorphism. For example 299 species of fish have been reported (as of August 2008) as living in the hypogean environment. Of those hypogean species, 184 have been described as having some kind of troglomorphism (Romero *et al.* 2009). In other words, there are slightly more species of hypogean fishes that are eyed and pigmented than there are blind and depigmented ones. As cave researchers start paying more attention to non-troglomorphic hypogean fauna, particularly in tropical countries, it is quite possible that the gap will widen: Trajano *et al.* (2002), for example, reported numerous non-troglomorphic fish species of at least eight genera from several caves in Thailand while finding only three troglomorphic species in those same caves. Bichuette and Trajano (2003a) reported for the São Domingos karst area in central Brazil the presence of five troglobitic species, whereas 22 species found there were non-troglobitic.

Sometimes variability within a single species can be very high. That is the case in the Mexican cave tetra *Astyanax fasciatus*. This species has been reported from numerous caves throughout its range, including Belize, Costa Rica, and Brazil; however, only those occurring in the San Luis de Potosí Area, east central Mexico (*c.* 22°05′N, 99°00′W), have developed troglomorphic populations, and not all of these populations consist of blind and depigmented fish. Some of them are fully eyed and pigmented fish; most are blind and depigmented; a handful of them show an intermediate phenotype (Mitchell *et al.* 1977; Romero 1983; Espinasa *et al.* 2001). As mentioned earlier, morphological variability can be found within individuals of the same cave population (Espinasa and Borowsky 2000).

Another confounding variable is that not all troglomorphisms can be explained as a direct consequence of the absence of light or even as an adaptation to the cave environment. The reduction in cuticle development and/or loss of cuticle among terrestrial insects, and of scales among fish, illustrates this dilemma. Both phenomena seem to be very common, although not universal. Functionally, the problem is the lack of a solid theory that explains why, for example, most fish have scales, because some fish groups (even those not living in caves) are scaleless. Thus, it is hard to understand the adaptive value of becoming scaleless in the hypogean environment. Neoteny could provide the explanatory mechanism for this character state, given that the loss of scales has been considered the product of neoteny among fishes in general (Banister 1984). Although that may be a mechanistic explanation, it does not explain the functional value of being scaleless: the loss of scales may not produce a significant loss of fitness, but, again, not knowing the ultimate functional value of having scales, we are not in a position to provide an illuminating explanation for their loss.

Some authors have reported the existence of 'albino' cave fauna. Albinism is a phenomenon yet to be fully understood in cave biology. Complete albinism is a rare occurrence among vertebrate groups. Uieda (2000) studied this phenomenon among bats and found that complete albinism among these mammals has been documented in eight families, 38 species, and at least 64 individuals. Of these, 39 individuals were observed and/or captured in sheltered roosts such as caves (51.3%), mines and galleries (20.5%), buildings (17.9%), and hollow trees and bird boxes (7.7%). Only one albino bat (2.6%) was captured in an external roost (foliage). This researcher suggested that sheltered roosts (such as caves) favor the survival of albino bats by offering protection against sunlight, water loss, and visually hunting predators.

However, albinism reported for cave fishes might be due to terminological confusion. There is no such thing as a 'white' pigment in the two species of cave fish in which it has been reported: *Trichomycterus itacarambiensis* from Brazil (Trajano 1995) and *Cottus carolinae* from West Virginia, USA (Williams and Howell 1979; Neely and Mayden 2003). Rather, what we see is a total lack of pigmentation, which fits the definition of albinism.

With reference to the reduction and/or loss of the gas (swim) bladder among hypogean fish, a functional explanation is more readily apparent: because hypogean waters tend to be very shallow, this organ no longer has any adaptive value that may increase the fitness of the species/population in question.

Body size is another issue that has yet to be explored. Apparently, reduction in body size and/or an elongated body should provide a competitive advantage in an ecosystem of reduced dimensions with an abundance of crevices that could be used to hide from predators and as either feeding or reproductive niches. However, the data available are inconclusive: some cave species/populations have larger body size compared with their epigean ancestors; others are smaller. This is certainly an area that requires more attention.

The general picture emerging from the information summarized above is one of complexity and even, sometimes, contradiction. It certainly does not support blanket generalizations about hypogean fauna in terms of their phenotype: in other words, there are no archetypical hypogean organisms. The reason for this conclusion is that it is impossible to make strong empirical generalizations about how each character trait affects individual fitness because the outcomes of natural selection are not always predictable.

Can it be assumed, then, that there is no point in trying to come up with a hypogean archetype? As Wagner (2001b, p. 9) put it: 'A character concept that only satisfies the aesthetic predilection of theorists is ultimately doomed, regardless of how true or elegant it may be.' Therefore the issue is not whether or not there are troglomorphic species or their relative number; the real issues are, for example, why some troglomorphic species exhibit those characters, why the changes in characters occur, and why there are so many hypogean organisms that do not show the characters that are normally used to depict cave organisms.

The phenotypic organization of any organism is a composite of morphological, physiological, and behavioral traits. That composite can be very complex since some of the character changes may be related to a single environmental condition (e.g. light) but yet be genetically independent. In other cases the phylogenetic history of the group (at the order, family, or genus level) to which the species in question belongs may have a large effect. Thus, it should not be surprising that not all of the organisms living in the hypogean environment develop the same set of phenotypes.

Later in this chapter the specifics of how and why these changes occur are discussed, but first it is necessary to answer one of the most intriguing – and controversial – questions in cave biology: how is the hypogean environment colonized?

3.3 Hypogean colonization

Colonization in general is one of those ecological–evolutionary phenomena that is riddled with speculation, largely because this is a process difficult to observe in natural conditions and whose replication in the laboratory depends on many assumptions. This is also true for the hypogean environment in general. A confounding variable in this whole issue is the fact that most biospeleologists, whose field experience is largely confined to temperate, energy-deprived caves, have always assumed that there are not any really good reasons why an organism would occupy a nutrient-poor habitat. Therefore, many researchers have espoused the idea that the only explanation for colonization of the hypogean environment is either an accident or some other very unusual circumstance (see, for example, Holsinger 2000). However, there are no empirical observations supporting such hypotheses; on the contrary, field observations and biological theory are not consistent with such notions. Part of such arguments is that once the organisms are in the hypogean environment, the only reason they stay there is because they become 'trapped' (see, for example, Wilkens 1979; Langecker 1989).

These hypotheses are based on a philosophical stance similar to Richard Goldschmidt's idea of 'hopeful monsters.' In the same way that modern developmental genetics clearly shows that we do not need these 'hopeful monsters' to imagine big leaps forward in morphological evolution (Akam 1998), both modern ecological theory as well as field observations lead us to conclude that we do not need these evolutionary events to be serendipitous.

Although passive dispersal has been documented for a number of organisms that have arrived at islands on floating objects, there is no such drastic and generalized spatial discontinuity between the hypogean and the epigean environments. Whether the cave colonizers reach the hypogean habitat by land, by air, or by periodic flooding, there is little that prevents them from returning to their original habitat (see Romero *et al.* 2002b); therefore the accidental-entrapment hypothesis cannot be used as a valid premise, much less as a generalization for the process of cave colonization.

Two biogeographic models have been proposed to explain the colonization of the hypogean environment: the climatic-relict model and the adaptive-shift model. Under the first model, one would find cool and moist habitats just south of the glacial maxima, which favored the ample distribution of invertebrates typical of such environments and which could be found in both caves and forests. As glaciers retreated 'these species became progressively restricted to the cool, moist interiors of caves, sinkholes, deep wooded ravines, and cool forest floors at higher altitudes' (Holsinger 2000, p. 403). According to this hypothesis, later warming extinguished the epigean populations, leaving the hypogean ones isolated and consequently inclined to evolve into obligatory cave species, ultimately producing the troglomorphic species present today. One of the classical objections to this hypothesis is that it does not explain the origin of troglomorphic faunas in the tropics. This objection has been countered by saying that although the tropical faunas did not experience the temperature variations of the temperate areas of the world, they were subject to changes in rainfall, and therefore caves may have served as refugia to these organisms. This hypothesis seems more plausible for certain marine cave fauna that show some relictual distribution, as mentioned in Chapter 2.

Notice that the two authors applying the climatic-relict model to lower latitudes are ichthyologists (Humphreys 1993; Trajano 1995); they were naturally preoccupied with the issue of water, leaving unexplained the issues of terrestrial hypogean fauna in these latitudes and why there are so many cave organisms that do not show the troglomorphisms that would allegedly result from this process. Also inconsistent with this model are data from molecular clock studies, which have shown that many cave species invaded that habitat well before the more recent glaciations occurred. For example, Chakraborty and Nei (1974) calculated the time of divergence between the cave and river populations of *A. fasciatus* as between 525,000 and 710,000 years ago. That is consistent with the geological data on the formation of caves where this species is found today. Other species have an even longer evolutionary history in the underground: blind hypogean mole rats of the genus *Spalax* originated in the Middle Eocene to early Oligocene (45–35 mya) and have persisted until the present. On the other hand, sometimes animals may look for a refugium in caves when it is too cold: Fenolio *et al.* (2005b) suggested that the seasonal movement patterns of pickerel frogs (*Rana palustris*) in an Ozark cave in Oklahoma were the result of these amphibians using caves as thermal refugia during the coldest months of the year.

Yet another objection to the climatic-relict hypothesis is that it does not explain current events of cave colonization (see, for example, Romero *et al.* 2002b). Thus, although the climatic-relict hypothesis may explain some specific cases (e.g. subterranean diving beetles in Australia (Leys *et al.* 2003), or some anchialine or marine fauna), it cannot be considered a universal explanation.

An alternative hypothesis on cave colonization is the adaptive-shift model; this model argues that preadapted ancestors actively invaded the hypogean environment to exploit new niches and became troglobites without disruption of the gene flow from their epigean relatives. This hypothesis has a number of pitfalls; first, it does not allow for allopatric or parapatric speciation. A number of troglobites occur whose presumed ancestors are unknown, since no similar species have ever been found in the epigean environment (for examples among fish, see Romero and Paulson 2001a); in some cases even new taxonomic classes and families have been erected for the classification of some troglobites because of their lack of obvious affinities with epigean species (see, for example, Koenemann *et al.* 2003; Yager 1994, respectively). The proponent of this model (Howarth 1973, 1981) works on lava-tube caves in Hawaii where some of the particular characteristics he describes may be common for that habitat and location, but that does not mean that the model has general applicability.

In many ways, this is a contrasting argument similar to the one in the 1980s regarding dispersal vs. vicariance distribution: on the one hand freshwater fish biologists were rabid proponents of vicariance for explaining the origin and distribution of their organisms because the dispersal of freshwater fish has so many barriers and is so slow that vicariance was thought to be the best explanation; on the other hand, ornithologists found the classical dispersal explanation to be the most logical since the organisms they studied experience fewer barriers when expanding their distributions. It all depended upon which explanation better fitted their own experiences. Obviously neither was universal.

The same can be said today of the refugia vs. the adaptive-shift models; it depends upon where one works; it will serve one purpose better than another, but in any case neither is universal, and therefore, they cannot be considered paradigmatic in the Kuhnian sense of the word (Kuhn 1970).

The question is, thus, are there field observations supporting some particular explanatory mechanism for the colonization of the hypogean environment? Romero (1984a, 1985a) carried out field studies at a pond in Costa Rica that receives water from a phreatic source. An assemblage of about 120 *A. fasciatus* lived in that pond. These fish were, morphologically speaking, identical to other epigean tetras, i.e. with full eyes and pigmentation. However, I found that unlike the typical epigean *A. fasciatus* population, the fish in the pool did not form shoals, which is a behavior typical of cave fish populations. Second, when floating food was dropped onto the surface of the water, the fish, almost without exception, pushed that food to the subterranean habitat, where it was then consumed. More interesting still, observations with low-light-sensitive equipment showed that the fish actually entered the subterranean flow of water at dusk.

A number of field observations and manipulations strongly suggest that fish both pushed the food into the subterranean cavity and also disappeared into that cavity at night to escape fishing bats of the species *Noctilio leporinus*. One of the site manipulations consisted of using white floodlights to illuminate the surface of the pool in order to create light conditions mimicking those of daytime. When those lights were turned on at night, the fish density on the pool increased to levels similar to those observed during daytime, which was followed by increased bat activity. The bats could apparently sense the fish because the oxygen content of the pool was low, and *A. fasciatus* could always be seen swimming near the surface of the water, where the oxygen content is higher by diffusion. When swimming near the surface, the fish created ripples that could be sensed by the bats' echolocation system. When the pool was covered almost at surface level by using a plastic sheet, the bat activity decreased significantly. In another manipulation the entrance to the underwater cavity was blocked before dusk, thus preventing the fish from entering that cavity. In response, the fish then tended to move to the edges of the pool, apparently to avoid bat predation.

These field manipulations were followed by laboratory studies with *A. fasciatus* individuals from both the pool connected to the subterranean cavity and from a nearby pool that has no connection to hypogean waters. Both populations of fish were kept separately in aquarium tanks under a 12 h day/12 h night cycle for nine months and then tested for their preferences for shaded or lighted halves of larger tanks. The fish from the pool connected to the subterranean cavity still preferred to move into the shaded area when the dark half of the cycle started, a response not witnessed among the fish from the open pool. All these results suggest not only that *A. fasciatus* was using the underground pool as a shelter from bat predation, but also that active colonization of underground waters may occur as a response to selective pressures, not by accidental exposure.

The idea of active colonization has also been proposed for ice caves in temperate regions (Racovitza 2000). Camp and Jensen (2007) showed that plethodontid salamanders in the Cumberland Plateau of northwestern Georgia use both cave and epigean habitats, moving into caves to avoid hot, dry conditions of the epigean environment. Other studies also suggest that the fauna found in some caves, such as the chemoautotrophic communities, may be the result of multiple colonization events over time (Sarbu 2000).

It is worth mentioning the fact that some troglomorphic populations may be ecologically replaced (even in a short period of time) by epigean ones, even if the epigean form is the reputed ancestor of the hypogean population in question. That is the case reported for the hypogean population of *Rhamdia quelen* from a cave in Trinidad, WI. Romero *et al.* (2002b) studied this fish population originally described by Norman (1926) on the basis of its reduced eyes and pigmentation as a new troglomorphic genus and species, *Caecorhamdia urichi*. Beginning in the 1950s, a number of specimens collected in the cave displayed variability in eye size and pigmentation. Later studies (Silfvergrip 1996) indicated that this cave population was, taxonomically speaking, part of the widely distributed epigean (surface, eyed/pigmented) catfish *Rhamdia quelen*. In 2000 and 2001 Romero and colleagues conducted field studies that included direct observation of individuals by means of infrared-sensitive equipment (video cameras and night-vision goggles) and echo-sounders as well as collection of some individuals for behavioral research (Romero and Creswell 2000; Romero *et al.* 2001). All available museum specimens of the cave population were also examined. The results suggested that the troglomorphic population had been completely replaced by the epigean

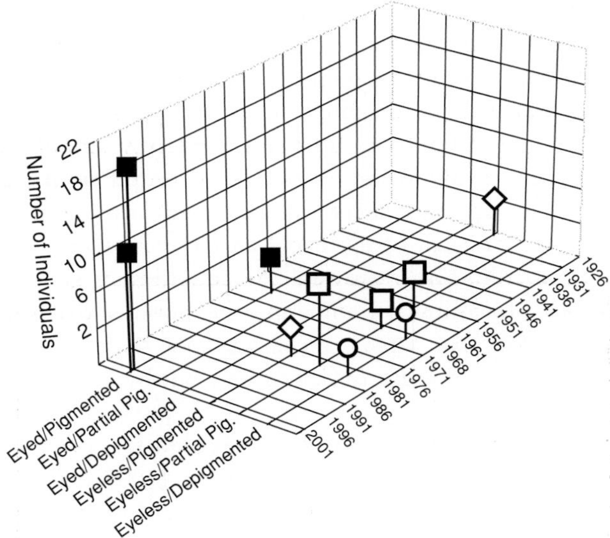

Figure 3.3 Changes in cave *Rhamdia quelen* morphs through time.

one of the same species in as little as 50 years (Fig. 3.3). It was hypothesized by these authors that the most important reason for this replacement was the reinvasion of epigean individuals of *R. quelen*, prompted by changes in precipitation regimes. Epigean individuals, because of their larger size, aggressive behavior, and generalist feeding nature, were well suited to outcompete troglomorphic individuals.

Another example of opportunism among cave colonizers was given by Reeves and McCreadie (2001). While studying the abundance of several species of insects in a cave in Georgia, USA, they found that the colonization patterns on carrion by cavernicoles differed between permanent and transient cave-dwelling species, and suggested that such variation could be due to the different reproductive strategies of each species.

Another question frequently asked concerns cave species that are found in several caves, whether connected or not. Are those populations the product of a single colonization event followed by hypogean dispersal, or are they the product of multiple colonization events? Verovnik *et al.* (2003) looked at this issue for the hypogean populations of the crustacean amphipod *Asellus aquaticus* in Slovenia and northeastern Italy. *A. aquaticus* is a generalist species, found today in several cave localities throughout most of Europe. Populations in these localities are isolated from the epigean ones; sometimes they are identified as the subspecies *A. a. aquaticus* and sometimes as the subspecies *A. a. subterraneus*. These populations may or may not display depigmentation, eye reduction, and appendage elongation, and even when they do, such troglomorphisms may be expressed with some variability. By using randomly amplified polymorphic DNA analysis, Verovnik and collaborators found evidence that the seven hypogean populations were the result of three separate invasions in both time and space. Surprisingly, two of the hypogean populations studied by these authors showed no reduction in genetic variability compared with the surface populations, suggesting that the bottleneck effect never took place and/or that the hypogean populations are sufficiently large and/or recent to maintain genetic heterogeneity. There is also the possibility that these and other polymorphic hypogean populations are actually the result of two or more colonization events.

Dowling *et al.* (2002) and Strecker *et al.* (2003) provided genetic analyses suggesting that at least some of the troglomorphic populations of the fish *A. fasciatus* in Mexico may have arisen from separate cave invasions. Similar results were obtained by Hoch and Howarth (1999), who demonstrated multiple cave invasions by species of the planthopper genus *Oliarus* in Hawaii. This further reinforces the improbability of the generalization that cave colonization is the result of a fortuitous entrapment; such a serendipitous event would not be likely to occur repeatedly in the same geographical area.

The next question is: are some species more likely to be successful hypogean colonizers than others? More importantly, why do some hypogean species undergo major phenotypic changes whereas others seem to remain phenotypically similar to their epigean ancestors?

3.4 The myth of preadaptation

As mentioned in Chapter 1, the idea of preadaptation is common in biospeleological jargon, and it has both a long history and firm roots in orthogenetic explanations of evolution in caves. We can trace the origin of this word in its biological sense to Lucien Cuénot, who, in his *La Genèse des Espèces Animales* (1911), vol. 4, p. 306, defined it as the possession or acquisition by an organism of heritable features that adapt it to an environment or mode of life that only later becomes available to it: in other words, adaptation in advance. Some of the architects of the modern synthesis criticized the validity of preadaptation as a phenomenon and were quick to identify it as part of the orthogenetic discourse (see, for example, Simpson 1944). However, this term is very popular among biospeleologists.

To the myths that describe cave species as types instead of variable elements in time and space, and that view caves as 'harsh' habitats (see Chapter 4) and cave colonization as a serendipitous process, needs to be added the omnipresent notion of preadaptation. Two examples of such a notion being accepted without question are supplied by Christiansen (1992, p. 464), who wrote, 'There is general agreement that pre-adaptation (or exaptation) is crucial for entrance into caves' and Holsinger (2000, p. 400): 'There is a consensus among biospeleologists that troglobites are ultimately derived from preadapted epigean propagules or founders that live in either terrestrial or aquatic environments.'

Again, this belief derives from the view of caves as habitats too inhospitable for any organism to live there. Weber (2000), for example, wrote: 'successful colonists have appropriate morphological, physiological and ethological adaptations that enable them to survive and reproduce in the cave habitat' (Weber, 2000, p. 110). This statement implies that all successful cave colonists are phenotypically peculiar because they are either troglomorphic or have some 'preadaptations' to the hypogean environment.

However, this ignores the fact that, as mentioned earlier, a very large proportion of cave organisms never show either troglomorphic characters or 'preadaptations' to the hypogean environment. Once more it must be asked: what is the evidence supporting the notion that an organism has to be preadapted to successfully colonize the hypogean environment? Holsinger (2000, p. 400), for example, gives nine references to substantiate what he calls a widespread agreement on this matter; however, none of those references provides hard evidence, but rather philosophical views on this issue.

Romero and Paulson (2001b,c) tested the preadaptation hypothesis among troglomorphic fishes. First, they tried to understand the meaning of the concept of 'preadaptation' among biospeleologists. By surveying the literature, they found that 'preadaptations' for the hypogean environment, when defined, consisted of one, two, or all three of the following morphological, physiological, or behavioral characteristics: (a) hyperdeveloped sensory organs (the assumption is that to survive in the darkness you must have other ways to 'sense' the environment by non-visual means); (b) low metabolism (the assumption being that caves are so

Table 3.3 *Fish families with troglomorphic representatives*

If any of the putative 'preadaptive' features had been reported in the family, that family was placed in the column of 'preadapted' families; otherwise, it was placed in the 'non-preadapted' column. Numbers represent the number of troglomorphic species in each family.

'Preadaptive' families		Non-'preadaptive' families	
Balitoridae	15	Cyprinidae	18
Ictaluridae	4	Cobitidae	1
Siluridae	2	Characidae	2
Claridae	3	Loricariidae	3
Pimelodidae	7	Bythitidae	7
Trichomycteridae	3	Poecilidae	1
Astroblepidae	2	Eleotridae	4
Sternopygidae	1	Gobiidae	4
Amblyopsidae	5		
Synbranchidae	4		
Total	46	Total	40

energy-depleted you must survive on very little food); and (c) nocturnal habits (the idea is that if one is accustomed to being active at night one has a better chance of thriving in caves) (see, for example, Holsinger 2000; Langecker 2000). Then 86 troglomorphic species of fish were grouped into their 18 respective families and a search was made for any of the above 'preadaptive' characters among those families (Table 3.3). Of all the 18 fish families with troglomorphic representatives, only ten have any of the 'preadaptive' features as part of their biological characteristics. The conclusion was that alleged 'preadaptations' to the hypogean environment are neither necessary nor sufficient to successfully colonize such a habitat.

Of course, it could be argued that the above conclusion may be faulty since very little is known of the biology of the vast majority of cave organisms to ascertain whether or not they posses 'preadaptive' features. To counter this, there follows (below) a summary of current knowledge about the cave organism that is probably the most studied.

The blind cave tetra, *Astyanax fasciatus*, is arguably the most studied troglomorphic fish and probably the cave organism most studied overall. This species can be found as both an epigean (eyed and pigmented) form and as a hypogean one (usually, but not always, blind and depigmented).

The epigean form has a broad distribution in the freshwaters of the New World from Texas to Argentina. Although cave populations of the eyed form have been reported in Belize (F. Bonaccorso, pers. comm.), Costa Rica (Romero 1984a), the Yucatán peninsula (Hubbs 1938), and Brazil (Trajano 2001), the only region in which they have developed into blind, depigmented individuals is the San Luis de Potosí Area, east central Mexico (*c.* 22°05′N, 99°00′W), where at least 31 caves supporting subterranean populations of this fish can be found (Espinasa *et al.* 2001). Not all the cave populations of this area display the same degree of morphological divergence from the surface forms, however. Some are completely blind and depigmented whereas others are only partly so. Three caves contain only individuals with full eyes and pigmentation. Eleven of these populations include both blind and eyed forms, as well as phenotypically intermediate forms (Mitchell *et al.* 1977; Romero 1983; Espinasa *et al.* 2001). At least one of them contains both eyed and blind forms with no intermediate forms (Espinasa and Borowsky 2000).

Besides blindness and depigmentation, the troglomorphic and surface morphs of *A. fasciatus* differ in many other morphological and behavioral characteristics. Troglomorphic populations also have a larger number of taste buds (Schemmel 1967). Unlike the epigean form, the blind hypogean one never shoals, is active all the time, and is not aggressive (Breder and Gresser 1941; Breder 1942; Boucquey *et al.* 1965; Erckens and Weber 1976). Although the blind form does produce an alarm substance, it does not respond to it (Pfeiffer 1966). Schemmel (1980) also reported differences between the two forms in the angle of inclination used when feeding from the bottom, with the blind form forming a more acute angle with the bottom. Differences in the level of phototactic responses among different populations have also been reported, indicating that even blind cave forms can respond to light, although the level of response differs depending on the population (Romero 1984c; Romero *et al.* 2003). Differences in behavior have also been found among troglomorphic species of the North American cavefish family Amblyopsidae, whose species display different responses to light (Green and Romero 1997).

The surface and troglomorphic forms of *A. fasciatus* interbreed in both natural and laboratory conditions, producing fertile hybrids with a phenotypically intermediate form in the F_1 generation and with an F_2 generation (after self-cross) whose individuals range from an almost completely blind and depigmented form to an almost fully eyed and pigmented one (Wilkens 1969; Sadoglu 1957; Peters and Peters 1973). Electrophoretic and karyotypic studies also support the contention that the cave and epigean forms are the same species (Avise and Selander 1972; Kirby *et al.* 1977).

This biological picture is not only complicated in space but also in time. When the troglomorphic form of *A. fasciatus* was originally described in 1936, the entire population in the Mexican type locality, La CuevaChica, consisted of a very uniform morph of blind and depigmented fishes. Romero (1983) analyzed the gross morphology of individuals that had been collected between 1936 and 1942 as well as those collected in 1982. He found that the La Cueva Chica population had evolved in 43 years or less into a morphologically intermediate population composed of individuals that were neither totally blind and depigmented nor fully eyed and pigmented. Romero concluded that this new morph was the result of introgressive hybridization that probably started in 1940 with the invasion of the cave environment by epigean individuals. Langecker *et al.* (1991) later reported a similar case of introgressive hybridization for a cave population of *A. fasciatus* in La Cueva de El Pachón.

With all this information at hand, no one has ever formulated a convincing description of what could have been the 'preadaptive' features of the comparably well studied epigean ancestor of *E. fasciatus*. Further, if the epigean *A. fasciatus* was 'preadapted,' why has it undergone such massive morphological, physiological, and behavioral changes to become a troglomorph? Equally telling is the fact that these fish in some caves have not developed any of the troglomorphisms typical of their counterparts in the San Luis de Potosí region of Mexico. This indicates, together with the existence of many species/populations of non-troglomorphic, hypogean fish (Chapter 2, p. 120), that fish do not have to develop troglomorphisms to reach an evolutionary adaptive peak in the hypogean environment, nor do they have to possess troglomorphic characteristics prior to entering the hypogean environment in order to be successful.

Another case that does not fit the 'preadaptation' explanation comes from the most unlikely of all possible examples, an alleged 'preadapted' organism itself. The Texas blindcat *Trogloglanis pattersoni*, which is found in deep phreatic layers of the Edwards Aquifer, has minute barbels, unlike those of other catfishes in the same family (Ictaluridae) (Langecker and Longley 1993). This is inconsistent with the generalization that enlarged sensory organs are required to enhance survival potential in the hypogean environment because one would expect those barbels to have increased in size or, at least, to have maintained the original size found throughout the family; however, they are reduced.

Holsinger (2000) has advanced the idea of applying the concept of exaptation, instead of 'preadaptation,' to the evolution of the troglobites. Gould and Vrba (1982) when they proposed the term 'exaptation', defined it as 'features that now enhance fitness but were not built by natural selection for their current role.' The problem with this terminological switch is that by reading Gould and Vrba's article (as well as the latest version of the concept in Gould 2002), it is clear that what they are referring to are specific structures that were previously developed for a particular role and are now being used for a different function. However, the main troglomorphisms, blindness and depigmentation, were not 'built' previously for anything else but rather are novel characters by default. For example, not a single instance is known of a cave organism that was blind and depigmented before invading the hypogean environment. Further, the existence of both a large number of fully eyed and pigmented organisms (Poly 2001) as well as intermediate forms (e.g. Burr *et al.* 2001) is, again, inconsistent with the necessity of either a 'preadaptation' or exaptation as a prelude to the successful colonization of the hypogean environment.

Of course, one could go to extremes by saying that if an organism lives in a habitat, it is because it is 'preadapted' to it, but that is a circular argument. So, to understand how and why organisms survive in caves, it is necessary to look at facts, not philosophies; recent research is providing very useful material.

This is why the concept of 'preadaptation', so popular among biospeleologists, is considered a relict at best among mainstream evolutionary biologists (e.g. Futuyma 1998, pp. 155–6; Pigliucci 2001b, p. 379). It is obvious from reading Chapter 1 of this book that, given the lack of evidence supporting this generalization, the concept of preadaptation is nothing more than a left-over from the orthogenetic hypotheses that have had such a strong influence in cave biology.

3.5 A case for phenotypic plasticity

After a critical look at many of the myths surrounding the evolution of hypogean organisms, it is time to address the most important issue of all: why have many cave organisms evolved by reducing and/or losing phenotypic characters?

A biological phenomenon that is rarely mentioned in the biospeleological literature and that the present author believes to play a major role in both the diversity of morphs and the evolution of cave fauna in general, is phenotypic plasticity. Caves around the world exhibit a variety of characteristics, including a wide range of temperatures, varying water supplies, and differing space availability (Juberthie 2000). The only thing they have in common is that for most, if not all, of their length, there is a lack of natural light. The two most noticeable organismal characters that closely correlate with light conditions are eyes and pigmentation. Both casual observations and experimental studies show that cave animals and their epigean ancestors can display responses to the presence or absence of light during the development of their pigmentation and their visual apparatus. The first observations were those of Rasquin (1947, 1949) who reported that when epigean *A. fasciatus* were raised under conditions of total darkness they displayed a lower degree of eye and pigment development. Similar observations for epigean crayfishes have also been reported (Cooper *et al.* 2001). On the other hand, if troglomorphic animals, even as adults, receive extended exposure to light, both pigmentation and the visual apparatus may become partly expressed, a finding that also holds true for other troglomorphic fishes such as *Typhlichthys subterraneus* (Woods and Inger 1957), *Rhamdia quelen* (Kenny, in Romero *et al.* 2002b), and *A. fasciatus* (Peters and Peters 1986).

Romero *et al.* (2002a); Romero and Green (2005) were able to confirm these initial observations by placing larvae of *A. fasciatus* 24 h old from three different populations, epigean (eye, pigmented), La Cueva de El Pachón (blind, depigmented), and their hybrids, under two different conditions (24 h light and total darkness) for a period of 30 days. Preliminary results showed that the eyes of the epigean larvae were much less developed when raised under conditions of darkness than when raised under light conditions. However, the most spectacular results were obtained with the El Pachón cave population: although those larvae that were raised under conditions of total darkness did not show any noticeable eye tissue, as expected, those raised under light conditions did (Fig. 3.4).

This strongly suggests that many troglomorphic animals are derived from epigean species by means of phenotypic plasticity. This is consistent with the fact that lack of light can trigger heterochrony, i.e. changes in the timing of development of features. Examples of phenotypic plasticity can be seen in (a) paedomorphs (animals that do not reach

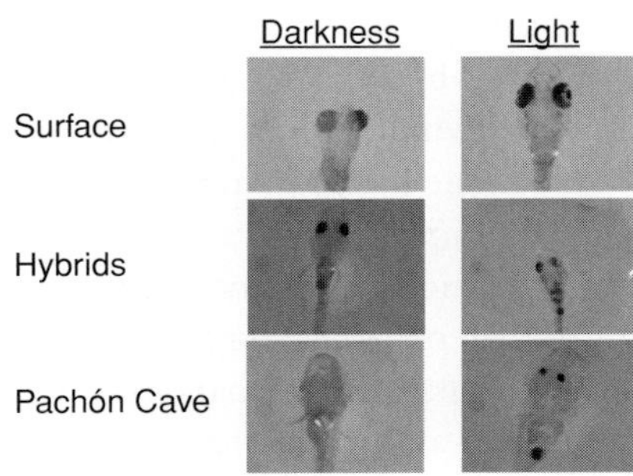

Figure 3.4 Development of eye tissue and pigmentation among different populations of *Astyanax fasciatus*. Photos by Aldemaro Romero. (See Plate 14.)

morphological maturity [metamorphs] reproducing as juveniles) and (b) neotenes (animals with slowed growth) (*sensu* Gould 1977). Many cave organisms are either paedomorphic or neotenic (Hobbs 2000; Langecker 2000; Weber 2000). Further, most troglobitic salamanders are paedomorphic, and half of all known paedomorphic salamanders are troglomorphic (Bruce 1979; Sweet 1986). Individuals living in the hypogean environment gain an advantage by becoming paedomorphic because this condition gives them the flexibility to survive in an unpredictable environment. Paedomorphosis in *Eurycea neotenes* appears to be a response to selection for the ability to survive dry periods in hypogean aquatic refugia (Sweet 1977). It is still unclear whether paedomorphism evolved before cave colonization or vice versa (Collazo and Marks 1994).

In addition, neoteny in hypogean animals, particularly fish, is well documented for reduced body size (Poulson 1964), loss of scales (Banister 1984), fin modifications (Greenwood 1976; Cooper and Kuhene 1974), and reduced ossification (Langecker and Longley 1993).

These examples also reinforce the idea that troglomorphisms are the result of natural selection. It is known that the direction and degree of response to environmental factors (reaction norm) is genetically variable and subject to natural selection (see Pigliucci 2001a for a full discussion of this phenomenon). Therefore, natural selection may favor those individuals with a higher capacity to express specific traits under appropriate conditions (Stearns 1983). Thus, phenotypic plasticity often provides a reproductive advantage over a genetically fixed phenotype because environmentally induced phenotypes have a higher probability of conforming to prevailing environmental conditions than genetically fixed ones (Whiteman 1994).

The present author believes that natural selection favors paedomorphs/neotenes by fixing their paedomorphic/neotenic alleles in the cave population. Given that most cave populations are small and subject to very similar selective pressures within the same cave, this evolutionary process can take a relatively short time. In fact, paedomorphosis can be achieved via a major gene effect (small genetic change generating a large phenotypic effect) (Voss and Shaffer 1997; but see Voss and Shaffer 2000), and that helps to explain why salamander evolution into a paedomorphic condition can take place quite rapidly (Semlitsch and Wilbur 1989). Several authors (Yamamoto and Jeffery 2000; Jeffery 2001; Strickler *et al.* 2001 for *A. fasciatus* and Brodsky *et al.* (2005) for hypogean blind mole rats) have shown that troglomorphic characters can arise via minor changes in developmental genes; this idea is consistent with the notion that regulatory loci produce environment-specific genetic effects. Only when there is a constant gene flow from the epigean environment (as was the case of introgression for *A. fasciatus* in La Cueva Chica or the replacement for *R. quelen* in the Cumaca Cave, Trinidad, described earlier) can such changes be prevented or reversed. In this respect, the recessive allele can be considered the 'troglomorphic gene' because it manifests a morphologically and ecologically differentiated phenotype that is reproductively isolated from the epigean ancestor, and genetic variance is affected by environmental conditions.

This explanation is further supported by the convergent nature of troglomorphic characters. Convergent evolutionary patterns are strong evidence of adaptation via natural selection (Endler 1986). Isolation would later lead toward speciation through genetic differentiation from the epigean ancestor. Many troglomorphic organisms are believed to have recently invaded the hypogean environment because their epigean ancestors are easily recognizable, and the populations can even interbreed and produce fertile hybrids (see, for example, Romero 1983).

The application of the concept of phenotypic plasticity to the evolution of troglomorphic fishes in particular and troglomorphic organisms in general, as proposed here, helps to explain many of the phenomena summarized earlier in this chapter. If troglomorphy is a condition that results from canalization as a developmental phenomenon, then that process should result in homeostasis. Homeostasis measures the degree of variation of a particular phenotype when it is perturbed, either by the environment or by a mutation. The more canalized the genotype, the more homeostatic the phenotype (Pigliucci 2001a, p. 95).

An example of canalization combined with phenotypic plasticity is the axolotl, *Ambystoma mexicanum*. This is a species in which a single genotype produces a discrete series of phenotypes. One cannot but wonder to what extent that may also be the case for some hypogean populations of diverse organisms that show an incipient level of troglomorphism while their epigean ancestor is also present. The similarities among some troglomorphic species/populations can be attributed to stabilizing selection for similar environments. Such convergence would be the result, thus, of similar reaction norms, rather than being due to specific developmental mechanisms. Conversely, the overall differences found even among troglomorphic organisms in terms of eye, pigmentation, and scale development must be the result of both different reaction norms and local environmental conditions. As pointed out earlier, not all hypogean environments are identical; great differences exist, particularly between tropical and temperate caves.

In fact, these cases of convergence are not limited to hypogean organisms. The same types of selection-induced change may be seen among deep-sea fishes (Poulson 2001) and fishes in murky rivers where phenotypic reduction/loss of eyes, pigmentation, fins, laterosensory canals, and odontodes (mineralized, tooth-like structures found as outgrowths of scales, rays, and bones) has occurred (Schaefer *et al.* 2005).

How, then, may the fact that the evolution of troglomorphic characters does not necessarily occur in parallel be explained? This is because (a) such characters are controlled by sets of genes independent from one another, (b) the degree of development of some of these characters (e.g. barbels in fish) is conditioned by their phylogenetic history, and (c) the selective pressures on each one of those characters may differ from cave to cave (Culver *et al.* 1995; Romero and Paulson 2001c). In addition to the reduction/loss of phenotypic characters, many troglomorphic organisms exhibit enhancement of sensory systems (chemical and mechanical) that are favored by natural selection, since these sensory systems increase their fitness by helping them to find food and/or mates. Complex, coordinated, and adaptive phenotypes such as a set of troglomorphisms can originate rapidly and with little genetic change via correlated shifts in the expression of plastic traits. This has been shown for blind hypogean mole rats (Brodsky *et al.* 2005) and for the fish *A. fasciatus*, which achieves a true phenotypic revolution with little genotypic change. Composite characters, such as those often observed among troglomorphic organisms, are produced by correlated phenotypic shifts that give the impression of a coevolved character set (West-Eberhard 1989).

What about all the non-troglomorphic species living in the hypogean environment? It is known that there is abundant genetic variation for plasticity within natural populations, which in turn is subject to selection. In addition, genetic variation for phenotypic plasticity is widespread, and the same population can harbor genetic variation for the plasticity of one trait while being invariant for the plasticity of another trait related to the same environmental variable. Again, this may explain the complexity observed in phenotypic responses among hypogean organisms. Some may display a high degree of blindness but very little depigmentation because the genes controlling one of the features are highly plastic whereas those controlling the other are not. The fact that genetic variation for phenotypic plasticity is widespread can help to explain why, for example, only cave populations of the fish *A. fasciatus* in the San Luis de Potosí area have developed troglomorphisms whereas those in Yucatán, Belize, Costa Rica, and Brazil have not, even though there is ample variation for plasticity among populations of the same species.

The ability of individuals of some troglomorphic species to regain some eye tissue and pigmentation, as reported here, may be the result of each population's retention of a substantial capability to alter its phenotype even if it represents an ecotype from a genetic viewpoint. This fits perfectly with current knowledge of population genetics for *A. fasciatus*, in which there are drastically different phenotypes (epigean and troglomorphic) but very little genetic differentiation, so the troglomorphic one could easily be characterized as an ecotype. An ecotype was originally defined as a population arising due to genetic response to a specific habitat, i.e. a population genetically specialized to a particular environmental condition. A phenotypically plastic genotype could yield what looks like an ecotype under extreme environmental conditions. Substantial convergence in the reaction norms of different populations can occur within certain ranges of environments.

Pigliucci (2001a, p.77) made three major points characterizing the interspecific variation for phenotypic plasticity that are relevant to the evolution of hypogean fauna: (1) closely related species can either differ substantially in their plasticities or present similar reaction norms; (2) plasticity can facilitate the evolution of specialized ecotypes starting from a generalist strategy; (3) closely related species can display very similar reaction norms early during their ontogeny, arriving at divergent phenotypes and plasticities only later in development. These conditions, again, serve to explain why some species in some families develop troglomorphs whereas others do not, and why a fish like *A. fasciatus*, which has no evident 'preadaptation,' has done so well in caves: it is a generalist, as evidenced by its wide distribution and occupancy of diverse ecological niches.

Plasticity can (and should) be maintained in fluctuating environments, especially when fluctuations in the environment are predictable to some extent. In another long-standing generalization about the cave environment, there is the belief that caves are so constant that no ecological fluctuations take place in them. However, this view has been challenged for some time. Hawes (1939), for example, was the first to provide specific examples of flooding being a periodic event in caves, leading to fluctuations in their ecological conditions. He showed how, despite other factors such as temperature and lack of light being constant, periodic floods provide conditions of a fluctuating environment and also play a role in colonization events.

Thus, it is not surprising that the organisms for which phenotypic plasticity has been demonstrated are all aquatic: crayfish, fishes, and salamanders. Many other examples, ranging from sponges to other arthropods, are provided in Chapter 2. Fluctuating environmental conditions are particularly factual in tropical caves where there are constant (but predictable) fluctuations in water level due to drastic seasonal changes in rainfall regimes. Is this one of the reasons why there are more troglomorphic species/populations in the tropics than in temperate regions? This question is certainly worth exploring, and that will be done in the next chapter.

3.6 Conclusions

Several points should be evident at the end of this chapter.

1. Not all hypogean organisms are troglomorphic.
2. Not all hypogean organisms show the same suite of troglomorphic characters.
3. Not all troglomorphic characters show the same level of development (or lack thereof) within the same troglomorphic species/population.
4. A single species can show highly divergent phenotypic morphs (troglomorphic vs. non-troglomorphic) that may or may not be dependent upon the environment they inhabit (as evidenced by fully eyed, pigmented hypogean fishes).

5. Troglomorphic populations can undergo dramatic phenotypic changes due to either introgressive hybridization with, or ecological replacement by, conspecific epigean individuals.

The above statements may be expanded or modified once more studies are conducted with other species. Unfortunately, most current knowledge comes from the study of a few species such as *A. fasciatus* and, to a certain extent, the fish family Amblyopsidae, whose troglomorphic individuals seem to be quite genetically distinct from any presumed ancestor (see Romero 2002b and references therein). The recent studies on *R. quelen* summarized above suggest that diversity is the rule, not the exception, when it comes to understanding the biological nature of hypogean organisms. That is why the conclusions above emphasize exceptions and variability, not uniformity or fixity.

The next set of questions that needs to be answered has less to do with the nature of the hypogean organisms themselves than with the environment in which they live. Such questions include (1) what kind of constraints does the hypogean environment impose upon evolution? (2) what is the interplay between phenotypic and genetic changes during hypogean colonization? and (3) what is the role played by behavior during the process of cave colonization and evolution?

This latter question may be highly important to understanding evolutionary processes in general. Mayr called behavior 'the pacemaker of evolution' (Mayr 1982, p. 612) and has argued for some time that changes in behavior precede changes in morphology. As I mentioned earlier, changes in behavior were recorded among individuals of a population of fishes at the entrance of a subterranean resurgence in Costa Rica (Romero 1984a).

Lee and his collaborators (Lee *et al.* 1996) used molecular genetics to study swiftlets, small insectivorous birds many of which nest in caves and are known to echolocate. Because of a lack of distinguishing morphological characters, the taxonomy of swiftlets is primarily based on the presence or absence of echolocating ability, together with nest characters. By analyzing cytochrome *b* mitochondrial DNA sequences from swiftlets and their relatives, they found that this bird group was not monophyletic. Their finding strongly suggested that echolocating swiftlets (*Aerodramus*) and the non-echolocating 'giant swiftlet' (*Hydrochous gigas*) can be grouped together, but the remaining non-echolocating swiftlets belonging to the genus *Collocalia* are not sister taxa to these swiftlets. They also suggested that echolocation abilities in *H. gigas* were secondarily lost and that echolocation may have propelled the phylogenetic divergence of these cave-inhabiting birds.

In fact the vocal behavior of these birds can be quite complex. Fullard *et al.* (1993) found that vocalizations of wild Atiu swiftlets (*Aerodramus sawtelli*) on a roost/nesting cave on Atiu Island in the Cook Islands are emitted as distinct single pulses rather than the double or multiple clicks typical of most swiftlets. Spectral analyses indicated that these birds do not adjust the peak frequencies of their calls as they fly within the cave and suggested they do not systematically structure the frequency content of their calls. These birds decrease their interpulse periods upon entering the cave and increase them upon exiting, presumably in response to differing light levels or space between the walls. As they land at their roost/nest site, these birds emit a train of low interpulse period calls that is occasionally followed by a vocalization, suggesting that it serves as an announcement to other birds on or near the nests.

Field study of the behavior of cave organisms, thus, remains a fascinating area with great potential for understanding evolutionary processes in the hypogean world.

4 · *The ecology of cave organisms*

This chapter is aimed at explaining the diversity of caves from an ecological viewpoint and the interactions among the different abiotic and biotic components of the hypogean environment. Particular emphasis is given to the ecological differences between caves in temperate and tropical environments, as most assumptions on cave ecology have been made based on caves in higher latitudes. These differences are also important because of their consequences in practical applications toward conservation issues.

4.1 Introduction

The first thing to be realized about the hypogean environment is that it is not a closed system. Not only do many cave creatures move in and out of this environment, but abiotic elements such as water, air, and many chemicals constantly flow through these ecosystems as well. Thus, to better understand how caves work from an ecological viewpoint it is necessary to look at them in a holistic way that includes the external ecosystems with which they interact.

The hypogean environment can be classified, for the purposes of this book, into three major classes: air, water-filled, and mixed. Sometimes the amounts of water can vary greatly, particularly in tropical areas, due to extreme variations of precipitation. Although many organisms live among the interstices of the soil particles, they are outside the scope of this book and are not considered directly in any depth. That does not mean that they are totally ignored, as mentioned in Chapters 2 and 3, since interstitial organisms sometimes represent transitional forms between epigean and hypogean environments.

4.2 Diversity and distribution

There are many types of hypogean habitat from a geological viewpoint. They include karsts, lava tubes, ice caves, and underground lakes and rivers without direct access by humans (phreatic, artesian). The most common and best known ones are karsts, which are formed in limestone areas (characterized by carbonate rocks). These caves are the result of rock dissolution by acidic waters (most rainfall is acidic). The landscape formed by these types of rock constitutes about 15% of the Earth's surface. Thus, cave and phreatic habitats can be found in most areas of the world. More than 100,000 caves have been described for Europe and about 50,000 for the USA alone.

The diversity of hypogean environments encompasses not only geology in general but geomorphology in particular. In terms of size they range from small crevices to extraordinarily long: when counting all its mapped passages, Mammoth Cave in Kentucky, the world's largest cave, has about 580 km of known passages. Caves can be horizontal, vertical, multilayered, or a combination of these. They can be found in the form of a single tunnel or an extensive underground network with multiple connections to the epigean environment. Among those that are aquatic in nature there are freshwater, marine, and anchialine (i.e. with restricted exposure to open air, one or more connections to the sea, and influenced by both the marine and terrestrial ecosystems with which they interface). Anchialine habitats are common in volcanic or limestone bedrocks (Sket 1996a). These types of geological formation are found in a wide range of latitudes around the world.

Therefore, it is not surprising that in the aforementioned diversity of habitats there is a corresponding diversity of biota, as sketched in Chapter 2. Sometimes the magnitude of hypogean biodiversity is not apparent, as is the case in the Edwards Aquifer in Texas and northeastern Mexico. This aquifer resides in the Edwards limestone and is about 282 km long and from 8 to 64 km wide. It consists of a recharge area and an artesian area (Longley 1981). More than 40 hypogean species have been described for these waters, from crustaceans to fishes. This must be a very small sample of the actual diversity of organisms contained therein because this biodiversity has been studied only when found in springs or pumped out from wells. Furthermore, when one considers that hypogean waters represent 97% of the world's freshwater, the potential for underground life in this environment is enormous (Marmonier *et al.* 1993).

A popular misconception about cave biodiversity and biomass is that such environments are always poor in both. Although it is true that many hypogean environments are small, lack primary producers, and have a depauperate fauna when compared with the epigean environment, it is

Table 4.1 *Summary of hypogean faunal surveys in selected regions of the world*

Latitude is represented by the average for the region in question.

Area/cave surveyed	Number of non-troglomorphic species	Number of troglomorphic species (% of the total in parenthesis)	Average latitude	Source
Southern Ontario, Canada	301	0 (0%)	50°	Peck 1988
Slovenia	1,066	190 (15.13%)	46°	Sket 1996b
France	4,218	218 (4.91%)	46°	Juberthie and Ginet 1994
Pennsylvania, USA	131	15 (10.27%)	41°	Mohr 1953; Holsinger 1976
New South Wales, Australia	422	83 (16.5%)	33°	Thurgate *et al.* 2001a
Northern Mexico	143	32 (18.29%)	25°	Reddell 1982
Eastern Australia	148	82 (35.65%)	20°	Thurgate *et al.* 2001b

not uncommon to find tropical caves with ceilings literally covered by bats, the soil covered by myriads of invertebrates, and water teeming with aquatic life, including hundreds if not thousands of fish in a single pool. The origin of this misconception stems from the fact that most cave research has been conducted in temperate caves (USA, Europe) where biodiversity and biomass are rather poor. Therefore, one should ask whether or not biodiversity indices follow a pattern that can be correlated with latitude. For example, it is interesting to notice that most karstic areas of the world are in temperate regions (see the frontispiece of Wilkens *et al.* 2000). Thus, one might expect that the highest cave biodiversity should also be found in mid-latitudes; however, that is not the case.

Table 4.1 summarizes the information of hypogean faunal surveys in selected regions of the world. There one can see that there is an increasing proportion of troglomorphic species as the region is located closer to the Equator; the exception is Slovenia, but this anomaly can be explained by the fact that almost the entire country is karstic in nature and that such a system is probably the most studied in the world, having been explored for much longer than even Mammoth Cave.

Canada is conspicuous for its lack of troglomorphic species (Peck 1988). This is important since much has been made of troglomorphisms as a result of lack of food availability (see Hüppop 2000, and discussion below).

As expected, biodiversity in caves increases in inverse proportion to latitude and it is not adventurous to predict that once more is learned about tropical caves, such a relation will become even more apparent. The other corollary to these data is that the effect of surrounding biota on caves needs to be considered; caves do not exist in a vacuum (as do some terrestrial fauna on remote oceanic islands) but they largely reflect the surrounding biodiversity in terms of both faunal origin and composition.

Hypogean biodiversity as a whole is also very surprising. According to Culver and Holsinger (1992), the total number of troglomorphic species is between 50,000 and 100,000. As shown in Chapter 2, that number is rather conservative. First of all, most of these authors' assumptions were based on the biodiversity of caves in the USA, in which, as was noted above, biodiversity is rather poor. Second, most caves, particularly in tropical countries, have not been thoroughly explored (Deharveng and Bedos 2000). Third, knowledge of phreatic ecosystems is, and will continue to be, very limited in the foreseeable future because what is known about such ecosystems is largely based on fortuitous findings since humans cannot explore them directly. Fourth, humans tend to be most impressed with megafauna, so most species recorded are those easily visible. Finally, the obsession of biospeleologists with dealing only with troglomorphic species leads many to ignore a large number of epigean species (many times higher in number than troglomorphic ones) that play a major role in hypogean ecosystems.

This highlights another issue of tremendous importance from the ecological viewpoint. In addition to the typical problems of calculating biodiversity values in caves and other hypogean environments, there is the added cultural problem of what is considered to be a 'true' cave organism. Take, for example, Weber (2000), who proposed that unless the animal in question shows clear troglomorphisms it cannot be considered what he called a 'true cavernicole.' That is, in the present author's opinion, a misjudgment. Animals in a particular environment cannot be considered 'true' members of that ecosystem based on specific morphological characteristics but rather on the role they play in that ecosystem. To corroborate this, consider one of the examples utilized by Weber to exclude certain species from being what he (and many others) considers to be a 'true cavernicole': cave birds.

As explained in Chapter 2, there are two groups of bird that use caves on a daily basis for resting and reproduction: the oilbird, *Steatornis caripensis* (Steatornithidae), and several species of swift of the genus *Collocalia* (Apodidae). Both of these not only utilize caves as a permanent habitat during the day for resting and nesting but are the only bird species that have developed echolocation abilities to navigate inside the caves. Like many nocturnal birds they have large eyes, which they use mostly outside the caves to forage. However, despite the fact that the development of echolocating abilities is clearly a major adaptation to life in caves which requires major neurological rewiring, they tend to be dismissed as not 'true cavernicoles.' More importantly, from an ecological perspective, the droppings of these bird species, as well as those of cave bats, have a great influence on the ecology of the cave they inhabit. Studies at Cumaca Cave in Trinidad, WI, indicated that oilbirds were a major component of the ecology of that cave, occupying the cliffs of most of the largest halls and displacing the bats to the smaller halls and towards the end of the cave (Romero and Creswell 2000; Romero *et al.* 2001, 2002a). The droppings of the oilbirds were prominent; although no quantitative studies have been conducted, it is difficult to imagine that such abundant organic material has no influence on the ecology of that particular cave.

The best example of a non-troglomorphic group of organisms playing a major role in cave ecology is the case of cave bats. Bat guano generates rich and complex invertebrate communities, particularly in tropical caves (Ferreira and Martins 1999). Bat guano has also been described as a source of food for fish (Romero 1983) and even salamanders. Fenolio *et al.* (2005a) reported coprophagy in salamanders from an Oklahoma cave and found that the nutritional value of guano was comparable to that of their invertebrate prey. They further suggested that bat guano may play an important role as a source of food among other cave vertebrates.

Needless to say, the effect of the presence of bat guano on microbial fauna must also be immense, but that is an area largely unstudied. Explorers of tropical caves know very well that caves with high levels of guano deposits have higher temperatures. This anecdotal observation has been confirmed empirically. Baudinette *et al.* (1994) found high and rather constant temperatures in caves inhabited by large bat colonies and considered that such heat was part of the microclimate created by the bats themselves, which, in turn, generates better conditions for maternity.

Another source of food for hypogean organisms can be plant roots. In many karstic areas tree roots penetrate the substrate all the way to the phreatic levels, where they can obtain water. There, root mats form a diverse and abundant biomass. Jasinska *et al.* (1996) reported 41 species of aquatic hypogean organism, including annelids, arthropods, and fish, from a cave in Australia that had root mats in its phreatic waters. Their study concluded that the root mats were the primary source of energy for all these organisms.

From a taxonomic viewpoint, as mentioned in Chapter 2 for fishes, it can be said that there are approximately equal numbers of non-troglomorphic and troglomorphic species/populations; the situation is similar for other groups of organisms normally found in caves.

Therefore, in order to gain a clear picture of the true biodiversity values in caves, it is not sufficient to look only at troglomorphic organisms. As explained in Chapter 1, this typological view of life, with its roots in eighteenth- and nineteenth-century essentialism and which was so prevalent until the introduction of the modern synthesis with its populational view of biology, impairs a clear view of reality (Romero 2007).

4.3 Cave ecosystem structure

As mentioned in Chapter 3, one of the major problems of cave biology is the proliferation of terms to describe either organisms that inhabit the hypogean environment based on their spatial distribution and/or different portions of the ecosystem itself. Although terms are useful to identify ideas, objects, or mechanisms, an overabundance of them leads to confusion and, above all, the misleading interpretation of nature as a series of well-defined compartments. The reality is different: in nature all is in flux and although basic terminology (e.g. herbivore, plankton, etc.) is well understood, other jargon can be confusing and highly artificial.

Ecologists confronted these problems in the early twentieth century when they stopped looking at natural associations as static components of nature and viewed them rather as dynamic systems in both time and space. That is when the concept of succession was fully adopted (Tansley 1935). Hence, the term ecosystem became universally accepted as one in four dimensions, i.e. the three spatial ones plus time.

Look, for example, at some of the terms frequently used in biospeleology, where even the term hypogean is somewhat misleading. Although this term is used frequently throughout this book and in the author's own research on fishes, this choice has been facilitated by the fact that all hypogean fishes are either cave or phreatic in terms of their habitats, i.e. within the realm of speleology: there are no interstitial (part of the meiofauna) or edaphic (soil-related) fish. The meiofauna is very peculiar in that it seems to be a temporary residence for many large organisms, some of which have characteristics typical of cave fauna (blindness and depigmentation); they have other characteristics that are due to the spatial constraints of where they live in terms of the reduced space in between the sand particles, for which reason they tend to have elongated bodies.

Although many of these terms may be useful, that does not mean that they are necessary; in fact, if overused they can be detrimental to the communication and understanding of scientific ideas. The hypogean environment should be viewed as a system rather than as a collection of units that need to be classified based only on external, superficial characters and without taking into consideration the temporal dimension of those objects.

Recently, Campbell Grant *et al.* (2007) proposed a view of caves as an example of an ecological dendritic network. They define dendritic networks as those spatial environments in which both the branches and the nodes serve as habitat and where the specific spatial arrangement and hierarchical organization of these elements interacts with a species' way of moving and distributing, which, in turn, will affect its abundance and community interactions. Because most caves do show some geometric similarity with this type of structure, this approach seems reasonable. Furthermore, these authors propose that one of the reasons for the high rate of endemism in cave biota is precisely the spatial organization of these habitats.

Therefore, to better understand how caves work as ecosystems, it is necessary to see them from a systemic viewpoint, interpreting their organization and the relationships between their components. One of the weaknesses of biospeleology as a science is the natural inclination of its practitioners towards an essentialist (typological) view of nature rather than seeing it in a spatio-temporal continuum.

Some authors even view cave species as quite separated from their epigean ancestors even if there is genetic evidence of their close relationships. Although the biological species concept (BSC) has been criticized for not being universal and lacking diagnosability for all cases, it is still far more logical than the evolutionary species concept (ESC) and the phylogenetic species concept (PSC), both of which are arbitrary, artificial, and non-biological, serving only diagnosability, which makes them germane to the typological concepts of the nineteenth century. It has been convincingly argued that diagnosability is not a sufficient criterion for a species definition and that the PSC describes species taxa rather than defining a species concept (Glaubrecht 2004). In other words, researchers should not forget that species are not elements in a periodic table.

The same happens with caves and their elements. As mentioned earlier, there are many types of cave; they come in different sizes and shapes, are found in many latitudes and ecological regions, and also vary in their origin, development, and age. On top of that, caves represent only one of the many available niches for the surrounding biota, which, ultimately, will influence the nature and composition of the cave itself.

4.4 Spatial organization

Little work has been done either on ecosystem structure or on information and energy transfer in the hypogean environment. Most cave students have seen caves as authentic islands of much reduced dimensions, in comparative terms, and in one-dimensional terms. However, caves have spatial and temporal dimensions that attest to their complexity (despite their apparent simplicity). Bussotti *et al.* (2006) used a multifactorial sampling design to examine the distribution of species assemblages within three different caves in southern Italy over a period of 11 months and found a pattern of change in the structure of the assemblages along the exterior–interior axis, as well as among areas, which suggested a highly complex structure for the biotic community.

From a spatial viewpoint the typical cave (if there is such a thing) has five spatial–conceptual axes. First, there is the terrestrial–horizontal one on which are found many terrestrial organisms, terrestrial invertebrates being the most evident to the casual observer. The second is defined by the length of the cave. It is well known that community structure and biodiversity distribution changes throughout the length of the cave; the lengthier the cave, the more complex that structure can be. The third is vertical and is largely defined by the differences between the biodiversity found on the ground and that roosting on walls or the ceiling of the cave. This is an important dimension since roosting animals, whether they are bats or birds, usually provide large amounts of nutrients to the cave. In addition, these animals usually move daily from inside the cave to the epigean environment; thus they represent one of the most important facilitators of the interactions between the hypogean and epigean environments. The fourth is water: whether a cave is permanently or periodically flooded with water makes a great difference not only to its biotic composition but also to its own dynamic and community structure. The fifth dimension that must be considered is that of the outside environment that influences the cave: whether it is the terrestrial community outside the cave determining the species composition and abundance of animals that frequent both sides of the equation, or water flowing in and out of the cave, the external environment can have a tremendous impact on cave ecology.

Of course, cave diversity is just too variable to attempt to categorize all caves with these components *sensu stricto* (and this would be, anyway, a form of typology). One could argue that, given the different biological microcosms, there is no reason to apply the theory of fractals to caves as they can be applied to nature in general. However, the way in which mainstream ecologists have been able to characterize ecosystem components is not because of their nature (which is clearly structured), but because these subdivisions, when not taken to extremes, are useful ways to understand how nature works.

For example, the way in which bats are distributed in a cave influences patchiness in that cave because of the heterogeneous way in which bat excrement will be deposited. This phenomenon has also been observed among mysid crustaceans, which deposit organic material in a patchy manner (Coma *et al.* 1997). These authors found that in a cave of the Medes Island in the northwestern Mediterranean, the species *Hemisysis speluncona* forms large swarms with daily migrations from the inner part of the cave, where they remain during the day, to the exterior, where they feed at night. The swarms of this species play a major role in transferring organic material into the cave in the form of fecal pellets. Even soil, in many caves, is carried inside from the exterior (see, for example, Foos *et al.* 2000).

Another remarkable example of the complexity of ecosystem structure in caves can be conveyed by looking at the ecological role played by the mite *Coprozercon scopaeus*, which was a species used to describe a new family of mesostigmatic mites, Coprozerconidae. This species was found in the feces of the woodrat, *Neotoma floridana magister*, in Mammoth Cave, Kentucky. This is the only species of its suborder (Epicrinea) whose life cycle seems to be restricted to the cavernicolous environment. The subspecies of woodrat associated with it lives most of its life in caves and rock slide crevasses in Appalachian areas from Pennsylvania to Tennessee. The woodrats always defecate in the same sites (dumps) (usually about 1 m away from each other), thus providing not only abundant but also stable sources of nutrients. These dumps also provide a source of energy to other arthropods. The dumps can be as high as 25 cm and contain fecal pellets of various ages (Moraza and Lindquist 1998).

In addition to these spatial dimensions, caves must also be seen from a temporal perspective. Caves have evolved, from a geological viewpoint, in many ways, depending upon their geology, location, and climate. Logically, it can be expected that organisms living in them have co-evolved. Unfortunately, and unlike the epigean environment, caves lack a meaningful fossil record that might give an idea of how those changes occurred at times before the most recent ice ages; caves tend to be very poor in terms of sediment preservation. Even when fossilized elements are found in caves, that fossil record refers mostly to terrestrial mammals that temporarily inhabit the cave during some portion of their life cycle. Thus, there are no real fossil records that can help to elucidate evolutionary changes from epigean species to troglobites.

The closest example is the case of *Paleozercon cavernicolus*, a species of mite known only from specimens embedded in calcium deposits of a stalagmite near a cave entrance (Blaszak *et al.* 1995); however, even this does not mean that these organisms lived exclusively in caves.

This paucity of fossil evidence is unfortunate in more than one way, not only because of the lack of hard evidence of how those changes occur from an anatomical viewpoint but also because it has given some biospeleologists a further impression that cave organisms are 'fixed' in time. The other aspect rarely taken into consideration is that of more short-term variations or even seasonal ones. As mentioned in Chapter 3, studies in La Cueva Chica in Mexico and at the Cumaca Cave in Trinidad have shown that changes in rainfall regimes can have an important impact on species inhabiting caves, even on short historical scales (a few decades) (Romero 1983; Romero *et al.* 2002a).

When considering temporal aspects in the evolution of populations, species, and/or communities in caves one must, therefore, take into consideration the temporal scale. However, given the lack of a fossil record, how is this possible? Molecular clocks could possibly be used, although the results of such clocks are far from definitive given the fact that different assumptions and methodologies may yield different outcomes. Another method is to use generation times. The reasoning is very simple: not all organisms reproduce the same number of times in fixed astronomical cycles; furthermore, as mentioned in Chapter 3, many organisms such as cave fishes have extended life cycles compared with those of their epigean ancestors. Such changes seem to be prompted by water cycles rather than by astronomical ones; this is only logical given the fact that the hypogean environment isolates obligatory organisms from astronomical clues.

A paradox also arises from this situation. As noted in Chapter 3, the morphological evolution of many cave organisms seems to be rather fast, aided by phenotypic plasticity; however, when becoming more troglomorphic many of those organisms have reduced considerably the number of generations per unit time. This means that within the same phylogenetic lines there will be different tempos of evolution; that is why the use of molecular clocks may not be the best way to ascertain the evolutionary pace for both phylogenetic lines and ecological communities.

This approach is not new, however. Ginzburg and Darnuth (2008) proposed something similar in the area of metabolic ecology.

4.5 Trophic structure

Some authors (e.g. Holsinger 2000) have argued that hypogean environments are 'harsh' because they are poor in nutrients. However, the available data do not support that statement as a valid generalization. Animals that colonize caves can find in those habitats food (see, for example, Ferreira and Martins 1999), reproductive niches (e.g. Rogowitz *et al.* 2001; Briggler and Puckette 2003), protection from predators (e.g. Romero 1985a; Tabuki and Hanai 1999), protection against desiccation (Jensen *et al.* 2002), and a place for hibernation (Zhang 1986; Resetarits 1986; for a general discussion on this see Bellés 1991). These ecological opportunities of the hypogean environment allow many different species of many different taxa to undergo extensive adaptive radiations, leading to many differentiated populations and/or species (Hoch and Howarth 1999). In addition, contrary to generalizations based on studies of caves in temperate regions (see, for example, Poulson and White 1969), many caves are very rich in nutrients, particularly in tropical regions (see, for example, Deharveng and Bedos 2000) and some are even chemoautotrophic (Airoldi and Cinelli 1996; Sarbu 2000; Sarbu *et al.* 2000; Hose *et al.* 2000) thanks to bacteria that produce organic matter by oxidizing sulfur. Both tropical and chemoautotrophic caves are usually very rich in species, with some of those species having large population sizes.

In fact, bacteria may play a much larger role in caves than previously thought. Engel *et al.* (2004b) found in Lower Kane Cave, Wyoming, USA, that filamentous aquatic *Epsilonproteobacteria* and *Gammaproteobacteria* colonize the carbonate substrates so common in many caves and

Figure 4.1 Gypsum from Mammoth Cave. Photo by Aldemaro Romero. (See Plate 15.)

through their metabolism generate sulfuric acid, which dissolves the substrate, not only shaping the interior of the cave but also enlarging its crevices and therefore increasing its size. The phenomenon known as sulfuric acid speleogenesis (SAS) was reported in the 1970s for the same cave but in the air only, where sulfuric acid oxidation replaced the aerial carbonate by gypsum (Fig. 4.1). Therefore, we can say that microbes play a major role in subsurface karstification.

The widely repeated yet unsupported generalization that the hypogean environment is very poor in nutrients has also led to a number of other equally unsubstantiated claims regarding the ecology of cave organisms. Weber (2000, p. 110), for example, has stated

> The requirements for a continual cave existence evidently explain the restriction of troglophilic and troglobitic vertebrates to fishes and amphibians. Birds and mammals, as homoeothermic animals, must eat more or less continuously to maintain their high activity and body temperature.

This statement fails to take into consideration three facts: (1) both birds (e.g. oilbirds) and mammals (especially bats) can easily move in and out of caves, and this allows them to utilize the resources available in both the hypogean and epigean environments at the same time; (2) many species of mammal spend long periods of time in caves while hibernating, precisely when their food requirements are at their lowest; and (3) all troglomorphic vertebrates are fish or amphibians, i.e. organisms that are highly dependent on the aquatic environment to survive, which limits their ability to abandon the cave they inhabit; the exceptions, such as populations of fish and amphibians living in caves that have water connections with the outside world, are usually characterized by hybridization (see, for example, Romero 1983; Romero *et al.* 2002b). Thus, it would be a disadvantage for mammals and birds that can and do utilize the resources of the epigean and the hypogean environments to develop troglomorphisms such as blindness or depigmentation, because that would place them at a competitive disadvantage once they were out of the cave. This same reasoning can be extended to reptiles, whose mobility is as good as that of non-flying, terrestrial mammals. Further, following Weber's reasoning, reptiles should become troglomorphic since they are poikilotherms; yet no troglomorphic reptile has ever been reported.

According to Weber (2000, p. 110) 'reptiles are terrestrial and food scarcity is stronger in the terrestrial than in the aquatic cave habitat (. . .) So it seems likely that, even for reptiles, food supply is too low.' Again, this reasoning is faulty since many cave inhabitants, such as bats and oilbirds, depend on a food supply from outside the cave, which they retrieve by active means (via large energy expenditures), something that reptiles could also do. Obviously, the most serious problem with Weber's explanation is to consider troglomorphs as the only 'true' cavernicoles, thus diminishing the important role played by these organisms in the life cycle of many other organisms as well as the differential mobility of different taxa.

Weber (2000, p. 110) also claims that 'one adaptation to the low food supply is the body size of troglobitic fishes and salamanders, which are usually small in comparison to epigean relatives . . .' This statement has a number of problems. First, there is no empirical evidence that all, or even most, cave organisms are smaller than their putative ancestors. The troglomorphic sculpins of the *Cottus carolinae* species group, for example, are actually larger than the surface form (G.L. Adams, pers. comm.). Further, even if that were true, there can be at least two alternative explanations for this alleged phenomenon: (1) many caves have a large number of crevices that can provide not only protection against potential predators but also means to move from one cave to another, so being smaller provides a selective advantage that has nothing to do with food supply; (2) as seen in Chapter 3, many if not most troglomorphic characters are the product of heterochrony, and small body size is precisely a product of that phenomenon.

The fatal blow to the assumption that cave organisms in general and fishes in particular look the way they look because of lack of nutrients is provided by the troglomorphic *A. fasciatus*, which has a resting metabolic rate nearly twice that of its epigean form (Schlagel and Breder 1947). This is not an aberration: several cave populations of amphipods show metabolism no lower than that of their epigean counterparts (Culver 1971; Gilbert and Mathieu 1980).

One question that could be explored further is whether water temperature may affect metabolic rate in hypogean aquatic organisms from an evolutionary viewpoint. That is difficult to answer because of the lack of data. On one hand, the example of the troglomorphic *A. fasciatus* mentioned in the previous paragraph corresponds to a tropical environment; this is one of the very few hypogean fish species for which metabolic rates have been examined. Data on water temperature are not generally available for most hypogean fishes, much less information on potential seasonal variability in temperate regions. Therefore, more data on both metabolic rate and environmental temperature are needed before making any predictions.

Another by-product of the myth that caves are very poor in nutrients is the popular misconception that troglomorphic organisms have reduced eyes and pigmentation as a response to the low availability of food. However, all empirical evidence indicates that the responses are physiological, not morphological, and that in those cave environments characterized by high levels of energy supply, metabolism actually increases rather than decreases and yet, reduction and/or elimination of phenotypic features still occurs.

Many hypogean organisms can and do undergo long periods of starvation. Several species of fish and salamander, for example, can experience periods of one year or more without food (Poulson 1964; Mathieu and Gilbert 1980; Hervant *et al.* 2001; Hervant and Renault 2002). The ability to survive prolonged periods of food deprivation is not unique to hypogean organisms. Numerous epigean animal species belonging to a wide variety of taxa undergo long periods of starvation during hibernation, aestivation, and/or spawning seasons. Their responses to such conditions do not take the form of reduction or loss of phenotypic structures, but are physiological in nature.

Hypogean organisms subjected to food deprivation respond in a fashion similar to that of epigean ones subjected to similar conditions. Mendez and Wieser (1993) first proposed a set of physiological strategic responses to these conditions that has now been found to occur in a wide variety of animal species, both epigean and hypogean. This physiological strategy consists of undergoing sequential phases, itemized as follows.

(1) Stress: this is the start of the starvation period, characterized by increased locomotory activity associated with food finding. This phase may last up to 60 days in the cave salamander *Proteus anguinus* (Hervant *et al.* 2001).
(2) Transition: this phase is characterized by a drastic reduction in activity and oxygen consumption.
(3) Adaptation: this is the longest phase, which may last a year or more. It is characterized by constant minimal rate of oxygen consumption, stable metabolic activity, and highly reduced locomotory behaviors.
(4) Recovery: this phase is characterized by exceptional hyperactivity and increase in oxygen consumption, both associated with searching for food.

Birds and mammals show a similar strategy, only they add a critical phase after the adaptation phase (Le Maho 1984).

Given that this is a convergent feature among long-fasting organisms, particularly many hypogean ones, it supports Mendez and Wieser's (1993) initial hypothesis that natural selection is the mechanism favoring this sequential energy strategy, whose overall characterization is one of a combination of 'sit and wait' behavior while no food is available, subsisting on internal energy reserves and low metabolic requirements during that period while showing high recovery abilities during re-feeding. The hypogean salamander *Proteus anguinus*, for example, can undergo periods of food deprivation for up to 96 months.

One of the by-products of both hibernation and lengthening of the life cycle in animals that live in caves is an increase in their longevity. The life span of cave fishes has been reported to be exceedingly long. The amblyopsid fish *Amblyopsis rosae* is slow-growing, with a long life span (*c.* 10 years); maturation takes at least four years (Poulson 1963; Robison and Buchanan 1988). A less hypogean species of this fish family, the spring cavefish *Forbesichthys agassizi*, has a life span of about three years (Smith and Welch 1978; Etnier and Starnes 1993). Among bats, hibernating species live, on average, six years longer than species that do not hibernate. In addition, bats that roost in caves live more than five years

Figure 4.2 Vegetation near caves can be abundant and does have an influence on the cave biota. Photo by Danté Fenolio. (See Plate 16.)

longer than bats that live elsewhere or do not roost (Wilkinson and South 2002), independent of the family to which they belong. So cave roosting improves the fitness of the species associated with that environment, since life span can be construed as a result of natural selection acting to maximize reproductive success.

For species that enter or use caves as temporary habitats, their relationship with those habitats is more complex than it may seem. For example, there are several species of harvestman (opilionid) that spend the daytime in caves to leave at night to predate on insects. One species of harvestman of the genus *Goniosoma* from Brazil is found in different parts of the cave system depending upon the vegetation outside, showing how external factors may influence the distribution of cave organisms (Fig. 4.2). Interestingly enough, this species is preyed upon inside the cave by insects and spiders (Machado *et al.* 2003), showing that the idea that so-called trogloxenes use caves to escape predators may be true in some cases but is not necessarily so for others.

There are also species of fish that enter and exit caves, playing a major role in the ecology of those environments. One example is the cardinal fish *Apogon imberbis*. This is a small fish distributed along the eastern Atlantic coast from Morocco to the Gulf of Guinea, including the

Azores. It can be solitary or form shoals and is common in environments ranging from small crevices to marine caves, where the fish can be found in large numbers. This species shows no troglomorphisms whatsoever, yet it plays a major role in transferring organic material to these marine caves, as mysid crustaceans do. Just like bats, they tend to stay in the caves during the day and leave the caves at night, presumably for feeding (Bussotti *et al.* 2003). Thus caves would be very different places if these 'trogloxenes' were not to be considered as an integral part of cave ecology just because they are not troglomorphic.

One aspect of cave ecology that has yet to be studied is how this vertical transfer of nutrients occurs, particularly from bats and cave birds to the terrestrial and aquatic organisms found on the bottom of the cave. Once those studies are carried out, it would not be surprising to find that such an energy transport occurred in a similar manner to energy flows elsewhere on Earth, i.e. with a strong vertical polarity with a lot of the energy concentrated at the top (e.g. bats) and at the bottom (e.g. guano), an adaptation to the way in which life on this planet receives its main source of energy, the Sun, from above (Margalef 1993).

In any case, some preliminary studies confirm the complexity of the trophic structures of caves. Graening (2005), while studying six subterranean stream habitats in the Ozarks, found that there were three trophic levels in those subterranean streams. The first one was formed by a detrital food base of clastic sediment, bat guano, and surface inputs; a second trophic level was formed by detritivores, primarily crustaceans and amphibians; and a third, top level is composed of predators, primarily fishes.

4.6 Is there succession in caves?

Because of the lack of primary producers, it has long been believed that caves lack any expression of meaningful ecological succession (a phenomenon first and mostly studied in vegetation). This has led to the idea of the so-called 'stability' of the cave ecosystem. Much has been written alleging that the cave ecosystem is stable. For example, Langecker (2000, p. 135) characterized caves as 'an environment that is relatively stable in its climatic characteristics' and Boutin and Coineau (2000, p. 434) affirmed that 'the relative temporal stability of subterranean habitats, postulated for a long time by many authors, has been demonstrated in many particular cases and constitutes one of the generally accepted paradigms of biospeleology'.

However, such statements are not really backed up by sufficient data to allow such a blanket generalization to be made. Perhaps because of the lack of primary producers, cave biologists think that there is no succession, and therefore that the system is a 'stable' one. In addition, succession tends to be slower in temperate environments than in tropical, humid ones. That is the reason why the life spans of animals tend to be longer in ecosystems with slow successions compared with those with rapid ones; that is why very long life spans are found among some troglomorphic organisms in temperate caves (e.g. amblyopsid fishes). In addition, tropical ecosystems, because they have higher levels of energy (in terms of both absolute and flow), allow for more fluctuations and more rapid succession, which in turn accelerate the pace of evolution, both at the individual (species/population) level and at the ecosystem one. However, primary producers are not necessary for succession to happen; mines provide a good example of this. Milanovich *et al.* (2006) reported that an abandoned mine in Arkansas had been recently invaded by the slimy salamander (*Plethodon albagula*) for nesting. They reported this phenomenon not only as a recent one but also one in which fecundity is influenced by precipitation.

Ashmole *et al.* (1992) described faunal succession in the lava caves of the Canary Islands. They found that the first hypogean communities were characterized by pioneering epigean species common in the surrounding areas that were opportunistically taking advantage of the new environment, mostly for either feeding or seeking protection from predators during the day. According to these authors, the presence of chemolithotrophic bacteria suggested the possibility of some primary production taking place early on. They further discussed the idea that as the lava caves age the animal community in them also changes by increasing the number of species. Therefore, succession does occur in caves. What may have happened in the past is that the typological concept of caves, as static and relatively isolated ecological units, created a philosophical barrier to understanding the dynamics involved in this process.

As mentioned earlier, ecological replacement has been reported between two populations of the catfish *Rhamdia quelen* in Trinidad, WI, where in fewer than 100 years an eyed, pigmented population has replaced one that was blind and depigmented (Romero *et al.* 2001). This is another example of the fluctuations that can take place among cave biota.

Another major impact of bacteria is their potential role in the contribution of cave formations per se, as mentioned earlier. Engel *et al.* (2004a) found that numerous bacteria colonize carbonate surfaces, generating sulfuric acid as a metabolic by-product which, in turn, lowers pH and contributes to the dissolution of the rocks. Therefore as the cave habitat changes, so does its biota.

If there is no regularity of 'laws' governing succession in 'lighted' ecosystems, should such regularities be expected among hypogean ones? Probably not; it is not easy to believe in the idea of ecosystems as self-organizing superorganisms. Caves, like any other environments, particularly extreme ones, will be invaded by living organisms following the most conspicuous of all of evolution's characteristics: opportunism. They may or may not interact with other invading organisms, but certainly there is no evidence that the resulting systems will be structured in one way or another. Furthermore, nobody to the author's knowledge has ever expressed the idea that hypogean ecosystems reach a 'climax' in the ecological sense. Changes in hypogean environments (and even in their organisms) seem to be asymmetrical.

Very little is really known about succession in hypogean environments, so at this point all that can be done is to speculate. One of those speculations, however, can also be a word of warning: do not expect to find regularities with universal applications. The best evidence that such a statement may be true is the differential biodiversity composition that is found among caves around the world.

And what is known about natural (non-anthropocentric) perturbations in the hypogean environments? The answer is: very little. It is known that, despite having lost circadian rhythmicity, some aquatic organisms adjust their breeding period to the availability of water.

It is too bad that caves are terrible places for fossilization; otherwise they could provide interesting clues about ecological succession. Since bats are such an important source of energy for many caves, one can only wonder how their explosive radiation in the Eocene (Teeling *et al.* 2005) may have changed the ecological landscapes of caves.

4.7 Interactions of cave habitats with the epigean environment

Until recently, caves have been seen as rather isolated habitats whose connections to the epigean environment were largely restricted to the cave entrance(s), whether those entrances were dry or wet. However, recent studies show that, in addition to ground, air, and/or water connectivity, caves can interact with the soil environment above them and, by extension, with a still greater portion of the epigean environment.

This fact has already been recognized by hydrogeologists, who have described the interactions between river waters and underground waters and all the hydrological linkages with adjacent aquifers as vitally important to understanding the flow and biochemical nature of groundwaters (for a review, see Hancock *et al.* 2005).

Gers (1998) provided evidence that there are exchanges of organic matter and living organisms between caves and the soil above them. He looked at vertical distributions of arthropods from leaf litter on the ground to caves underneath and found links between hypogean, endogean (soil) and epigean species. That connection is due largely to the existence of the MSS (*milieu souterrain superficiel*) or superficial underground section. This section is made of weathered bedrock with heterogeneous spaces in rocky material and can be found between the soil and the cave. It can be populated by a great diversity of arthropods regardless of the nature of the rock (Juberthie *et al.* 1981). Some organic material is passively transported by percolation from the soil to the caves, but Gers (1998) found that there is also active migration of arthropods, not only from the epigean environment to the cave, but also from the cave to the epigean environment, with the MSS being the area where the food webs of both environments interlink.

These connections are particularly important in some troglobitic beetles such as *Speonomus hydrophilus*. Crouau-Roy *et al.* (1992) found that the energy base for these insects ultimately derives from epigean primary productivity and can therefore be subject to both the geological structure on top of the cave and the normal seasonal fluctuations, since energy is transported into the cave via the MSS.

This is not to say that the fauna found in percolating water is the same as the one found in caves. In fact, it contains not only species from both the epigean and cave environments but also its own peculiar fauna. That is why it can be considered an ecotone (Prous *et al.* 2004; Pipan *et al.* 2006).

An ecotone has been defined as the transition zone between two ecosystems. These areas tend to have species richness higher than that of either of the two contiguous zones, with elements from both. The question is, can cave entrances be considered ecotones, and if so how are they characterized in terms of their biodiversity? Culver and Poulson (1970) studied the fauna at the entrance of Cathedral Cave in Missouri and suggested that such an entrance area had more biodiversity similarities

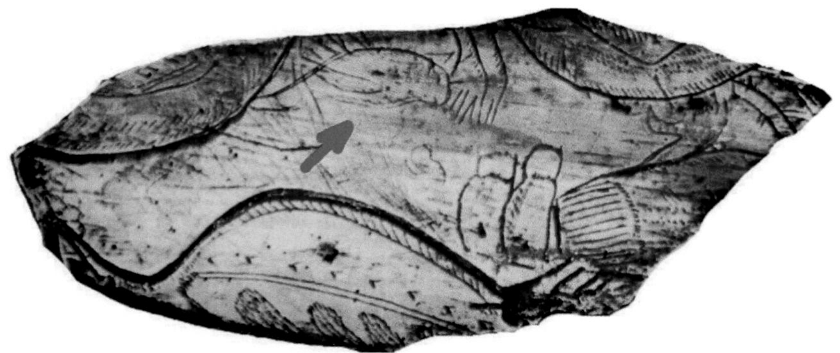

Plate 1 The earliest known human representation of cave fauna dates back to *c.* 22,000 YBP (years before the present) (Upper Paleolithic). It is a carved drawing of a wingless cave cricket, *Troglophilus* sp., on a bison (*Bison bonasus*) bone found in the Grotte des Trois Frères (Three Brothers Cave) in the central Pyrenees, France (Chopard 1928). Line drawing by Amy Awai-Barber from a photograph of the original.

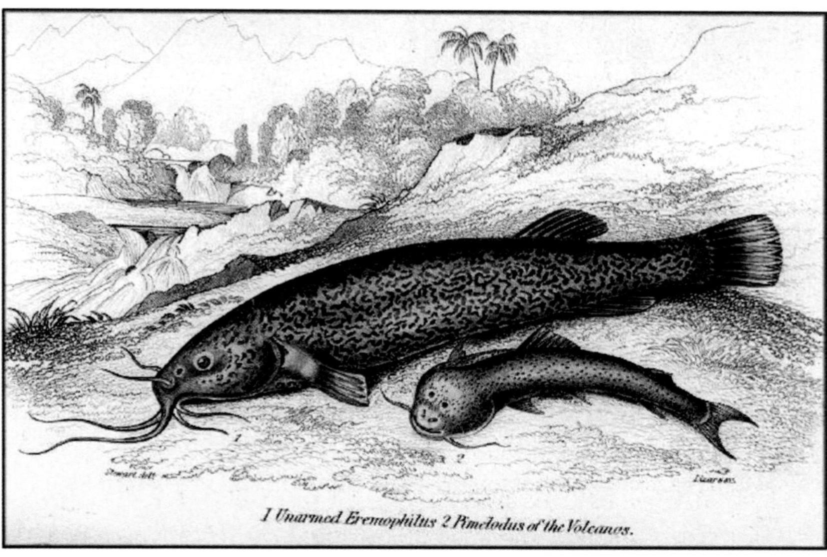

Plate 2 Illustration of the alleged subterranean fishes from a volcano in Ecuador by Humboldt (1805).

Plate 3 Nineteenth-century illustration on a postcard of Bottomless Pit at Mammoth Cave by an anonymous artist.

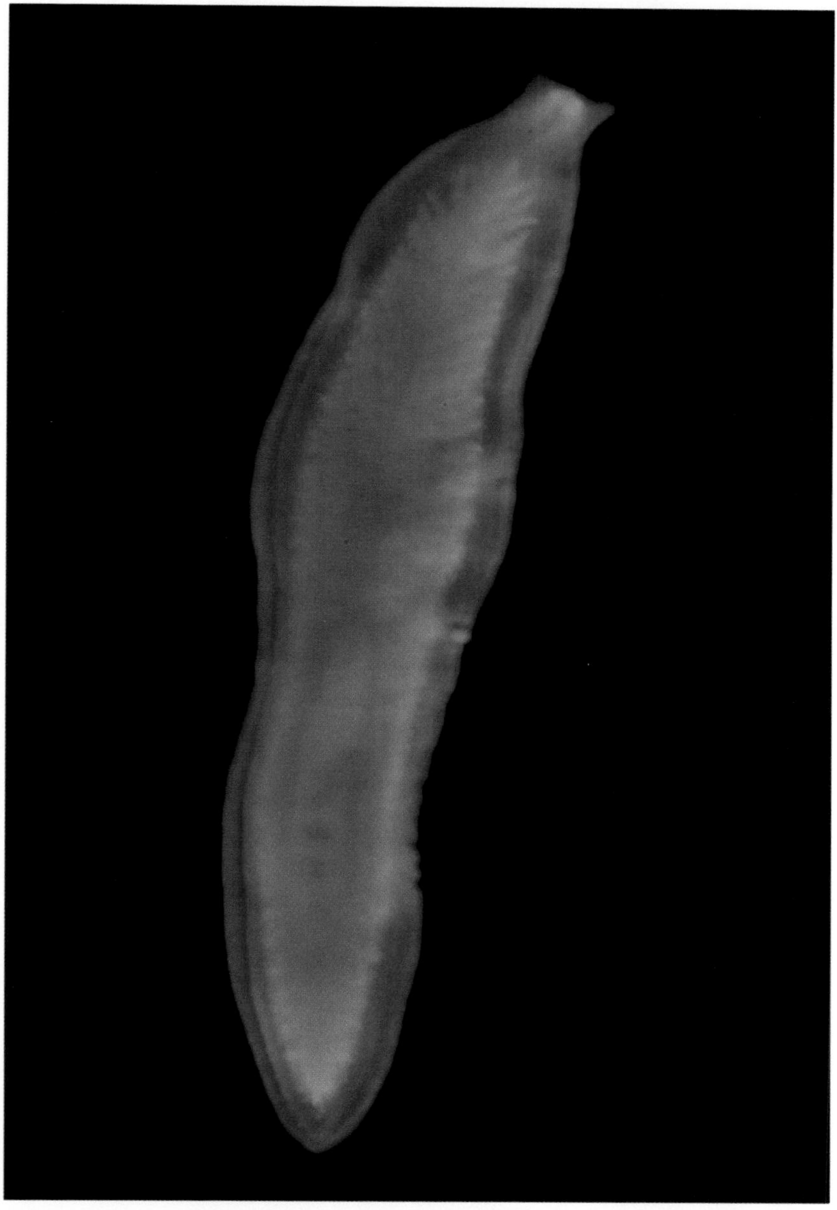

Plate 4 Sphalloplana percaeca from Big Mouth Cave, Grundy County, Tennessee. Photo by Danté Fenolio.

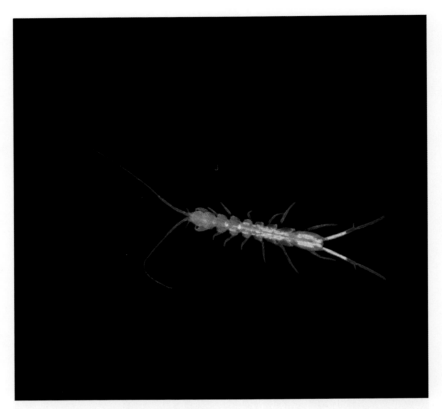

Plate 5 Caecidotea sp. Photo by Danté Fenolio.

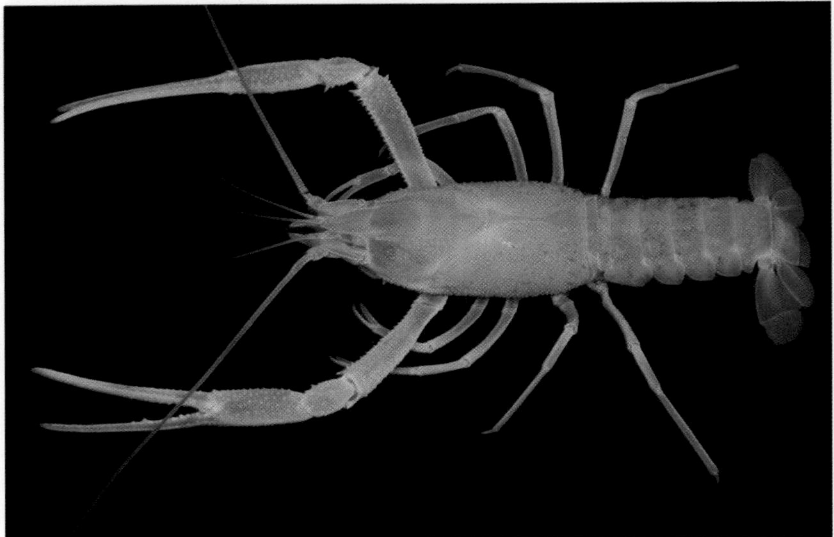

Plate 6 Procambarus lucifugus. Photo by Danté Fenolio.

Plate 7 A cave opilionid showing the typical blindness and depigmentation of troglomorphic species. Photo by Danté Fenolio.

Plate 8 A cave millipede from Blevins Cave, Arkansas. Photo by Danté Fenolio.

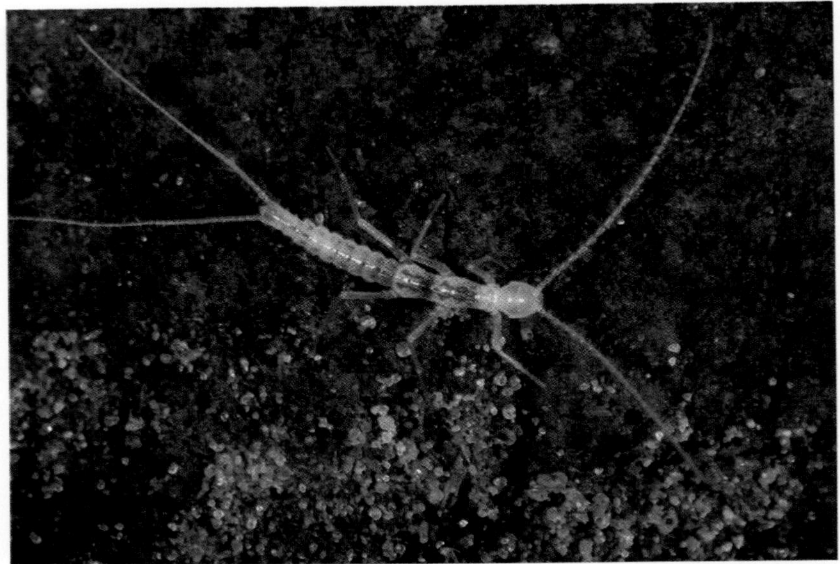

Plate 9 A Campodeidae dipluran from the Ozarks in Oklahoma. Photo by Danté Fenolio.

Plate 10 Pritella phreatophila from the Edwards Aquifer in Texas. Photo by Danté Fenolio.

Plate 11 A still undescribed species of *Eurycea* from a cave in southern Texas. Photo by Danté Fenolio.

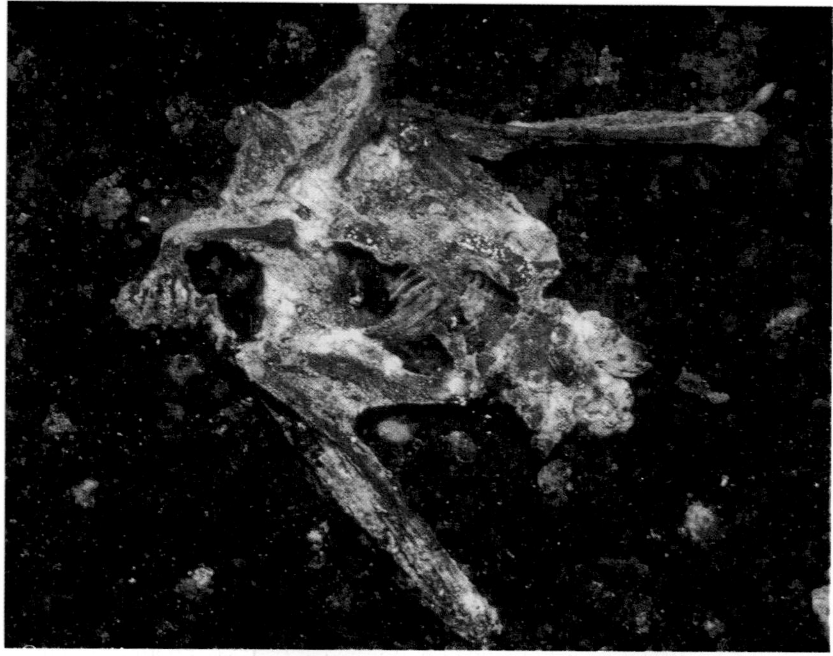

Plate 12 A decomposing bat from the Ozarks of Arkansas. Photo by Danté Fenolio.

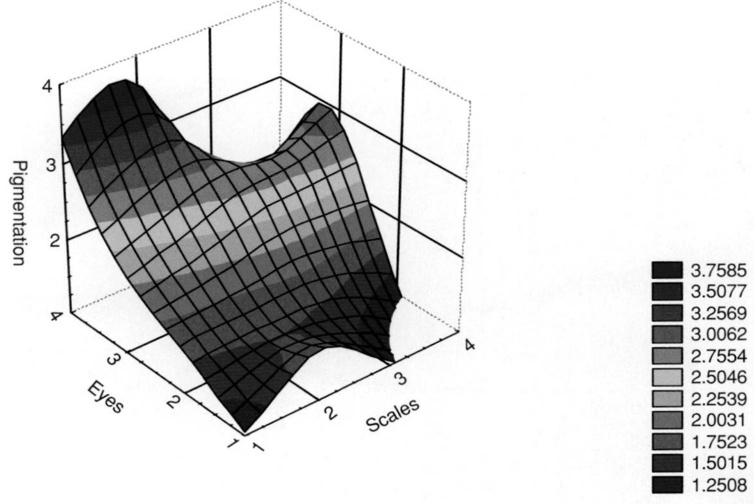

Plate 13 A landscape representation of the character state for all troglomorphic fish species. The irregular landscape illustrates the lack of complete (or even partial) convergence in character development for all these fish species.

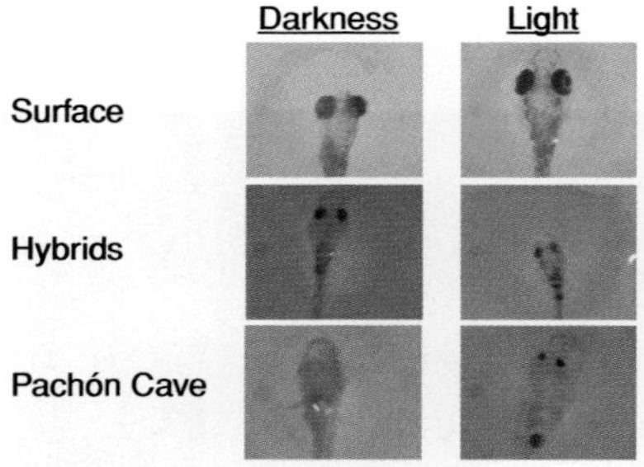

Plate 14 Development of eye tissue and pigmentation among different populations of *Astyanax fasciatus*. Photos by Aldemaro Romero.

Plate 15 Gypsum from Mammoth Cave. Photo by Aldemaro Romero.

Plate 16 Vegetation near caves can be abundant and does have an influence on the cave biota. Photo by Danté Fenolio.

Plate 17 Heavy use of caves, as in this one in Bermuda, can cause serious environmental damage not only to the resident organisms but also to the geology of these karst formations. Notice how many stalactites have been cut to make space for tourists visiting the cave. Photo by Aldemaro Romero.

Plate 18 The building of staircases like this one in the main entrance of Mammoth Cave disrupts the movements of biota in and out of caves. Photo by Aldemaro Romero.

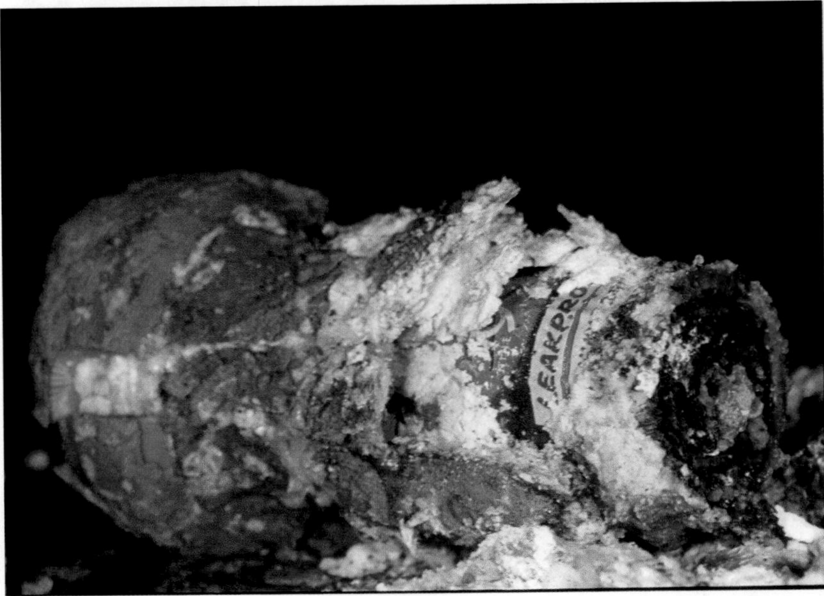

Plate 19 An old battery in Cottonwood Cave, Sequoia Co. The disposal of refuse that contains heavy metal represents a serious danger to the ecology of caves, given that they have very little capacity to recycle pollutants. Photo by Danté Fenolio.

Plate 20 Mexican free-tailed bats leaving a cave in Oklahoma at dusk. Photo by Danté Fenolio.

Plate 21 Building a bat gate above a sink opening. Photo by Danté Fenolio.

with the hypogean fauna than with the epigean one. On the other hand Prous *et al.* (2004) conducted a similar study in two caves in Brazil and found the opposite: a larger similarity in biodiversity composition between the epigean environment and the ecotone. The invertebrate richness of the ecotone in one cave was similar to that of the epigean environment, whereas in the other it was intermediate between the epigean and hypogean environments.

In other cases it is difficult to determine any clear-cut transition area between the epigean and the hypogean environment based on physical characteristics of the cave alone. Such is the case of marine caves that penetrate from the ocean directly into karstic areas of 100 m or more in length. However, many organisms seem to delimit that transition zone based on both light penetration and salinity. This has been documented for the cave at Pont d'En Gil in Menorca (Balearic Islands, Spain) where different species of mysid crustacean distribute themselves based on light intensity and salinity (Wittmann 2004).

This gives an even more complex picture of the organization of the trophic structure of caves, and leads to the issue of connectivity (see Margalef and Gutiérrez 1983). The concept of food web connectivity (C) is an ecological measure of the linkage patterns between or among different food webs. Because the idea of caves is as highly isolated habitats, it could have been said in the past that the number of links (or connectivity) between the hypogean environment and the epigean one was very poor. However, studies like the one described above suggest a much more complicated structure with a higher number of links, which can affect the community structure and function of both the hypogean environment and its surrounding epigean one (for more on the issue of connectivity, see Dunne *et al.* 2002).

Of course, the biggest implication of the higher connectivity than expected is that it is now possible to better understand the fact that the differences between cave ecosystems in temperate and tropical areas are the result not of intrinsic differences between types of cave but of differences between the types of ecological conditions outside those caves: in temperate ecosystems there is a periodic interruption (or diminishing) of epigean activities in winter that is more acute the higher the latitude. This means that activities such as colonization and competition are severely reduced in those areas; this, in turn, means that caves are poorer in terms of biodiversity in high latitudes.

Another issue little studied in cave communities is that of connectivity among the different elements of the cave environment and, therefore, how energy and information flows from one to another. This is surprising since these ecosystems are generally supposed to be simplified (see above) because of the general lack of primary producers. Since energy is reduced by 90% from one trophic level to another, this explains why there are no large predators in caves (even snakes are very rare and mostly limited to cave entrances).

Another aspect little studied beyond the taxonomic viewpoint is the role of parasites in the hypogean environment. Internal and external parasites seem to be as common among hypogean fauna as they are among the epigean one. Energy is transferred from the host to the parasite; if, as some assume, the hypogean environment is poor in nutrients, the question is whether the parasitic relationship between hypogean hosts and their parasite differ from that of epigean organisms?

Finally, there is the issue of competition. Three factors are important: the two organisms/populations that compete, and the resource for which they compete. Again very little is known about this process in caves. Some observations suggest that there is a strong competition for space among animals that occupy similar niches in caves, such as between bats and cave birds for ceilings and cliffs. New research, particularly among marine invertebrates (cited in Chapter 2), suggests that competition for light and nutrients plays a major role in the distribution of those organisms in the hypogean environment.

It is clear that the ecology of caves is a largely unexplored subject. Many of the suppositions that have been made in the past are generalizations based on philosophy rather than on science.

4.8 Caves as record keepers of climate change

Given the growing interest in climate change, it is not surprising that the hypogean environment has been looked at as a source of long-term environmental information. Ku and Li (1998), for example, looked at the isotopic compositions of oxygen, carbon, magnesium, and strontium in speleothems in limestone caves in China and were able to reconstruct regional changes in precipitation, temperature, and vegetation over the past 500 years. They found that there had been 14 precipitation cycles with a periodicity of 30–40 years, probably reflecting fluctuations in the strength of the East Asian summer monsoons reaching northeastern China. They also found evidence of the ‘Little Ice Age’ that took place after the year 1620, as well as anthropogenic activities of fossil fuel CO_2 combustion in recent decades and regional deforestation between the thirteenth and the sixteenth centuries when Beijing was expanding in both population size and large construction projects. Therefore, caves seem to provide useful information for understanding climate change in the recent past.

Caves can also provide a view into a longer span of time. Wang *et al.* (2008) used high-resolution speleothem records from Sanbao Cave in central China to look at the East Asian monsoons for the past 224,000 years. They found that the monsoon record was dominated by 23,000 year cycles and that these tropical/subtropical monsoons responded dominantly and directly to changes in Northern Hemisphere summer insulation on orbital timescales, showing that the ages of the events were exceptionally well constrained and may serve as benchmarks for correlating and calibrating climate records.

5 · *Cave conservation and management*

This chapter deals with what has been learned so far regarding conservation, legal protection, and management (including the little known about restoration) of cave habitats. This issue is examined from habitat, species, population, and genetic perspectives.

5.1 Introduction

Caves and associated ecosystems (mostly karst) represent resources of great value. These values can be grouped into three general clusters: ecologic–scientific, economic, and cultural.

As described in previous chapters, caves have attracted the interest of researchers for many centuries. They provide a wealth of information not only about biodiversity and their intrinsic processes such as ecology and evolution, but also about geology, paleontology, chemistry, archaeology, and history.

From the economic viewpoint the importance of karstic areas is overwhelming: more than 25% of the world's population either lives on or obtains its water from karst aquifers. In the United States alone, 20% of the land surface is karstic in nature and 40% of the groundwater used for drinking comes from karst aquifers. Every year about 20 million tourists visit caves worldwide.[1] This activity brings economic well-being not only to cave owners but also to the surrounding communities. In karstic areas a number of other human activities of economic importance take place: agriculture, mining (including guano extraction), animal breeding, and fungus cultivation, as well as the exploitation of biological resources such as the harvesting of cave swiftlet and oilbird nests. Some caves are also used as sanatoria in the belief that they can cure respiratory conditions.

[1] *Source*: Karst Waters Institute (KWI): http://www.karstwaters.org/kwitour/whatiskarst.htm

From the cultural viewpoint caves are also important: they provide us with a wealth of information about human evolution, history, and religion. However, all these values are threatened by human activities. Anthropogenic impacts on caves are magnified by two major factors. The first is their relatively small size, which makes the effects of any disturbance disproportionately large. In addition, most populations of cave organisms, particularly in temperate regions, tend to be relatively small and with limited hypogean dispersal capabilities in comparison with their epigean counterparts. The second major factor is that, because caves are relatively closed environments, recycling of substances introduced into them is slower than in other ecosystems. This is particularly true in the case of underground water.

Throughout this book a view of caves as complex, heterogeneous, and very dynamic environments has been proposed. This idea runs counter to the conventional wisdom usually expressed in speleological circles, according to which caves are simple, homogeneous, highly stable habitats. As will be shown below, anthropogenic effects on these environments reinforce only the more dynamic and intricate view.

This chapter analyzes, with examples, how humans have impacted and continue to impact the cave ecosystem, how complex those impacts can be, and what kinds of measures have been taken in order to ameliorate those impacts.

In order to better understand anthropogenic effects on hypogean ecosystems, impacts are classified according to a modified version of the proposal by van Beynen and Townsend (2005) to quantitatively measure anthropogenic effects on karst ecosystems. This general scheme is summarized in Table 5.1.

Although Table 5.1 represents a good checklist, its application must take into consideration a number of factors. One is that there are diverse types of karst around the globe that differ in size and location, and in their geological and chemical composition. The other issue is that the checklist takes into consideration a number of factors whose evaluation requires an interdisciplinary team capable of assessing each one of them as objectively as possible. The quality of the information available is also crucial. Therefore, this list must be applied with great caution (Calò and Parise 2006).

It is also important to remember that most karst systems are threatened not by a single factor but by a combination of two or more. An example of this can be found in a list generated by the Karst Waters Institute (KWI) during a scientific conference that took place in February 1997,

Table 5.1 *Slightly modified list of indicators by categories and attributes listed by van Beynen and Townsend (2005) in their schematization of factors to be measured in order to develop a disturbance index for karst environments*

These can include not only caves but also phreatic ecosystems.

Category	Attribute	Indicator
Geomorphology	Surface landforms	Quarrying/mining
		Flooding by anthropogenic constructions
		Stormwater drainage
		Infilling
		Dumping
	Soils	Erosion
		Compaction
	Subsurface karsts	Human-induced flooding
		Structure removal
		Mineral and sediment removal
		Floor sediment compaction/destruction
		Temperature
Atmosphere	Air quality	Humidity
		Composition
		Corrosion
Hydrology	Water quality (surface)	Agrochemicals
		Industrial and oil pollution
	Water quality (springs)	Algal blooms
	Water quantity	Changes in level of the water table
		Changes in cave drip water
Biota	Vegetation disturbance	Vegetation removal
	Terrestrial hypogean biota	Species richness
		Population density
	Aquatic hypogean biota	Species richness
		Population density
Cultural	Human artifacts	Destruction/removal
		Regulatory protection
	Stewardship	Enforcement of regulations
		Public education
	Building infrastructure	Building of roads
		Building over karst features
		Artificial illumination
		Construction within caves

Table 5.2 *List of the ten most endangered karst systems of the world according to the Karst Waters Institute (KWI)*

Name	Location	Threats
Blue River Basin	Southern Indiana, USA	Commercial and residential development
Cape Range Peninsula	Australia	Water extraction, urban development, quarrying, oil exploration
Church and Bitumen Caves	Bermuda	Commercial and residential development, water pollution
Cueva del Viento System	Canary Islands, Spain	Sewage dumping, solid wastes, residential development
Fricks Cave	Georgia, USA	Commercial and residential development
Ha Tien-Hon Chong	Vietnam	Industrial development
Jollyville Plateau	Texas, USA	Road building, chemical spills, commercial, industrial, and residential development, exotic species
Koloa Lava Tube System	Hawaii, USA	Agriculture, urbanization, refuse dumps, deforestation, mining, invasion of alien species
Lez Karst System	France	Over-extraction of water
South Central Kentucky Karst	Kentucky, USA	Agriculture, oil and gas extraction, expanding transportation corridors, urban development

Source: Mylroie and Tronvig 1998.

entitled *Conservation and Protection of the Biota of Karst*. They produced a list of the ten most endangered karst systems based on the threats they faced (Mylroie and Tronvig 1998). The list is presented in Table 5.2.

Most anthropogenic physical impacts on caves can be grouped as follows: (1) changes in the physical properties of the air (temperature, humidity, carbon dioxide) due to human visitation; (2) changes in hydrological conditions due to water pumping and pollution; (3) enlargement (and/or obstruction) of entrance(s) and walls; (4) building of stairs; (5) installation of lights, creating the condition for

Figure 5.1 Heavy use of caves, as in this one in Bermuda, can cause serious environmental damage not only to the resident organisms but also to the geology of these karst formations. Notice how many stalactites have been cut to make space for tourists visiting the cave. Photo by Aldemaro Romero. (See Plate 17.)

photosynthesis (by introducing photosynthetic organisms) or scaring away some (if not all) of the natural inhabitants of the cave; (6) compaction of soils and/or mining/quarrying of geological material; and (7) the introduction of foreign biological agents such as bacteria and fungi. Most of these impacts can be traced to the development of tourist amenities.

Many 'show caves' (caves open to commercial tourism) already suffer from an excess number of visitors because of a lack of studies into the maximum number of humans that can visit a cave over a particular period of time without significant effects (carrying capacity) (Fig. 5.1). Caves open to the public are either managed by governmental authorities or by private owners. The first are sometimes pressured by either the public or policy makers to make caves available to as many people as possible. In the case of privately owned caves, visitor numbers are usually driven by financial considerations. In both cases the needs of the visitors to marvel about the physical and biological attributes of caves seem to take precedence over the effects of those very same visitors on their natural features. Thus, their carrying capacity in terms of number of visitors is usually overlooked. Some attempts have been made to establish the maximum number of visitors that a cave can have to minimize the effects caused by humans, as in the Grotta di Castellana (Cave of Castellana) and Grotta Grande del Vento (Big Wind Cave) in Italy, based on the changes in temperature, humidity, and CO_2 concentrations (Cigna 1993b).

These anthropogenic factors are sometimes difficult to study owing to the fact that environmental parameters in caves are influenced by natural fluctuations. For example, carbon dioxide (CO_2) concentrations vary owing to rainfall and the local geology (Denis *et al.* 2005). Therefore, without a clear-cut baseline (prior to human intervention), it is not easy to precisely assess anthropogenic impacts on caves. To make things worse, many of these major impacts are difficult to ascertain because many caves have been used by humans for a long time. Thus, on many occasions there is no real snapshot of how those caves originally functioned under natural conditions.

However, researchers have been able to obtain reliable data on the anthropogenic impacts on caves, showing that they can be quite large and multifaceted, as described below with a number of examples.

Now let us analyze each one of the factors listed in Table 5.1.

5.2 Effects on geomorphology

5.2.1 Quarrying/mining

Limestone quarrying has been carried out since ancient times; all areas of the world that are rich in karst have been utilized in one way or another to extract construction material. Today this is particularly true in regions such as Southeast Asia (Clements *et al.* 2006) and the Balkans (see, for example, Parise *et al.* 2004). When quarrying takes place, the geology of many areas that contain hypogean organisms is affected in many ways, including destruction of the karstic landscape, changes in hydrological balances such as water table levels and quality, the creation of artificial pools and spring discharges, as well as the generation of sinkholes and the outright destruction of caves, particularly when explosives are used. Rarely, if ever, is karst stripping followed by any kind of restoration, leaving the soils totally denuded and vulnerable to further erosion. Needless to say, all these changes directly affect the ecology of hypogean organisms in ways that may be irreversible (Wood *et al.* 2002).

Changes in the geology of caves also take place through natural causes. These include seismotectonic events (i.e. earthquakes) as well as graviclastic events (i.e. rocks falling under their own weight). The morphologies that these factors leave on speleothems are different from those caused by explosions, quarrying, and/or vandalism (Crispim 1999). Therefore, it is possible to tell which caused which, even when a new cave is discovered as a result of quarrying/mining and later vandalized. This is important because it allows a baseline to be established of what is natural and what is not in the geological evolution of a cave.

Quarrying has been found to have a major impact on the stability of karstic areas in southern Italy (Calò and Parise 2006). These effects have also been recorded in developing countries such as Trinidad and Tobago, where, together with forestry, urban development, and tourism, they have destroyed much of this landscape with little, if any, consideration of its importance when carrying out conservation plans (Day and Chenowerh 2004).

Even when quarrying is focused on a particular element of the karst system, the effects can be multiple. An example is the gypsum extraction at Sorbas, in southeastern Spain, an area that contains hundreds of dolines and numerous highly unusual exo- and endokarstic forms with large caverns adorned with numerous unique speleothems. The extraction of the gypsum has impacted not only the landscape but also the local flora, fauna, and hydrological regime by increasing percolation and affecting air quality (Pulido-Bosch *et al.* 2004).

5.2.2 Urbanization

Because karst spring waters represent a resource valuable to humans, it is not surprising that ancient civilizations developed in areas where such a resource was available for both agriculture and direct human consumption. LaMoreaux and LaMoreaux (2007) summarized the history of hydrological research in karst areas. According to them, this type of research is first described in cuneiform tablets dating back to 852 BC in the headwaters of the Tigris, whose source is a karst spring. The Bible mentions that the main source of water for the ancient city of Palmyra, Syria, was a hot sulfur spring named Efca, believed to have curative powers. Other ancient references to karstic waters being used by humans include Li Daoyuan's book *Annotation on Water Scripture*, published in the second century AD. Another Chinese reference to early uses of karstic waters is that of the water from Lisban Spring, in China, recorded in 1134 BC as being used for medicinal purposes by many monarchies. The Romans were also aware of the potential benefits of these underground waters, as evidenced by the public baths built around the hot springs in Bath, England (LaMoreaux and LaMoreaux 2007).

The ancient Greeks developed water management technologies as far back as 3,000 years ago. In fact, the presence of karst areas with available water resources from springs and caves were key in the settlement and urbanization planning of many a Greek *polis*. However, the urbanization that accompanied Greek civilization brought with it important changes in the hydrological regimes of karstic areas by increasing runoff, changing the points of entry, creating flooding, and diminishing the available water supply (Crouch 1993, 2004).

Urbanization can also have direct impacts on the biological resources of caves. Petit *et al.* (2006) concluded that urban sprawl had diminished the populations of columnar cacti on Curaçao on which most bat species feed and that this, in turn, resulted in significant reduction of bat populations inhabiting caves in that Caribbean island in the span of 10 years.

Urbanization also increases the sedimentation in karst watersheds. Using a sediment budget approach, Hart and Schurger (2005) were able to trace recent sedimentation and suspended sediments to urbanization, with sediments that could be stored for centuries. A similar situation has been described for the entire region of central Texas, USA, which includes the cities of San Antonio and Austin. There, Mahler *et al.* (1999) found a high organic carbon content that gave sediments an increased potential to transport contaminants. Further, they predicted that the volume of these sediments was likely to increase with continued urbanization of the watershed.

Urbanization is taking place in areas that are critical to survival of some species. That is the case of the Alabama cavefish, *Speoplatyrhinus poulsoni*, a species catalogued as federally endangered and restricted to Key Cave in northwestern Alabama, where the total population is estimated to be fewer than 100 individuals (Kuhajda and Mayden 2001), making it one of the most endangered fish species in the world (Romero 1998b). A similar situation is occurring with the diverse aquatic crustacean fauna of Slovenia and elsewhere in Europe (Sket 1999).

5.2.3 Agriculture, cattle raising, and deforestation

Although agriculture and deforestation are activities that take place outside caves, their impact on the hypogean environment is beyond question. Water quantity and flow is affected by agriculture, generating both loss and creation of aquatic habitats, elimination or introduction of organisms, and changes in the food chains; there can be

Figure 5.2 A researcher conducting a bat guano pile study. Photo by Danté Fenolio.

dramatic transformations in the water quality owing to the introduction of agrochemicals (pesticides, herbicides, and fertilizers) which can change the trophic nature of the hypogean communities, diversity composition and abundance, and the composition of sediments (Gunn *et al.* 2000). In addition, the use of heavy machinery impacts the soil, changing the nature of the recharge areas that feed the water that these ecosystems have.

Because guano deposits can be analyzed stratigraphically (Fig. 5.2), it is possible to detect changes in agricultural practices via changes in the pollen composition in those deposits (Maher 2006). In addition, because agriculture is a more extensive activity in terms of total area, its impact on the hypogean aquatic environment can be more generalized than the effects generated by mining (Moraes *et al.* 2002).

Delivery of fecal material to sinking streams has been linked to cattle raising (Gunn *et al.* 2000). Boyer and Pasquarell (1996, 1999) found that cattle raising considerably impacted karstic waters of the Appalachian Region, USA, in the form of both increased nitrification and input of fecal bacteria. This was particularly true in dairies that did not apply best management practices to control animal wastes. Water pollution has led to the endangerment of a number of hypogean species (see, for example, Koppelman and Figg 1995).

When an epigean source of pollution is eliminated, that does not mean that the positive effects are going to be seen immediately. Rózkowski (1998) calculated that pollution caused by agriculture and industry took between 3 and 50 years to percolate from the surface to the underground waters in the Krakow Upland (southern Poland). The exact rate varied by location and depended on whether the limestone was highly permeable or covered by overburden.

5.2.4 Flooding by anthropogenic constructions

Flooding changes the entire water regime of a karstic area. The flooding can be as large as covering an entire karstic valley or as small as reservoirs in rural areas. Floods can destabilize slopes; an extreme example is the three Gorges Dam in China.

Flooding can have a detrimental effect on cave communities because flood waters can bring in exogenous species that disturb the structure of hypogean communities (Ducarme *et al.* 2004a). They also can modify the morphology of caves by infilling side passages with sediments, disrupting water flow, or by clearing out passages and connecting previously unconnected fragments of the cave (Howard and Groves 1995). Sometimes they even carry vertebrate remains to areas not originally inhabited by such fauna (Simms 1994).

Sometimes, action to prevent flooding and its consequences may not be very effective at all. For example, the Wonderfontein Valley and Spruit in South Africa is on dolomitic aquifers that have been heavily exploited since the nineteenth century during gold-mining excavations. In order to avoid flooding to the valley, large-scale de-watering of some of those aquifers was carried out. As a consequence a number of sinkholes and dolines were formed; although many of the sinkholes were refilled, they were reactivated owing to the continuous flooding (Swart *et al.* 2003).

5.2.5 Stormwater drainage

Because karsts allow rapid drainage, they have been commonly used by planners and engineers as drainage areas that not only modify the water regime but also absorb pollutants. Thus, many industries have been placed next to dolines as a convenient way to dispose of stormwater. As a result there have been serious issues with water quantity and quality in many areas of the world (see, for example, Emmett and Telfer 1994).

5.2.6 Infilling

Sinkholes are commonly filled in order to take advantage of the area for construction purposes. This limits the amount of water going into the karst, generating flooding in the adjacent surface areas. Because sometimes the sinkholes reappear after filling, this also represents a danger to constructions as there is a risk of subsequent collapse. To make things worse, the heterogeneity of karst geology structure and function is being impacted via dissolution by acidic water, making this substrate unstable in the long term. Careful studies of any karst on which construction takes place are fundamental in order to make such constructions feasible, whether the construction is a building or a road (see, for example, Nichol 1998). This includes studies of all the patterns of fracture enlargement in the karst aquifer in order to proceed with the appropriate infilling (Howard and Groves 1995). In certain parts of the world where there is frequent heavy rain, the problem is compounded by sediments generated by the erosion caused by precipitation (James 1993).

5.2.7 Dumping

Sinkholes are often used as 'natural' landfills, or landfills are built right in karstic areas. Such activities lead to heavy pollution of underground waters by substances that may include heavy metals (Gutiérrez *et al.* 2004).

5.2.8 Soils

Karstic areas do not usually have much soil on top of them. One reason is that water tends to percolate very easily and in consequence little water is retained at the surface (LaFleur 1999). This, in turn, makes soils above karstic areas very fragile; their mismanagement usually carries immediate and lasting effects.

Erosion by agriculture and deforestation

Since the Paleolithic, farming and deforestation have led to soil erosion in karstic areas of Europe (Sauro 1993). Karst areas that have been deforested show an increase in soil erosion of about 20% due to precipitation that washes out the unprotected soil (Allred 2004). Deforestation for developmental purposes is also causing serious soil erosion problems in countries such as China, leading to cases of desertification (Wang *et al.* 2004a,b). This problem is magnified in areas of karst collapse, producing sinkholes where soil erosion accelerates (Lolcama *et al.* 2002). Restoration of soil cover is possible but is labor-intensive and vulnerable to climatic fluctuations and activities by feral animals; pastoral activities must therefore be closely monitored. Some experiments along these lines have been carried out in Australia (Gillieson *et al.* 1996). The erosion of soils may continue long after deforestation and agricultural activities have ceased to take place (Midriak and Liptak 1995).

Compaction

Livestock and human use compacts the soil reducing percolation and changing the recharge dynamics of the underlying aquifer. Covelli *et al.* (1998) reported that, for Grotta Grande (Big Cave) in northern Italy, both human development and agricultural activities had permanently affected the percolation dynamics and water quality in the recharge zone of this very large karst cave, which attracts many tourist visitors.

5.2.9 Subsurface karst

Caves whose development has taken place above the level of the current water table, as well as those only partly shaped by water, have also been affected by anthropogenic factors as enumerated below. In some cases such effects are the result of direct human intervention to modify the cave itself by enlarging and/or obstructing passages to the cave, building stairs, and introducing artificial lights (Fig. 5.3). All of these interfere with the ecology of the cave by modifying the habitat of many animals and microbial biota, but it is artificial lighting that tends to create the worst problems. Artificial illumination creates the condition for photosynthesis by introduced photosynthetic organisms and may scare away some (if not all) of the original inhabitants of the cave. For example, the Slovenian brown bear (*Ursus arctos*) population, the only viable population in Central and Western Europe, prefers long caves with small entrances located more than 540 m from the closest human settlement (Petram *et al.* 2004). American black bears (*Ursus americanus*) have recolonized western Texas because of the availability of undisturbed caves that they use as dens (Mitchell *et al.* 2005).

Other vertebrates for which the use of caves is an essential part of their life cycle may be surprising: an example is the critically endangered Mediterranean monk seal (*Monachus monachus*), which uses marine caves as dens in the Mediterranean (Gucu *et al.* 2004).

Figure 5.3 The building of staircases like this one in the main entrance of Mammoth Cave disrupts the movements of biota in and out of caves. Photo by Aldemaro Romero. (See Plate 18.)

Human-induced flooding

An increasing issue in terms of conservation in karst areas is flooding of such areas during the construction and maintenance of water reservoirs for hydroelectric plants. There are numerous examples in Serbia and, increasingly, in China. Developing countries, which require more and more energy and water supply for their economic activities and increasing human population, have opted for the construction of large and numerous hydroelectric plants. This means changes in the hydrological regime of many karstic areas that lead towards inundation of caves and the destruction of their biota as well as of their archaeological and geological features (Milanovic 2002).

Structure removal

One of the most evident results of vandalism in caves is the removal of speleothems (mostly stalactites and stalagmites) from caves to be used as decorations or simply because of pointless destruction. I have personally observed this in lava caves of Hawaii where some caves have been denuded of all of their natural structures by unconscious tourists and even locals.

Mineral and sediment removal
Other removals of materials from caves include the exploitation of phosphate and nitrates (mostly for the manufacturing of gunpowder), guano (for its use as fertilizer), other minerals, and crystals, particularly in gypsum caves. This not only affects the natural beauty of caves but also disturbs their ecology by removing nutrients, disrupting surfaces, and affecting the delicate organic balance generated by microorganisms.

Floor sediment compaction/destruction
Heavy use of caves also means compaction of their soils and damage to rocky substrates, leading to the destruction of habitats for many animals.

5.3 Effects on the atmosphere of caves

Human activities in caves affect their air quality, composition, and humidity and may even lead to corrosion of their geological and cultural features.

One of the best studied cases in which tourism has impacted a cave is that of the Cueva de las Maravillas (the Cave of Marvels) in Aracena, southern Spain. According to Pulido-Bosch *et al.* (1997), this cave, which is visited by about 160,000 people a year, has seen a reduced amount of water due to pumping; increased temperature and CO_2 concentration due to breathing by humans; and decreased relative humidity and invasion of photosynthetic plants due to artificial lighting. Similar situations have been recorded in other caves visited by large numbers of people, such as Grotta Grande del Vento (Big Wind Cave) in central Italy, which receives nearly 100,000 visitors per year (Bertolani *et al.* 1991, cited in Pulido-Bosch *et al.* 1997).

Sometimes it is possible to study the effects of human visitation by researching the natural conditions in a cave before it is opened to the public. Calaforra *et al.* (2003) studied changes in cave air temperatures in the Cueva del Agua (Water Cave) de Iznalloz, Granada, southern Spain. This is a cave with great tourist potential. Because the cave had been kept closed to the public for more than 30 years previous to the study, it was possible to investigate the potential thermal impact by humans before it could be made available to tourists. These researchers studied the effects of external weather conditions and observed the thermal recovery (return to the normal temperature conditions) after two large experimental visits by tourists (980 and 2,088 visitors on two different days). They recorded how as soon as the visitors came to the cave (two and a half minutes) the temperature of the air increased, reaching a peak between 30 and 70 minutes after the visit began. After the visitors left it took between five and six hours for the air temperature to return to normal. These results show that human visitation can quickly affect air temperatures in caves, and that a cave may take a long while to recover its natural conditions after humans have left. In a way these results should not be surprising: it is known that caves with large bat colonies have higher air temperatures than those without such mammal populations.

Another important issue that must be taken into consideration is the fact that air conditions throughout caves are not homogeneous but rather composed of a number of microclimates that vary with location. Bourges *et al.* (2006) studied these differences in the limestone cave Aven d'Orgnac (The Sinkhole of Orgnac) in southern France. They found that, at the entrance of the cave, air temperature was highly correlated with the external temperature, with ventilation occurring in the winter when the colder, denser air penetrated the cave. Deeper into the cave, however, there are virtually no changes in temperature through time, basically because that temperature is directly influenced not by external air but by the large volume of rock, the temperature of which is considered constant.

Another question is whether gating has any impact on cave air temperature. Martin *et al.* (2006) studied the impact of gating with horizontal bars on the air temperature of a cave in northeastern Oklahoma in both summer and winter. They found that such an impact was minimal and without effects on the endemic fauna.

Sometimes it is not the temperature alone that causes problems in the cave but also the humidity generated by the presence of humans, even when that presence is minimal. Fernández-Cortes *et al.* (2006b) studied the impact of human visitation on the microclimate processes of a mine, El Geodo de Pulpí (Geode of Pulpí) in Almería, southern Spain, and found a significant impact of condensation on the surface of the gypsum crystals as a result of increased temperature and water vapor caused by human breathing. Visits of as few as two or three people for longer than 10 min could lead to corrosion of the crystals. Such effects could be long-lasting: these researchers found that the total recovery time required to resume the initial natural thermal and humidity conditions after a visit of this type was 27 h.

Slow air circulation also causes rapid rises in concentrations of CO_2 generated by human visitors. This lack of appropriate oxygen for breathing may impact both cave animal populations and humans, especially when visiting the cave in large numbers (Fernandez-Cortes *et al.* 2006a). Glowworms in New Zealand began declining when a new entrance was opened, leading to desiccation (Bowie *et al.* 2006).

5.4 Hydrology

The list of anthropogenic effects on the hydrology of karstic areas in general and on caves in particular is a long and growing one. As mentioned earlier, environmental effects on caves are not only the results of direct human contact inside the caves but also of what humans do around the caves. They include not only effects on the quantity and quality of water (the latter due to the influence of agrochemicals, industrial waste, and oil pollution), but also organic pollution by human and animal wastes (mostly through sewage) in springs, which leads to algal blooms (see, for example, Bartsch and Tittley 2004). Others include accidental spills of hazardous materials, oil and/or gas exploration/exploitation, and intentional dumping of hazardous waste into sinkholes and sinking streams. There have also been documented cases of sedimentation and runoff as a consequence of farming and mining activities, logging and/or deforestation, and road and building construction (urbanization) as well as runoff and erosion from rainfall.

During these processes a number of chemicals come into contact with the soil; because of the highly permeable nature of limestone, the most common geology around caves, those chemicals percolate until they reach both the groundwater and the caves themselves. Agents causing this type of pollution include, but are not limited to, fecal bacteria, organics from manure, septic leachate, sewage sludge, sediment, and toxic concentrations of metals (see, for example, Graening and Brown 2003) (Fig. 5.4).

In terms of water quantity, changes in the hydrological regime can occur due to impoundments, quarrying, and the digging of wells and/or water extraction. The most significant pressure is created by pumping water out of the phreatic zones (or even from the caves themselves) to be used to supply newly urbanized areas or for agriculture. Excessive extraction of underground water, for example, severs the links with epigean ecosystems and with other aquifers, affecting species distribution and abundance (Hancock *et al.* 2005).

To make things worse, because of the increasing demands for fresh water in coastal areas, wells are pumping out fresh water, which is replaced by saline water from the sea. This is creating a crisis of water quality in

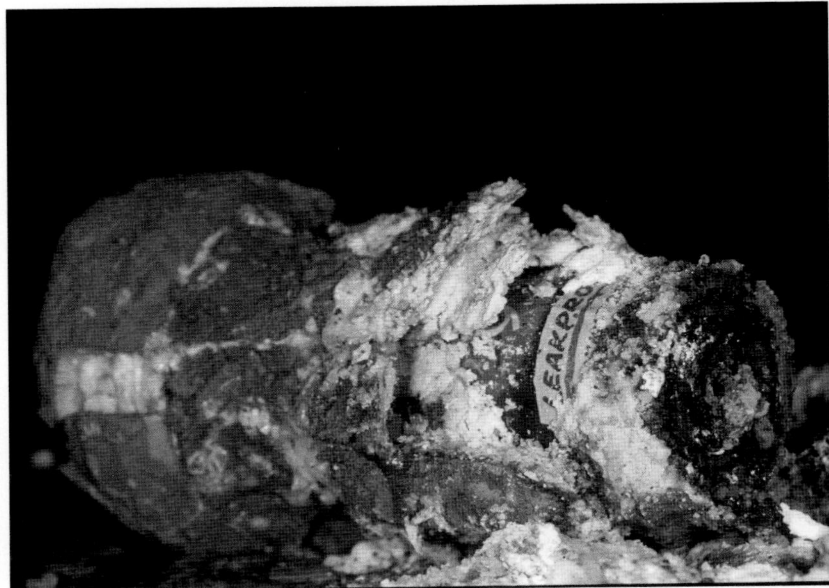

Figure 5.4 An old battery in Cottonwood Cave, Sequoia Co. The disposal of refuse that contains heavy metal represents a serious danger to the ecology of caves, given that they have very little capacity to recycle pollutants. Photo by Danté Fenolio. (See Plate 19.)

many coastal regions of the world, which are usually the ones with the largest population densities (for a more detailed synthesis of these problems, see Danielopol *et al.* 2003).

Sometimes these anthropogenic effects are gradual and slowly mounting; sometimes they occur in the form of a sudden catastrophe. In November 1981 about 80,000 l of liquid ammonium nitrate and urea fertilizer was spilled at a pipeline break near Dry Fork Creek in the recharge area for Maramec Spring, Missouri, USA. Seven days following the break, dissolved oxygen at Maramec Spring, 21 km from the break site, dropped to less than 1 mg l^{-1} for nine days, resulting in a loss of over 37,000 fish. The concentration of ammonia and nitrate nitrogen remained elevated in the spring for more than 38 days. Among the hypogean organisms killed were 10,000 individuals of the rare Salem cave crayfish *Cambarus hubrichti* and about 1,000 individuals of the southern cavefish *Typhlichthys subterraneus* (Crunkilton 1984).

When caves are located on islands, as is the case for many anchialine caves with their unique fauna, problems are magnified owing to small island size and high population density. That is the case on Bermuda, where organic pollutants have been detected since the 1980s (Illiffe and Jickells 1984). There, as in many other caves, the list of pollutants of epigean origin is a long one: heavy metals (mercury, cadmium, lead), organics (toluene, benzene, and vinyl chloride from mining and other industrial operations), agrochemicals, fossil fuels, sewage of human and animal origin, solid wastes, mineral alloys, and paints. New developments can make things even worse for those anchialine caves in Bermuda where plans to build golf courses are threatening the habitat of the endemic copepod *Speleophria bivexilla* (Knight 1997).

Unfortunately, as can be seen by some of the examples mentioned above, in most cases there is not just a single threat to caves from changes in water quantity and quality but a combination of several factors (see, for example, Gunn *et al.* 2000).

5.5 Effects on the biota

Needless to say, the above-mentioned factors not only impact the physico-chemical features of caves but, more importantly, their biodiversity. This phenomenon has now been widely documented.

Because the Marine Biology Station of Naples, Italy (founded in 1872), became an active field site so long ago, data collected over more than a century has yielded revealing historical information on changes of biodiversity in nearby marine caves. Essentially, species of mysid crustacean have disappeared from the more urbanized areas and are now found only in the less urbanized, insular ones (Wittmann 2001). However, sometimes it is not necessary to go so far back in time to notice changes: water quality deteriorated in less than 20 years (1983–2002) sufficiently to endanger the survival of the Benton cave crayfish (*Cambarus aculabrum*) in several caves in Arkansas, USA, owing to septic system discharge and runoff from animal feeding operations (Graening *et al.* 2006b). Even changes in vegetation in the areas surrounding caves does affect water balance in caves, as has been found in Australia (Humphreys 2006). Koppelman and Figg (1995) and Verovnik *et al.* (2003) found that hypogean populations of crustaceans that show low genetic variability may be the result of pollution affecting the population size.

Petit *et al.* (2006) surveyed the bat populations of Curaçao, Netherlands Antilles, between 1993 and 2003 and found significantly fewer individuals of a wide range of species. These authors pointed out major disturbances in caves as the cause of population depletion and even imminent extinction of some of the local species, with cascading effects on the local ecology due to the fact that some of those bat species are pollinators.

One factor little studied is the introduction of foreign biological agents such as bacteria and fungi when humans visit a cave. The major problem with studying this is that in order to make sure that this type of biota can be compared before and after human visitation, it is necessary to find caves that have never been explored by humans before, such as caves discovered during excavations or as a result of ceiling collapse. The caves then have to be explored by properly trained personnel in sterile clothing, to collect samples before any casual visit may be made to the cave. Obviously these conditions are extremely difficult to meet.

Removal of vegetation from areas surrounding caves may have a detrimental effect on the cave fauna itself. In addition to the effects on bat populations reported above, vegetation removal can also have a detrimental effect on invertebrates. Taylor *et al.* (2005) found that cave crickets (*Ceuthophilus* spp.) from Big Red Cave in Texas travel during the night as far as 105 m outside the cave to forage on grass, leaf litter, and herbaceous vegetation. Since many cave terrestrial invertebrate species are considered endangered, that means that the protection of the cave itself is not enough to ensure their survival; there is also a need to protect the surrounding areas (Culver *et al.* 2000).

Another issue directly affecting the biota of caves is the overcollecting of organisms. As mentioned earlier, population numbers of cave biota, particularly vertebrates in temperate regions, tend to be small and, thus, collecting can seriously affect their ecological health. Most of the threats come from commercial utilization of cave species.

For example, the swiftlet (*Collocalia fuciphaga*) is eaten by the locals of the Andaman and Nicobar Islands, in the Gulf of Bengal, India. In fact they are considered of high economic value. Sankaran (2001) found that the population of this bird on those islands had been reduced by more than 80% in 10 years in 322 caves. It seems that the only hope to save this species is by ex-situ breeding, as in the experimental farm for them that has been established in Indonesia.

Other vertebrates have been the subject of overcollection, such as the Ozark cavefish (*Amblyopsis rosae*) in Arkansas, USA (Romero 1998b). Because part of the problem is collection for scientific purposes, some researchers have been developing a number of non-lethal techniques that allow the collection of information on cave species without having to impact their populations (see, for example, Bowie *et al.* 2006).

Caves are also a magnificent repository of information about past biodiversity for particular areas. Burney *et al.* (2001) discovered a cave on the south coast of Kaua'i in the Hawaiian Islands through coring and excavations in a large sinkhole. There they found a remarkably well preserved diversity of plant and animal remains, ranging from diatoms to vertebrates that pre-dated the human habitation of those islands. What they encountered was evidence of highly diverse pre-human ecological conditions in the Hawaiian lowlands, conditions that changed profoundly through the decline or extirpation of most native species and their replacement with introduced ones. The fossils included undescribed extinct species of snail as well as records of deforestation, overgrazing, and soil erosion. Among the species introduced by Polynesians was the Pacific rat (*Rattus exulans*) more than 800 years ago. Similar examples of caves as historical museums of past biodiversity have been reported for New Zealand (Clark *et al.* 1996) and Europe (Vigne and Valladas 1996).

5.5.1 Bats as ecological indicators of the environmental health of caves

Many species of bat use caves and mines extensively as nursery roosts, swarming sites, and hibernacula. Thus, it is not surprising that bats represent one of the best indicators of the health of caves. Furthermore, bats depend upon food resources found in areas surrounding caves while bringing into the caves the by-product of that food in the form of guano (Fig. 5.5).

To get a full picture of the importance of bats as ecological indicators, we need to look at their conservation status as a whole. There are 1,001 species of bat, all of which are grouped within the order Chiroptera. This is the second most diverse mammal group (after Rodentia), accounting for about 20% of all mammalian species.

Something that is very interesting is the apparent ease with which bat populations, isolated in underground environments, can give rise to new species. Molecular work in mines, for example, suggests that such environments can give rise to new species in a relatively short period of time (Armstrong 2006). The inference that can be drawn is that one of the reasons that the order Chiroptera is so diverse is that caves cause population isolation, which, in turn, leads to speciation. In fact, there seems to be a positive correlation between the number of caves in an area and the number and abundance of bat species (see, for example, O'Malley *et al.* 2006).

Figure 5.5 Mexican free-tailed bats leaving a cave in Oklahoma at dusk. Photo by Danté Fenolio. (See Plate 20.)

One type of behavior that seems to accentuate population isolation is the fact that at least some species of bat show a great deal of site fidelity (Weyandt *et al.* 2005). This presents a conservation challenge: attempts to have bats recolonize caves after the local population has been extirpated may be a task more difficult than originally imagined.

Many species of bats have been severely impacted by humans: 12 bat species have become extinct in the past 500 years, 238 are threatened according to the IUCN (International Union for the Conservation of Nature) and about the same number are considered to be facing one or another environmental problem. Probably the most important threat to bat survival is the loss or modification of foraging habitats and roost localities (Mickleburgh *et al.* 2002).

Caves and abandoned mines represent one of the most important habitats for bats. For example, 60 of the 134 Mexican species of bat regularly roost in caves (Arita 1993) and the world's largest bat colony is found in Bracken Cave, Texas, USA, which contains nearly 20,000,000 individuals (McCracken 1986).

The same caves can be used by many species of bat (see, for example, Arita 1996) and most caves in areas where there are several species of bat are inhabited by more than one species. The more diverse the cave is in terms of microhabitats, the more diverse the bat species composition is (Brunet and Medellin 2001). Furthermore, bat diversity and population sizes per cave can also fluctuate with the different seasons (Furman and Ozgul 2002; Parsons *et al.* 2003; Galindo *et al.* 2004). Bats in caves can be found from near the entrance to the deepest areas although they tend to avoid being within 30 m of the entrance (Arita and Vargas 1995; O'Donnell 2002).

Sometimes anthropogenic effects can be significant even when no apparent physical modification to the cave has taken place. Mann *et al.* (2002) found that even cave tours can have a negative effect on bat populations. They studied the behavioral responses of a maternity colony of about 1,000 cave myotis (*Myotis velifer*) in the Kartchner Caverns in southeastern Arizona, USA, by experimentally exposing those roosting colonies to cave tours; they found that light intensity and noise produced increased bat activity (number of takeoffs, landing, vocalization intensity) which can be detrimental to breeding colonies.

In order to protect bats from anthropogenic disturbances, many cave entrances have been protected by using horizontal steel bars (see, for example, Hsu 1997) which in theory should allow bats to fly in and out of the cave while keeping human intruders away. However, the effectiveness of such gates has been controversial (Fig. 5.6).

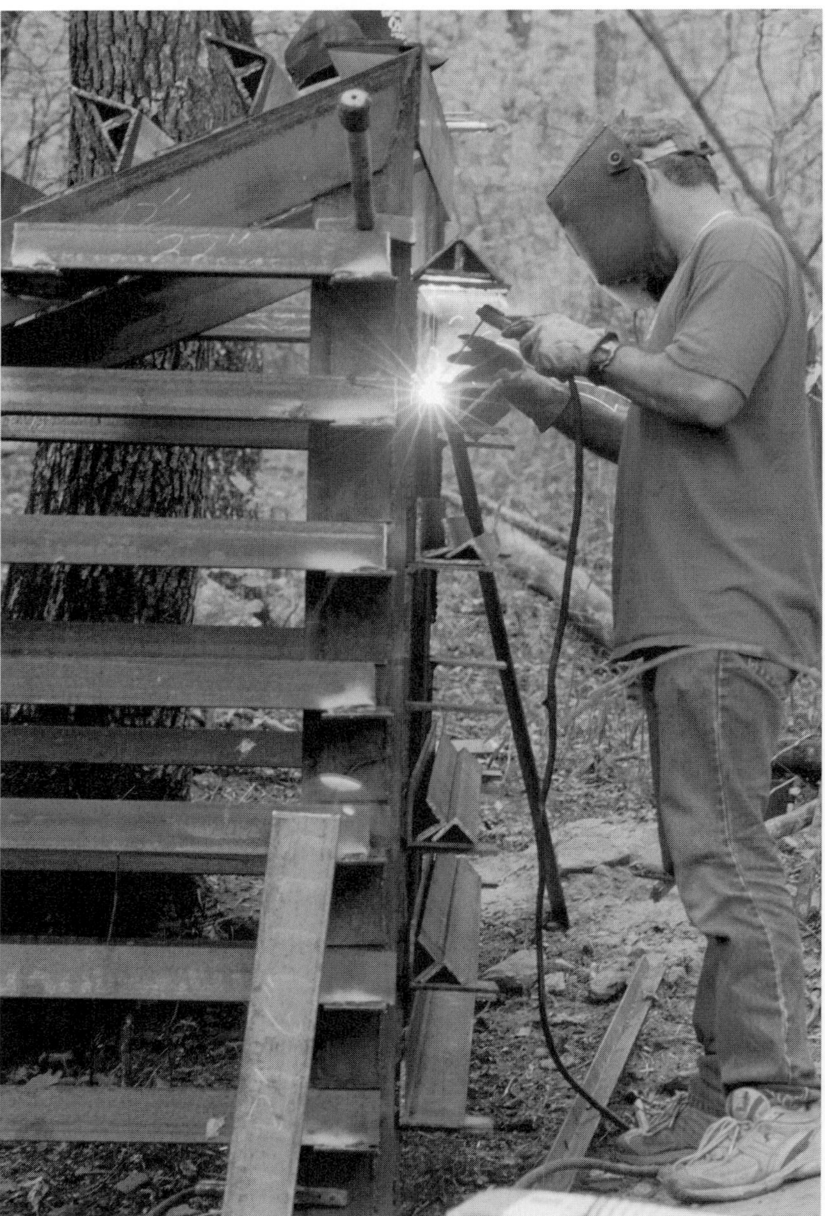

Figure 5.6 Building a bat gate above a sink opening. Photo by Danté Fenolio. (See Plate 21.)

Ludlow and Gore (2000) studied the impact of such gates on the emergence patterns of two species of bat: the southeastern myotis (*Myotis austroriparius*) and the gray bat (*M. grisescens*) at Old Indian Cave in northern Florida, USA. These authors counted the number of emerging bats at a gated entrance and an open entrance on a monthly basis for one year before and one year after the gate was removed. They found statistically significant differences in the number of bats emerging from the entrance with bars after the bars were removed: before the removal of the gate, 7.8% of the bats used the gated entrance but after the bars were removed 47.9% did so. This is interesting because it shows that removal of steel-bar gates can affect emergence patterns of two different species of bat even if another ungated entrance is available. Since bats play such a major role in cave ecology it has been recommended to use perimeter fencing as an alternative to steel-bar gates at caves where trespassing and vandalism are not chronic problems.

On the other hand Martin *et al.* (2003) reported a study of 25 cave entrances in northeastern Oklahoma, USA in which they assessed the impact of those gates on colonies of endangered gray bats (*Myotis grisescens*) from 1981 to 2001. These authors found a statistically significant increase in the number of gray bats, from 60,130 in 1981 to 70,640 in 2001. They also compared initiations of emergences at three gated and three open-passage caves in June and July 1999–2000 and found no significant differences in timing of initiation of emergence between colonies in gated versus open-passage caves.

Spanjer and Fenton (2005) measured the behavioral responses (flight speeds, flight behavior, and vocalizations) of bats at 28 caves and mines (16 with and 12 without gates) from Ontario to Tennessee, USA. They found that bats always circled and retreated more often and passed directly through less often at gates. Furthermore, the smaller the gate size, the more fly–retreat and circling behavior occurred. This led them to conclude that in order to minimize the impact of gates on bats, gates should be built in larger areas, with a larger opening on the top of the gate, be placed on flat profiles instead of inclines, and be erected gradually so the bats could grow accustomed to them. Furthermore, Pugh and Altringham (2005), based on experimental studies, calculated that the minimum spacing between horizontal bars in gates should be 15 cm.

Of course caves cannot be seen as totally isolated islands and that is particularly true in the case of species that move in and out of caves, such as bats. Conservation of adjacent areas is essential; even ecological corridors have been proposed to ensure that these species can access their feeding areas (Stoner *et al.* 2003). Some bat species depend upon a particular non-cave food source to survive. In the Mexican state of Nuevo León, colonies of the Mexican long-nosed bat (*Leptonycteris nivalis*), which is nectarivorous, are heavily dependent on the availability of blooming agaves (*Agave* spp.) (Moreno-Valdez *et al.* 2004).

Another example is that of the nectar-feeding bat *Leptonycteris curasoae*, which depends upon the availability of flowers and fruits of columnar cacti. These bats roost in nearby caves. Increasing deforestation in the area is placing this species in danger of imminent extinction (Penalba *et al.* 2006).

Another example of how pollution outside caves can affect bats roosting in the hypogean environment is that of bats found dead in caves. A study was made of gray bats (*Myotis grisescens*), an endangered species. Analyses showed that their bodies had lethal levels of dieldrin and heptachlor (Clark *et al.* 1978, 1980, 1983). Sometimes it is possible to trace a pollutant directly to its source. In Australia high concentrations of organochlorines and certain metals in the southern bent-wing bat (*Miniopterus schreibersii bassanii*) at Bat Cave have been attributed to insecticides that have been bioaccumulated by these insect-feeding bats (Allinson *et al.* 2006).

5.6 Cultural heritage

Caves represent not only a showcase of biodiversity but also a repository of human history. However, much of that history is being endangered owing to multiple causes, which include illegal collection of artifacts, vandalism, and many of the physical and chemical factors mentioned earlier. Lighting, for example, degrades caves by corroding and degrading artwork on their walls (Mangin *et al.* 1999). However, these effects are not only caused by chemicals and physical factors but also by bacteria (Schabereiter-Gurtner *et al.* 2002), as has been found on the famous paintings in the Altamira Cave in Spain.

5.7 Climate change

Climate change (through either variations in the precipitation regimes or direct impact on water temperature) represents another threat to the cave biota. Chevaldonné and Lejeune (2003) reported that in some caves of the French Mediterranean, *Hemimysis speluncola*, a species of mysid crustacean typical of colder waters, now has a much more restricted distribution due to progressive warming while being replaced by its congener *H. margalefi*, which shows a much wider tolerance to warmer waters.

The genetic response of species to climate change has been studied by using molecular approaches on organisms that were around when the last major climate changes took place. Hadly *et al.* (2004) reported their studies on genetic population and population size variations on two geographically widespread rodent species (*Microtus montanus* and *Thomomys talpoides*) during late Holocene (2,500–1,000 YBP) climatic change. They used ancient DNA to compare two independent estimates of population size (ecological and genetic) and corroborated their results with gene diversity and serial coalescent simulations. Their study suggested that those climate changes resulted in population size decrease, which, in turn, produced (in some cases) declining genetic diversity. This declining diversity would place those populations in an even more precarious position by making them more vulnerable to epidemics or other environmental factors.

5.8 Legal protection

A number of countries, states, and provinces around the world have moved to create a legal framework to protect caves and their associated environments. The first state cave protection act passed in the United States was that of Colorado in 1883 (although it was repealed in 1971). Now about half of the states of that country have state laws that protect the caves. The federal government has also enacted legislation in that regard. The most important of these laws is the Federal Cave Resources Protection Act of 1988, which directs cave conservation for many federal land management agencies. Other laws, such as The Endangered Species Act of 1973 and the Federal Archaeological Resources Protection Act of 1976, have broad applicability to the conservation of cave resources on federal lands and elsewhere. However, there is still the problem of enforcement, which in many instances is weak (Huppert 1995).

In the United Kingdom a number of caves have been designated as Sites of Special Scientific Interest (SSSI), and the Wildlife and Countryside Act 1981 was enacted for the planning and management of natural areas of human activities carried out within SSSI boundaries. Both of these legal actions have had a positive impact on the protection of caves in that country (Hardwick and Gunn 1996).

5.9 Conclusions

Based on all the information provided in this chapter, it is clear that the monitoring of the hypogean environment requires comprehensive, detailed, and constant study to really understand the dynamics of these habitats, which greatly vary depending upon size, structure, and geographic location. Some specific recommendations have been produced (see, for example, Watson *et al.* 1997). Yet there is much to learn before specific procedures for each case can be agreed. It seems that the appropriate management of each cave, particularly when the goal is to balance the conservation of its resources and its utilization, as is the case for tourism, will require not only constant monitoring but also baseline information about the ecological parameters of those caves before they start to be utilized in any significant way. And that is, for the most part, impossible.

6 · *Epilogue*

With young researchers in mind, this book ends with a summary of some of the unanswered questions in biospeleology.

6.1 The role played by behavior in the evolution of cave organisms

It is commonly assumed that behavior plays a major role in the colonization of new niches, since behavior is the most plastic part of the phenotype. Although changes in behavior are well documented and present even in transitional forms (Romero 1984a), the role of behavior in the changes in other phenotypic characters is unknown. Behavioral changes usually precede external morphological evolution (Mayr 1982; Wcislo 1989; McPeek 1995). Behavioral plasticity thus enables animals to compensate for morphological and physiological changes generated by genetic changes; after all, individual adaptability is the main object of selection (Wright 1931). Behavioral invasion of a new environment by adults exposes the reaction norm of their progeny. Since hormonal production is closely linked to behavior and hormones play a role in many developmental processes, there is a great potential for hormones to produce (or act as) developmental constraints (Hayes 1997). Therefore, the arrest in development of features could be due to diminishing hormonal production as a physiological consequence of adaptation to the hypogean environment (i.e. many behaviors are no longer performed under conditions of darkness). This, in turn, could lead to the differential regulation of developmental genes.

6.2 Integrative molecular genetics

The importance of understanding how behavior-mediated hormonal production affects the phenotype is rooted at the molecular level of genetics. It is known that hormones can shape the organism in response to its genetic programming as well as carrying information from environmental receptors, thus, triggering a genotype-specific reaction that develops into phenotypic plasticity. This means that there are specific short upstream sequences that regulate the response of genes to a variety of environmental signals and limit gene transcription to specific organs or tissues. So the question is, what are the molecular mechanisms for silencing, or in other words for the reduction and/or loss of, morphologic features? An assortment of proteins and, sometimes, RNAs, pull the strings, telling the genes when and where to turn on or off. Gene activity is influenced by the proteins that package the DNA into chromatin and by enzymes that modify both those proteins and the DNA itself. The chromatin-modifying enzymes are now considered the 'master puppeteer' of gene expression. Epigenetic changes can enable cells to respond to environmental signals conveyed by hormones, growth factors, and other regulatory molecules without having to alter the DNA itself. Thus, patterns of gene expression, not genes themselves, define each cell type. That is what Yamamoto and Jeffery (2000) found when they transplanted the lens of the eye of an embryo of an epigean *A. fasciatus* into the optic cup of a cave fish, resulting in the restoration of optic tissues that otherwise would not have been expressed in the troglomorphic form. Conversely, eye growth and development were retarded after transplantation of a cave fish lens into an epigean fish optic cup or lens extirpation. These results showed that evolutionary changes in an inductive signal from the lens are involved in cave fish eye degeneration. This is interesting because it shows that changing the internal environment of an organ while development takes place can have a major influence on how that organ is shaped. But if the optic tissues in the troglomorphic *A. fasciatus* could be restored, would that change the behavioral visual responses of a fish that otherwise would be blind?

Romero *et al.* (2001) and Romero and Green (2005) explored this issue by examining phototactic behavior in epigean and troglomorphic forms of *A. fasciatus* whose eyes were modified during embryogenesis by removing one or both lens vesicles from the epigean form or by transplanting the lens vesicle from an epigean fish into the optic cup of a blind cave form. As mentioned earlier, lens removal results in eye degeneration and blindness in adult epigean fish, whereas lens transplantation stimulates growth of the eye, inducing the development of optic tissues in the normally eyeless adult cave fish. It was shown that epigean fish with a degenerate eye and cave fish with an induced eye both develop retinotectal projections but that the size of their optic tectum is essentially unaffected. Fish photoresponsiveness was examined by placing fish in an aquarium with one half illuminated and the other half dark, and scoring their presence in the illuminated or the dark half. Both the eyeless epigean fish and the cave fish with induced eyes appeared to be indifferent to the illumination, whereas the surface forms were scotophilic, suggesting that optic development and phototactic behavior can be experimentally decoupled.

These combinations of studies clearly show that the only way to begin to understand some basic questions in evolutionary biology is via interdisciplinary approaches rather than through purely reductionist views.

6.3 Trophic structure of caves

It is amazing how little is known about the ecology of caves in general, particularly when it comes to their trophic structure. This might be the result of the old concept of caves as 'poor' from an ecological viewpoint. However, in the present author's view, once researchers start looking at caves from the point of view of energy transfer (including energy from the epigean environment), their views of caves as habitats will be profoundly modified.

Another question is: what kinds of constraint does the hypogean environment impose on the evolution of cave organisms? In other words, how is it possible to decipher the interplay of lack of light and other factors affecting specific hypogean conditions, upon different groups of organisms, their genetic makeup, and their phenotypic responses?

6.4 Other biological questions

There is a need for a better understanding of the functional architecture of cave organisms, i.e. the set of pathways that clarifies the relationship between genotypes and phenotypes. It should be remembered that most character differentiation arises late in development, and that is why most phenotypic differentiation is the result of genetic differentiation at the developmental level, not purely structural. This is why the reduction and/or loss of structure can occur so rapidly in evolutionary terms.

Some (if not all) phenotypic characters are expressed at irregular intervals (after disappearing for portions of a life cycle, they reappear in subsequent generations). Therefore they are 'polyphyletic' with respect to cell lineages, and their phylogenetic continuity may be partly independent of any continuity at the level of particular genes, or any repetition of particular patterns of gene expression (Roth 2001, p. 105). Is this why there are so many morphotypes among some cave species? After all, phenotypic variance is directly correlated with environmental variance, and environmental variance is usually higher than can be observed in a single period of time, especially on evolutionary time scales. Maybe what is being observed is an interaction among three factors: environmental variance, mutations with major developmental effects, and phenotypic plasticity. If this is the case, how does the interaction work?

Many underground environments (including caves) show high levels of the radioactive gas radon (see, for example, Gillmore *et al.* 2000). Do these levels that influence the rate of mutation among hypogean organisms?

Of course the problem with all this is that, as bizarre as troglomorphic organisms may look, they are the product of the same biological phenomenon found elsewhere: parasites are highly simplified yet very successful organisms in the history of life. For example, there are parasitic plants characterized by the loss of chlorophyll; many birds and insects living on islands and/or high mountains are limbless and/or flightless (Darlington 1943; Byers 1969; Livezey and Humphrey 1986; Roff 1990; Finston and Peck 1995); many fishes and dolphins living in the murky waters of tropical rivers have reduced pigmentation and eyes, as do many species living in abyssal waters; snakes have lost their ancestral legs and cetaceans have had their ancestral limbs highly reduced; further, there is nothing among the terrestrial ancestors (the mesonychids) of cetaceans to indicate that they were 'preadapted' to their colonization of the aquatic environment (which was one of the most remarkable evolutionary transitions in the history of life and the adaptations to which have been attributed to neoteny as well; Sedmera *et al.* 1997). Despite all this, it is doubtful whether anyone would be taken seriously who used cetaceans as an example of 'regressive evolution', given the sophisticated acoustic abilities and social structure in many species. Those who have explored the notion of an arrow in evolutionary time, which is not the same as a time arrow in ecology, have dismissed it. As Maynard Smith put it (1970, p. 271): 'If there is a 'law of complexity', it refers not to a single species (. . .) but to the ecosystem as a whole. The complexity of the most complex species may increase, but not all species become more complex.'

Furthermore, take the example of humans: according to Diamond and Stermer (1999) the features reduced or lost in modern humans from their immediate ancestors include loss of the tail, loss of body hair, loss of the ability to synthesize vitamin C, and reductions in the size of teeth, the size of the vermiform appendix, the thickness of the skull, and in the thickness of the bony brow ridges. Are humans the product of 'regressive evolution'? Nonsense. What is more, biospeleologists who use the term 'regressive evolution' always have trouble answering the question of regressive to where (see Romero 1985b for discussion of these semantic issues).

The sad part of this controversy is that modern explanations have already been offered in the past to describe the evolution of troglomorphisms. Dobzhansky (1970, pp. 405–7) did an excellent job summarizing some of the major concepts regarding this phenomenon. In his very brief but illuminating discussion on phenotypic reductions, he clearly established that: (i) evolution is opportunistic, (ii) adaptation to a new environment may decrease the importance of some organs/functions, which may become vestigial and disappear, (iii) there are numerous examples of rudimentations/losses of organs among both animals and plants, (iv) acquisition/enlargement of organs can occur among organisms that otherwise show 'regressions' for other organs/functions, (v) cave animals provide some of the best examples of this phenomenon but they are not the only ones (some cave organisms do not display regressions and regressions may be found among non-cave animals), (vi) there is a great deal of variation among these characters even within the same species/population, and (vii) both genes and phenotypic plasticity are responsible for troglomorphic characters.

Therefore, this book is not saying anything essentially new; it is simply an attempt to reconcile the facts with modern evolutionary biology while staying away, as far as humanly possible, from philosophical theories that predispose to a biased view of life. If nothing else, one can learn from the evolution of hypogean fishes that such evolution, as indeed is all evolution, is opportunistic (Romero 2001a). No wonder life is ubiquitous on Earth, as is being shown by studying extremophiles (see, for example, Kristjánsson and Hreggvidsson 1995; Horikoshi and Grant 1998). The ability of life to succeed under such a variety of environments has led some to predict the presence of life on many other planets, including those in this solar system (Nealson and Conrad 1999). Curiously, it has been hypothesized that if life exists on some other planet or planetoid, it will probably be in a non-light-based environment, such as the ones found on Earth in hydrothermal vents or sulfur-based caves (Santini and Galleni 2001).

As George Gaylord Simpson (1949, p. 160), another of the architects of the Modern Synthesis, put it: 'The course of evolution follows opportunity rather than plan.' Opportunism as a biological phenomenon is not just another philosophical idea but a well established fact. There is empirical evidence in the literature that shows that opportunistic evolution can take advantage of a previous condition (Andersson 1990), to fill empty adaptive zones (Bronson 1979; Benton 1983; Harries *et al.* 1996), for feeding (Jaksĭć and Braker 1983), breeding (Tindle 1984), and for social behavior (McKenna 1979). Opportunism has been proven to lead to mutualism (Fiedler 2001), intraspecific parasitism (Tinsley 1990; Field 1992), and reproduction (Kasyanov *et al.* 1997). Opportunism has been described as a major factor for colonizing species (Martin and Braga 1994) and as a major factor in colonizing extreme environments (Tunnicliffe 1991). There is a correlation between behavioral plasticity and opportunism (Brown 1990; Werdelin and Asa Fortelius 1999; Johnson 2000). Lefebvre *et al.* (1997) found links between opportunism and phenotypic evolution and stated that innovation rate in the field may be a useful measure of behavioral plasticity. Opportunism has even been described at the molecular level (Doolittle 1988; Meléndez-Hevia *et al.* 1996; Green 2001). Therefore, opportunism is probably much more important in natural systems than is generally appreciated (Berry 1989). Some have even defined evolution as a by-product of disrupted communities in which momentary opportunities for divergence are created (Dimichele *et al.* 1987).

Therefore, the evolution of hypogean fauna must be considered as a natural phenomenon in biology, which is driven by opportunism and processed by phenotypic plasticity. The question is: is it possible to test for opportunism?

6.5 Concluding questions for historians, philosophers, and sociologists of science

Finally, this book addresses some questions for historians, philosophers, and sociologists of science. A baffling question about the evolutionary biology of hypogean organisms is why so many researchers are attracted to ideas of directional evolution of cave faunas by calling the process of loss of, for example, eyes and pigmentation, 'regressive evolution.' Why consider cave fish species to be relatively fixed in time and space? Further, why did these orthogenic ideas of evolution have to be justified by the notion of 'preadaptation'? Why was the colonization of the cave environment seen as an 'accidental, tough luck' scenario? In other words, why this finalistic view of life?

This may be the result of the long history of determinism in the development of biology. Determinism is an idea that may have a place in physics, but not in biology, particularly when one attributes change to natural selection, with its emphasis on the chance nature of variation (Berry 1989).

Why is there such a tendency among humans to see the universe as a pre-programmed entity? Even Darwin held some orthogenetic ideas early on (Herbert 1977, pp. 199–200). These ideas have been very popular among anthropologists, especially paleoanthropologists (White 1959). However, the supposed mechanisms behind this alleged 'direction' were always vague and filled with a mystical aura. Lull (1921), for example, just talked about an internal driving force. George Gaylord Simpson (1944) had an ambiguous position regarding orthoselection, linearity, or trends. Supporters of orthogenetic explanations were troubled by the idea of the reversal of the process of evolution away from supposed 'perfection'. Such reversals were epitomized by troglomorphic organisms, therefore, whose form must be due to 'regressive' evolution.

Maybe humans are hard-wired against the idea that there is no purpose in nature. However, that seems to be a question for evolutionary psychologists beyond the scope of this book. Still, in the present author's view, many classical biospeleologists are unable to distinguish metaphor and metaphysics from science.

Appendix 1

Glossary of terms frequently used in biospeleology

Some of these terms are purely geological in origin, but they are also employed by biologists. References to the Oxford English Dictionary (OED) are for its electronic edition as per June 2008. Terms in bold within a definition are explained elsewhere in this appendix.

accidental An organism that is rarely found in caves, and when found there, it is not because the organism is making any real use of the habitat. Notice that this is a very ad hoc definition: in theory, when an individual of a species that later may become a permanent inhabitant of caves first enters a cave, it could also be called an 'accidental.' This term was introduced in biospeleology by Schiner (1854) and it was later replaced by the term **trogloxene** by Racovitza (1907). 'Accidental' as a term is still utilized, probably as a consequence of applying the terminology of the five classes of association used by the Braun-Blanquet (1928) school of phytosociology (also known as the Zürich–Montpellier School) in the description and classification of plant communities. To Braun-Blanquet, accidentals were rare species in a community, present as chance invaders from another community.

aeolian caves Caves formed by wind erosion. Caves of this type tend to be short in length. They can be found in coastal areas of Oregon State (USA), the American Southwest, the Canary Islands, southern Africa, Israel, and Tasmania.

amphibites Species that require both surface and hypogean waters in order to fulfill their life cycles. This is a term rarely used in biospeleology.

anastomotic caves Caves with a series of tubes that sometimes intersect with each other many times, forming a complex grid with a three-dimensional structure; also known as maze caves. One classic example is Crystal Cave, southern Sierra Nevada, California.

anchi(h)aline This term refers to aquatic habitats with a restricted exposure to open air, with one or more non-surface connections to the sea; they are thus influenced by both the marine and the terrestrial ecosystems with which they interface. They are common in volcanic or limestone bedrock. Since the 1980s, 1 new class, 3 new orders, 7 new families, 75 new genera, and more than 300 species (mostly crustaceans) have been described from anchialine habitats around the world. This term was introduced by Holthuis (1973) and later redefined (Stock *et al.* 1986). Riedl (1966) called such habitats *Randhoelen* or marginal caves.

aquifer A body of permeable rock (e.g. unconsolidated gravel or a sand stratum) that is capable of storing significant quantities of water, that is underlain by impermeable material and through which groundwater moves. Aquifers are permeable enough to transmit groundwater, yielding such waters to wells and springs (see **artesian**). This term has been used since at least 1901 (Todd 1901).

artesian Originally describing wells made in the French province of Artois in the eighteenth century, such that a perpendicular boring into a synclinal fold or basin of the strata produced a constant supply of water rising spontaneously to the surface of the ground. Thus, it is applied to water obtainable by artesian boring. This term is frequently used interchangeably with **phreatic**. Charles Lyell popularized the term in his 1830–3 *Principles of Geology*.

aven A hole in a cave roof. It is the same as a shaft seen from above.

biofilm A thin layer of microorganisms covering a hard substrate. This term became popular among the microbiological community in the 1980s.

biospeleology The study of life in caves and other underground environments except for **interstitial** ones and the **meiofauna**. It also applies to the recreational exploration of caves. This term was coined by Armand Viré (as 'biospeleologie') in 1904.

blue hole A shaft-like depression flooded with abundant sea water. Blue holes are usually found on coral islands. This term is employed in the

Bahamas to designate **sinkholes** from which cooler water rises during the high tide, and in Belize, Jamaica, Florida, and the Red Sea for water resurgences. The deepest one is the Dean's Blue Hole of the Bahamas, which is about 320 m in depth (Wilson 1994). The blue color is due to the presence of algae in the water (see Dill *et al.* 1998; Huys and Iliffe 1998; Fosshagen and Iliffe 2003).

breakdown Rock material, found mostly on cave floors, that is the product of ceiling collapses.

cave A natural underground or underwater hollow place with an opening that is more or less horizontal. For cavers, a cave is any natural hole, vertical (also known as potholes), horizontal, or a combination of both, which can be penetrated by humans. This definition does not include mines or tunnels or any other cavity of anthropogenic origin. Depending upon their geologic origin, caves can be classified as limestone, sandstone, hydrothermal, lava, glacier, or tectonic. Although this definition is arbitrary and anthropocentric, it is a practical one, since only those caves that can be penetrated by humans can be studied directly. Howarth (1983) broadens this definition by designating the different voids of caves, based on their size, as follows: microcavernous (<0.1 cm), mesocavernous (0.1–20 cm), and macrocavernous (>20 cm). The term cave has been used since Ancient Rome, and in English since at least the thirteenth century (OED). Among the combined forms in which it is used, we find cave-deposit (any geological formation deposited in caves) and cave-dweller (one who dwells in a cave), which includes all sorts of cave organisms such as cave salamanders, cave fish, cave crustaceans, etc.

cavern A synonym for a **cave** or cave chamber. This term is vaguer and more poetic, usually giving a sense of vastness.

cavernicole (n), cavernicolous (adj.) These terms refer to any organisms living in caves, whether permanently or just for part of their life cycle. They were probably first used in English in relation to biospeleology in a short note published in the *American Naturalist* in 1878 (Anonymous 1878).

cenote The word *cenote* is Spanish but derived from the Mayan word *tzonot* or *conot,* which is somewhat loosely used in the Yucatán Peninsula of Mexico to refer to various types of bodies of water contained in vertical cavities in the limestone, which makes up the flat plain that constitutes that peninsula. A cenote is defined today as a flooded, natural depression carved out in limestone with a collapsed ceiling. Cenotes contain varied aquatic fauna. This term has been used by the Spaniards since their visits to the Yucatán Peninsula in the early sixteenth century and in English since at least 1841 (Stephens 1841).

chemolithotrophy The process of extracting nutrients from the substrate carried out by some microbial organisms. This term was probably first used by Goldman (1960) and is increasingly utilized today in the field of microbial ecology.

clastic sediments Broken material, here in the form of particles that have been eroded from rocks and that have become deposited in caves. Clastic sediments appear in the form of both mud and **breakdown**.

closed depressions Slumps or dips on the surface of karstic areas that can be quite extensive and funnel-shaped (see **doline**).

crenobionts Organisms normally found in springs and spring brooks, i.e. at the edge of the hypogean environment. This term became more or less popular in the 1990s (see, for example, Galassi and Pesce 1991).

doline The same as a **closed depression**.

edaphobiont, edaphobite An organism living in deep soil.

edaphon Refers collectively to organisms living in the soil and was apparently coined by R. H. Francé (1913).

endogean Refers to the environment underneath the Earth's surface. In theory this term is a synonym of **hypogean** and should include **cave**, **phreatic**, **artesian**, **interstitial**, and edaphic (soil) environments, as well as the **meiofauna**. However, except for most artesian and phreatic environments, all the others have organisms that in different degrees enter and exit those habitats with relative frequency. Endogean is the opposite of **epigean**. It is not clear why this term is much less popular than hypogean. The word was probably borrowed from botany, where the naturalist De Candolle (1813) used it to refer to a plant in which new wood is developed in the interior of the stem.

epigean Refers to the surface environment as opposed to the **hypogean** or **endogean** one. It also applies to organisms living there. It was probably used for the first time in English in the field of biospeleology by Alpheus S. Packard in 1888, and is now universally accepted.

epikarst The upper section of the percolation area of the **karst** between the unconsolidated material (soil, sediment, and vegetation debris) and the carbonate rock that is partly saturated with water. This layer is capable of storing, delaying, and/or rerouting vertical infiltration to the deeper regional **phreatic** zone of the underlying karst **aquifer** (Jones *et al.* 2004). This term was probably first used by Mangin (1973) and was popularized by Blavoux and Mudry (1986).

evaporite The remaining substance, usually sodium chloride, that results from the evaporation of water containing salts.

glacier cave A cave carved out of the ice inside a glacier; it is different from an **ice cave**. Glacier caves tend to be poor in terms of biodiversity, essentially as a consequence of being in latitudes where biodiversity per se is also very low.

grotto A section of a cave that is well decorated with calcite or is otherwise aesthetically impressive. This term is also used to identify local, more or less organized groups of cavers. This term has been employed in English since the seventeenth century (OED).

guano An accumulated deposit of animal excrement. Most guano in caves is produced by bats, but some is also produced by cave birds such as swifts and oilbirds. Guano deposits play a major role in the ecology of many caves, particularly in the tropics where they constitute a major source of energy. In fact many species of cave animal thrive in areas of high concentrations of guano.

guanobite An organism that inhabits and/or makes extensive use of guano as a source of food.

guanophage An organism that feeds on **guano**.

gypsum A mineral of hydrous calcium sulphate.

hydrothermal cave A cave formed or modified by water at high temperatures. Such caves are particularly interesting because of the microorganisms associated with them. This term has been used in geology since the mid seventeenth century (OED).

hypogean Refers to the subsurface or subterranean environment as opposed to the **epigean** one. It also applies to organisms living there. In the biospeleological context it was probably first used by Badham (1852).

hyporheic zone The interstitial space within the sediments of a streambed, representing the transition zone between the surface waters and **hypogean** ones. It is a widely used term probably first introduced by Coleman and Hynes (1970).

ice cave Cave with rock walls, containing either seasonal or permanent ice. Cf. **glacier cave**.

interstitial Referring to the spaces in between particles. Interstitial has been used in the English language since the seventeenth century (OED).

karren German word that means fissures or furrows.

karst From the Serbo-Croat *Kras* and the German *der Karst*, a limestone region of Ljubljana in the northwestern area of the former Yugoslavia near the border with Italy. In geology, karst is a landscape resulting from a combination of high rock solubility and well-developed secondary solubility in well-drained areas. Karst areas are characterized by having sinking streams, caves, closed depressions, fluted rock outcrops, and large springs. The first usage in the scientific literature in English was probably in an article by the Foreign Secretary of the Royal Society of London in 1860–62 (OED).

lava cave A cave formed by flowing molten material; cavities form as the hot material cools. These cavities are also known as lava tubes; the most famous ones are in Hawaii. This term was already being used in the scientific literature in English towards the end of the nineteenth century (Lucas 1898).

limestone caves Caves that occur in rock containing at least 50% calcium carbonate. Many limestone caves are porous and therefore permeable, and can be modified by water. This term appeared in the scientific literature in the second half of the nineteenth century (Pengelly *et al.* 1873).

meiofauna In general, meiofauna are animals intermediate in size between the macro- and the microfauna. This term was originally used by soil researchers and then utilized in the 1950s and 1960s by aquatic biologists to refer to animals that will pass through a 500 μm sieve but are retained by a 40 μm sieve.

MSS Acronym for the French *milieu souterrain superficiel* or mesovoid shallow stratum. MSS refers to the **interstitial** spaces deep in the soil–bedrock interface; it is typical of glacially fragmented zones. This is a rarely used term.

paleokarst Any geological evidence of former karstic activity.

phreatic Refers to an underground natural source of water. The phreatic zone is also the zone of saturated rock below the water table. Our knowledge of the organisms living there is only indirect, because they cannot be studied directly by humans. The fauna we know have been pumped out from wells or collected at springs. Occasionally some phreatic areas become accessible to humans owing to erosion; they are then called phreatic caves. This term is sometimes used interchangeably with **artesian**. It was probably first used in the context of speleological studies (*phréatique*) by Daubrée (1887).

saltpeter A white crystalline substance, usually composed of potassium nitrate, that was used during the nineteenth century to produce gunpowder and for medicinal purposes.

sandstone cave A cave in sandstone rocks. Such caves are mostly dissolutional in origin. They can be either horizontal or vertical. The first reference in the scientific literature is probably that of Howitt *et al.* (1862).

scotophilia The tendency to stay away from light exhibited by many hypogean organisms, including blind ones (they use other sensory systems to detect light). With reference to the behavior of cave animals, this term was probably first used by Romero (1984d).

sea caves Caves formed by the action of waves on sea cliffs. These caves can be formed in a variety of geologies and can be of many different lengths, up to more than 100 m. They usually have a large chamber immediately inside the entrance.

sinkhole Any natural, surface depression, usually through which foul matter runs and contaminates the groundwater. In speleology it means a hole, cavern, or funnel-shaped cavity made in the earth by the action of water on the soil, rock, or underlying strata, and frequently forming the course of an underground stream. The general term was used as early as the fifteenth century (OED). A synonym is *swallet*.

solution caves Caves formed by the chemical action of water on the surrounding rock. Solution caves can be formed in many types of rock, but the most common ones are in limestone formations, and they are called **limestone** or dolomite caves. The gypsum caves of the south-western United States are also solution caves.

spel(a)ean Pertaining to caves. This term has been used in English since the nineteenth century (OED).

speleogenesis The origin and development of caves. The term appears in some documents by the National Speleological Society (USA) in the late 1950s.

speleology The scientific study of caves; also refers to the hobby of exploring caves. Édouard-Alfred Martel was the first to use this term in published form (1894a,b) as *spélaeologie*; although Martel himself claims that the term was invented by Emile-Valere Rivière DePrecourt. The current French spelling, *spéléologie*, was first used by Martel in 1895. It was later introduced into English in a paper presented at the 6th Geographical Congress in 1895 (the proceedings were published the following year; Martel 1896) when he referred to speleology as something more than a mere sport. Martel (1897) further introduced the term in more popular English literature. An alternative French spelling, *spéologie*, was introduced by Louis de Nussac (1892, p. 3), and it is sometimes used in the form of *biospéologie* (Vandel 1964). Alternative terms have been used in other languages to conceptualize cave science, such as the German *Höhlenkunde* (Schmidl 1850, p. 564), the English *caveology* (Forwood 1870, p. 172), and the French *grottologie* by Martel (Martel 1889, p. 239). Although

Höhlenkunde is still used by German authors, speleology and its derived forms in other languages continue to be the terms most universally employed (Martel 1900).

speleothem Any structure that is generated in a cave by the deposition of minerals from water. Examples are **stalactites** and **stalagmites**.

spring An English word used since medieval times, referring to the natural point of emergence of underground water onto the surface (OED).

stalactite A formation of calcium carbonate generated from the roof or sides of a cave.

stalagmite A vertical formation of calcium carbonate on the floor of a cave.

stygobiont An organism that inhabits groundwater. This term became especially popular among European researchers in the 1980s (Barr and Holsinger 1985).

stygobite Any hypogean organism that shows some sort of specialization to the underground environment. Adaptations may include, but are not limited to, eye reduction, depigmentation, reduction of scale number and development in fish, hyperdevelopment of some sensory organs, reduction in metabolic rates, reduction or disappearance of circadian rhythms, reduction in fecundity, increased egg size, increased life span, increased starvation resistance, and the reduction or disappearance of certain behaviors such as aggressiveness, schooling, and response to alarm substances. Stygobites are considered 'obligatory' residents of the underground environment. This term is similar in meaning to **troglobite**.

stygofauna Collective term for the animals inhabiting the underground water environment. This term may have been introduced by Ginet and Decou (1977).

stygomorphic Describes an organism that displays the convergent phenotypic (morphological, physiological, and behavioral) characteristics of **stygobites**. This term is similar in meaning to **troglomorphic**.

stygophile An aquatic organism that can complete its life cycle in caves but may also do so outside of caves (see **troglophile**). It has been used infrequently but particularly with reference to amphipods (see, for example, Notenboon 1991).

stygoxene An organism that can be found accidentally in the hypogean environment. This term is similar in meaning to **trogloxene**.

suffosional caves Caves produced by sediments flushed by stormwaters. They are usually small in size, and the typical ones are found in the Badlands National Monument in western South Dakota, USA.

sump A flooded section of a cave.

talus caves Openings between piles of boulders that are sufficiently large to allow a human being to pass through them.

tectonic cave A cave formed by ground movement, mostly landsliding in jointed rocks. Tectonic caves do not depend on dissolution for their formation.

travertine A solid block of limestone that can be used for construction.

troglobite Any of the organisms found in caves that display convergent phenotypes (morphological, physiological, and behavioral) such as loss of eyes and pigmentation. The term was first used by J. B. Schiner in A. Schmidl *Grötten und Höhlen von Adelsberg* (1854). Troglobite is sometimes used interchangeably with **troglobiont** and **stygobite**.

troglodyte A term used in the English language since the sixteenth century that refers to people or animals that venture into or live in caves (OED). Although it is very rarely used in modern biospeleological scientific literature, it is sometimes employed in the popular press.

troglomorphic This term was proposed by Christiansen (1962) and is widely used today (see also **stygomorphic**). It refers to organisms that show reduction or loss of phenotypic characteristics related to the hypogean environment.

troglophile An organism that can complete its life cycle in caves but may also do so outside of caves (see **stygophile**). It was first used by J. B. Schiner in A. Schmidl *Grötten und Höhlen von Adelsberg* (1854).

trogloxene An organism that habitually enters caves but must return periodically to the outside for certain of its living requirements, usually food. Bats and cave birds are good examples (see **stygoxene**). This term was introduced by Racovitza (1907) to replace **accidental** or 'occasional guest' used by Schiner in Schmidl (1854).

vadose cave A vadose (or unsaturated) cave is one that underwent most of its development above the water table.

vadose zone The zone of rock above the water table.

volcanic caves See **lava caves**.

References

Agassiz, E. C. 1890. *Louis Agassiz. His Life and Correspondence.* Boston, MA: Houghton, Mifflin and Company.

Agassiz, L. 1847 [1848]. [Plan for an investigation of the embryology, anatomy and effect of light on the blind-fish of the Mammoth Cave, *Amblyopsis spelaeus*]. *Proceedings of the American Academy of Arts and Sciences* **1**:1–180.

Agassiz, L. 1851. Observations on the blind fish of the Mammoth cave. *American Journal of Science* **11**:127–8.

Agassiz, L. 1859. *An Essay on Classification.* London: Longman, Brown, Green, Longmans, Roberts.

Agrios, G. N. 2004. *Plant Pathology*, 5th edition. San Diego, CA: Academic Press.

Airoldi, L. & F. Cinelli. 1996. Variability of fluxes of particulate material in a submarine cave with chemolithoautotrophic inputs or organic carbon. *Marine Ecology Progress Series* **139**:205–17.

Airoldi, L., A. J. Southward, I. Niccolai & F. Cinelli. 1997. Sources and pathways of particulate organic carbon in a submarine cave with sulphur water springs. *Water, Air and Soil Pollution* **99**:353–62.

Akam, M. 1998. Hox genes, homeosis and the evolution of segment identity: no need for hopeless monsters. *International Journal of Developmental Biology*, special issue **42**:445–51.

Alberti, L. 1550. *Descrittione di tvtta Italia.* Bologna: Anselmo Giaccarelli.

Allinson, G., C. Mispagel, N. Kajiwara *et al.* 2006. Organochlorine and trace metal residues in adult southern bent-wing bat (*Miniopterus schreibersi bassanii*) in south-eastern Australia. *Chemosphere* **64**:1464–71.

Allouc, J. & J. G. Harmelin. 2001. Mn-Fe deposits in shallow cryptic marine environment: examples in northwestern Mediterranean submarine caves. *Bulletin de la Société Géologique de France* **172**:765–78.

Allred, K. 2004. Some carbonate erosion rates of Southeast Alaska. *Journal of Cave and Karst Studies* **66**:89–97.

Anderson, L. 1976. Charles Bonnet's taxonomy and Chain of Being. *Journal of the History of Ideas* **37**:45–58.

Andersson, M. 1990. Evolution: a case of male opportunism. *Nature* **343**:20.

Andre, H. M. & X. Ducarme. 2003. Rediscovery of the genus *Pseudotydeus* (Acari: Tydeoidea), with description of the adult using digital imaging. *Insect Systematics and Evolution* **34**:373–9.

Anker, A. & T. M. Iliffe. 2000. Description of *Bermudacaris harti*, a new genus, and species (Crustacea: Decapoda: Alpheidae) from anchialine caves of Bermuda. *Proceedings of the Biological Society of Washington* **113**:761–75.

Anonymous. 1833. Cabinet of nature. Cavern of the guacharo. *Monthly Repository* **4**:24–8.

Anonymous. 1878. [A note on *Proteus anguinus*.] *American Naturalist* **12**:321.

Anonymous. 1889. Edible mushrooms of the United States. *Science* **13**:453–5.

Anonymous. 1981. Stephen L. Bishop. 1821–1857. Explorer and Guide. Mammoth Cave. *Journal of Spelean History* **15**:11.

Anonymous. 1992. Bishop, Stephen, pp. 82–3, in: John. E. Kleber (ed.). *Kentucky Encyclopedia*. Lexington, KY: University Press of Kentucky.

Appel, T. A. 1988. *The Cuvier-Geoffroy Debate: French Biology in the Decades before Darwin*. New York: Oxford University Press.

Argyll, Duke. of. 1867. *The Reign of Law*. London: Alexander Strahan.

Ariani, A. P., M. M. Camassa & K. J. Wittmann. 1999. Faunistic and biocenotic aspects of a semi-hypogean water system: the 'spunnulate' of Torre Castiglione (Apulia, southern Italy), p. 31, in: D. Holcer & M. Sasic (eds.) *Abstracts of the 14th International Symposium of Biospeleology*, Makarska, Croatia, 19–26 September 1999.

Arita, H. T. 1993. Conservation biology of the cave bats of Mexico. *Journal of Mammalogy* **74**:693–702.

Arita, H. T. 1996. The conservation of cave-roosting bats in Yucatan, Mexico. *Biological Conservation* **76**:177–85.

Arita, H. T. & J. A. Vargas. 1995. Natural-history, interspecific association, and incidence of the cave bats of Yucatan, Mexico. *Southwestern Naturalist* **40**:29–37.

Armstrong, K. N. 2006. Phylogeographic structure in *Rhinonicteris aurantia* (Chiroptera: Hipposideridae): implications for conservation. *Acta Chiropterologica* **8**:63–81.

Arnedo, M. A., P. Oromi, C. Muria, N. Macias-Hernandez & C. Ribera. 2007. The dark side of an island radiation: systematics and evolution of troglobitic spiders of the genus *Dysdera* Latreille (Araneae: Dysderidae) in the Canary Islands. *Invertebrate Systematics* **21**:623–60.

Artigas, M., T. F. Glick & R. A. Matínez. 2006. *Negotiating Darwin. The Vatican Confronts Evolution, 1877–1902*. Baltimore, MD: The Johns Hopkins University Press.

Ashmole, N. P. & M. J. Ashmole. 1997. The land fauna of Ascension Island: new data from caves and lava flows, and a reconstruction of the prehistoric ecosystem. *Journal of Biogeography* **24**:549–89.

Ashmole, N. P., P. Oromí, M. J. Ashmole & J. L. Martín. 1992. Primary faunal succession in volcanic terrain: lava and cave studies on the Canary Islands. *Biological Journal of the Linnean Society* **46**:207–34.

Avise, J. C. & R. K. Selander. 1972. Evolutionary genetics of cave-dwelling fishes of the genus *Astyanax*. *Evolution* **26**:1–19.

Ayala, F. 1971. Dobzhansky, Theodosius, pp. 233–42, in: C. C. Gillispie (ed.) *Dictionary of Scientific Biography*. Vol. 4. New York: Scribner.

Badham, C. D. 1852. Prose halieutics. *Fraser's Magazine* **46**:271.

Baker, J. K. 1962. The manner and efficiency of raptor depredations on bats. *The Condor* **64**:500–4.

Baker, K. M. 2004. On Condorcet's "sketch". *Daedalus* **133**:56–64.

Baldock, R. N. & H. B. S. Womersley. 2005. Marine benthic algae of the Althorpe Islands, South Australia. *Transactions of the Royal Society of South Australia* **129**:116–27.

Banister, K. E. 1984. A subterranean population of *Garra barreimiae* (Teleostei: Cyprinidae) from Oman, with comments on the concept of regressive evolution. *Journal of Natural History* **18**:927–38.

Banta, A. M. 1909. *The Fauna of Mayfield's Cave*. Washington, D.C.: Carnegie Institution of Washington.

Banta, A. M. 1921. An eyeless daphnid, with remarks on the possible origin of eyeless cave animals. *Science* **53**:462–3.

Barnes, D. K. A. & J. J. Bell. 2002. Coastal sponge communities of the West Indian Ocean: morphological richness and diversity. *African Journal of Ecology* **40**:350–9.

Barr, T. C. 1962a. The blind beetles of Mammoth Cave, Kentucky. *American Midland Naturalist* **68**:278–84.

Barr, T. C. 1962b. Studies on the cavernicole *Ptomaphagus* of the United States (Coleoptera: Catopidae) *Psyche* **70**:50–8.

Barr, T. C. 1966. Evolution of cave biology in the United States, 1822–1965. *National Speleological Society Bulletin* **28**:15–21.

Barr, T. C. 1967. Observations on the ecology of caves. *The American Naturalist* **101**: 475–91.

Barr, T. C. 1986. Mammoth Cave in the years 1836–1855. *Journal of Spelean History* **20**:39–40.

Barr, T. C. & J. R. Holsinger. 1985. Speciation of cave faunas. *Annual Review of Ecology and Systematics* **16**:313–37.

Barranco, P. & J. G. Mayoral. 2007. A new species of *Eukoenenia* (Palpigradi, Eukoeneniidae) from Morocco. *Journal of Arachnology* **35**:318–24.

Barrett, L., D. Gaynor, D. Rendall, D. Mitchell & S. P. Henzi. 2004. Habitual cave use and thermoregulation in chacma baboons. *Journal of Human Evolution* **46**:215–22.

Bartels, P. J. & D. R. Nelson. 2006. A large-scale, multihabitat inventory of the Phylum Tardigrada in the Great Smoky Mountains National Park, USA: a preliminary report. *Hydrobiologia* **558**:111–18.

Barton, H. A. & F. Luiszer. 2005. Microbial metabolic structure in a sulfidic cave hot spring: potential mechanisms of biospeleogenesis. *Journal of Cave and Karst Studies* **67**:28–38.

Barton, H. A. & N. R. Pace. 2005. Discussion: persistent coliform contamination in Lechuguilla Cave pools. *Journal of Cave and Karst Studies* **67**:55–7.

Barton, H. A., J. R. Spear & N. R. Pace. 2001. Microbial life in the underworld: biogenicity in secondary mineral formations. *Geomicrobiology Journal* **18**:359–68.

Bartsch, I. & I. Tittley. 2004. The rocky intertidal biotopes of Helgoland: present and past. *Helgoland Marine Research* **58**:289–302.

Bateson, W. 1922. Evolutionary faith and modern doubts. *Science* **55**:1412.

Baudinette, R. V., R. T. Wells, K. J. Sanderson & B. Clark. 1994. Microclimatic conditions in maternity caves of the bent-wing bat, *Micropterus schreibersii* – an attempted restoration of a former maternity site. *Wildlife Research* **21**:607–19.

Bell, J. J. 2002. The sponge community in a semi-submerged temperate sea cave: density, diversity and richness. *Marine Ecology-Pubblicazioni della Stazione Zoologica di Napoli I.* **23**:297–311.

Bellés, X. 1991. Survival, opportunism and convenience in the processes of cave colonization by terrestrial faunas. *Oecologia Aquatica* **10**:325–35.

Bellon, R. 2001. Joseph Dalton Hooker's ideals for a professional man of science. *Journal of the History of Biology* **34**:51–82.

Benedetti-Cecchi, L., L. Airoldi, M. Abbiati & F. Cinelli. 1998. Spatial variability in the distribution of sponges and cnidarians in a sublittoral marine cave with sulphur-water springs. *Journal of the Marine Biological Association of the United Kingdom* **78**:43–58.

Benoit, J. B., J. A. Yoder, L. W. Zettler & H. H. Hobbs. 2004. Mycoflora of a trogloxenic cave cricket, *Hadenoecus cumberlandicus* (Orthoptera: Rhaphidophoridae), from two small caves in Northeastern Kentucky. *Annals of the Entomological Society of America* **97**:989–93.

Benton, M. J. 1983. Dinosaur success in the Triassic: a noncompetitive ecological model. *Quarterly Review of Biology* **58**:29–55.

Berg, L. S. 1926. *Nomogenesis; or, Evolution determined by Law.* London: Constable.

Bergson, H. 1907. *L'Evolution Créatrice.* Paris: Félix Alcan.

Bernasconi, R. 1999. *Paladilhia bessoni* n.sp. (Gastropoda Prosobranchia Hydrobiidae) from karstic groundwater of Haute Soule, Pyrenees Atlantiques, France. *Revue Suisse de Zoologie* **106**:385–92.

Berra, T. M. & J. D. Humphrey. 2002. Gross anatomy and histology of the hook and skin of forehead brooding male nurseryfish, *Kurtus gulliveri*, from northern Australia. *Environmental Biology of Fishes* **65**:263–70.

Berry, R. J. 1989. Ecology: where genes and geography meet. Presidential address to the British Ecological Society, December 1988. *Journal of Animal Ecology* **58**:733–59.

Besson, J. 1569 [1969]. *L'art et Science de Trouver les Eaux et Fontaines Cachees sous Terre: Autrement que par les Moyens Vulgaires des Agriculteurs et Architectes.* Orléans: E. Gibier. [Facsimile reproduction by Editions Coral, Columbus, OH.]

Besuchet, C. 1981. Description of *Scydmaenus aelleni*, a new species of cavernicolous scydmaenid beetle from New Caledonia. *Revue Suisse de Zoologie* **88**:459–62.

Bichuette, M. E. & E. Trajano. 2003a. Epigean and subterranean ichthyofauna from the São Somingos karst area, Upper Tocantins River basin, Central Brazil. *Journal of Fish Biology* **63**:1100–21.

Bichuette, M. E. & E. Trajano. 2003b. A population study of epigean and subterranean *Potamolithus* snails from southeast Brazil (Mollusca: Gastropoda: Hydrobiidae). *Hydrobiologia* **505**:107–17.

Biota Environmental Sciences Pty Ltd (BESPL). 2005. *Barrow Island Gorgon Gas Development.* North Perth, Western Australia, Australia: Biota Environmental Sciences Pty Ltd.

Blanc, M., P. Banarescu, J.-L. Gaudet & J. C. Hureau. 1971. *European Inland Water Fish. A Multilingual Catalogue.* London: Fishing News (Book) Ltd.

Blaszak, C., J. C. Cokendolpher & V. J. Polyak. 1995. *Paleozercon cavernicolous*, n.gen., n. sp., fossil mite from a cave in the southwestern U.S.A. (Acari, Gamasida,

Zerconidae), with a key to neartic genera of Zerconidae. *International Journal of Acarology* **21**:253–9.

Blavoux, B. & J. Mudry. 1986. Influence of the summer rainfalls on the quality of the reserves of the karstic aquifers - the effect of the soil and of the epikarst in the concentration of chlorides. *Bulletin de la Societé Geologique de France* **2**:667–74.

Bocking, S. 1988. Alpheus Spring Packard and cave fauna in the evolution debate. *Journal of the History of Biology* **21**:425–56.

Bodon, M., S. Cianfanelli, E. Talenti, G. Manganelli & F. Giusti. 1999. *Litthabitella chilodia* (Westerlund, 1886) in Italy (Gastropoda: Prosobranchia: Hydrobiidae). *Hydrobiologia* **411**:175–89.

Boero, F., F. Cicogna, D. Pessani & R. Pronzato. 1991. In situ observations on contraction behavior and diel activity of *Halcampoides purpurea* var. *mediterranea* (Cnidaria, Anthozoa) in a marine cave. *Marine Ecology* **12**:185–92.

Boesgaard, T. & R. Kristensen 2001. Tardigrades from Australian marine caves. With a redescription of *Actinarctus neretinus* (Arthrotardigrada). *Zoologischer Anzeiger* **240**:253–64.

Boltovskoy, D., M. J. Gibbons, L. Hutchings & D. Binet. 1999. General biological features of the South Atlantic, pp. 1–42, in: D. Boltovskoy (ed.). *Zooplankton of the South Atlantic*. Leiden: Backhuys Publishers.

Bosque, C. & O. De Parra. 1992. Digestive efficiency and rate of food passage in oilbird nestlings. *Condor* **94**:557–71.

Boucquey, C., G. Thines & C. Van Der Borght. 1965. Étude comparative de la capacité photopathique et de l'activité chez le poisson cavernicole *Anoptichthys antrobius*, chez la forme epigee ancestrale *Astyanax mexicanus*, et chez les hybrides F_1 (*Astyanax* × *Anoptichthys*) et F_2, pp. 79–103, in: J. Mendioni (ed.). *La Distribution Temporelle des Activités Animales et Humaines*. Paris: Masson et Cie.

Bourdier, F. 1971. Cuvier, Georges, pp. 521–8, in: C. C. Gillispie (ed.) *Dictionary of Scientific Biography*. vol. 3. New York: Scribner.

Bourdier, F. 1972a. Gaudry, Albert Jean, pp. 295–7, in: C. C. Gillispie (ed.) *Dictionary of Scientific Biography*. vol. 5. New York: Scribner.

Bourdier, F. 1972b. Geoffroy Saint-Hilaire, Ètienne, pp. 355–8, in: *Dictionary of Scientific Biography* (C. C. Gillispie, ed.), vol. 5. New York: Scribner.

Bourges, F., P. Genthon, A. Margin & D. D'Hulst. 2006. Microclimates of l'Aven d'Orgnac and other French limestone caves (Chauvet, Esparros, Marsoulas). *International Journal of Climatology* **26**:1651–70.

Boutin, C. & N. Coineau. 2000. Evolutionary rates and phylogenetic age in some stygobiontic species, pp. 433–51, in: H. Wilkens, D. C. Culver & W. F. Humphries (eds.). *Subterranean Ecosystems*. Amsterdam: Elsevier.

Bowie, M. H., S. Hodge, J. C. Banks & C. J. Vink. 2006. An appraisal of simple tree-mounted shelters for non-lethal monitoring of weta (Orthoptera: Anostostomatidae and Rhaphidophoridae) in New Zealand nature reserves. *Journal of Insect Conservation* **10**:261–8.

Bowler, P. J. 1983. *The eclipse of Darwinism. Anti-Darwinian Evolution Theories in the Decades around 1900*. Baltimore, MD: The Johns Hopkins University Press.

Bowler, P. J. 2005. Revisiting the eclipse of Darwinism. *Journal of the History of Biology* **38**:19–32.

Bowman, T. E., J. Yager & T. M. Iliffe. 1985. *Speonebalia cannoni*, n. gen., n. sp., from the Caicos Islands, the first hypogean leptostracan (Nebaliacea: Nebaliidae). *Proceedings of the Biological Society of Washington* **98**:439–46.

Boxshall, G. A. & D. Jaume. 2000. Discoveries of cave misophrioids (Crustacea: Copepoda) shed new light on the origin of anchialine faunas. *Zoologischer Anzeiger* **239**:1–19.

Boyer, D. G. & G. C. Pasquarell. 1996. Agricultural land use effects on nitrate concentrations in a mature karst aquifer. *Water Resources Bulletin* **32**:565–73.

Boyer, D. G. & G. C. Pasquarell. 1999. Agricultural land use impacts on bacterial water quality in a karst groundwater aquifer. *Journal of the American Water Resources Association* **35**:291–300.

Brancelj, A. 2000. *Morariopsis dumonti* n.sp (Crustacea: Copepoda: Harpacticoida) – a new species from an unsaturated karstic zone in Slovenia. *Hydrobiologia* **463**: 23–80.

Brancelj, A. 2006. The epikarst habitat in Slovenia and the description of a new species. *Journal of Natural History* **40**:403–13.

Braun-Blanquet, J. 1928. *Pflanzensoziologie. Grundzuge der Vegetationskunde*. Berlin: Springer.

Breder, C. M. 1942. Descriptive ecology of La Cueva Chica, with especial reference to the blind fish, *Anoptichthys*. *Zoologica* **27**:7–15.

Breder, C. M. & E. B. Gresser. 1941. Correlations between structural eye defects and behavior in the Mexican blind characin. *Zoologica* **26**:123–31.

Briggler, J. T. & W. L. Puckette. 2003. Observations on reproductive biology and brooding behavior of the Ozark zigzag salamander, *Plethodon angusticlavius*. *The Southwestern Naturalist* **48**:96–100.

Brindle, A. 1980. The cavernicolous fauna of Hawaiian lava tubes 12. A new blind troglobitic earwig *Anisolabis howarthi*, new species (Dermaptera, Carcinophoridae) with a revision of the related surface living earwigs of the Hawaiian Islands USA. *Pacific Insects* **21**:261–74.

Brodsky, L. I., J. Jacob-Hirsch, A. Avivi *et al.* 2005. Evolutionary regulation of the blind subterranean mole rat, *Spalax*, revealed by genome-wide gene expression. *Proceedings of the National Academy of Sciences of the United States of America* **102**:17047–52.

Bronson, F. H. 1979. The reproductive ecology of the house mouse. *Quarterly Review of Biology* **54**:265–99.

Brooks, W. K. 1909. Biographical memoir of Alpheus Hyatt (1838–1902). *Biographical Memoirs of the National Academy of Sciences* (USA) **6**:311–25.

Brown, J. S. 1990. Habitat selection as an evolutionary game. *Evolution* **44**:732–46.

Bruce, R. C. 1979. Evolution of paedomorphosis in salamanders of the genus *Gyrinophilus*. *Evolution* **33**:998–1000.

Brunet, A. K. & R. A. Medellin. 2001. The species-area relationship in bat assemblages of tropical caves. *Journal of Mammalogy* **82**:1114–22.

Brusca, R. C. & G. J. Brusca. 1990. *Invertebrates*. Sunderland, MA: Sinauer.

Buchanan, J. 1936. Notes on an American cave flatworm, *Sphalloplana percaeca* (Packard). *Ecology* **17**:194–211.

Budel, B., D. C. J. Wessels & D. Mollenhauer. 1993. Mass development of *Nostoc microscopicum* (Carmichael) Harvey ex Bornet and Flahault in a cave in

Clarens-Sandstone of the Drakensberg Mountains, South Africa (Golden Gate Highlands National Park). *Archiv für Protistenkunde* **143**:229–35.

Buffenstein, R. 1996. Ecophysiological responses to a subterranean habitat; a Bathyergid perspective. *Mammalia* **60**:591–605.

Buhlmann, K. 2001. A biological inventory of eight caves in northwestern Georgia with conservation implications. *Journal of Cave and Karst Studies* **63**: 91–8.

Burda, H., S. Begall, O. Grutjen & A. Scharff. 1999. How to eat a carrot? Convergence in the feeding behavior of subterranean rodents. *Naturwissenschaften* **86**:325–7.

Burkhardt, F. & S. Smith (eds.). 1987. *The Correspondence of Charles Darwin*. Volume 3. *1844–1846*. Cambridge: Cambridge University Press.

Burkhardt, F. & S. Smith (eds.). 1989. *The Correspondence of Charles Darwin*. Volume 5. *1851–1855*. Cambridge: Cambridge University Press.

Burkhardt, F. & S. Smith (eds.). 1990. *The Correspondence of Charles Darwin*. Volume 6. *1856–1857*. Cambridge: Cambridge University Press.

Burkhardt, R. W. 1977. *The Spirit of the System. Lamarck and Evolutionary Biology*. Cambridge, MA: Harvard University Press.

Burney, D. A., D. McCloskey, D. Kikushi *et al.* 2001. Fossil evidence for a diverse biota from Kaua'i and its transformation since human arrival. *Ecological Monographs* **71**:615–41.

Burr, B. M., G. L. Adams, J. K. Krejca, R. J. Paul & M. L. Warren, Jr. 2001. Troglomorphic sculpins of the *Cottus carolinae* species group in Perry County, Missouri: distribution, external morphology, and conservation status. *Environmental Biology of Fishes* **62**:279–96.

Bussotti, S., P. Guidetti & G. Belmonte. 2003. Distribution patterns of the cardinal fish, *Apogon imberbis*, in shallow marine caves in southern Apulia (SE Italy). *Italian Journal of Zoology* **70**:153–7.

Bussotti, S., A. Terlizzi, S. Fraschetti, G. Belmonte & F. Boero. 2006. Spatial and temporal variability of sessile benthos in shallow Mediterranean marine caves. *Marine Ecology Progress Series* **325**:109–19.

Byers, G. W. 1969. Evolution of wing reduction in crane flies (Diptera: Tipulidae). *Evolution* **23**:346–54.

Calaforra, J. M., A. Fernández-Cortés, F. Sánchez-Martos, J. Gisbert & A. Pulido-Bosch. 2003. Environmental control for determining human impact and permanent visitor capacity in a potential show cave before tourist use. *Environmental Conservation* **30**:160–7.

Calder, D. R. & J. S. Bleakney. 1965. Microarthropod ecology of a porcupine-inhabited cave in Nova Scotia. *Ecology* **46**:895–9.

Calò, F. & M. Parise. 2006. Evaluating the human disturbance to karst environments in southern Italy. *Acta Carsologica* **35**:47–56.

Camp, C. D. & J. B. Jensen. 2007. Use of twilight zones of caves by Plethodontid salamanders. *Copeia* **2007**:594–604.

Campbell Grant, E. H., W. H. Lowe & W. F. Fagan. 2007. Living in the branches: population dynamics and ecological processes in dendritic networks *Ecology Letters* **10**:165–75.

Canaveras, J. C., S. Sanchez-Moral, V. Soler & C. Saiz-Jimenez. 2001. Microorganisms and microbially induced fabrics in cave walls. *Geomicrobiology Journal* **18**:223–40.

Carey, P. G., A. J. Sargent, A. M. Taberner, G. Ramon & G. Moya. 2001. Ecology of cavernicolous ciliates from the anchihaline lagoons of Mallorca. *Hydrobiologia* **448**:193–201.

Carpenter, J. H. 1970. Systematics and ecology of cave planarians of the United States. *American Zoologist* **10**:543.

Carr, J. 1973. Lister, Martin, pp. 415–17, in: C. C. Gillispie (ed.) *Dictionary of Scientific Biography*. vol. 8. New York: Scribner.

Casale, A., P. M. Giachino, & B. Jalzic. 2004. Three new species and one new genus of ultraspecialized cave dwelling Leptodirinae from Croatia (Coleoptera, Cholevidae). *Natura Croatica* **13**:301–17.

Castleberry, S. B., W. M. Ford, P. B. Wood, N. L. Castleberry & M. T. Mengak. 2001. Movements of Allegheny woodrats in relation to timber harvesting. *Journal of Wildlife Management* **65**:148–56.

Causey, N. B. & D. L. Tiemann. 1969. A revision of the bioluminescent millipedes of the genus *Motyxia* (Xystodesmidae, Polydesmida). *Proceedings of the American Philosophical Society* **113**:14–33.

Chakraborty, R. & M. Nei. 1974. Dynamics of gene differentiation between incompletely isolated populations of unequal sizes. *Theoretical Population Biology* **5**: 460–9.

Chamberlin, J. C. & D. R. Malcolm. 1960. The occurrence of false scorpions in caves with special reference to cavernicolous adaptation and to cave species in the North American fauna (Arachnida-Chelonethida). *American Midland Naturalist* **64**:105–15.

Chelius, M. K. & J. C. Moore. 2004. Molecular phylogenetic analysis of archaea and bacteria in Wind Cave, South Dakota. *Geomicrobiology Journal* **21**:123–34.

Chen, Y.-R., J.-X. Yang & Z. G. Zhu. 1994. A new fish of the genus *Sinocyclocheilus* from Yunnan with comments on its characteristic adaptation (Cypriniformes: Cyprinidae). *Acta Zootaxonomica Sinica* **19**:246–53.

Chevaldonné, P. & C. Lejeune. 2003. Regional warming-induced species shift in north-west Mediterranean marine caves. *Ecology Letters* **6**:371–9.

Chopard, L. 1928. Sur une gravure d'insecte de l'epoque magdalénienne. *Comptes Rendus de la Societé de Biogeographie* **5**:64–7.

Christian, E. 2005. Palpigradi (micro-whipscorpions), arachnids in a lightless world. *Denisia* **2004 (12)**:473–83.

Christiansen, K. A. 1962. Proposition pour la classification des animaux cavernicoles. *Spelunca Memoires* **2**:76–8.

Christiansen, K. A. 1965. Behavior and form in the evolution of cave Collembola. *Evolution* **19**:529–37.

Christiansen, K. A. 1992. Biological processes in space and time. Cave life in the light of modern evolutionary theory, pp. 453–78, in: A. I. Camacho (ed.). Monogr. 7, *The Natural History of Biospeleology*. Madrid: Museo Nacional de Ciencias Naturales.

Christiansen, K. & D. Culver. 1987. Biogeography and the distribution of cave Collembola. *Journal of Biogeography* **14**:459–77.

Christman, M. C., D. C. Culver, M. K. Madden & D. White. 2005. Patterns of endemism of the eastern North America cave fauna. *Journal of Biogeography* **32**:1441–52.

Cianficconi, F., C. Romano & P. Salerno. 2001. Checklist dei Tricotteri del Parco di Monte Cucco (Umbria, PG). *Rivista di Idrobiologia* **40**:379–400.

Ciarniello, L. C., M. S. Boyce, D. C. Heard & D. R. Seip. 2005. Denning behavior and den site selection of grizzly bears along the Parsnip River, British Columbia, Canada. *Ursus* **16**:47–58.

Cigna, A. A. 1993a. *Speleology by Titus Lucretius Carus. Atti del Simposio Internazionale sulla Protostoria della Speleologia*. Città di Castello, Italy: Edizioni Nuova Prhomos.

Cigna, A. A. 1993b. Environmental-management of tourist caves – the examples of Grotta di Castellana and Grotta Grande del Vento, Italy. *Environmental Geology* **21**:173–80.

Clark, B. K., & B. S. Clark. 1994. Use of caves by eastern woodrats (*Neotoma floridana*) in relation to bat populations, internal cave characteristics and surface habitats. *American Midland Naturalist* **131**:359–64.

Clark Jr., D. R., R. L. Clawson & C. J. Stafford. 1983. Gray bats killed by Dieldrin at two additional Missouri caves: aquatic microinvertebrates found dead. *Bulletin of Environmental Contamination and Toxicology* **30**:214–18.

Clark Jr., D. R., R. K. LaVal & A. J. Krynitsky. 1980. Dieldrin and Heptachlor residues in dead gray bats, Franklin County, Missouri – 1976 versus 1977. *Pesticides Monitoring Journal* **13**:137–40.

Clark, D. R. Jr., R. K. LaVal & D. M. Swineford. 1978. Dieldrin-induced mortality in an endangered species, the Gray Bat (*Myotis grisaceus*). *Science* **199**:1357–9.

Clark, G. R., P. Petchey, M. S. McGlone & P. Bristow. 1996. Faunal and floral remains from Earnscleugh cave, central Otago, New Zealand. *Journal of the Royal Society of New Zealand* **26**:363–80.

Clayton, D. H., R. D. Price & R. D. M. Page. 1996. Revision of *Dennyus* (*Collodennyus*) lice (Phthiraptera: Menoponidae) from swiftlets, with descriptions of new taxa and a comparison of host-parasite relationships. *Systematic Entomology* **21**:179–204.

Clements, R., N. S. Sodhi, M. Schilthuizen & P. K. L. Ng. 2006. Limestone karsts of Southeast Asia: imperiled arks of biodiversity. *BioScience* **56**:733–42.

Clottes, J. 2003. *Return to Chauvet Cave: Excavating the Birthplace of Art: the First Full Report*. London: Thames and Hudson.

Coddington, J. A. 2005. Phylogeny and classification of spiders, pp. 18–24, in: Ubick, D., P. Paquin, P. E. Cushing & V. Roth (eds.). *Spiders of North America: an Identification Manual*. Poughkeepsie, NY: American Arachnological Society.

Coleman, M. J. & H. B. N. Hynes. 1970. The vertical distribution of the invertebrate fauna in the bed of a stream. *Limnology and Oceanography* **15**:31–40.

Coleman, W. 1964. *Georges Cuvier, Zoologist: a Study in the History of Evolution Theory*. Cambridge, MA: Harvard University Press.

Collazo, A. & S. B. Marks. 1994. Development of *Gyrinophilus porphyriticus*: identification of the ancestral developmental pattern in the salamander family Plethodontidae. *Journal of Experimental Zoology* **268**:239–58.

Colp, R. 1986. "Confessing a murder": Darwin's first revelations about transmutation. *Isis* **77**:9–32.

Coma, R., M. Carola, T. Riera & M. Zabala. 1997. Horizontal transfer of matter by a cave-dwelling mysid. *Marine Ecology. Pubblicazioni della Stazione Zoologica di Napoli* **18**:211–26.

Condorcet, J.-A. N. de. 1793–4. *Esquisse d'un Tableau Historique des Progrès de l'Esprit Human*. Paris: Agasse.

Condorcet, J.-A. N. de C. 1802. *Outlines of an Historical View of the Progress of the Human Mind, being a Posthumous Work of the late M. de Condorcet*. Baltimore, MD: G. Fryer, for J. Frank.

Cook, G. 1975. Cave-dwelling aquatic Oligochaeta (Annelida) from eastern United States. *Transactions of the American Microscopical Society* **94**:24–37.

Cooper, H. M., M Herbin & E. Nevo. 1993. Visual system of a naturally microphthalmic mammal: the blind mole rat, *Spalax ehrenbergi*. *Journal of Comparative Neurology* **328**:313–50.

Cooper, J. E. & R. A. Kuhene. 1974. *Speoplatyrhynus poulsoni*, a new genus and species of subterranean fish from Alabama. *Copeia* **1974**:486–93.

Cooper, R. L., H. Li, Y. Long, J. L. Cole & H. L. Hopper. 2001. Anatomical comparisons of neural systems in sighted epigean and troglobitic crayfish species. *Journal of Crustacean Biology* **21**:360–74.

Cope, E. D. 1864. On a blind silurid from Pennsylvania. *Proceedings of the Academy of Natural Sciences of Philadelphia* **1864**:231–3.

Cope, E. D. 1872. On the Wyandotte Cave and its fauna. *American Naturalist* **6**:406–22.

Cope, E. D. 1896. *The Primary Factors of Organic Evolution*. Chicago, IL: Open Court.

Corbera, J. 2002. Amphi-Atlantic distribution of the Mancocimatinae (Cumacea: Bodotriisae), with description of a new genus dwelling in marine lava caves of Tenerife (Canary Islands). *Zoological Journal of the Linnean Society* **134**:453–61.

Corsi, P. 2005. Before Darwin: transformist concepts in European natural history. *Journal of the History of Biology* **38**:67–83.

Covelli, S., F. Cucchi & R. Mosca. 1998. Monitoring of percolation water to discriminate surficial inputs in a karst aquifer. *Environmental Geology* **36**:296–304.

Crispim, J. A. 1999. Seismotectonic versus man-induced morphological changes in a cave on the Arrabida chain (Portugal). *Geodinamica Acta* **12**:135–42.

Crouau-Roy, B., Y. Crouau & C. Ferre. 1992. Dynamic and temporal structure of the troglobitic beetle *Speonomus hydrophilus* (Coleoptera: Bathysciinae). *Ecography* **15**:12–18.

Crouch, D. P. 1993. *Water Management in Ancient Greek Cities*. New York: Oxford University Press.

Crouch, D. P. 2004. *Geology and Settlement. Greco-Roman Patterns*. Oxford: Oxford University Press.

Crum, H. 1983. *Mosses of the Great Lakes*. Ann Arbor, MI: University of Michigan Herbarium.

Crunkilton, R. 1984. Subterranean contamination of Maramec Spring by ammonium nitrate and urea fertilizer and its implications for rare cave biota. *Missouri Speleology* **25**:151–9.

Cuénot, L. 1911. *La Genesis de las Especes Animals*. Paris: Librairie Félix Alcan.

Culver, D. C. 1970. Analysis of simple cave communities I. Caves as islands. *Evolution* **24**:463–74.

Culver, D. C. 1971. Analysis of simple cave communities. III. Control and abundance. *American Midland Naturalist* **85**:173–87.

Culver, D. C. & J. R. Holsinger. 1992. How many species of troglobites are there? *National Speleological Society Bulletin* **54**:79–80.

Culver, D., J. R. Holsinger & R. Baroody. 1973. Toward a predictive cave biogeography: the Greenbriar Valley as a case study. *Evolution* **27**:689–95.

Culver, D. C., T. C. Kane & D. W. Fong. 1995. *Adaptation and Natural Selection in Caves. The Evolution of* Gammarus minus. Cambridge, MA: Harvard University Press.

Culver, D. C., L. M. Lawrence, M. C. Christman & H. H. Hobbs III. 2000. Obligate cave fauna of the 48 contiguous United States. *Conservation Biology* **14**:386–401.

Culver, D. C. & T. L. Poulson. 1970. Community boundaries: faunal diversity around a cave entrance. *Annales Spéléologie* **25**:853–60.

Culver, D. & W. White. 2005. *Encyclopedia of Caves.* Amsterdam: Elsevier.

Cunningham, J. A., G. D. Hopkins, C. A. Lebron & M. Reinhard. 2000. Enhanced anaerobic bioremediation of groundwater contaminated by fuel hydrocarbons at Seal Beach, California. *Biodegradation* **11**:159–70.

Cunningham, K. I., D. E. Northup, R. M. Pollastro, W. G. Wright & R. J. LaRock. 1995. Bacteria, fungi, and biokarst in Lechuguilla Cave, Carlsbad Caverns National Park, New Mexico. *Environmental Geology* **25**:2–8.

Danielli, H. M. C. & M. A. Edington. 1983. Bacterial calcification in limestone caves. *Geomicrobiology Journal* **3**:1–16.

Danielopol, D. L., A. Baltanás & W. F. Humphreys. 2000. *Danielopolina kornickeri* sp. n. (Ostracoda, Thaumatocypridoidea) from a western Australian anchialine cave: morphology and evolution. *Zoologica Scripta* **29**:1–16.

Danielopol D. L., C. Griebler, A. Gunatilaka & J. Notenboom. 2003. Present state and future prospects for groundwater ecosystems. *Environmental Conservation* **30**:104–30.

Darlington, P. J. 1943. Carabidae of mountains and islands: data on the evolution of isolated faunas, and on atrophy of wings. *Ecological Monographs* **13**:37–61.

Darwin, C. 1859. *On the Origin of the Species by Means of Natural Selection.* London: J. Murray.

Darwin, C. 1861. *On the Origin of the Species by Means of Natural Selection* (3rd edn.). London: J. Murray.

Darwin, F. 1896. *The Life and Letters of Charles Darwin.* New York: D. Appleton and Company.

Daubrée, A. 1887. *Eaux Souterraines a l'Epoque Actuelle.* Paris: Dunod.

Davidson, J. P. 1997. *The Bone Sharp. The Life of Edward Drinker Cope.* Philadelphia, PA: The Academy of Natural Sciences of Philadelphia.

Davis, P. G. 1997. The bioerosion of bird bones. *International Journal of Osteoarchaeology* **7**:388–401.

Day, M. J. & M. S. Chenoweth. 2004. The karstlands of Trinidad and Tobago, their land use and conservation. *Geographical Journal* **170**:256–66.

De Beer, G. 1973. Lankester, Edwin. Ra., pp. 26–27, in: C.C. Gillispie (ed.) *Dictionary of Scientific Biography*, vol. 8. New York: Scribner.

De Candolle, A. P. 1813. *Théorie Élémentaire de la Botanique; ou, Exposition des Principes de la Classification Naturelle et de l'Art de Décrire et d'Étudier les Végétaux*. Paris: Déterville.

De Chardin, T. 1955. *Le Phénomène Humain*. Paris: Du Seuill.

DeKay, J. E. 1842. *Zoology of New York or the New-York Fauna*, Part IV, *Fishes*. Albany, NY: W. & A. White & J. Visscher.

Deharveng, L. & A. Bedos. 2000. The cave fauna of southeast Asia. Origin, evolution and ecology, pp. 603–32, in: H. Wilkens, D. C. Culver & W.F. Humphries (eds.) *Subterranean Ecosystems*. Amsterdam: Elsevier.

Denis, A., R. Lastennet, F. Huneau & P. Makaurent. 2005. Identification of functional relationships between atmospheric pressure and CO2 in the cave of Lascaux using the concept of entropy of curves. *Geophysical Research Letters* **32 (5)**:Art. No. L05810.

Desimone, L. R. L. & N. Moracchiolin. 1994. Hydrobiidae (Gastropoda, Hydrobioidea) from the Ribeira valley, Se Brazil, with descriptions of 2 new cavernicolous species. *Journal of Molluscan Studies* **60**:445–59.

Desmond, R. 1972. Hooker, Joseph Dalton, pp. 488–92, in: C. C. Gillispie (ed.) *Dictionary of Scientific Biography*, vol. 6. New York: Scribner.

Dexter, R. W. 1965. The "Salem secession" of Agassiz zoologists. *Essex Institute Historical Collections* **101**:27–39.

Dexter, R. W. 1979. The impact of evolutionary theories on the Salem Group of Agassiz Zoologists (Morse, Hyatt, Packard, Putnam). *Essex Institute Historical Collections* **115**:144–71.

Dhondt, J. L. & J. G. Harmelin. 1993. Redescription of *Alcyonidum duplex* Prouho, 1892 (Bryozoa, Ctenostomida). Description and ecology. *Cahiers de Biologie Marine* **34**:65–75.

Diamond, J. & D. Stermer. 1999. Evolving backward. *Discover* **19**:64–8.

Dill, R. F., L. S. Land, L. E. Mack & H. P. Schwartz. 1998. A submerged stalactite from Belize: petrography, geochemistry, and geochronology of massive marine cementation. *Carbonates and Evaporites* **13**:189–97.

Dimichele, W. A., T. L. Phillips, & R. G. Olmstead. 1987. Opportunistic evolution: abiotic environmental stress and the fossil record of plants. *Review of Palaeobotany and Palynology* **50**:151–78.

Dirig, R. 1994. Lichens of pine-barrens, dwarf pine plains, and ice-cave habitats in the Shawangunk Mountains, New York. *Mycotaxon* **52**:523–58.

Dobzhansky, T. 1968. Teilhard de Chardin and the orientation of evolution. *Zygon* **3**:242–58.

Dobzhansky, T. 1970. *Genetics of the Evolutionary Process*. New York: Columbia University Press.

Doolittle, R. F. 1988. Lens proteins. More molecular opportunism. *Nature* **336**: 18.

Doran, N. E., A. M. M. Richardson & R. Swain. 2001. The reproductive behaviour of the Tasmanian cave spider *Hickmania troglodytes* (Araneae: Austrochilidae). *Journal of Zoology* **253**:405–18.

Dove, S., J. C. Ortiz, S. Enriquez *et al.* 2006. Response of holosymbiont pigments from the scleractinian coral *Montipora monasteriata* to short-term heat stress. *Limnology and Oceanography* **51**:1149–58.

Dowling, T. E., D. P. Martasian & W. R. Jeffery. 2002. Evidence for multiple genetic forms with similar eyeless phenotypes in the blind cavefish, *Astyanax mexicanus*. *Molecular Biology and Evolution* **19**:446–55.

Ducarme, X., H. M. André, G. Wauthy & P. Lebrun. 2004a. Comparison of endogeic and cave communities: microarthropod density and mite species richness. *European Journal of Soil Biology* **40**:129–38.

Ducarme, X., G. Wauthy, H. M. Andre & P. Lebrun. 2004b. Survey of mites in caves and deep soil and evolution of mites in these habitats. *Canadian Journal of Zoology* **82**:841–50.

Dumnicka, E. 2005. Worms, pp. 614–18, in: Culver, D. & W. White (eds.) *Encyclopedia of Caves*. Amsterdam: Elsevier.

Dumnicka, E. & K. Wojtan. 1990. Differences between cave water ecological-systems in the Krakow Czestochowa upland. *Stygologia* **5**:241–7.

Dumont, H. J. 1995. The evolution of groundwater Cladocera. *Hydrobiologia* **307**:69–74.

Dumont, H. J. & S. Negrea. 1996. A conspectus of the Cladocera of the subterranean waters of the world. *Hydrobiology* **325**:1–30.

Dunne, J. A., R. J. Williams & N. D. Martinez. 2002. Food-web structure and network theory: the role of connectance and size. *Proceedings of the National Academy of Sciences of the United States of America* **99**:12917–22.

Eddy, J. H. 1994. Buffon's *Histoire naturelle*. History? A critique of recent interpretations. *Isis* **85**:644–61.

Edgecombe, G. D. 2006. A troglobitic cryptopid centipede (Chilopoda: Scolopendromorpha) from western Queensland. *Record of the Australian Museum* **23**:193–8.

Eigenmann, C. H. 1890. The Point Loma blind fish and its relatives. *Zoe* **1**:65–96.

Eigenmann, C. H. 1898. A new blind fish. *Proceedings of the Indiana Academy of Sciences* **897**:231.

Eigenmann, C. H. 1903. In search of blind fishes in Cuba. *World Today* **5**:1131–6.

Eigenmann, C. H. 1909. *Cave Vertebrates of America. A Study in Degenerative Evolution*. Washington, D.C.: Carnegie Institution of Washington.

Eigenmann, C. H. 1919. *Trogloglanis pettersoni*, a new blind fish from San Antonio, Texas. *Proceedings of the American Philosophical Society* **58**:397–400.

Eimer, T. 1887–1888. *Die Entstehung der Arten auf Grund von Vererben erwobener Eigenschaften nach den Gesetzen organischen Wachsens. Ein Beitrag zur einheitlichen Auffassung der Lebewelt*. Jena: G. Fischer.

Emberton, K. C., T. A. Pearce, P. F. Kasigwa, P. Tattersfield & Z. Habibu. 1997. High diversity and regional endemism in land snails of eastern Tanzania. *Biodiversity and Conservation* **6**:1123–36.

Emmett, A. J. & A. L. Telfer. 1994. Influence of karst hydrology on water-quality management in southeast South-Australia. *Environmental Geology* **23**:149–55.

Endler, J. A. 1986. *Natural Selection in the Wild*. Princeton, NJ: Princeton University Press.

Engel, A. S., M. L. Porter, B. K. Kinkle & T. C. Kane. 2001. Ecological assessment and geological significance of microbial communities from Cesspool Cave, Virginia. *Geomicrobiology Journal* **18**:259–74.

Engel, A. S., M. L. Porter, L. A. Stern, S. Quinlan & P. C. Bennett. 2004a. Bacterial diversity and ecosystem function of filamentous microbial mats from aphotic (cave) suflidic springs dominated by chemolithoautotrophic "*Epsilonproteobacteria*". *FEMS Microbiological Ecology* **51**:31–53.

Engel, A. S., L. A. Stern & P. C. Bennett. 2004b. Microbial contributions to cave formation: new insights into sulfuric acid speleogenesis. *Geology* **32**:369–72.

Erckens, W. & F. Weber. 1976. Rudiments of an ability for time measurements in cavernicole fish *Anoptichthys jordani* Hubbs & Innes (Pisces: Characidae). *Experientia* **32**:1297–9.

Erdbrink, D. P. B. 1983. Eleven bones: more fossil remains of cave lions and cave hyaenas from the North Sea area. *Bijdragen tot de Dierkunde* **53**:1–12.

Erkens, K., M. Lademan, K. Tintelnot *et al.* 2002. Histoplasm ose-Gruppenerkrankung bei Fledermausforschern nach Kubaaufenthalt. *Deutsche medizinische Wochenschrift* **127**:21–5.

Erseus, C. 1986. A new species of *Phallodrilus* (Oligochaeta, Tubificidae) from a limestone cave on Bermuda. *Sarsia* **71**:7–9.

Espinasa, L. & R. Borowsky. 2000. Re-acquisition of the eyed condition in a population of blind cave fish *Astyanax fasciatus* in a karst window, p. 146, in: *Program Book and Abstracts, 80th Annual Meeting of the American Society of Icthyologists and Herpetologists, La Paz, Baja California Sur, Mexico, June 14–20*. La Paz, Mexico: American Society of Ichthyologists and Herpetologists.

Espinasa, L. & A. Fisher. 2006. A cavernicolous species of the genus *Anelpistina* (Zygentoma: Nicoletiidae) from San Sebastian Cave, Oaxaca, Mexico. *Proceedings of the Entomological Society of Washington* **108**:655–60.

Espinasa, L., P. Rivas-Manzano & H. E. Perez. 2001. A new blind cave fish population of genus *Astyanax*: geography, morphology and behavior. *Environmental Biology of Fishes* **62**:339–44.

Etnier, D. A. & W. E. Starnes. 1993. *The Fishes of Tennessee*. Knoxville, TN: University of Tennessee Press.

Ewan, J. 1975. Rafinesque, Constantine Samuel, pp. 262–4, in: C. C. Gillispie (ed.) *Dictionary of Scientific Biography*, vol. 11. New York: Scribner.

Faimon, J., J. Stelcl, S. Kubesova & J. Zimak. 2003. Environmentally acceptable effect of hydrogen peroxide on cave "lamp-flora", calcite speleothems and limestones. *Environmental Pollution* **122**:417–22.

Fain, A. & A. V. Bochkov. 2002. A new genus and species of cheyletid mite (Acari: Cheyletidae) from a cave in Western Australia. *International Journal of Acarology* **28**:37–40.

Farber, P. L. 1975. Buffon and Daubenton: divergent traditions within the *Histoire naturelle*. *Isis* **66**:63–74.

Faust, B. 1967. Saltpere mining in Mammoth Cave, Kentucky. *Journal of Spelean History* **1**:3–9.

Fenolio, D. B., G. O. Graening, B. A. Collier & J. F. Stout. 2005a. Coprophagy in a cave-adapted salamander; the importance of bat guano examined through nutritional and stable isotope analyses. *Proceedings of the Royal Society* B**273**:439–43.

Fenolio, D. B., G. O. Graening & J. F. Stout. 2005b. Seasonal movement patterns of pickerel frogs (*Rana palustris*) in an Ozark cave and trophic implications supported by stable isotope evidence. *Southwestern Naturalist* **50**:385–9.

Fenton, M. B. 1975. Acuity of echolocation in *Collocalia hirundinacea* (Aves: Apodidae), with comment on the distributions of echolocating swiftlets and molossid bats. *Biotropica* **7**:1–7.

Ferguson, L. M. 1996. *Condeicampa langei*, new genus and species of Dipluran (Diplura: Campodeidae) from Whipple Cave, Nevada, U.S.A. *Memoires de Biospéologie* **23**:133–41.

Fernández-Cortes, A, J. M. Calaforra & F. Sanchez-Martos. 2006a. Spatiotemporal analysis of air conditions as a tool for the environmental management of a show cave (Cueva del Agua, Spain). *Atmospheric Environment* **40**:7378–94.

Fernández-Cortes, A., J. M. Calaforra, F. Sanchez-Martos & J. Gisbert. 2006b. Microclimate processes characterization of the giant Geode of Pulpi (Almeria, Spain): technical criteria for conservation. *International Journal of Climatology* **26**:691–706.

Ferreira, R. L. & R. P. Martins. 1999. Trophic structure and natural history of bat guano invertebrate communities, with special reference to Brazilian caves. *Tropical Zoology* **12**:231–52.

Ferreira, R., X. Prous & R. P. Martins. 2007. Structure of bat guano communities in a dry Brazilian cave. *Tropical Zoology* **20**:55–74.

Fiedler, K. 2001. Ants that associate with Lycaeninae butterfly larvae: diversity, ecology and biogeography. *Diversity and Distributions* **7**:45–60.

Field, J. 1992. Intraspecific parasitism as an alternative reproductive tactic in nest-building wasps and bees. *Biological Reviews* **67**:79–126.

Fiers, F., & T. M. Iliffe. 2000. *Nitocrellopsis texana* n. sp. from central TX (USA) and *N. ahaggarensis* n. sp. from the central Algerian Sahara (Copepoda, Harpacticoida). *Hydrobiologia* **418**:81–7.

Finston, T. L. & S. B. Peck. 1995. Population structure and gene flow in *Stomion*: a species swarm of flightless beetles of the Galapagos Islands. *Heredity* **75**:390–7.

Fiorina, A, F. Olivo, G. Caretta, P. Cassini & E. Savino. 2000. Study of microfungi and bacteria in the air of a karst cave in Toirano (Savona, Italy). *Micologia Italiana* **29**:65–73.

Fliermans, C. B. & E. L. Schmidt. 1977. *Nitrobacter* in Mammoth Cave. *International Journal of Speleology* **9**:1–19.

Foddai, D. & A. Minelli. 1999. A troglomorphic geophilomorph centipede from France (Chilopoda: Geophilomorpha: Geophilidae). *Journal of Natural History* **33**:267–87.

Foissner, W. 2003. Two remarkable soil spathidiids (Ciliophora: Haptorida), *Arcuospathidium pachyoplites* sp. n. and *Spathidium faurefremieti* nom. n. *Acta Protozoologica* **42**:145–59.

Foos, A. M., I. D. Sasowsky, E. J. La Rock & P. N. Kambesis. 2000. Detrital origin of a sedimentary fill, Lechuguilla Cave, Guadalupe Mountains, New Mexico. *Clays and Clay Minerals* **48**:693–8.

Foreign Secretary. 1860–1862. Notice of recent scientific researches carried on abroad. *Proceedings of the Royal Society of London* **11**:45–53.

Forwood, W. S. 1870. *An Historical and Descriptive Narrative of the Mammoth Cave of Kentucky: Including Explanations of the Causes Concerned in its Formation, its Atmospheric Conditions, its Chemistry, Geology, Zoology, etc., with Full Scientific Details of the Eyeless Fishes*. Philadelphia, PA: J.B. Lippincott & Co.

Fosshagen, A. & T. M. Iliffe. 2003. Three new genera of the Ridgewayiidae (Copepoda, Calanoida) from anchialine caves in the Bahamas. *Sarsia* **88**:16–35.

Francé, R. H. 1913. *Das Edaphon: Untersuchungen zur Oekologie der bodenbewohnenden Mikroorganismen*. München, Germany: Verlag der Deutschen Mikrologischen Gesellschaft.

Fullard, J. H., R. M. R. Aarclay & D. W. Thomas. 1993. Echolocation in free-flying atiu swiftlets (*Aerodramus sawtelli*). *Biotropica* **25**:334–9.

Furman, A. & A. Ozgul. 2002. Distribution of cave-dwelling bats and conservation status of underground habitats in the Istanbul area. *Ecological Research* **17**:69–77.

Futuyma, D. J. 1998. *Evolutionary Biology*. Sunderland, MA: Sinauer.

Gabriel, R. & J. W. Bates. 2003. Responses of photosynthesis to irradiance in bryophytes of the Azores laurel forest. *Journal of Bryology* **25**:101–5.

Galassi, D. P. & G. L. Pesce.1991. *Elaphoidella mabelae* n. sp., a crenobiont harpacticoid from Italy (Copepoda, Canthocamptidae). *Crustaceana* **60**:1–6.

Galindo, C., A. Sanchez, R.H. Quijano & L. G. Herrera. 2004. Population dynamics of a resident colony of *Leptonycteris curasoae* (Chiroptera: Phyllostomidae) in central Mexico. *Biotropica* **36**:382–91.

Garbacki, N., L. Ector, I. Kostikov & L. Hoffmann. 1999. Contribution to the study of the flora of caves in Belgium. *Belgian Journal of Botany* **132**:43–76.

Gemma, J. N., R. E. Koske & T. Flynn. 1992. Mycorrhizae in Hawaiian Pteridophytes: occurrence and evolutionary significance. *American Journal of Botany* **79**:843–52.

Gentner, D. R. 1968. The scientific basis of some concepts of Pierre Teilhard de Chardin. *Zygon* **3**:432–41.

Gers, C. 1998. Diversity of energy fluxes and interactions between arthropod communities: from soil to cave. *Acta Oecologica* **19**:205–13.

Gifford, G. E. 1967. An American in Paris, 1841–1842: four letters from Jefferies Wyman. *Journal of the History of Medicine and Allied Sciences* **22**:274–85.

Gilbert, J. & J. Mathieu. 1980. Relations entre les teneurs en proteins, glucides et lipids au cours du jeûne experimental, chez deux espèces de *Niphargus* peuplant des biotopes differents. *Crustaceana* (Supplement) **6**:137–47.

Gillieson, D., P. Wallbrink & A. Cochrane. 1996. Vegetation change, erosion risk and land management on the Nullarbor plain, Australia. *Environmental Geology* **28**:145–53.

Gillmore, G. K., M. Sperrin, P. Phillips & A. Denman. 2000. Radon hazards, geology, and exposure of cave users: a case study and some theoretical perspectives. *Ecotoxicology and Environmental Safety* **46**:279–88.

Ginet, R. & V. Decou. 1977. *Initiation à la Biologie et à l'Écologie Souterraines*. Paris: Delarge.

Ginzburg, L. & J. Darnuth. 2008. The space-lifetime hypothesis: viewing organisms in four dimensions, literally. *American Naturalist* **171**:125–31.

Girard, C. F. 1859. Ichthyological notes. *Proceedings of the Academy of Natural Sciences of Philadelphia* **1859**:63–4.

Giribet, G., G. D. Edgecombe, W. C. Wheler & C. Babbitt. 2002. Phylogeny and systematic position of Opinioles: a combined analysis of Chelicerate relationships using morphological and molecular data. *Cladistics* **18**:5–70.

Giribet, G. & C. Ribera. 2000. A review of arthropod phylogeny: new data based on ribosomal DNA sequences and direct character optimization. *Cladistics* **16**:204–31.

Gittleson, S. M. & R. L. Hoover. 1969. Cavernicolous protozoa – review of the literature and new studies in Mammoth Cave, Kentucky. *Annales de Spéléologie* **24**:737–76.

Glaubrecht, M. 2004. Leopold von Buch's legacy: treating species as dynamic natural entities, or why geography matters. *American Malacological Bulletin* **19**:111–34.

Gnaspini, P. 1996. Population ecology of *Goniosoma spelaeum*, a cavernicolous harvestman from south-eastern Brazil (Arachnida: Opiliones: Gonyleptidae). *Journal of Zoology* **239**:417–35.

Gnaspini, P. & A. J. Cavalheiro. 1998. Chemical and behavioral defenses of a neotropical cavernicolous harvestman: *Goniosoma spelaeum* (Opiliones, Laniatores, Gonyleptidae). *Journal of Arachnology* **26**:81–90.

Gnaspini, P., F. H. Santos & S. Hoenen. 2003. The occurrence of different phase angles between contrasting seasons in the activity patterns of the cave harvestman *Goniosoma spelaeum* (Arachnida, Opiliones). *Biological Rhythm Research* **34**:31–49.

Golovatch, S. I., J. J. Geoffroy & J. P. Mauries. 2006. Four new Chordeumatida (Diplopoda) from caves in China. *Zoosystema* **28**:75–92.

Golovatch, S. & J. Wytwer. 2004. The South American millipede genus *Phaneromerium* Verhoeff. 1941, with the description of a new cavernicolous species from Brazil (Diplopoda: Polydesmida: Fuhrmannodesmidae). *Annales Zoologici* **54**:511–14.

Goldman, C. R. 1960. Primary productivity and limiting factors in three lakes of the Alaska Peninsula. *Ecological Monographs* **30**:207–30.

Goode, C. E. 1986. *World Wonder Saved. How Mammoth Cave became a National Park.* Mammoth Cave, KY: The Mammoth Cave National Park Association.

Goodnight, C. J. & M. L. Goodnight. 1960. Speciation among cave opilionids of the United States. *American Midland Naturalist* **64**:34–8.

Goudge, T. A. 1973. Bergson, Henri Louis, pp. 8–12, in: C.C. Gillispie (ed.) *Dictionary of Scientific Biography*, vol. 2. New York: Scribner.

Gould, S. J. 1977. *Ontogeny and Phylogeny*. Cambridge, MA: Harvard University Press.

Gould, S. J. 2002. *The Structure of Evolutionary Theory*. Cambridge, MA: The Belknap Press of Harvard University Press.

Gould, S. J. & E. S. Vrba. 1982. Exaptation – a missing term in the science of form. *Paleobiology* **8**:4–15.

Graening, G. O. 2003. Subterranean biodiversity of Arkansas, part 2: Status update of the Foushee cavesnail, *Amnicola cora* Hubricht, 1979 (Mollusca: Gastropoda: Hydrobiidae). *Journal of the Arkansas Academy of Science* **57**:195–6.

Graening, G. O. 2005. Trophic structure of Ozark cave streams containing endangered species. *Oceanological and Hydrobiological Studies* **34**:3–17.

Graening, G. O. & A. V. Brown. 2003. Ecosystem dynamics and pollution effects in an Ozark cave stream. *Journal of the American Water Resources Association* **39**:1497–507.

Graening, G. O., M. E. Slay & C. Bitting. 2006a. Cave fauna of the Buffalo National River. *Journal of Cave and Karst Studies* **68**:153–63.

Graening, G. O., M. E. Slay, A. V. Brown & J. B. Koppelman. 2006b. Status and distribution of the endangered benton cave crayfish, *Cambarus aculabrum* (Decapoda: Cambaridae). *Southwestern Naturalist* **51**:376–81.

Granger, G. 1971. Condorcet, Marie-Jean-Antoine-Nicolas, Marquis de, pp. 383–99, in: C. C. Gillispie (ed.) *Dictionary of Scientific Biography*, vol. 3. New York: Scribner.

Grayson, D. K. 2000. Mammalian responses to middle Holocene climatic change in the great basin of the western United States. *Journal of Biogeography* **27**:181–92.

Green, B. R. 2001. Was 'molecular opportunism' a factor in the evolution of different photosynthetic light-harvesting pigment systems? *Proceedings of the National Academy of Sciences of the United States of America* **98**:2119–21.

Green, S. & A. Romero. 1997. Responses to light in two blind cave fishes (*Amblyopsis spelaea* and *Typhlichthys subterraneus*) (Pisces: Amblyopsidae). *Environmental Biology of Fishes* **50**:167–74.

Greene, J. C. 1959. *The Death of Adam: Evolution and its Impact on Western Thought.* Ames, IA: Iowa State University Press.

Greenwood, P. H. 1976. A new and eyeless cobitid fish (Pisces, Cypriniformes) from the Zagros Mountains, Iran. *Journal of Zoology* **180**:129–37.

Grgic, T. & I. Kos. 2001. Temperature preference in some centipede species of the genus *Lithobius* Leach, 1814 (Chilopoda: Lithobiidae). *Acta Biologica Slovenica* **44**:3–12.

Griffin, D. R. 1953. Acoustic orientation in the oil bird, *Steatornis*. *Proceeding of the National Academy of Sciences* **39**:884–93.

Griffith, D. M. & T. L. Poulson. 1993. Mechanisms and consequences of intraspecific competition in a carabid cave beetle. *Ecology* **74**:1373–83.

Grimaldi, S. D. & M. G. D'Addabbo. 2001. Further data on the Mediterranean Sea tardigrade fauna. *Zoologischer Anzeiger* **240**:345–60.

Grimoult, C. 1998. *Évolutionnisme et Fixisme en France. Histoire d'un Combat 1800–1882.* Paris: CNRS Éditions.

Grishkan, I., E. Nevo & S. P. Wasser. 2004. Micromycetes from the saline Arubotaim Cave: Mount Sedom, the Dead Sea southwestern shore, Israel. *Journal of Arid Environments* **57**:431–43.

Grobbelaar, J. U. 2000. Lithophytic algae: a major threat to the karst formation of show caves. *Journal of Applied Phycology* **12**:309–15.

Grobe, P. & C. Luter. 1999. Reproductive cycles and larval morphology of three recent species of *Argyrotheca* (Terebratellacea: Brachiopoda) from Mediterranean submarine caves. *Marine Biology* **134**:595–600.

Groth, I. & C. Saiz-Jimenez. 1999. Actinomycetes in hypogean environments. *Geomicrobiology Journal* **16**:1–8.

Gucu, A. C., G. Gucu & H. Orek. 2004. Habitat use and preliminary demographic evaluation of the critically endangered Mediterranean monk seal (*Monachus monachus*) in the Cilician Basin (Eastern Mediterranean). *Biological Conservation* **116**:417–31.

Guerrero, R., C. Martin & O. Bain. 2003. *Litomosoides yutajensis* n. sp., first record of this filarial genus in a mormoopid bat. *Parasite. Journal de la Societé Française de Parasitologie* **10**:219–25.

Gunn, J., P. Hardwick & P. J. Wood. 2000. The invertebrate community of the Peak-Speedwell cave system, Derbyshire, England: pressures and considerations for conservation management. *Aquatic Conservation-Marine and Freshwater Ecosystems* **10**:353–69.

Gutierrez, M., H. Neill & R. V. Grand. 2004. Metals in sediments of springs and cave streams as environmental indicators in karst areas. *Environmental Geology* **46**:1079–85.

Guzman-Cornejo, G., L. Garcia-Prieto, J. B. Morales-Malacara & G. P. P. De Leon. 2003. Acarine infracommunities associated with the Mexican free-tailed bat, *Tadarida brasiliensis mexicana* (Chiroptera: Molossidae) in arid regions of Mexico. *Journal of Medical Entomology* **40**:996–9.

Haacke, W. 1893. *Gestaltung und Vererbung: eine Entwickelungsmechanik der Organismen.* Leipzig: T. O. Weigel.

Hadly, E. A., U. Ramakrishnan, Y. L. Chan *et al.* 2004. Genetic response to climatic change: insights from ancient DNA and phylochronology. *Public Library of Science Biology* **2**:1600–9.

Halliday, R. B. 2001. Mesostigmatid mite fauna of Jenolan Caves, New South Wales (Acari: Mesostigmata). *Australian Journal of Entomology* **40**:299–311.

Halloy, S. 1991. Islands of life at 6000 m altitude: the environment of the highest autotrophic communities on earth (Socompa Volcano, Andes). *Arctic and Alpine Research* **23**:247–62.

Hanamura, Y. & T. Kase. 2003. *Palaumysis pilifera*, a new species of cave-dwelling mysid (Crustacea: Mysidacea) from Okinawa, southwestern Japan, with an additional note on *P. simonae* Bacescu & Iliffe, 1986. *Hydrobiologia* **497**:145–52.

Hancock, P. J., A. J. Boulton & W. F. Humphreys. 2005. Aquifers and hyporheic zones: towards an ecological understanding of groundwater. *Hydrogeology Journal* **13**:98–111.

Hardwick, P. & J. Gunn. 1996. The conservation of Britain's limestone cave resource. *Environmental Geology* **28**:121–7.

Hardy, J. D. 1957. Bat predation by the Cuban boa, *Epicrates angulifer. Copeia* **1957**:151–2.

Harmelin, J. G. 1990. Interactions between small sciaphilous scleractinians and epizoans in the northern Mediterranean, with particular reference to bryozoans. *Marine Ecology-Pubblicazioni della Stazione Zoologica di Napoli I* **11**:351–64.

Harmelin, J. G. 1997. Diversity of bryozoans in a Mediterranean sublittoral cave with bathyal like conditions: role of dispersal processes and local factors. *Marine Ecology Progress Series* **153**:139–52.

Harries, P. J., E. G. Kauffman & T. A. Hansen. 1996. Models for biotic survival following mass extinction, pp. 41–60, in: *Biotic Recovery from Mass Extinction Events*. Special Publication 102. London: Geological Society.

Harris, A. 2006. Animalia/Kinorhyncha. The Virtual Zoo. Accessed 11 April 2006. www.virtualzoo.org/classifications/class.php?Style=S&PhylumID=0000000021.

Hart, C. W., R. B. Manning & T. M. Iliffe. 1985. Fauna of the Atlantic marine caves: evidence of dispersal by sea floor spreading while maintaining ties to deep water. *Proceedings of the Biological Society of Washington* **98**:288–92.

Hart, E. A. & S. G. Schurger. 2005. Sediment storage and yield in an urbanized karst watershed. *Geomorphology* **70**:85–96.

Harvey, J. 1999. A focal point for feminism, politics, and science in France. The Clémence Royer Centennial Celebration of 1930. *Osiris* **14**:86–101.

Harvey, M. S. 2002. The neglected cousins: what do we know about the smaller arachnid orders? *Journal of Arachnology* **30**:357–72.

Hawes, R. S. 1939. The flood factor in the ecology of caves. *Journal of Animal Ecology* **8**:1–5.

Hayami, I. & T. Kase. 1996. Characteristics of submarine cave bivalves in the northwestern Pacific. *American Malacological Bulletin* **12**:59–65.

Hayes, T. B. 1997. Hormonal mechanisms as potential constraints on evolution: examples from the Anura. *American Zoologist* **37**:482–90.

Hecht, M. K. & W. C. Steere. 1970. *Essays in Evolution and Genetics in Honor of Theodosius Dobzhansky*. New York: Appleton-Century-Crofts.

Hedin, M. C. 1997. Speciational history in a diverse clade of habitat-specialized spiders (Araneae: Nesticidae: *Nesticus*): inferences from geographic-based sampling. *Evolution* **51**:1929–45.

Herbert, S. 2005. The Darwinian revolution revisited. *Journal of the History of Biology* **38**:51–66.

Hernando, C., P. Aguilera & I. Ribera. 2001. *Limnius stygius* sp. nov., the first stygobiontic riffle beetle from the Palearctic Region (Coleoptera: Elmidae). *Entomological Problems* **32**:69–72.

Hershler, R. & J. R. Holsinger. 1990. Zoogeography of North-American hydrobiid cavesnails. *Stygologia* **5**:4–16.

Hershler, R. & G. Longley. 1986. Phreatic hydrobiids (Gastropoda: Prosobranchia) from the Edwards (Balcones Fault Zone) Aquifer region, South-Central Texas. *Malacologia* **27**:127–72.

Hervant, F., J. Mathieu & J. Durand. 2001. Behavioural, physiological and metabolic responses to long-term starvation and refeeding in a blind cave-dwelling (*Proteus anguinus*) and a surface-dwelling (*Euproctus asper*) salamander. *Journal of Experimental Biology* **204**:269–81.

Hervant, F. & D. Renault. 2002. Long-term fasting and realimentation in hypogean and epigean isopods: a proposed adaptive strategy for groundwater organisms. *Journal of Experimental Biology* **205**:2079–87.

Heth, G., E. Nevo, & J. Todrank. 1996. Seasonal changes in urinary odors and in responses to them by blind subterranean mole rats. *Physiology and Behavior* **60**:963–8.

Heuss, T. 1991. *Anton Dohrn: a Life for Science*. New York: Springer-Verlag.

Hickman, C., L. Roberts & A. Larson. 2000. *Animal Diversity*. New York: McGraw-Hill.

Hill, C. R. 1974. The sources and influence of the *Descrittione di tutta Italia* of Fra Leandro Alberti. Ph.D. dissertation, University of Edinburgh.

Hill, L. 1969. Feeding and food habits of the spring cavefish, *Chologaster agassizi*. *American Midland Naturalist* **82**:110–16.

Hintzsche, E. 1972. Henle, Friedrich Gustav Jacob, pp. 268–70, in: C. C. Gillispie (ed.) *Dictionary of Scientific Biography*, vol. 6. New York: Scribner.

Hintzsche, E. 1973. Koellikeer, Rudolf Albert von, pp. 437–40, in: C. C. Gillispie (ed.) *Dictionary of Scientific Biography*, vol. 7. New York: Scribner.

Hobbs, H. H. 2000. Crustacea, pp. 95–107, in: H. Wilkens, D. C. Culver & W. F. Humphries (eds.) *Subterranean Ecosystems*. Amsterdam: Elsevier.

Hoch, H. & F. G. Howarth. 1999. Multiple cave invasions by species of the planthopper genus *Oliarus* in Hawaii (Homoptera: Fulgoroidea: Cixiidae). *Zoological Journal of the Linnean Society* **127**:453–75.

Hoenen, S. & P. Gnaspini. 1999. Activity rhythms and behavioral characterization of two epigean and one cavernicolous harvestmen (Arachnida, Opiliones: Gonyleptidae). *Journal of Arachnology* **27**:159–64.

Holmes, A. J., N. A. Tujula, M. Holley *et al.* 2001. Phylogenetic structure of unusual aquatic microbial formations in Nullarbor caves, Australia. *Environmental Microbiology* **3**:256–64.

Holsinger, J. R. 1976. The cave fauna of Pennsylvania, pp. 72–87, in: W. B. White (ed.) *Geology and Biology of Pennsylvania Caves*. Harrisburg, PA: Geological Survey.

Holsinger, J. R. 2000. Ecological derivation, colonization, and speciation, pp. 399–415 in: H. Wilkens, D. C. Culver & W. F. Humphries (eds.) *Subterranean Ecosystems*. Amsterdam: Elsevier.

Holthuis, L. B. 1973. Caridean shrimp found in land locked saltwater pools at four Indo-West Pacific localities (Sinai Peninsula, Funafuti Atoll, Maui and Hawaii Islands), with the description of one new genus and four new species. *Zoologisches Verhandelingen* **128**:1–48.

Horder, T. J. 1998. Why do scientists need to be historians? *Quarterly Review of Biology* **73**:175–87.

Horikoshi, K. & W. D. Grant. 1998. *Extremophiles: Microbial Life in Extreme Environments*. New York: Wiley-Liss.

Hose, L. D., A. N. Palmer, M. V. Palmer *et al.* 2000. Microbiology and geochemistry in a hydrogen-sulphide-rich karst environment *Chemical Geology* **69**:399–423.

Howard, A. D. & C. G. Groves. 1995. Early development of karst systems. 2. Turbulent flow. *Water Resources Research* **31**:19–26.

Howard, M. 1981. *The Franco-Prussian War: The German Invasion of France, 1870–1871*. London: Routledge.

Howarth, F. G. 1973. The cavernicolous fauna of Hawaiian lava tubes. Introduction. *Pacific Insects* **15**:139–51.

Howarth, F. G. 1981. Non-relictual terrestrial troglobites in the tropic Hawaiian caves. *Proceedings of the 8th International Speleological Congress of Speleology* **2**:539–41.

Howarth, F. G. 1983. Ecology of cave arthropods. *Annual Review of Entomology* **28**:365–89.

Howitt, A. W., R. O'Hara Burke, J. King *et al.* 1862. Exploring expedition from Victoria to the Gulf of Carpentaria, under the Command of Mr. Robert O'Hara Burke. *Journal of the Royal Geographical Society of London* **32**:430–529.

Hsu, M. J. 1997. Population status and conservation of bats (Chiroptera) in Kenting National Park, Taiwan. *Oryx* **3**:295–301.

Hsu, M. J. & G. Agoramoorthy. 2001. Occurrence and diversity of thermophilous soil microfungi in forest and cave ecosystems of Taiwan. *Fungal Divers Research Series* **7**:27–33.

Hubbs, C. L. 1938. Fishes from the caves of Yucatan. *Carnegie Institution of Washington Publications* **491**:261–95.

Hubbs, C. L. 1964. David Starr Jordan. *Systematic Zoology* **13**:195–200.

Humboldt, A. von. 1793. *Florae Fribergensis Specimen, Plantas Cryptogamicas Praesertim Subterraneas Exhibens*. Berolini: H.A. Rottmann.

Humboldt, A. von. 1805. Mémoire sur une nouvelle espèce de pimelode, jetée par les volcans du Royaume de Quito, in: A. von Humboldt & A. Bompland (eds.) *Voyage de Humboldt et Bonpland*, deuxième partie. *Observations de Zoologie et d'Anatomie comparée*, vol. 1.

Humboldt. A. von. 1817. Mémoire sur le Guacharo de la caverne de Caripe. *Recueil d'Observations de Zoologie Et d'Anatomie* no. 2.

Humphreys, W. 1991. Experimental re-establishment of pulse-driven populations in a terrestrial troglobite community. *Journal of Animal Ecology* **60**:609–23.

Humphreys, W. F. 1993. Cave fauna in semi-arid tropical Western Australia: a diverse relict wet-forest litter fauna. *Mémoires de Biospéologie* **20**:105–10.

Humphreys, W. F. 2006. Aquifers: the ultimate groundwater-dependent ecosystems. *Australian Journal of Botany* **54**:115–32.

Hunter, A. J., D. E. Northup, C. N. Dahm & P. J. Boston. 2004. Persistent coliform contamination in Lechuguilla Cave pools. *Journal of Cave and Karst Studies* **66**:102–10.

Huppert, G. N. 1995. Legal protection for caves in the United States. *Environmental Geology* **26**:121–3.

Hüppop, K. 2000. How do cave animals cope with the food scarcity in caves?, pp. 159–88, in: H. Wilkens, D. C. Culver & W. F. Humphries (eds.) *Subterranean Ecosystems*. Amsterdam: Elsevier.

Husband, R. W. & B. M. O'Conner. 2003. A new genus and species of mite (Acari: Tarsonemia: Podapolipidae), ectoparasite of the Peruvian cockroaches, *Blaberus parabolicus* (Walker) and *Eublaberus distanti* (Kirby) (Blattodea: Blaberidae). *International Journal of Acarology* **29**:331–8.

Huys, R. & T. M. Iliffe. 1998. Novocriniidae, a new family of harpacticoid copepods from anchihaline caves in Belize. *Zoologica Scripta* **27**:1–15.

Ignatov, M. S. & E. A. Ignatova. 2001. On the zoochory of *Schistostega pennata* (Schistostegaceae, Musci). *Arctoa* **10**:83–96.

Iliffe, T. M. & T. D. Jickells. 1984. Organic pollution of an inland marine cave from Bermuda. *Marine Environmental Research* **12**:173–89.

Iwaniuk, A. N., C. P. Heesy, M. I. Hall & D. R. W. Douglas. 2008. Relative Wulst volume is correlated with orbit orientation and binocular visual field in birds. *Journal of Comparative Physiology A-Neuroethology, Sensory, Neural and Behavioral Physiology* **194**:267–82.

Jackson, J. R. & W. C. Kimler. 1999. Taxonomy and the personal equation: the historical fates of Charles Girard and Louis Agassiz. *Journal of the History of Biology* **32**:509–55.

Jager, P. 2005. New large-sized cave-dwelling *Heteropoda* species from Asia, with notes on their relationships (Araneae: Sparassidae: Heteropodinae). *Revue Suisse de Zoologie* **112**:87–114.

Jaksĭć, F. M. & H. E. Braker. 1983. Food-niche relationships and guild structure of diurnal birds of prey: competition versus opportunism. *Canadian Journal of Zoology* **61**:2230–41.

James, J. M. 1993. Burial and infilling of a karst in Papua New Guinea by road erosion sediments. *Environmental Geology* **21**:144–51.

Jasinska, E. J., B. Knott & A. J. McComb. 1996. Root mats in ground water: a fauna-rice cave habitat. *Journal of the North American Benthological Society* **15**:508–19.

Jaume, D., G. A. Boxshall & W. F. Humphreys. 2001. New stygobiont copepods (Calanoida; Misophrioida) from Bundera Sinkhole, an anchialine cenote in north-western Australia. *Zoological Journal of the Linnean Society* **133**:1–24.

Jeannel, R. G. 1926. *Faune Cavernicole de la France avec une Étude des Conditions d'Existence dans le Domaine Souterrain*. Paris: P. Lechevalier.

Jeannel, R. G. 1950. *La Marche de l'Evolution*. Paris: Presses Universitaires de France.

Jeffery, W. R. 2001. Cavefish as a model system in evolutionary developmental biology. *Developmental Biology* **231**:1–12.

Jensen, J. B., C. D. Camp & J. L. Marshall. 2002. Ecology and life history of the pigeon salamander. *Southeastern Naturalist* **1**:3–16.

Johnson, K. H. 2000. Trophic-dynamic considerations in relating species diversity to ecosystem resilience. *Biological Reviews of the Cambridge Philosophical Society* **75**:347–76.

Jones, B. 1995. Processes associated with microbial biofilms in the twilight zone of caves – examples from the Cayman Islands. *Journal of Sedimentary Research Section A* **65**:552–60.

Jones, B. 2001. Microbial activity in caves: a geological perspective. *Geomicrobiology Journal* **18**:345–57.

Jones, W. K., D. C. Culver & J. S. Herman. 2004. *Epikarst. Proceedings of the Symposium held October 1–4, 2003, Shepherstown, West Virginia, U.S.A.* Charles Town, West Virginia: Karst Waters Institute.

Juberthie, C. 2000. The diversity of the karstic and pseudokarstic hypogean habitats in the world, pp. 17–39, in: H. Wilkens, D. C. Culver & W. F. Humphries (eds.) *Subterranean Ecosystems*. Amsterdam: Elsevier.

Juberthie, C., M. Bouillon & B. Delay. 1981. Sur l'existence du milieu souterrain superficiel en zone calcaire. *Mémoires de Biospéologie* **8**:77–93.

Juberthie, C. & R. Ginet. 1994. France, pp. 665–692, in: Juberthie, C. & Decu, V. (eds.) *Encyclopaedia Biospeologica*. Moulis: Societé de Biospeléologie.

Juget, J., M. C. D. Chatelliers & P. Rodriguez. 2006. *Troglodrilus* (Annelida, Oligochaeta, Tubificidae), a new genus from subterranean habitats in south-western Europe. *Hydrobiologia* **564**:7–17.

Južnič, S. 2006. Karst research in the 19th century – Karl Dežman's (1821–1889) work. *Acta Carsologica* **35/1**:139–48.

Kajihiro, E. S. 1965. Occurrence of dermatophytes in fresh bat guano. *Applied Microbiology* **13**:720–4.

Kano, Y., S. Chiba & T. Kase. 2002. Major adaptive radiation in neritopsine gastropods estimated from 28S rRNA sequences and fossil records. *Proceedings of the Royal Society of London Series* **269**:2457–65.

Kano, Y. & T. Kase. 2002. Anatomy and systematics of the submarine-cave gastropod *Pisulina* (Neritopsina: Neritiliidae). *Journal of Molluscan Studies* **68**:365–83.

Karaman, G. S. & S. G. Matocec. 2006. *Niphargus echion*, a new species of amphipod (Crustacea Amphipoda, Niphargidae) from Istra, Croatia. *Zootaxa* **1150**:53–68.

Karamanlidis, A. A., R. Pires, N. C. Silva & H. C. Neves. 2004. The availability of resting and pupping habitat for the critically endangered Mediterranean monk seal *Monachus monachus* in the archipelago of Madeira. *Oryx* **38**:180–5.

Kasyanov, V. L., O. M. Korn & A. V. Rybakov. 1997. Reproductive strategy of cirripedes (Thecostraca, Cirripedia). 2. Asexual reproduction, fecundity and reproductive cycles. *Biologiya Morya* (Vladivostok) **23**:337–44.

Kerrigan, R. W., D. M. Carvallho, P. A. Horgen & J. B. Anderson. 1995. Indigenous and introduced populations of *Agaricus bisporus*, the cultivated 'button mushroom', in eastern and western Canada. *Canadian Journal of Botany* **73**:1925–38.

Kirby, R. F., K. W. Thompson & C. Hubbs. 1977. Karyotypic similarities between the Mexican and blind tetras. *Copeia* **1977**:578–80.

Kircher, A. 1665. *Mundus Subterraneus, in XII libros digestus; quo divinum subterrestris mundi opificium, mira ergasteriorum naturæ in eo distributio, verbo pantámorphou Protei regnum, universæ denique naturæ majestas & divitiæ summa rerum varietate exponuntur.* Amsterdam: J. Janssonium and E. Weyerstraten.

Knight, J. 1997. Subterranean blues. *New Scientist* **(2099)**:26.

Koch, C. L. 1835–8. *Deutschlands Crustaceen, Myriapoden und Arachniden: ein Beitrag zur Deutschen Fauna.* Regensburg: F. Pustet.

Koenemann, D., T. M. Iliffe & J. Van der Ham. 2003. Three new sympatric species of Remipedia (Crustacea) from Great Exuma Island, Bahamas Islands. *Contributions to Zoology* **72**:227–52.

Koilraj, A. J., G. Marimuthu, K. Natarajan, S. Saravanan, P. Maran & M. J. Hsu. 1999. Fungal diversity inside caves of Southern India. *Current Science* **77**:1081–4.

Koilraj, A., V. Sharma, G. Marimuthu & M. Chandrashekaran. 2000. Presence of circadian rhythms in the locomotor activity of a cave-dwelling millipede *Glyphiulus cavernicolus sulu* (Cambalidae, Spirostreptida). *Chronobiology International* **17**:757–65.

Konishi M. & E. I. Knudsen. 1979. The oilbird: hearing and echolocation. *Science* **204**:425–7.

Könnecker, G. & A. Freiwald. 2005. *Plectroninia celtica* n. sp. (Calcarea, Minchinellidae), a new species of "pharetronid" sponge from bathyal depths in the northern Porcupine Seabight, NE Atlantic. *FACIES* **51**:57–63.

Koppelman, J. B. & D. E. Figg. 1995. Genetic estimates of variability and relatedness for conservation of an Ozark cave crayfish species complex. *Conservation Biology* **9**:1288–94.

Kornicker, L. S. & J. Yager. 2002. Description of *Spelaeoecia saturno*, a new species from an anchialine cave in Cuba (Crustacea: Ostracoda: Myodocopa: Halocyprididae). *Proceedings of the Biological Society of Washington* **115**:153–70.

Kristjánsson, J. K. & G. O. Hreggvidsson. 1995. Ecology and habitats of extremophiles. *World Journal of Microbiology and Biotechnology* **11**:17–25.

Ku, T. L. & H. C. Li. 1998. Speleothems as high-resolution paleoenvironment archives: records from northeastern China. *Proceedings of the Indian Academy of Sciences – Earth and Planetary Sciences* **107**:321–30.

Kuehn, K. A. & R. D. Koehn. 1991. Fungal populations isolated from Ezell Cave in South Texas. *Stygologia* **6**:65–76.

Kuehn, K. A., R. M. O'Neil & R. D. Koehn. 1992. Viable photosynthetic microalgal isolates from aphotic environments of the Edwards Aquifer (Central Texas). *Stygicola* **7**:129–42.

Kuhajda, B. R. & R. L. Mayden. 2001. Status of the federally endangered Alabama cavefish, *Speoplatyrhinus poulsoni* (Amblyopsidae), in Key Cave and surrounding caves, Alabama. *Environmental Biology of Fishes* **62**:215–22.

Kuhn, T. S. 1970. *The Structure of Scientific Revolutions*. Chicago, IL: The University of Chicago Press.

Kuntner, M., B. Sket & A. Blejec. 1999. A comparison of the respiratory systems in some cave and surface species of spiders (Araneae, Dysderidae). *Journal of Arachnology* **27**:142–8.

Kurta, A., J. O. Whitaker, W. J. Wrennm & J. A. Soto-Centeno. 2007. Ectoparasitic assemblages on mormoopid bats (Chiroptera: Mormoopidae) from Puerto Rico. *Journal of Medical Entomology* **44**: 953–8.

LaFleur, R. G. 1999. Geomorphic aspects of groundwater flow. *Hydrogeology Journal* **7**:78–93.

Laing, C., G. Carmody & S. Peck. 1976a. How common are sibling species in cave-inhabiting invertebrates? *The American Naturalist* **110**:184–9.

Laing, C., G. Carmody & S. B. Peck. 1976b. Population genetics and evolutionary biology of the cave beetle *Ptomophagus hirtus*. *Evolution* **30**:484–98.

LaMoreaux, P. E. & J. LaMoreaux. 2007. Karst: the foundation for concepts in hydrogeology. *Environmental Geology* **51**:685–8.

Landoldt, J. C., S. L. Stephenson & C. W. Stihler. 1992. Cellular slime molds in West Virginia caves including notes on the occurrence and distribution of *Dictyostelium rosarium*. *Mycologia* **84**:399–405.

Langecker, T. G. 1989. Studies on the light reaction of epigean and cave populations of *Astyanax fasciatus* (Characidae, Pisces). *Mémoires de Biospéologie* **16**:169–76.

Langecker, T. G. 2000. The effects of continuous darkness on cave ecology and cavernicolous evolution, pp. 135–57, in: H. Wilkens, D. C. Culver & W. F. Humphries (eds.) *Subterranean Ecosystems*. Amsterdam: Elsevier.

Langecker, T. G. & G. Longley. 1993. Morphological adaptations of the Texas blind catfishes *Trogloglanis pattersoni* and *Satan eurystomus* (Siluriformes: Ictaluridae) to their underground environment. *Copeia* **1993**:976–86.

Langecker, T. G., H. Wilkens & P. Junge. 1991. Introgressive hybridization in the Pachon Cave population of *Astyanax fasciatus* (Teleostei: Characidae). *Ichthyological Exploration of Freshwaters* **2**:209–12.

Lankester, E. R. 1880. *Degeneration: a Chapter in Darwinism*. London: Macmillan.

Lankester, E. R. 1893. Blind animals in caves. *Nature* **47**:389.

Larson, A., D. W. Weisrock & K. H. Kozak. 2003. Phylogenetic systematics of salamanders (Amphibia: Urodela), a review, pp. 31–108, in: D. M. Selver (ed.) *Reproductive Biology and Phylogeny of Urodela*. Enfield, NH: Science Publishers, Inc.

Larson, D. J. & J. R. Labonte. 1994. *Stygoporus oregonensis*, a new genus and species of subterranean water beetle (Coleoptera: Dytiscidae: Hydroporini) from the United States. *Coleopterists Bulletin* **48**:371–9.

Laurenti, J. N. 1768. *Specimen medicum, exhibens synopsin reptilium emendatam cum experimentis circa venena et antidota reptilium Austriacorum*. Wien: Joan Thomae.

Lavoie, K. H., K. L. Helf & T. L. Poulson. 2007. The biology and ecology of North American cave crickets. *Journal of Cave and Karst Studies* **69**:114–34.

Lee, P. L. M., D. H. Clayton, R. Griffiths & R. D. M. Page. 1996. Does behavior reflect phylogeny in swiftlets (Aves: Apodidae)? A test using cytochrome b mitochondrial DNA sequences. *Proceedings of the National Academy of Sciences of the United States of America* **93**:7091–6.

Lee, S. & H. Kim. 2006. A fern aphid, *Neomacromyzus cyrtomicola* Lee, new genus and new species (Hemiptera: Aphididae) on *Cyrtomium falcatum* (Dryopteridaceae) in basalt rock caves. *Proceedings of the Entomological Society of Washington* **108**:493–501.

Lefebvre, L., P. Whittle & E. Lascaris. 1997. Feeding innovations and forebrain size in birds. *Animal Behaviour* **53**:549–60.

Lehnert, H. 1998. *Thrombus jancai* new species (Porifera, Demospongiae, Astrophorida) from shallow water off Jamaica. *Bulletin of Marine Science* **62**:181–7.

Leith, J. A. 1989. L'Evolution de l'idée de progrès à travers l'histoire. *Transactions of the Royal Society of Canada* **4**:3–8.

Le Maho, Y. 1984. Adaptations métaboliques au jeûne prolongé chez les oiseaux et les mammifères. *Bulletin d'Ecophysiologie* **2**:129–48.

Lewis, J. J. 2000. *Caecidotea cumberlandensis*, a new species of troglobitic isopod from Virginia, with new records of other subterranean Caecidotea (Crustacea: Isopoda: Asellidae). *Proceedings of the Biological Society of Washington* **113**:458–64.

Lewis, J. J. 2005. Six new species of Pseudotremia from caves of the Tennessee Cumberland Plateau (Diplopoda: Chordeumatida: Cleidogonidae). *Zootaxa* **1080**:17–31.

Lewis, W. C. 1989. Histoplasmosis: a hazard to new tropical caves. *National Speleological Society Bulletin* **51**:52–65.

Leys, R., C. H. S. Watts, S. J. B. Cooper & W. F. Humphreys. 2003. Evolution of subterranean diving beetles (Coleoptera: Dytisicidae: Hydroporini, Bidessini) in the arid zone of Australia. *Evolution* **57**:2819–34.

Leys, S. P., E. Cheung, & N. Boury-Esnault. 2006. Embryogenesis in the glass sponge *Oopsacas minuta*: formation of syncytia by fusion of blastomeres. *Integrative and Comparative Biology* **46**:104–17.

Li, W., D. Wu, A. Chen & J. Tao. 1997. Histological study on the horn-like projection of the head of *Sinocyclocheilus rhinocerous*. *Journal of Yunnan University* **19**:426–8.

Lidgard, D. C., O. Kiely, E. Rogan & N. Connolly. 2001. The status of breeding grey seals (*Halichoerus grypus*) on the east and south-east of Ireland. *Mammalia* **65**:283–94.

Lister, M. 1674. An account of two uncommon mineral substances, found in some coal and iron-mines of England; as it was given by the intelligent and learned Mr. Jessop of Bromhal in York-Shire to the ingenious Mr. Lister, and by him communicated to the publisher in a letter of January 7. 1663/74. *Philosophical Transactions of the Royal Society of London* **8**:6179–81.

Livezey, B. C. & P. S. Humphrey. 1986. Flightlessness in steamer-ducks (Anatidae: Tachyeres): its morphological bases and probable evolution. *Evolution* **40**:540–58.

Logan, A. 2005. A new lacazelline species (Brachiopoda, Recent) from the Maldive Islands, Indian Ocean. *Systematics and Biodiversity* **3**:97–104.

Logan, A. & H. Zibrowius. 1994. A new genus and species of rhynchonellid (Brachiopoda, Recent) from submarine caves in the Mediterranean Sea. *Marine Ecology – Pubblicazioni della Stazione Zoologica di Napoli I* **15**:77–88.

Lolcama, J. L., H. A. Cohen & M. J. Tonkin. 2002. Deep karst conduits, flooding, and sinkholes: lessons for the aggregates industry. *Engineering Geology* **65**:151–7.

Longley, G. 1981. The Edwards Aquifer: Earth's most diverse groundwater ecosystem? *International Journal of Speleology* **11**:123–8.

Longrás Otín, L. 2002. Francisco de Tauste (1626–1685), pp. 9–38, in: M.A. Pallarés Jiménez (ed.). *Arte y Bocabvlario de la lengva de los Indion Chaymas, Cvmanagotos, Cores, Parias, y otros diversos de la Provincia de Cvmana, o Nueva Andalvcia.* Zaragoza, Spain: Instituto Aragonés de Antropología.

Lourenco, W. R. 1995. *Chaerilus sabinae*, a new species of anophthalmous scorpion from the caves of matampa in India (Scorpiones, Chaerilidae). *Revue Suisse de Zoologie* **102**:847–50.

Lourenco, W. R. 2007. First record of the family Pseudochactidae Gromov (Chelicerata, Scorpiones) from Laos and new biogeographic evidence of a Pangaean palaeodistribution. *Comptes Rendus Biologies* **330**:770–7.

Lourie, S. A. & D. M. Tompkins. 2000. The diets of Malaysian swiftlets. *Ibis* **142**:596–602.

Lozouet, P. 2004. The European Tertiary Neritiliidae (Mollusca, Gastropoda, Neritopsina): indicators of tropical submarine cave environments and freshwater faunas. *Zoological Journal of the Linnean Society* **140**:447–67.

Lucas, F. A. 1898. Biological Society of Washington, 296th meeting, Saturday November 5. **8**:717–20.

Ludlow, M. E. & J. A. Gore. 2000. Effects of a cave gate on emergence patterns of colonial bats. *Wildlife Society Bulletin* **28**:191–6.

Lull, R. S. 1921. *Organic Evolution.* New York: Macmillan.

Lurie, E. 1960. *Louis Agassiz. A Life in Science.* Chicago: University of Chicago Press.

Lurie, E. 1970. Agassiz, Jean Louis Rodolphe, pp. 72–4, in: C. C. Gillispie (ed.) *Dictionary of Scientific Biography*, vol. 1. New York: Scribner.

Luter, C., G. Worheide & J. Reitner. 2003. A new thecideid genus and species (Brachiopoda, Recent) from submarine caves of Osprey Reef (Queensland Plateau, Coral Sea, Australia). *Journal of Natural History* **37**:1423–32.

Lydeard, C., R. H. Cowie, W. F. Ponder *et al.* 2004. The global decline of nonmarine mollusks. *BioScience* **54**:321–30.

Lyell, C. 1830–1833. *Principles of Geology.* London: J. Murray.

MacElroy, R. D. 1974. Some comments on the evolution of extremophiles. *Biosystems* **6**:74–5.

Machado, G. & P. S. Oliveira. 1998. Reproduction biology of the neotropical harvestman (*Goniosoma longipes*) (Arachnida, Opiliones: Gonyleptidae): mating and ovoposition behaviour, brood mortality, and parental care. *Journal of Zoology* **246**:359–67.

Machado, G., R. L. G. Raimundo & P. S. Oliveira. 2000. Daily activity schedule, gregariousness, and defensive behavior in the Neotropical harvestman *Goniosoma longipes* (Opiliones: Gonyleptidae). *Journal of Natural History* **34**:587–96.

Machado, S. F., R. L. Ferreira & R. P. Martins. 2003. Aspects of the population ecology of *Goniosoma* sp. (Arachnida, Opiliones, Gonyleptidae). *Tropical Zoology* **16**:13–31.

Mader, B. 2003. Archdure Ludwig Salvator and *Leptodirus hohenwarti* from Postojnska jama. *Acta Carsologica* **32/2**:289–98.

Magniez, G. J. 2001. New data on *Stenasellus strinatii* (Crustacea, Isopoda, Asellota, Stenasellidae), stygobiont from Sumatra (Indonesia). *Revue Suisse de Zoologie* **108**:551–7.

Maher, L. J. 2006. Environmental information from guano palynology of insectivorous bats of the central part of the United States of America. *Palaeogeography, Palaeoclimatology, Palaeoecology* **237**:19–31.

Mahler, B. J., L. Lynch & P. C. Bennett. 1999. Mobile sediment in an urbanizing karst aquifer: implications for contaminant transport. *Environmental Geology* **39**:25–38.

Mahunka, S. 2001. Cave-dwelling oribatid mites from Greece (Acari: Orbatida). *Revue Suisse de Zoologie* **108**:165–88.

Makarov, S. E., B. M. Mitic & S. B. Curcic. 2002. On two new cave diplopods from Serbia (Diplopoda, Julida). *Israel Journal of Zoology* **48**:235–42.

Makarov, S. E., L. R. Lucic, V. T. Tomic & I. M. Karaman. 2003a. Two new glomeridellids (Glomeridellidae, Diplopoda) from Montenegro and Macedonia. *Periodicum Biologorum* **105**:473–7.

Makarov, S. E., B. M. Mitic & S. B. Curcic. 2003b. *Svarogosoma bozidarcurcici*, n. g., n. sp. (Diplopoda, Anthroleucosomatidae) from the Balkan Peninsula, with notes on its phylogeny. *Periodicum Biologorum* **105**:465–72.

Makarov, S. E., B. M. Mitic & T. Rada. 2003c. On some endemic diplopods from Croatia (Polydesmida, Diplopoda). *Periodicum Biologorum* **105**:163–6.

Makarov, S. E., T. Rada, V. T. Tomic, B. M. Mitic & S. Vujcic-Karlo. 2006. *Typhloiulus gellianae* n. sp., a new cave-dwelling diplopod from Croatia (Myriapoda, Diplopoda, Julidae). *Periodicum Biologorum* **108**:97–9.

Makol, J. & G. Gabrys. 2005. *Caecothrombium deharvengi* sp. nov. (Acari: Actinotrichida: Eutrombidiidae) from Vietnam, with a proposal of Caethrombiinae subfam. nov. *Zoologischer Anzeiger* **243**:227–37.

Mangin, A. 1973. Sur la dynamique des transferts en aquifère karstique, pp. 157–62, in: International Union of Biospeleology *Proceedings of the 6th International Congress on Speleology, Olomouc*. Prague: Academia.

Mangin, A., F. Bourges & D. d'Hulst. 1999. La conservation des grottes ornéss: un problème de stabilité d'un système natural (l'exemple de la grotte préhistorique de Gargas, Pyrénées françaises). *Comptes Rendus de l'Academie des Sciences, Serie II, Fascicule a* **328**:295–301.

Mann, S. L., R. J. Steidl & V. M. Dalton. 2002. Effects of cave tours on breeding *Myotis velifer*. *Journal of Wildlife Management* **66**:618–24.

Manoleli, D. G., D. J. Klemm & S. M. Sarbu. 1998. *Haemopis caeca* (Annelida: Hirudinea: Arhynchobdellida: Haemopidae), a new species of troglobitic leech from a chemoautotrophically based groundwater ecosystem in Romania. *Proceedings of the Biological Society of Washington* **111**:222–9.

Margalef, R. 1974. *Ecología*. Barcelona, Spain: Omega.

Margalef, R. 1993. *Teoría de los Sistemas Ecológicos*. Barcelona, Spain: Universidad de Barcelona.

Margalef, R. & E. Gutierrez. 1983. How to introduce connectance in the frame of an expression for diversity. *American Naturalist* **121**:601–7.

Mariani, S. 2003. Recruitment in invertebrates with short-lived larvae: the case of the bryozoan *Disporella hispida* (Fleming). *Helgoland Marine Research* **57**:47–53.

Mariani, S., T. Alcoverro, M. J. Uriz & X. Turon. 2005. Early life histories in the bryozoan *Schizobrachiella sanguinea*: a case study. *Marine Biology* **147**:735–45.

Marmonier, P., P. Vervier, J. Gilbert & M.-J. Dole-Olivier. 1993. Biodiversity in ground waters. *Trends in Ecology and Evolution* **8**:392–5.

Martel, E. A. 1889. Sous terre (1er. Campagne). *Annales du Club Alpine de France* **15**(for 1888):238–94.

Martel, E. A. 1894a. *Les Abîmes*. Paris: Delagrave.

Martel, E. A. 1894b. La spélaeologie. *Comptes Rendus de la Association Française pour l'Advancement des Sciences* **22**:60.

Martel, E. A. 1896. Speleology, pp. 721–6, in *Report of the Sixth International Geographical Congress: held in London, 1895*. London: J. Murray.

Martel, E. A. 1897. British caves and speleology. *Geographical Journal* **10**:500–11.

Martel, E. A. 1900. *La spéléologie: ou Science des Cavernes*. Paris: Gauthier-Villars.

Mathieu, J. & J. Gilbert. 1980. Evolution des teneurs en proteins, glucides et lipids de *Niphargus renorhodanensis* Schellenberg comparé entre l'elevage en milieu naturel reconstitué et le jeûne experimental. *Crustaceana* (Suppl.) **6**:128–36.

Marti, R., M. J. Uriz, E. Ballesteros & X. Turon. 2004. Temporal variation of several structure descriptors in animal-dominated benthic communities in two Mediterranean caves. *Journal of the Marine Biological Association of the United Kingdom* **84**:573–80.

Marti, R., M. J. Uriz & X. Turon. 2005. Spatial and temporal variation of natural toxicity in cnidarians, bryozoans and tunicates in Mediterranean caves. *Scientia Marina* **69**:485–92.

Martin, J. M. & J. C. Braga. 1994. Messinian events in the Sorbas Basin in south-eastern Spain and their implications in the Recent history of the Mediterranean. *Sedimentary Geology* **90**:257–68.

Martin, G. R., L. M. Rojas, F. Ramirez, & R. McNeil. 2004a. The eyes of oilbirds (*Steatornis caripensis*): pushing at the limits of sensitivity. *Naturwissenschaften* **91**: 26–9.

Martin, G. R., L. M. Rojas, F. Ramirez, M. Yleana & R. McNeil. 2004b. Binocular vision and nocturnal activity in oilbirds (*Steatornis caripensis*) and pauraques (*Nyctidromus albicollis*): Caprimulgiformes. *Ornitologia Neotropical* **15**:233–42.

Martin, J. W. & G. E. Davis. 2006. Historical trends in crustacean systematics. *Crustaceana* **79**:1347–68.

Martin, K. W., D. M. Leslie, M. E. Payton, W. L. Puckette & S. L. Hensley. 2003. Internal cave gating for protection of colonies of the endangered gray bat (*Myotis grisescens*). *Acta Chiropterologica* **5**:143–50.

Martin, K. W., D. M. Leslie, M. E. Payton, W. L. Puckette & S. L. Hensley. 2006. Impacts of passage manipulation on cave climate: conservation implications for cave-dwelling bats. *Wildlife Society Bulletin* **34**:137–43.

Martuscelli, P. 1995. Avian predation by the round-eared bat (*Tonatia bidens*, Phyllostomidae) in the Brazilian Atlantic forest. *Journal of Tropical Ecology* **11**:461–4.

Matjašič, J. & B. Sket. 1971. Jamski hydroid s slovenskega krasa. *Biološki Vestnik* **19**:139–45.

Maynard Smith, J. 1970. Time in evolutionary process. *Studium Generale* **23**:266–72.

Mayr, E. 1960. The emergence of evolutionary novelties, pp. 349–80, in: S. Tax (ed.) *The Evolution of Life. Its Origin, History, and Future*. Chicago IL: The University of Chicago Press.

Mayr, E. 1982. *The Growth of Biological Thought: Diversity, Evolution, and Inheritance*. Cambridge, MA: Belknap Press.

McAllister, C. & C. Bursey. 2004. Endoparasites of the dark-sided salamander, *Eurycea longicauda melanopleura*, and the cave salamander, *Eurycea lucifuga* (Caudata: Plethodontidae), from two caves in Arkansas, USA. *Comparative Parasitology* **71**:61–6.

McCracken, G. F. 1986. Why are we losing our Mexican free-tailed bats? *Bats* **3**:1–4.

McCracken, G. F. 1989. Cave conservation: special problems of bats. *Bulletin of the National Speleological Society* **51**:47–51.

McFarlane, D. A. 1986. Cave bats of Jamaica. *Oryx* **20**:27–30.

McFarlane, D. A. & J. Lundberg. 2005. The 19th century excavation of Kent's Cavern, England. *Journal of Cave and Karst Studies* **67**:39–47.

McGrew, W. C., J. K. McKee, & C. E. G. Tutin. 2003. Primates in caves: two new reports of *Papio* spp. *Journal of Human Evolution* **44**:521–6.

McKenna, J. J. 1979. The evolution of allomothering behavior among colobine monkeys: function and opportunism in evolution. *American Anthropologist* **81**:818–40.

McLaughlin, P. 2002. Naming biology. *Journal of the History of Biology* **35**:1–4.

McMurray, D. N. & L. H. Russell. 1982. Contribution of bats to the maintenance of *Histoplasma capsulatum* in a cave microfocus. *American Journal of Tropical Medicine and Hygene* **31**:527–31.

McPeek, M. A. 1995. Morphological evolution mediated by behavior in the damselflies of two communities. *Evolution* **49**:749–69.

Mejia-Orriz, L. M., R. G. Hartnoll, J. A. Viccon-Pale. 2003. A new stygobitic crayfish from Mexico, *Procambarus cavernicola* (Decapoda: Cambaridae), with a review of cave-dwelling crayfishes in Mexico. *Journal of Crustacean Biology* **23**:391–401.

Melendez-Hevia, E., T. G. Waddell & M. Cascante. 1996. The puzzle of the Krebs citric acid cycle: assembling the pieces of chemically feasible reactions, and opportunism in the design of metabolic pathways during evolution. *Journal of Molecular Evolution* **43**:293–303.

Melim, L. A., K. M. Shinglman, P. J. Boston *et al.* 2001. Evidence for microbial involvement in pool finger precipitation, Hidden Cave, New Mexico. *Geomicrobiology Journal* **18**:311–29.

Mendez, G. & W. Wieser. 1993. Metabolic responses to food-deprivation and refeeding in juveniles of *Rutilus rutilus* (Teleostei, Cyprinidae). *Environmental Biology of Fishes* **36**:73–81.

Meroz-Fine, E., S. Shefer & M. Ilan. 2005. Changes in morphology and physiology of an East Mediterranean sponge in different habitats. *Marine Biology* **147**:243–50.

Mesibov, R. 2005. A new genus of burrowing and cave-dwelling millipedes (Diplopoda: Polydesmida: Dalodesmidae) from Tasmania, Australia. *Zootaxa* **1034**:21–42.

Messana, G. 2004. Africa: biospeleology, pp. 24–25, in: J. Gunn (ed.) *Encyclopedia of Caves and Karst Science*. New York: Fitzroy Dearborn.

Messana, G., M. Baratti & D. Benvenuti. 2002. *Pongycarcinia xiphidiourus* n. gen. n. sp., a new Brazilian Calabozoidae (Crustacea, Isopoda). *Tropical Zoology* **15**:243–52.

Meyer-Rochow, V. B. & A. R. Liddle. 1988. Structure and function of the eyes of two species of opilioid from New Zealand glow-worm caves (*Megalopsalis tumida*: Palpatores, and *Hendea myersi cavernicola*: Laniatores). *Proceedings of the Royal Society of London, Series B* **233**:293–319.

Mickleburgh, S. P., A. M. Hutson & P. A. Racey. 2002. A review of the global conservation status of bats. *Oryx* **36**:18–34.

Midriak, R. & J. Liptak. 1995. Erosion and reforestation of abandoned lands in the Slovak Karst Biosphere Reserve. *Ekologia-Bratislava* **14**:111–24.

Milanovich, J. R., S. E. Trauth, R. R. Jordan & D. A. Saugey. 2006. Fecundity, reproductive ecology, and influence of precipitation on clutch size in the western slimy salamander (*Plethodon albagula*). *Herpetologica* **62**:292–301.

Milanovic, P. 2002. The environmental impacts of human activities and engineering constructions in karst regions. *Episodes* **25**:13–21.

Miller, J. A. 2005. Cave adaptation in the spider genus *Anthrobia* (Araneae, Linyphiidae, Erigoninae). *Zoologica Scripta* **34**:565–92.

Minio-Paluello, A. 1970. Aristotle, pp. 250–81, in: C. C. Gilliespie (ed.) *Dictionary of Scientific Biography*, vol. 1. New York: Scribner.

Miquelarena, A., S. Ortubay & V. Cussac. 2005. Morphology, osteology and reductions in the ontogeny of the scaleless characid *Gymnocharacinus bergi*. *Journal of Applied Ichthyology* **21**:511–19.

Missouri State Parks and Historic Sites. Rock State Memorial Park. Accessed 11 April 2006. http://www.mostateparks.com/rockbridge/geninfo.htm.

Mitchell, F. S., D. P. Onorato, E. C. Hellgren, J. R. Skiles & L. A. Harveson. 2005. Winter ecology of American black bears in a desert montane island. *Wildlife Society Bulletin* **33**:164–71.

Mitchell, R. W. 1970. Cave adapted flatworms of Texas – systematics, natural history, and responses to light and temperature. *American Zoologist* **10**:547.

Mitchell, R. W. & S. B. Peck. 1977. *Typhlochactas sylvestris*, a new eyeless scorpion from Montane forest litter in Mexico (Scorpionida, Chactidae, Typhlochactinae). *Journal of Arachnology* **5**:159–68.

Mitchell, R. W., W. H. Russel & W. R. Elliot. 1977. *Mexican Eyeless Characin Fishes, Genus* Astyanax: *Environment, Distribution, and Evolution*. Special Publications No. 12. Lubbock, TX: Texas University Press.

Mivart, St. G. J. 1871. *Genesis of Species*. London: Macmillan & Co.

Mohr, C. E. 1953. Animals that live in Pennsylvania caves. *National Speleological Society Bulletin* **15**:15–23.

Molinari, J., E. E. Gutierrez, A. A. De Ascencao *et al.* 2005. Predation by giant centipedes, *Scolopendra gigantea*, on three species of bats in a Venezuelan cave. *Caribbean Journal of Science* **41**:340–6.

Monod, J. 1970. *Le Hasard et la Necessité*. Paris: Seuil.

Montalembert, M.-R. 1748. Observations de physique générale. *Histoire de l' Académie Royale des Sciences* **1748**:27–8.

Moore, J. 1996. Survey of the biota and trophic interactions within Wind Cave and Jewel Cave, South Dakota: Final Report. University of Northern Colorado.

Accessed 11 April 2006. http://www.nps.gov/wica/Abstract-Moore Survey_of_the_Biota_and_Trophic_Interactions_Within_Wind_Cave_and_Jewel_Cave.htm.

Moore-Landecker, E. 1996. *Fundamentals of the Fungi*. New York: Prentice-Hall.

Moraes, R., W. G. Landis & S. Molander. 2002. Regional risk assessment of a Brazilian rain forest reserve. *Human and Ecological Risk Assessment* **8**:1779–803.

Moravec, F., T. Scholz, C. VivasRodriguez, J. VargasVazquez & E. Mendoza-Franco. 1996. Systematic status and first description of male of *Dujardinia cenotae* Pearse, 1936 [equals *Hysterothylacium cenotae* (Pearse, 1936) Moravec *et al.* 1995] (Nematoda Anisakidae). *Systematic Parasitology* **33**:143–8.

Moraz, M. L. & E. E. Linquist. 1998. Coprozerconidae, a new family of zerconoid mites from North America (Acari: Mesostigmata: Zerconoidea). *Acarologia* **39**:291–313.

Moraza, M. L. 2004. *Rhodacarella*, a new genus of Rhodacaridae mites from North America (Acari: Mesostigmata: Rhodacaridae). *Zootaxa* **470**:1–10.

Moraza, M. L. & E. E. Lindquist. 1998. Coprozerconidae, a new family of Zerconoid mites from North America (Acari: Megostigmata: Zerconoidea). *Acarologia* **39**:291–313.

Moreno-Valdez, A., R. L. Honeycutt & W. E. Grant. 2004. Colony dynamics of *Leptonycteris nivalis* (Mexican long-nosed bat) related to flowering agave in Northern Mexico. *Journal of Mammalogy* **85**:453–9.

Morgan, R. 1943. Caves in world history. *Bulletin of the National Speleological Society* **5**:1–16.

Morris, P. J. 1997. Louis Agassiz's arguments against Darwinism and his additions to the French translation of the *Essay on Classification*. *Journal of the History of Biology* **30**:121–34.

Morton, B., F. Velkovrh & B. Sket. 1998. Biology and anatomy of the 'living fossil' *Congeria kusceri* (Bivalvia: Dreissenidae) from subterranean rivers and caves in the Dinaric karst of the former Yugoslavia. *Journal of Zoology* **245**:147–74.

Motas, C. 1962. Emil G. Racovitza: founder of biospeleology. *National Speleological Society Bulletin* **24**:3–8.

Muchmore, W. B. 1997. *Tuberochernes* (Psuedoscorpionida, Chernetidae), a new genus with species in caves in California and Arizona. *Journal of Arachnology* **25**:206–12.

Muchmore, W. B. 2001. An unusual new species of *Mundochthonius* from a cave in Colorado, with comments on *Mundochthonius montanus* (Pseudoscorpiones, Chthoniidae). *Journal of Arachnology* **29**:135–40.

Muchmore, W. B. & R. B. Pape. 1999. Description of an eyeless, cavernicolous *Albiorix* (Pseudoscorpionida: Ideoronidae) in Arizona, with observations on its biology and ecology. *The Southwestern Naturalist* **44**:138–47.

Murakami, Y. 1975. The cave myriapods of the Ryukyu islands, Japan. Part 1. *Bulletin of the National Science Museum* Series A **1**:85–113.

Mylroie, J & K. Tronvig. 1998. Karst Waters Institute creates top ten list of endangered karst ecosystems. *National Speleological Society News* (February):41–3.

Mystakidou, K., E. Tsilika, E. Parpa, E. Katsouda & L. Vlahos. 2004. Death and grief in the Greek culture. *Omega, Journal of Death and Dying* **50**:23–34.

National Park Service. 2005. Cave biology, Sequoia and Kings Canyon National Parks. http://www.nps.gov/seki/snrm/wildlife/cave_biology.htm.

Nealson, K. H. & P. G. Conrad. 1999. Life: past, present and future. *Philosophical Transactions of the Royal Society of London Series B* **354**:1923–39.

Neely, D. A. & R. L. Mayden. 2003. Phylogenetic relationships, diversity, and zoogeography of western *Cottus*. San Diego, CA: American Fisheries Society, Western Division.

Nelson, J. S. 2006. *Fishes of the World*. New York: John Wiley & Son.

Nevo, E. 1979. Adaptive convergence and divergence of subterranean mammals. *Annual Review of Ecology and Systematics* **10**:269–308.

Ng, P. K. L. 2002a. New species of cavernicolous crabs of the genus Sesarmoides from the Western Pacific, with a key to the genus (Crustacea: Decapoda: Brachyura: Sesarmidae). *Raffles Bulletin of Zoology* **50**:419–35.

Ng, P. K. L. 2002b. On a new species of cavernicolous *Neoliomera* (Crustacea: Decapoda: Brachyura: Xanthidae) from Christmas Island and Ryukyus, Japan. *Raffles Bulletin of Zoology* **50**:95–9.

Nichol, D. 1998. Sinkholes at Glan Llyn on the A55 North Wales Coast Road, UK. *Engineering Geology* **50**:101–9.

Nicholas, G. 1960. Checklist of macroscopic troglobitic organisms of the United States. *American Midland Naturalist*. **64**:123–60.

Nicholas, G. 1962. Checklist of troglobitic organisms of Middle America. *American Midland Naturalist* **68**:165–88.

Norman, J. R. 1926. A new blind catfish from Trinidad, with a list of the blind cave-fishes. *Annals and Magazine of Natural History* **18**:324–31.

Northup, D. E., S. M. Barns, L. E. Yu *et al.* 2003. Diverse microbial communities inhabiting ferromanganese deposits in Lechuguilla and Spider Caves. *Environmental Microbiology* **5**:1071–86.

Northup, D. E., C. N. Dahm, L. A. Melin *et al.* 2000. Evidence for geomicrobiological interactions in Guadalupe caves. *Journal of Cave and Karst Studies* **62**:80–90.

Northup, D. E. & K. H. Lavoie. 2001. Geomicrobiology of caves: a review. *Geomicrobiology Journal* **18**:199–222.

Notenboom, J. 1991. Marine regressions and the evolution of groundwater dwelling amphipods (in mammals and molluscs, Crustacea and correlations). *Journal of Biogeography* **18**:437–54.

Novak, T., J. Sambol & F. Janžerovič. 2003. Faunal dynamics in the Železna jama Cave. *Acta Carsologica* **33/2**:249–67.

Nussac, L. de. 1892. *Essai Élémentaire de Spéologie Naturelle du Bas-Limousin (départment de la Corrèze)*. Brive, France: Roche.

O'Donnell, C. F. J. 2002. Variability in numbers of long-tailed bats (*Chalinolobus tuberculatus*) roosting in Grand Canyon Cave, New Zealand: implications for monitoring population trends. *New Zealand Journal of Zoology* **29**:273–84.

Okuno, J. 1999. *Palaemonella hachijo*, a new species of shrimp (Crustacea: Decapoda: Palaemonidae) from a submarine cave in southern Japan. *Proceedings of the Biological Society of Washington* **112**:739–45.

O'Malley, R., T. King, C. S. Turner *et al.* 2006. The diversity and distribution of the fruit bat fauna (Mammalia, Chiroptera, Megachiroptera) of Danjugan Island, Cauayan, Negros Occidental, Philippines (with notes on the Microchiroptera). *Biodiversity and Conservation* **15**:43–56.

Olivier, G. 1967. Teilhard de Chardin et le transformisme. *Annales de l'Université de Paris* **37**:358–65.

Oppenheimer, J. M. 1982. Ernest Heinrich Haeckel as an intermediary in the transmutation of an idea. *Proceedings of the American Philosophical Society* **126**:347–55.

Osawa, M., Y. Fugita & J. Okuno. 2006. Two new species of *Pagurixus* (Crustacea: Decapoda: Anomura: Paguridae) from submarine caves of the Ryukyu Islands, southwestern Japan. *Zootaxa* **1148**:27–45.

Osawa, M. & M. Takeda. 2004. Hermit crabs (Crustacea: Decapoda: Anomura: Paguroidea) from submarine caves in the Ryukyu Islands, south-western Japan. *Journal of Natural History* **38**:1097–132.

Osborn, H. F. 1934. *Aristogenesis, the Creative Principle in the Origin of Species*. New York.

Osella, G. & A. M. Zuppa. 2006. *Otiorhynchus* (*Podonebistus*) *gasparoi* n. sp., a blind weevil from Greece (Coleoptera, Curculionidae, Entiminae, Otiorhynchini). *Revue Suisse de Zoologie* **113**:67–75.

Ozbek M. & M. O. Guloglu. 2005. A new cave amphipod from Turkey: *Gammarus ustaoglui* sp nov. *Israel Journal of Zoology* **51**:147–55.

Packard, A. S. 1871. The Mammoth Cave and its inhabitants. *American Naturalist* **5**:739–61.

Packard, A. S. 1888. On certain factors of evolution. *American Naturalist* **22**:808–21.

Packard, A. 1901. *Lamarck, the Founder of Evolution, his Life and Work*. New York: Longmans, Green, and Co.

Packard, A. S. & F. W. Putnam. 1872. *The Mammoth Cave and its Inhabitants*. Salem: Naturalist Agency.

Pansini, M. & G. L. Pesce. 1998. *Higginsia ciccaresei* sp. nov. (Porifera: Demospongiae) from a marine cave on the Apulian coast (Mediterranean Sea). *Journal of the Marine Biological Association of the United Kingdom* **78**:1083–91.

Parise, K., P. Qiriazi & S. Sala. 2004. Natural and anthropogenic hazards in karst areas of Albania. *Natural Hazards and Earth System Sciences* **4**:569–81.

Parsons, K. N., G. Jones, I. Davidson-Watts & F. Greenaway. 2003. Swarming of bats at underground sites in Britain – implications for conservation. *Biological Conservation* **111**:63–70.

Peck, S. B. 1968. A new cave catopid beetle from Mexico, with a discussion of its evolution. *Psyche* **75**:91–8.

Peck, S. B. 1970. The Catopinae (Coleoptera; Leiodidae) of Puerto Rico. *Psyche* **77**:237–42.

Peck, S. B. 1974. The invertebrate fauna of tropical American caves, part II: Puerto Rico, an ecological and zoogeographic analysis. *Biotropica* **6**:14–31.

Peck, S. B. 1975. A review of the New World Onychophora, with the description of a new cavernicolous genus and species from Jamaica. *Psyche* **82**:341–58.

Peck, S. B. 1988. A review of the cave fauna of Canada, and the composition and ecology of the invertebrate fauna of caves and mines in Ontario. *Canadian Journal of Zoology* **66**:1197–213.

Peck, S. B. 1990. Eyeless arthropods of the Galapagos Islands, Ecuador: composition and origin of the cryptozoic fauna of a young, tropical, oceanic archipelago. *Biotropica* **22**:366–81.

Peck, S. B. 1998. A summary of diversity and distribution of the obligate cave-inhabiting faunas of the United States and Canada. *Journal of Cave and Karst Studies* **60**:18–26.

Peck, S. B. & P. Gnaspini. 1997. *Ptomaphagus inyoensis* n.sp., a new microphthalmic montane beetle from California (Coleoptera; Leiodidae; Cholevinae; Ptomaphagini). *Canadian Entomologist* **129**:769–76.

Peck, S. B., A. E. Ruiz-Baliu & G. F. Garces Gonzalez. 1998. The cave inhabiting beetles of Cuba (Insecta: Coleoptera): diversity, distribution, and ecology. *Journal of Cave and Karst Studies* **60**:156–66.

Penalba, M. C., F. Molina-Ferrer & L. L. Rodriguez. 2006. Resource availability, population dynamics and diet of the nectar-feeding bat *Leptonycteris curasoae* in Guaymas, Sonora, Mexico. *Biodiversity and Conservation* **15**:3017–34.

Pengelly, W., G. Busk, J. Evans *et al.* 1873. Report on the exploration of Brixham Cave, conducted by a committee of the Geological Society, and under the superintendence of Wm. Pengelly, Esq., F.R.S., aided by a local committee; with descriptions of the animal remains by George Busk, Esq., F.R.S., and of the flint implements by John Evans, Esq., F.R.S. Joseph Prestwich, F.R.S., F.G.S., &c., Reporter. *Philosophical Transactions of the Royal Society of London* **163**:471–572.

Penuelas, J. & I. Filella. 2003. Deuterium labelling of roots provides evidence of deep water access and hydraulic lift by *Pinus nigra* in a Mediterranean forest of NE Spain. *Environmental and Experimental Botany* **49**:201–8.

Perez, T. 1996. Particle uptake by a hexactinellid sponge, *Oopsacas minuta* (Leucopsacasidae): the role of the reticulum. *Comptes Rendus de l'Academie des Sciences, Serie III* **319**:385–91.

Perez, T., J. Vacelet, G. Bitar & H. Zibrowius. 2004. Two new lithistids (Porifera: Demospongiae) from a shallow eastern Mediterranean cave (Lebanon). *Journal of the Marine Biological Association of the United Kingdom* **84**:15–24.

Pesce, G. L. & T. M. Iliffe. 2002. New records of cave-dwelling mysids from the Bahamas and Mexico with description of *Palaumysis bahamensis* n. sp. (Crustacea: Mysidacea). *Journal of Natural History* **36**:265–78.

Peters, N. & G. Peters. 1973. Problemes genetiques de l'evolution regressive des cavernicoles, pp. 187–201, in: L.H. Schroeder (ed.) *Genetics and Mutagenesis in Fish*. New York: Springer-Verlag.

Peters, N. & G. Peters. 1986. Zur genetischen Interpretation morphologischer Gesetzmussigkeiten der degenerativen Evolution. Untersuchungen am Auge einer Hohlenform von *Poecilia sphenops* (Poeciliidae, Pisces). *Zeitschrift für Morphologie und Ökologie der Tiere* **62**:211–44.

Petit, S., A. Rojer & L. Pors. 2006. Surveying bats for conservation: the status of cave-dwelling bats on Curacao from 1993 to 2003. *Animal Conservation* **9**:207–17.

Petram, W., F. Knauer & P. Kaczensky. 2004. Human influence on the choice of winter dens by European brown bears in Slovenia. *Biological Conservation* **119**:129–36.

Pfeiffer, W. 1966. Uber die Vererbung des Schreckreaktion bei *Astyanax* (Characidae, Pisces). *Zeitschrift für Vererbungslehre* **98**:97–105.

Pflieger, W. L. 1997. *The Fishes of Missouri*, revised edition. Jefferson City, MO: Missouri Department of Conservation.

Pigliucci, M. 2001a. *Phenotypic Plasticity. Beyond Nature and Nurture*. Baltimore, MD: The John Hopkins University Press.

Pigliucci, M. 2001b. Characters and environment, pp. 363–88, in: G.P. Wagner (ed.) *The Character Concept in Evolutionary Biology*. San Diego, CA: Academic Press.

Pilet, P. E. 1973. Bennet, Charles, pp. 286–7, in: C. C. Gillispie (ed.) *Dictionary of Scientific Biography*, vol. 2. New York: Scribner.

Pinto da Rocha, R. & A. B. Bonaldo. 2007. A new species of *Cryptocellus* (Arachnida, Ricinulei) from Oriental Amazonia. *Zootaxa* **1386**:47–51.

Pinto da Rocha, R. & A. B. Kury. 2003. Third species of *Guasiniidae* (Opiliones, Laniatores) with coments on familial relationships. *Journal of Arachnology* **31**:394–9.

Pinto da Rocha, R., G. Machado & P. Weygolt. 2002. Two new species of *Carinus* (Simon, 1892) from Brazil with biological notes (Arachnida; Amblypygi; Charinidae). *Journal of Natural History* **36**:107–18.

Pipan, T., A. Blejec & A. Brancelj. 2006. Multivariate analysis of copepod assemblages in epikarstic waters of some Slovenian caves. *Hydrobiologia* **559**:213–23.

Plate, L. H. 1913. *Selektionsprinzip und Probleme der Artbildung; ein Handbuch des Darwinismus*. Leipzig: Engelmann.

Plug, I. 2004. Resource exploitation: animal use during the middle stone age at Sibudu Cave, Kwazulu-Natal. *South African Journal of Science* **100**:151–8.

Poey, F. 1858. *Memorias sobre la Historia Natural de la Isla de Cuba*, 2 volumes. La Habana: Barcina.

Pohlman, J. W., T. M. Iliffe & L. A. Cifuentes. 1997. A stable isotope study of organic cycling and the ecology of an anchialine cave ecosystem. *Marine Ecology Progress Series* **155**:17–27.

Poly, W. J. 2001. Nontroglobitic fishes in Bruffey-Hills Creek Cave, West Virginia, and other caves worldwide. *Environmental Biology of Fishes* **62**:73–83.

Ponder, W. F., S. A. Clark, S. Eberhard & J. B. Studdert. 2005. A radiation of hydrobiid snails in the caves and streams at Precipitous Bluff, southwest Tasmania, Australia (Mollusca: Caenogastropoda: Rissooidea: Hydrobiidae sl). *Zootaxa* **1074**:3–66.

Ponder, W. F. & D. R. Lindberg. 2008. Molluscan evolution and phylogeny, pp. 1–17, in: W. F. Ponder & D. R. Lindberg (eds.) *Phylogeny and Evolution of Mollusca*. Berkeley, CA: University of California Press.

Potter, V. R. 1968. Teilhard de Chardin and the concept of purpose. *Zygon* **3**:367–76.

Poulson, T. L. 1963. Cave adaptation in amblyopsid fishes. *American Midland Naturalist* **70**:257–90.

Poulson, T. L. 1964. Animals in aquatic environments: animals in caves, pp. 749–71, in: D. B. Dill (ed.) *Handbook of Physiology*. Washington, D.C.: American Physiological Society.

Poulson, T. L. 2001. Adaptations of cave fishes with some comparisons to deep-sea fishes. *Environmental Biology of Fishes* **62**:345–64.

Poulson, T. L., K. H. Lavoie & K. Helf. 1995. Long-term effects of weather on the cricket (*Hadenoecus subterraneus*, Orthoptera, Rhaphidophoridae) guano community in Mammoth Cave National Park. *American Midland Naturalist* **134**:226–36.

Poulson, T. L. & W. B. White. 1969. The cave environment. *Science* **165**:971–81.

Preciado, I. & M. Maldonado. 2005. Reassessing the spatial relationship between sponges and macroalgae in sublittoral rocky bottoms: a descriptive approach. *Helgoland Marine Research* **59**:141–50.

Price, J. J., K. P. Johson, S. E. Bush & D. H. Clayton. 2005. Phylogenetic relationsips of the Papuan Swiftlet *Aerodramus papuensis* and implications for the evolution of avian echolocation. *Ibis* **147**:790–6.

Price, J. J., K. P. Johnson, & D. H. Clayton. 2004. The evolution of echolocation in swiftlets. *Journal of Avian Biology* **35**:135–43.

Price, L. 1996. The cave racer – *Elaphe taeniura. Malayan Naturalist* **50**:24–5.

Prous, X., R. L. Ferreira & R. P. Martins. 2004. Ecotone delimitation: epigean-hypogean transition in cave ecosystems. *Austral Ecology* **29**:374–82.

Pugh, M. & J. D. Altringham. 2005. The effect of gates on cave entry by swarming bats. *Acta Chiropterologica* **7**:293–9.

Pulido-Bosch, A., J. M. Calaforra, P. Pulido-Leboeuf & S. Torres-García. 2004. Impact of quarrying gypsum in a semidesert karstic area (Sorbas, SE Spain). *Environmental Geology* **46**:583–90.

Pulido-Bosch, A., W. Martín-Rosales, M. López-Chicano, C. M. Rodríguez-Navarro & A. Vallejos. 1997. Human impact in a tourist karstic cave (Aracena, Spain). *Environmental Geology* **31**:142–9.

Putnam, F. W. 1872. The blind fishes of the Mammoth Cave and their allies. *American Naturalist* **6**:6–30.

Putnam, F. W. 1875. On some of the habits of the blind crawfish, *Cambarus pellucidus*, and the reproduction of lost parts. *Proceedings of the Boston Society of Natural History* **18**:16–19.

Qian, X.-M. & B. Li. 2002. Relevant record of the blind fish in *Yi Ban Lu. China Historical Materials of Science and Technology* **23**:81–2.

Rabaud, E. 1941. *Introduction aux Sciences Biologiques*. Paris: Armand Colin.

Racovitza, E. G. 1907. Éssai sur les problèmes biospéleologiques. *Archives du Zoologie Experimentale et Generale* **6**:371–488.

Racovitza, E. G. 2000. Ice caves in temperate regions, pp. 561–8, in: H. Wilkens, D. C. Culver & W. F. Humphries (eds.) *Subterranean Ecosystems*. Amsterdam: Elsevier.

Rafinesque, C. S. 1815. *Analyse de la Nature, or, Tableau de l'Univers et des Corps Organisés*. Palermo, Sicily: published by the author.

Rafinesque, C. S. 1822. On two salamanders of Kentucky. *Kentucky Gazette, Lexington* (n.s.) **1**:3.

Rafinesque, C. S. 1832. The caves of Kentucky. *Atlantic Journal and Friend of Knowledge* **1**:27–30.

Rambla, M. & C. Juberthie. 1994. Opiliones, pp. 215–230, in: Juberthie, C. & V. Decu (eds.) *Enciclopaedia Biospeologica*, vol. 1. Moulis and Bucarest: Société de Biospéologie.

Raper, K. B. 1984. *The Dictyostelids*. Princeton, NJ: Princeton University Press.

Rasquin, P. 1947. Progressive pigmentary regression in fishes associated with cave environments. *Zoologica* **32**:53–42.

Rasquin, P. 1949. Spontaneous depigmentation in the catfish *Ameirus nebulosus*. *Copeia* **1949**:246–51.

Reddell, J. R. 1982. A checklist of the cave fauna of Mexico. VII. Northern Mexico. *Association Mexican Cave Studies Bulletin* **8**:249–83.

Reddell, J. R. & G. Veni. 1996. Biology of the Chiquibil Cave System, Belize and Guatemala. *Journal of Cave and Karst Studies* **58**:131–8.

Reeves, W. K. 2000. New faunal and fungal records from caves in Georgia, USA. *Journal of Cave and Karst Studies* **62**:169–79.

Reeves, W. K. 2001. Bionomics of *Cimex adjunctus* (Heteroptera: Cimicidae) in a maternity cave of *Myotis austroriparius* (Chiroptera: Vespertilionidae) (South Carolina, USA). *Journal of Entomological Science* **36**:74–7.

Reeves, W. K., L. A. Durden & W. J. Wrenn. 2004. Ectoparasitic chiggers (Acari: Trombiculidae, Leeuwenhoekiidae), lice (Phthiraptera), and Hemiptera (Cimicidae and Reduviidae) from South Carolina, USA. *Zootaxa* **647**:1–20.

Reeves, W. K. & J. W. McCreadie. 2001. Population ecology of cavernicoles associated with carrion in caves of Georgia, USA. *Journal of Entomological Science* **36**:305–11.

Reinhart, K., J. Ambler & M. McGuffie. 1985. Diet and parasitism at Dust Devil Cave. *American Antiquity* **50**:819–24.

Resetarits, S. J., Jr. 1986. Ecology of cave use by the frog *Rana palustris*. *American Midland Naturalist* **116**:256–66.

Rhodes, R. 1962. The evolution of the crayfishes of the genus *Orconectes*. *Ohio Journal of Science* **62**:65–96.

Richards, R. 1992. *The Meaning of Evolution. The Morphological Construction and Ideological Reconstruction of Darwin's Theory.* Chicago, IL: The University of Chicago Press.

Richards, R. 2002. *The Romantic Conception of Life. Science and Philosophy in the age of Goethe.* Chicago, IL: The University of Chicago Press.

Richards, R. L. 1972. The woodrat in Indiana: recent fossils. *Proceedings of the Indiana Academy of Science* **81**:370–5.

Richards, R. L. 1980. Rice rat (*Oryzomys* cf. *palustris*) remains from southern Indiana caves. *Proceedings of the Indiana Academy of Science* **89**:425–31.

Richards, R. L. 1982. Hunting Indiana bears. *Outdoor Indiana* **47**:16–18.

Richards, R. L. 1983. Getting down to the bear bones. *Outdoor Indiana* **48**:32–4.

Riedl, R. 1966. *Biologie der Meereshöhlen: Topographie, Faunistik und Ökologie eines unterseeischen Lebensraumes: eine Monographie.* Hamburg: Paul Parey.

Rigotti, F. 1986. Biology and society in the Age of Enlightenment. *Journal of the History of Ideas* **47**:215–33.

Rippon, J. W. 1988. *Medical Mycology. The Pathogenic Fungi and the Pathogenic Actinomycetes*, 3rd edition. Philadelphia, PA: W. B. Saunders.

Risse, G. B. 1971. Döllinger, Ignaz, pp. 146–7, in: C.C. Gilliespie (ed.) *Dictionary of Scientific Biography*, vol. 4. New York: Scribner.

Rivera, M. A. J., F. G. Howarth, S. Taita & G. K. Roderick. 2002. Evolution in Hawaiian cave-adapted isopods (Oniscidea: Philosciidae): vicariant speciation or adaptive shifts? *Molecular Phylogenetics and Evolution* **25**:1–9.

Roberts, L. P. 2000. Deep in the heart of Texas. *Endangered Species Bulletin* **25**:14–15.

Robison, H. W. & T. M. Buchanan. 1988. *Fishes of Arkansas*. Fayetteville, AK: Arkansas University Press.

Rodriguez, G. A. & D. P. Reagan. 1984. Bat predation by the Puerto Rican boa, *Epicrates inornatus*. *Copeia* **1984**:219–20.

Rodriguez-Duran, A. 1998. Nonrandom aggregations and distribution of cave-dwelling bats in Puerto Rico. *Journal of Mammalogy* **79**:141–6.

Roff, D. A. 1990. The evolution of flightlessness in insects. *Evolution* **60**:389–421.

Roger, J. 1973. Buffon, Georges-Louis Leclerc, Compte de, pp. 576–82, in: C. C. Gillispie (ed.) *Dictionary of Scientific Biography*, vol. 2. New York: Scribner.

Roger, J. 1997. *Buffon. A Life in Natural History.* Ithaca, NY: Cornell University Press.

Rogowitz, G. L., C. L. Candelaria, L. E. Denizard & L. J. Melendez. 2001. Seasonal reproduction of a neotropical frog, the cave coqui (*Eleutherodactylus cooki*). *Copeia* **2001**:542–7.

Rojas, L. M., Y. Ramirez, R. McNeil, M. Mitchell & G. Marin. 2004. Retinal morphology and electrophysiology of two caprimulgiformes birds: the cave-living and nocturnal oilbird (*Steatornis caripensis*), and the crepuscularly and nocturnally foraging common pauraque (*Nyctidromus albicollis*). *Brain Behavior and Evolution* **64**:19–33.

Roldan, M., E. Clavero, T. Canals, *et al.* 2004. Distribution of phototrophic biofilms in cavities (Garraf, Spain). *Nova Hedwigia* **78**:329–51.

Romero, A. 1983. Introgressive hybridization in a population of *Astyanax fasciatus* (Pisces: Characidae) at La Cueva Chica. *National Speleological Society Bulletin* **45**:81–5.

Romero, A. 1984a. Behavior in an "intermediate" population of the subterranean-dwelling characid *Astyanax fasciatus*. *Environmental Biology of Fishes* **10**:203–7.

Romero, A. 1984b. Charles Marcus Breder, Jr. 1897–1983. *National Speleological Society News* **42**:8.

Romero, A. 1984c. Cave colonization by fish: role of bat predation. *American Midland Naturalist* **113**:7–12.

Romero, A. 1984d. *Responses to light in cave and surface populations of* Astyanax fasciatus *(Pisces: Characidae): an evolutionary interpretation*. Ph.D. dissertation. Coral Gables, FL: University of Miami.

Romero, A. 1985a. Cave colonization by fish: role of bat predation. *American Midland Naturalist* **113**:7–12.

Romero, A. 1985b. Can evolution regress? *National Speleological Society Bulletin* **47**:86–8.

Romero, A 1985c. Ontogenetic change in phototactic responses of surface and cave populations of *Astyanax fasciatus* (Pisces: Characidae). *Copeia* **1985**:1004–11.

Romero, A. 1986a. Charles Breder and the Mexican blind characid. *National Speleological Society News* **44**:16–18.

Romero, A. 1986b. He wanted to know them all: Eigenmann and his blind vertebrates. *National Speleological Society News* **44**:379–81.

Romero, A. 1998a. Threatened fishes of the world: *Amblyopsis rosae* (Eigenmann, 1842) (Amblyopsidae). *Environmental Biology of Fishes* **52**:434.

Romero, A. 1998b. Threatened fishes of the world: *Speoplatyrhinus poulsoni* Cooper and Kuehne, 1974 (Amblyopsidae). *Environmental Biology of Fishes* **53**:293–4.

Romero, A. 1999a. The blind cave fish that never was. *National Speleological Society News* **57**:180–1.

Romero, A. 1999b. Myth and reality of the alleged blind cave fish from Pennsylvania. *Journal of Spelean History* **33**:67–75.

Romero, A. 2000. The speleologist who wrote too much. *National Speleological Society News* **58**:4–5.

Romero, A. 2001a. Evolution is opportunistic, not directional. *BioScience* **51**:2–3.

Romero, A. 2001b. Scientists prefer them blind: the history of hypogean fish research. *Environmental Biology of Fishes* **62**:43–71.

Romero, A. 2002a. The life and work of a little known biospeleologist: Theodor Tellkampf. *Journal of Spelean History* **36**:68–76.

Romero, A. 2002b. Between the first blind cave fish and the last of the Mohicans: the scientific romanticism of James E. DeKay. *Journal of Spelean History* **36**:19–29.

Romero, A. 2004. Pisces: Amblyopsidae, pp. 595–7, in: J. Gunn (ed.) *Encyclopedia of Cave and Karst Science*. London: Fitzroy Dearborn Publishers.

Romero, A. 2007. The discovery of the first Cuban blind cave fish: the untold story. *Journal of Spelean History* **41**:16–22.

Romero, A. 2008. Typological thinking strikes again. *Environmental Biology of Fishes* **81**:359–63.

Romero, A. & J. Creswell. 2000. In search of the elusive 'eyeless' cave fish of Trinidad, W.I. *National Speleological Society News* **58**:282–3.

Romero, A. & S. M. Green. 2005. The end of regressive evolution: examining and interpreting the evidence from cave fishes. *Journal of Fish Biology* **67**:3–32.

Romero, A., S. M. Green, A. Romero, M. M. Lelonek & K. C. Stropnick. 2003. One eye but no vision: troglomorphic *Astyanax fasciatus* (Pisces: Characidae) with induced eyes do not respond to light. *Journal of Experimental Zoology (Molecular and Developmental Evolution)* **300B**:72–9.

Romero, A., W. Jeffery & Y. Yamamoto. 2002a. When cave fish see the light: reaction norm to light exposure during development in epigean, troglomorphic, and hybrids of *Astyanax fasciatus*, p. 225, in: *Program Book and Abstracts*. Joint Meeting of Ichthyologists and Herpetologists, July 3–8, 2002. Kansas City, MO: American Society of Ichthyologists and Herpetologists.

Romero, A. & Z. Lomax. 2000. Jacques Besson, cave eels and other alleged European fishes. *Journal of Spelean History* **34**:72–7.

Romero, A. & K. M. Paulson. 2001a. It's a wonderful hypogean life: a guide to the troglomorphic fishes of the world. *Environmental Biology of Fishes* **62**:13–41.

Romero, A. & K. M. Paulson. 2001b. Scales not necessary: the evolution of scalelessness among troglomorphic fishes, p.114, in: *Program Book and Abstracts*. Joint Meeting of Ichthyologists and Herpetologists. 81st Annual Meeting of the American Society of Ichthyologists and Herpetologists. State College, Pennsylvania, July 5–10, 2001.

Romero, A. & K. M. Paulson. 2001c. Unparalleled evolution: blindness, depigmentation, and scalelessness do not run hand in hand among troglomorphic fishes, p. 64, in: *2001 NSS Convention. A Cave Odyssey*. July 23–27, 2001, Mount Vernon, Kentucky, Program Guide.

Romero, A. & K. M. Paulson. 2001d. Humboldt's alleged subterranean fish from Ecuador. *Journal of Spelean History* **36**:56–9.

Romero, A. & A. Romero. 1999. On Cope, caves, and skeletons in the closet. *National Speleological Society News* **57**:341–43.

Romero, A., A. Singh, A. McKie, M. Manna, R. Baker & K. M. Paulson. 2001. Return to the Cumaca Cave, Trinidad, W.I. *National Speleological Society News* **59**:220–1.

Romero, A., A. Singh, A. McKie *et al.* 2002b. Replacement of the troglomorphic population of *Rhamdia quelen* (Pisces: Pimelodidae) by an epigean population of the same species in the Cumaca Cave, Trinidad, W.I. *Copeia* **2002**:938–42.

Romero, A. & J. Woodward. 2005. On white fish and black men: did Stephen Bishop really discover the blind cave fish of mammoth cave? *Journal of Spelean History* **39**:23–32.

Romero, A., Y. Zhao & Y. Chen. 2008. The hypogean fishes of China. Abstract 0187. In *Joint Meeting of Ichthyologists and Herpetologists Abstracts CD 2008.*

Rossmässler, E. A. 1838–44. *Iconographie der Land- und Süßwassermollusken, mit vorzüglicher Berücksichtigung der europäischen noch nicht abgebildeten Arten.* 4 vols. Dresden, Leipzig: Arnold.

Roth, L. M. 1988. Some cavernicolous and epigean cockroaches with six new species, and a discussion of the Nocticolidae (Dictyoptera: Blattaria). *Revue Suisse de Zoologie* **95**:297–321.

Roth, V. L. 2001. Character replication, p. 10, in: G. P. Wagner (ed.) *The Character Concept in Evolutionary Biology*. San Diego, CA: Academic Press.

Rowland, J. M. & J. R. Reddell. 1979. The order Schizomida (Arachnida) in the New World. I. Protoschizomidae and *Dumitrescoae* group (Schizomidae: *Schizomus*). *Journal of Arachnology* **6**:161–96.

Rowland, S. M. 2001. Archaeocyaths – a history of phylogenetic interpretation. *Journal of Paleontology* **75**:1065–78.

Rózkowski, J. 1998. Endangering of the Upper Jurassic karst-fissured aquifer in the Krakow Upland (southern Poland). *Environmental Geology* **33**:274–8.

Rudwick, M. J. S. 1997. *Georges Cuvier, Fossil Bones, and the Geological Catastrophes: New Translations and Interpretations of the Primary Texts*. Chicago, IL: University of Chicago Press.

Ruecker, H. W. 1988. A new species of the genus *Holoparamecus* Curtis Coleoptera Merophysidae from Curaçao, Netherlands Antilles. *Revue Suisse de Zoologie* **95**:1027–30.

Ruhberg, H. & M. L. Hamer. 2005. A new species of *Opisthopatus* Purcell, 1899 (Onychophora: Peripatopsidae) from KwaZulu-Natal, South Africa. *Zootaxa* **1039**:27–38.

Ruse, M. 1996. *Monad to Man. The Concept of Progress in Evolutionary Biology*. Cambridge, MA: Harvard University Press.

Ryckman, R. E. 1956. Parasitic and some nonparasitic arthropods from bat caves in Texas and Mexico. *American Midland Naturalist* **56**:186–90.

Sadoglu, P. 1957. Mendelian inheritance in the hybrids between the Mexican blind cave fishes and their overground ancestor. *Verhandlungen Deutsche Zoologische Gesellschaft* **1957**:432–9.

Sand, W. 1997. Microbial mechanisms of deterioration of inorganic substrates – a general mechanistic overview. *International Biodeterioration and Biodegredation* **40**:183–90.

Sanford, W. F. 1965. Dana and Darwinism. *Journal of the History of Ideas* **26**:531–46.

Sankaran, R. 2001. The status and conservation of the Edible-nest Swiftlet (*Collocalia fuciphaga*) in the Andaman and Nicobar Islands. *Biological Conservation* **97**:283–94.

Santini, F. & L. Galleni. 2001. Non-light based ecosystems and bioastronomy. *Revista di Biologia* **94**:427–42.

Santos, F. H. & P. Gnaspini. 2002. Notes on the foraging behavior of the Brazilian cave harvestman *Goniosoma spelaeum* (Opiliones, Gonyleptidae). *Journal of Arachnology* **30**:177–80.

Sara, M & G. Bavestrello. 1995. *Tethya omanensis*, a remarkable new species from an Oman cave (Porifera, Demospongiae). *Bollettino di Zoologia* **62**:23–7.

Sarbu, S. M. 2000. Movile Cave: a chemoautotrophically based groundwater ecosystem, pp. 319–43, in: H. Wilkens, D. C. Culver & W. F. Humphries (eds.) *Subterranean Ecosystems*. Amsterdam: Elsevier.

Sarbu, S. M., S. Galdenzi, M. Menichetti & G. Gentile. 2000. Geology and biology of the Grotte di Frasassi (Frasassi Caves) in central Italy: an ecological multidisciplinary study of a hypogenic underground karst system, pp. 361–81, in: H. Wilkens, D. C. Culver & W. F. Humphries (eds.) *Subterranean Ecosystems*. Amsterdam: Elsevier.

Sarbu, S. M., T. C. Kane & B. K. Kinkle. 1996. A chemoautotrophic based cave ecosystem. *Science* **272**:1953–5.

Sauro, U. 1993. Human impact on the karst of the Venetian Fore Alps, Italy. *Environmental Geology* **21**:115–21.

Sawicki, T. R., J. R. Holsinger, M. Ortiz & A. Perez. 2003. *Bahadzia patilarga*, a new species of subterranean amphipod crustacean (Hadziidae) from Cuba. *Proceedings of the Biological Society of Washington* **116**:198–205.

Schabereiter-Gurtner, C., C. Saiz-Jimenez, G. Pinar, W. Lubitz & S. Rolleke. 2002. Altamira cave Paleolithic paintings harbor partly unknown bacterial communities. *FEMS Microbiology Letters* **211**:7–11.

Schaefer, S. A., F. Provenzano, M. de Pinna & J. N. Baskin. 2005. New and noteworthy Venezuelan glanapterygine catfishes (Siluriformes, Trichomycteridae), with discussion of their biogeography and psammophily. *American Museum Novitates* **3496**:1–27.

Scheller, U. 1996. A new troglobitic species of *Hanseniella* Bagnall (Symphyla: Scutigerellidae) from Tasmania. *Australian Journal of Entomology* **35**:203–7.

Scheller, U., B. P. M. Curcic & S. E. Marakov. 1997. *Pauropus furcifer* Silvestri (Pauropodidae, Pauropoda): towards an adaptation for life in caves. *Revue Suisse de Zoologie* **104**:517–22.

Schemmel, C. 1967. Vergleichende Untersuchungen an den Hautsinnesorganen ober- und unterirdisch lebender *Astyanax* -Formen, ein Beitrag zur Evolution der Cavernicolen. *Zeitschrift für Morphologie der Tiere* **61**:255–316.

Schemmel, C. 1980. Studies on the genetics of feeding behaviour in the cave fish *Astyanax mexicanus* f. *Anoptichthys*. An example of apparent monofactorial inheritance by polygenes. *Zeitschrift für Tierpsychologie* **53**:9–22.

Schilthuizen, M., A. S. Cabanban & M. Haase. 2005. Possible speciation with gene flow in tropical cave snails. *Journal of Zoological Systematics and Evolutionary Research* **43**:133–8.

Schiner, J. R. 1854. Fauna der Adelsberg, Lueger und Magdalener-grotte, p. 316, in: Schmidle, A. (ed.) *Die Grotten und Hölen von Adelsberg, Lueg, Planina und Lass*. Wien: Braunmüller.

Schiödte, J. C. 1849. *Specimen Faunæ Subterraneae. Bidrag til den Underjordiske Fauna*. Kjöbenhavn: Bianco Luno.

Schlagel, S. R. & C. M. Breder. 1947. A study of oxygen consumption of blind and eyed cave characins in light and darkness. *Zoologica* **32**:17–28.

Schmidl, A. 1850. Beitrag zur Höhlenkunde des Karst. *Sitzungsberichte der Kaiserlichen Akademie der Wissenschaften in Wien. Mathematisch-Naturwissenschaftliche Klasse* **5**:464–79.

Schmidl, A. (ed.) 1854. *Die Grotten und Höhlen von Adelsberg, Lueg, Planina und Laas.* Wien, Austria: Wilh. Braumüller.

Schmidt, F. 1832. Beitrag zu Krain's fauna. *Illÿrfches Blatt* **21**:9–10

Schwendinger, P. J. & G. Giribet. 2005. The systematics of the south-east Asian genus *Fangensis* Rambla (Opiliones: Cyphophthalmi: Stylocellidae). *Invertebrate Systematics* **19**:297–323.

Schwendinger, P. J., G. Giribet & H. Steiner. 2004. A remarkable new cave-dwelling *Stylocellus* (Opiliones, Cyphophthalmi) from peninsular Malaysia, with a discussion on taxonomic characters in the family Stylocellidae. *Journal of Natural History* **38**:1421–35.

Secord, D. & G. Muller-Parker. 2005. Symbiont distribution along a light gradient within an intertidal cave. *Limnology and Oceanography* **50**:272–8.

Sedmera, D., I. Misek & M. Klima. 1997. On the development of cetacean extremities. 2. Morphogenesis and histogenesis of the flippers in the spotted dolphin (*Stenella attenuata*). *European Journal of Morphology* **35**:117–23.

Semlitsch, R. D. & H. M. Wilbur. 1989. Artificial selection for paedomorphosis in the salamander *Ambystoma talpoideim*. *Evolution* **43**:105–12.

Sendra, A., V. M. Ortuno, A. Moreno, S. Montagud & S. Teruel. 2006. *Gollumjapyx smeagol* gen. n., sp n., an enigmatic hypogean japygid (Diplura: Japygidae) from the eastern Iberian Peninsula. *Zootaxa* **1372**:35–52.

Seryodkin, I. V., A. V. Kostyria, J. M. Goodrich *et al.* 2003. Denning ecology of brown bears and Asiatic black bears in the Russian Far East. *Ursus* **14**:153–61.

Sharratt, N. J., M. D. Picker & M. J. Samways. 2000. The invertebrate fauna of the sandstone caves of the Cape Peninsula (South Africa): patterns of endemism and conservation priorities. *Biodiversity and Conservation* **9**:107–43.

Shaw, T. R. 1992. *History of Cave Science. The Exploration and Study of Limestone Caves, to 1900.* Broadway: Sydney Speleological Society.

Shear, W. 1969. A synopsis of the cave millipedes of the United States, with an illustrated key to genera. *Psyche* **76**:126–43.

Shear, W. A. 2003. A second species of the rare millipede family Apterouridae (Diplopoda: Chordeumatidae: Striarioidea). *Proceedings of the Biological Society of Washington* **116**:509–14.

Shor, E. N. 1973. Jordan, David Starr, pp. 169–70, in: C. C. Gillispie (ed.) *Dictionary of Scientific Biography*, vol. 7. New York: Scribner.

Silfvergrip, A. M. C. 1996. *A Systematic Revision of the Neotropical Catfish Genus* Rhamdia *(Teleostei, Pimelodidae).* Stockholm: Swedish Museum of Natural History.

Silliman, B. 1851. On the Mammoth Cave of Kentucky. *American Journal of Science*, ser. 2, **10**:332–9.

Simms, M. J. 1994. Emplacement and preservation of vertebrates in caves and fissures. *Zoological Journal of the Linnean Society* **112**:261–83.

Simon, K. S., E. F. Benfield & S. A. Macko. 2003. Food web structure and the role of epilithic biofilms in cave streams. *Ecology* **84**:2395–406.

Simpson, G. G. 1944. *Tempo and Mode in Evolution*. New York: Columbia University Press.

Simpson, G. G. 1949. *The Meaning of Evolution*. New Haven, CT: Yale University Press.

Sket, B. 1996a. The ecology of anchihaline caves. *Trends in Ecology and Evolution* **11**:221–5.

Sket, B. 1996b. Biotic diversity of hypogean habitats in Slovenia and its cultural importance, pp. 59–74, in: A. Cimerman & N. Gunde-Cimerman (eds.) *Biodiversity*. International Biodiversity Seminar ECC XIV Meeting, June 30–July 4, 1995, Godz Martuljek, Slovenia. Ljubijana: National Institute of Chemistry.

Sket, B. 1999. High biodiversity in hypogean waters and its endangerment – the situation in Slovenia, the Dinaric Karst, and Europe. *Crustaceana* **72**:767–79.

Skey, B. 2004. Anchialine habitats, pp. 64–5, in: J. Gunn (ed.) *Encyclopedia of Caves and Karst Science*. New York: Fitzroy Dearborn.

Sloan, P. R. 1975. The Buffon-Linnaeus controversy. *Isis* **67**:356–75.

Sluys, R. & M. Benazzi, 1992. A new finding of a subterranean dendrocoelid flatworm from Italy (Platyhelminthes, Tricladida, Paludicola). *Stygologia* **7**:213–17.

Smith, D. C. & H. W. Brown, Jr. 2000. Louis Agasiz, the Great Deluge, and early Maine geology. *Northeastern Naturalist* **7**:157–77.

Smith, P. W. & N. M. Welch. 1978. A summary of the life history and distribution of the Spring Cavefish, *Chologaster agassizi* Putnam, with population estimates for the species in southern Illinois. *Illinois Natural History Survey, Biological Notes*. **1978**:104.

Smithers, P. 2005. The diet of the cave spider *Meta menardi* (Latreille 1804) (Araneae, Tetragnathidae). *Journal of Arachnology* **33**:243–6.

Sorensen, M. V., A. Jorgensen & T. M. Boesgaard. 2000. A new *Echinoderes* (Kinorhyncha: Cyclorhagida) from a submarine cave in New South Wales, Australia. *Cahiers de Biologie Marine* **4**:167–79.

Sötje, I. & G. Jarms. 1999. Detailed description of *Thecoscyphus zibrowii* Werner, 1984 (Scyphozoa, Coronatae) with remarks on the life cycle. *Mitteilungen aus dem Hamburgischen Zoologischen Museum und Institut* **96**:5–13.

Southward, A. J., M. C. Kennicutt, J. Alcala Herrera *et al.* 1996. On the biology of submarine caves with sulphur springs: appraisal of C-13/C-12 ratios as a guide to trophic relations. *Journal of the Marine Biological Association of the United Kingdom* **76**:265–85.

Spanjer, G. R. & M. B. Fenton. 2005. Behavioral responses of bats to gates at caves and mines. *Wildlife Society Bulletin* **33**:1101–12.

Stanton, W. 1971. Dana, James Dwight, pp. 549–54, in: C. C. Gilliespie (ed.) *Dictionary of Scientific Biography*, vol. 3. New York: Scribner.

Stearns, S. C. 1983. The evolution of life-history traits in mosquitofish since their introduction to Hawaii in 1905: rates of evolution, heritabilities, and developmental plasticity. *American Zoologist* **23**:65–75.

Stephens, J. L. 1841. *Incidents of Travel in Central America, Chiapas, and Yucatan*. New York: Harper & Brothers.

Stepien, C. A., B. Morton, K. A. Dabrowska *et al.* 2001. Genetic diversity and evolutionary relationships of the troglodytic 'living fossil' *Congeria kusceri* (Bivalvia: Dreissenidae). *Molecular Ecology* **10**:1873–9.

Stock, J. H., T. M. Iliffe & D. Williams 1986. The concept "anchialine" reconsidered. *Stygologia* **2**:90–2.

Stoev, P. 2001. A synopsis of the Bulgarian cave centipedes (Chilopoda). *Arthropoda Selecta* **10**:31–54.

Stoev, P. 2004. The first troglomorphic species of the millipede genus *Paracortina* Wang & Zhang, 1993 from south Yunnan, China (Diplopoda: Callipodida: Paracortinidae). *Zootaxa* **441**:1–8.

Stoev, P. & H. Enghoff. 2005. A new cave-dwelling millipede of the genus *Bollmania* Silvestri, 1896 from Yunnan, China, with remarks on the reduction of the second female leg-pair (Diplopoda: Callipodida: Caspiopetalidae). *Journal of Natural History* **39**:1875–91.

Stone, A. J. 1995. *Images from the Underworld: Naj Tunich and the Tradition of Maya Cave Painting*. Austin, TX: University of Texas Press.

Stoner, K. E., K. A. O. Salazar, R. C. R.-Fernández & M. Quesada. 2003. Population dynamics, reproduction, and diet of the lesser long-nosed bat (*Leptonycteris curasoae*) in Jalisco, Mexico: implications for conservation. *Biodiversity and Conservation* **12**:357–73.

Strecker, U., L. Bernatchez & H. Wilkens. 2003. Genetic divergence between cave and surface populations of *Astyanax* in Mexico (Characidae, Teleostei). *Molecular Ecology* **12**:699–710.

Strickler, A. G., Y. Yamamoto & W. R. Jeffery. 2001. Early and late changes in *Pax6* expression accompany eye degeneration during cavefish development. *Development, Genes and Evolution* **211**:138–44.

Suarez-Morales, E. & T. M. Iliffe. 2005. A new Exumella (Crustacea: Copepoda: Ridgewayiidae) from anchialine waters of the western Caribbean, with comments on regional biogeography. *Bulletin of Marine Science* **77**:409–23.

Sustr, V., D. Elhottova, V. Kristufek *et al.* 2005. Ecophysiology of the cave isopod *Mesoniscus graniger* (Frivaldszky, 1865) (Crustacea: Isopoda). *European Journal of Soil Biology* **41**:69–75.

Swart, C. J. U., E. J. Stoch, C. F. van Jaarsveld & A. B. A. Brink. 2003. The Lower Wonderfontein Spruit: an exposé. *Environmental Geology* **43**:635–53.

Sweet, S. S. 1977. Natural metamorphosis in *Eurycea neotenes*, and the generic allocation of the Texas *Eurycea* (Amphibia: Plethodontidae). *Herpetologica* **33**:364–75.

Sweet, S. S. 1986. Caudata, pp. 734–740, in: L. Botosaneanu (ed.) *Stygofauna Mundi. A Faunistic, Distributional, and Ecological Synthesis of the World Fauna inhabiting Subterranean Waters (including the Marine Interstitial)*. Leiden: E.J. Brill.

Tabuki, R. & T. Hanai. 1999. A new sigillid ostracod from submarine caves of the Ryukyu Islands, Japan. *Palaeontology* **42**:569–93.

Taguchi, I. & K. Makiya. 1982. House centipede *Thereuonema hilgendorfi* as a predator of mosquitoes. *Medical Entomology and Zoology* **33**:33–40.

Talarico, G., J. G. Palacios-Vargas, M. F. Silva & G. Alberti. 2006. Ultrastructure of tarsal sensilla and other integument structures of two *Pseudocellus* species (Ricinulei, Arachnida). *Journal of Morphology* **267**:441–63.

Tansley, A. G. 1935. The use and abuse of vegetational concepts and terms. *Forest Ecology and Management* **16**:284–307.

Tarburton, M. K. 2003. The breeding biology of the Mountain Swiftlet, *Aerodramus hirundinaceus*, in Irian Jaya. *Emu* **103**:177–82.

Tauste, F. 1678. *Relación de las Misiones de los Religiosos Capuchinos en la provincia de Cumaná*. (Unpublished manuscript.)

Taylor, G. 1970. Bentham, George, pp. 614–15, in: C. C. Gillispie (ed.) *Dictionary of Scientific Biography*, vol. 1. New York: Scribner.

Taylor, J. 1964. Noteworthy predation on the guano bat. *Journal of Mammalogy* **45**:300–1.

Taylor, S. J., J. K. Krejca & M. L. Denight. 2005. Foraging range and habitat use of *Ceuthophilus secretus* (Orthoptera: Rhaphidophoridae), a key trogloxene in central Texas cave communities. *American Midland Naturalist* **154**:97–114.

Teeling, E. C., M. S. Springer, O. Madsen *et al.* 2005. A molecular phylogeny for bats illuminates biogeography and the fossil record. *Science* **307**:580–4.

Tellkampf, T. 1844a. Beschreibung einiger neuer in der Mammuth-Höhle in Kentucky aufgefundener Gattungen von Gliederthieren. *Archives Vereins Freund Naturliche Mecklenburg* **10**:318–22.

Tellkampf, T. 1844b. Uber den blinden Fisch der Mammuthhöhle in Kentucky. *(Muller's) Archives für Anatomie und Physiologie* **1844**:381–95.

Tétry, A. 1971a. Caullery, Maurice, pp. 148–9, in: C. C. Gillispie (ed.) *Dictionary of Scientific Biography*, vol. 3. New York: Scribner.

Tétry, A. 1971b. Cuénot, Lucien, pp. 492–4, in: C. C. Gillispie (ed.) *Dictionary of Scientific Biography*, vol. 3. New York: Scribner.

Thinés, G. 1969. *L'Evolution Regressive des Poissons Cavernicoles et Abyssaux*. Paris: Masson et Cie.

Thomas, M. L. H., A. Logan, K. E. Eakins & S. M. Mathers. 1992. Biotic characteristics of the anchialine ponds of Bermuda. *Bulletin of Marine Science* **50**:133–57.

Thomassen, J. A., R.J. den Tex, M.A.G. de Bakker & G. D. E. Povel. 2005. Phylogenetic relationships amongst swifts and swiftlets: a multi locus approach. *Molecular Phylogenetics and Evolution* **37**:264–77.

Thompson, R. S., T. R. Van Devender, P. S. Martin, T. Foppe & A. Long. 1980. Shasta ground sloth (*Nothrotheriops shastense* Hoffstetter) at Shelter Cave, New Mexico: environment, diet, and extinction. *Quaternary Research* **14**:360–76.

Thurgate, M. E., J. S. Gough, A. Spate & S. Eberhard. 2001a. Subterranean biodiversity in New South Wales: from rags to riches. *Records of the Western Australian Museum Supplement* **64**:37–47.

Thurgate, M. E., J. S. Gough, A. K. Clarke, P. Serov & A. Spate. 2001b. Stygofauna diversity and distribution in Eastern Australian cave and karst areas. *Records of the Western Australian Museum Supplement* **64**:49–62.

Tindle, R. 1984. The evolution of breeding strategies in the flightless cormorant (*Nannopterum harrisi*) of the Galapagos. *Biological Journal of the Linnean Society* **21**:157–64.

Tinsley, R. C. 1990. Host behaviour and opportunism in parasite life cycles. Parasitism and host behaviour, pp. 158–92, in: C. J. Barnard & J. M. Behnke (eds.) *Parasitism and Host Behaviour*. London: Taylor and Francis.

Todaro, M. A., F. Leasi, K. Bizzarri & P. Tongiorgi. 2006. Meiofauna densities and gastrotrich community composition in a Mediterranean sea cave. *Marine Biology* **149**:1079–91.

Todd, J. E. 1901. Some problems of the Dakota artesian system. *Science* **14**:794.

Todrank, J. & G. Heth. 1996. Indiviual odours in two chromosomal species of blind, subterranean mole rat (*Spalax ehrenbergi*): conspecific and cross-species discrimination. *Ethology* **102**:806–11.

Tompkins, D. A. 1999. Impact of nest-harvesting on the reproductive success of black-nest swiftlets (*Aerodramus maximus*). *Wildlife Biology* **5**:33–6.

Trajano, E. 1995. Evolution of tropical troglobites: applicability of the model of Quaternary climatic fluctuations. *Memoires de Biospeleologie* **22**:203–9.

Trajano, E. 2000. Cave faunas in the Atlantic tropical rain forest: composition, ecology, and conservation. *Biotropica* **37**:882–93.

Trajano, E. 2001. Ecology of subterranean fishes: an overview. *Environmental Biology of Fishes* **62**:133–60.

Trajano, E., N. Mugue, J. Krejca, C. Vidthayanon, D. Smart & R. Borowsky. 2002. Habitat, distribution, ecology and behavior of cave balitorids from Thailand (Teleostei: Cypriniformes). *Ichthyological Exploration of Freshwaters* **13**:169–84.

Triplehorn, C. A. & N. F. Johnson. 2005. *Borror and DeLong's Introduction to the Study of Insects*. Belmont, CA: Thompson.

Trissino, G. G. 1537. Letter dated 5 March. In: Alberti, L. 1550.

Tunnicliffe, V. 1991. The biology of hydrothermal vents: ecology and evolution. *Oceanography and Marine Biology: An Annual Review* **29**:319–407.

Ubelaker, J. & M. Dailey. 1969. *Trichuroides myoti*, a new nematode from the gray bat, *Myotis grisescens*. *American Midland Naturalist* **85**:284–6.

Uieda, W. 2000. A review of complete albinism in bats with five new cases from Brazil. *Acta Chiropterologica* **2**:97–105.

United States Department of Agriculture. 2002. Water quality and aquatic biological assessment of Hunter's and Devil's Icebox caves. Agricultural Research Service, United States Department of Agriculture. Accessed 11 April 2006. Https://fsb.missouri.edu/ARS/LerchB/Cave_PO.htm.

Unwin, R. W. 1995. A provincial man of science at work: Martin Lister, F.R.S., and his illustrators 1670–1683. *Notes and Records of the Royal Society of London* **49**:209–30.

Uriz, M. J., D. Rosell & D. Martin. 1992. The sponge population of the Cabrera Archipelago (Balearic Islands) – characteristics, distribution, and abundance of the most representative species. *Marine Ecology – Pubblicazioni della Stazione Zoologica di Napoli I* **13**:101–17.

Uschmann, G. 1972. Haeckel, Ernst Heirich Philipp August, pp. 6–11, in: C. C. Gillispie (ed.) *Dictionary of Scientific Biography*, vol. 6. New York: Scribner.

Vacelet, J., N. Bouryesnault & J. G. Harmelin. 1994. Hexactinellid cave, a unique deep-sea habitat in the scuba zone. *Deep-Sea Research Part I – Oceanographic Research Papers* **41**:965–73.

Vacelet, J. & E. Duport. 2004. Prey capture and digestion in the carnivorous sponge *Asbestopluma hypogea* (Porifera: Demospongiae). *Zoomorphology* **123**:179–90.

Valvasor, J. W. 1687. An extract of a letter written to the Royal Society out of Craniola, being a full and accurate description of the wonderful Lake of Kirknitz in that country. *Philosophical Transactions of the Royal Society of London* **16**:411–27.

Valvasor, J. W. 1689. *Die Ehre des Herzogthums Krain*. Ljubljana, Slovenia: Endter.

Van Beynen, P. & K. Townsend. 2005. A disturbance index for karst environments. *Environmental Management* **36**:101–16.

Vandel, A. 1964. *Biospéologie: la Biologie des Animaux Cavernicoles*. Paris: Gauthier-Villars.

Vandel, A. 1965. *Biospeleology. The Biology of Cavernicolous Animals*. Oxford: Pergamon Press.

Van Dyck, S. 1982. *Antechinus puteus* (Marsupialia: Dasyuridae), a new fossil species from the Texas caves, Southeastern Queensland. *Australian Mammology* **5**:59–68.

Verovnik, R., B. Sket, S. Prevorcnik & P. Trontelj. 2003. Random amplified polymorphic DNA diversity among surface and subterranean populations of *Asellus aquaticus* (Crustacea: Isopoda). *Genetica* **119**:155–65.

Vidlicka, L., P. Vrsansky & D. E. Shcherbakov. 2003. Two new troglobitic cockroach species of the genus *Spelaeoblatta* (Blattaria: Nocticolidae) from North Thailand. *Journal of Natural History* **37**:107–14.

Vigne, J. D. & H. Valladas. 1996. Small mammal fossil assemblages as indicators of environmental change in northern Corsica during the last 2500 years. *Journal of Archaeological Science* **23**:199–215.

Villoria Moreno, S. 1996. New genus and species of the deep-sea family Coronarctidae (Tardigrada) from a submarine cave with a deep-sea like condition. *Sarsia* **81**:275–83.

Vinogradova, O., O. V. Kovalenko, S. P. Wasser, E. Nevo & M. Weinstein-Evron. 1998. Species diversity gradient to darkness stress in blue-green algae/cyanobacteria: a microscale test in a prehistoric cave, Mount Carmel, Israel. *Israel Journal of Plant Sciences* **46**:229–38.

Viré, A. 1899. *Essai sur la faune obscuricole de France, étude particulière de quelques formes zoologiques*. Thesis. Paris.

Viré, A. 1904. La biospéologie. *Comptes Rendus de l'Académie des Sciences du Paris* **139**.

Voisin, J. F., Y. V. Quang & P. Nguyen Quang. 2005. The diet of the white nest swiftlet (*Aerodramus fusciphagus germani*) in Vietnam. *Aves* **42**:142–8.

Von Sternberg, R. & M. Schotte. 2004. A new anchialine shrimp of the genus *Procaris* (Crustacea: Decapoda: Procarididae) from the Yucatan Peninsula. *Proceedings of the Biological Society of Washington* **117**:514–22.

Voss, S. R. & H. B. Shaffer. 1997. Adaptive evolution via a major gene effect: paedomorphosis in the Mexican axolotl. *Proceedings of the National Academy of Sciences of the United States of America* **94**:14185–9.

Voss, S. R. & H. B. Shaffer. 2000. Evolutionary genetics of metamorphic failure using wild-caught vs. laboratory axolotls (*Ambystoma mexicanum*). *Molecular Ecology* **9**:1401–7.

Waddell, D. R. & K. T. I. Duffy. 1986. Breakdown of self/nonself recognition in cannibalistic strains of the predatory slime mold, *Dictyostelium caveatum*. *Journal of Cell Biology* **102**:298–305.

Wagner, G. P. 2001a. *The Character Concept in Evolutionary Biology*. San Diego, CA: Academic Press.

Wagner, G. P. 2001b. Characters, units and natural kinds: an introduction, pp. 1–10, in: G. P. Wagner, *The Character Concept in Evolutionary Biology*. San Diego, CA: Academic Press.

Wallace, D. R. 1999. *The Bonehunters' Revenge. Dinosaurs, Greed, and the Greatest Scientific Feud of the Gilded Age*. Boston, MA: Houghton Mifflin Company.

Wallich, N. 1851. *Specimen Faunæ Subterraneæ: being a Contribution towards the Subterranean Fauna*. London.

Wang, S. J., R. L. Li, C. X. Sun *et al.* 2004a. How types of carbonate rock assemblages constrain the distribution of karst rocky desertified land in Guizhou Province, PR China: phenomena and mechanisms. *Land Degradation and Development* **15**:123–31.

Wang, S. J., Q. M. Liu & D. F. Zhang. 2004b. Karst rocky desertification in southwestern China: geomorphology, landuse, impact and rehabilitation. *Land Degradation and Development* **15**:115–21.

Wang, Y., H. Cheng, R. L. Edwards *et al.* 2008. Millennial- and orbital-scale changes in the East Asian monsoon over the past 224,000 years. Nature **451**:1090–3.

Warren, L. 2004. *Constantine Samuel Rafinesque. A Voice in the American Wilderness*. Lexington, KY: The University Press of Kentucky.

Watson, J., E. Hamilton-Smith, D. Gillieson & K. Kiernan. 1997. *Guidelines for Cave and Karst conservation*. Cambridge, UK: IUCN.

Watson, P. J. 1974. *Archaeology of the Mammoth Cave Area*. New York: Academic Press.

Wcislo, W. T. 1989. Behavioral environment and evolutionary change. *Annual Review of Ecology and Systematics* **20**:137–69.

Weber, A. 2000. Fish and amphibian, pp. 109–32, in: H. Wilkens, D. C. Culver & W. F. Humphreys (eds.) *Subterranean Ecosystems*. Amsterdam: Elsevier.

Welbourn, W. 1999. Invertebrate cave fauna of Kartchner Caverns, Arizona. *Journal of Cave and Karst Studies* **61**:93–101.

Went, F. W. 1969. Fungi associated with stalactite growth. *Science* **166**:385–6.

Werdelin, L. N. & M. Asa Fortelius. 1999. Testicondy and ecological opportunism predict the rapid evolution of elephants. *Evolutionary Theory* **12**:39–45.

West-Eberhard, M. J. 1989. Phenotypic plasticity and the origins of diversity. *Annual Review of Ecology and Systematics* **20**:249–78.

Weyandt, S. E., R. A. Van Den Bussche, M. J. Hamilton & D. M. Leslie. 2005. Unraveling the effects of sex and dispersal: Ozark big-eared bat (*Corynorhinus townsendii ingens*) conservation genetics. *Journal of Mammalogy* **86**:1136–43.

Weygoldt, P. 1994. Amblypygi, pp. 241–7, in: Juberthie, C. & V. Decu (eds.) *Encyclopaedia Biospéologica*, vol. 1. Moulis and Bucarest: Société de Biospéologie.

White, L. A. 1959. *The Evolution of Culture; the Development of Civilization to the Fall of Rome*. New York: McGraw-Hill.

White, R. E. 1983. *A Field Guide to the Beetles*. Boston, MA: Houghton Mifflin. www.zin.ru/animalia/coleoptera/eng/koval3.htm, accessed April 2005.

Whiteman, H. H. 1994. Evolution of facultative paedomorphosis in salamanders. *Quarterly Review of Biology* **69**:205–21.

Wiens, J. J., P. T. Chippindale & D. M. Hillis. 2003. When are phylogenetic analyses misled by convergence? A case study in Texas cave salamanders. *Systematic Biology* **52**:501–14.

Wilkens, H. 1969. Beitrage zur Degeneration des Auges bei Cavernicolen, Genzahl und Manifestationsart. *Zoologisches Anzeiger* **180**:454–64.

Wilkens, H. 1979. Reduktionsgrad und phylogenetisches Alter: ein Beitrag Besiedlungsgeschichte der Limnofauna Yukatans. *Zeitschrift für Zoologische Systematik und Evolutionsforschung* **17**:262–72.

Wilkens, H., D. C. Culver & W. F. Humphreys (eds.). 2000. *Subterranean Ecosystems*. Amsterdam: Elsevier.

Wilkinson, G. S. & J. M. South. 2002. Life history, ecology and longevity in bats. *Aging Cell* **1**:124–31.

Willemart, R. H. & P. Gnaspini. 2004a. Breeding biology of the cavernicolous harvestman *Goniosoma albiscriptum* (Arachnida, Opiliones, Laniatores): sites of oviposition, egg batches, characteristics and subsocial behavior. *Invertebrate Reproduction and Development* **45**:15–28.

Willemart, R. H. & P. Gnaspini. 2004b. Spatial distribution, mobility, gregariousness, and defensive behavior in a Brazilian cave harvestman *Goniosoma albiscriptum* (Arachnida, Opiliones, Gonyleptidae). *Animal Biology* **54**:221–35.

Willems, L., P. Comer, F. Hatert *et al.* 2002. Karst in granitic rocks, South Cameroon: cave genesis and silica and taranakite speleothems. *Terra Nova* **14**:355–62.

Williams, J. D. & W. M. Howell. 1979. An albino sculpin from a cave in the New River drainage of west Virginia (Pisces: Cottidae). *Brimleyana* **1**:141–6.

Wilson, L. G. 1973. Lyell, Charles, pp. 563–77, in: C. C. Gillispie (ed.) *Dictionary of Scientific Biography*, vol. 8. New York: Scribner.

Wilson, W. L. 1994. Morphometry and hydrology of Dean's Blue Hole, Long Island. *Bahamas Journal of Science* **2**:10–14.

Winkler, W. G. & D. B. Adams. 1972. Utilization of southwestern bat caves by terrestrial carnivores. *American Midland Naturalist* **87**:191–200.

Wittmann, K. J. 2001. Centennial changes in the near-shore mysid fauna of the Gulf of Naples (Mediterranean Sea), with description of *Heteromysis riedli* sp. n. (Crustacea, Mysidacea). *Marine Ecology – Pubblicazioni della Stazione Zoologica di Napoli* **22**:85–109.

Wittmann, K. J. 2004. *Retromysis nura* new genus and species (Mysidacea, Mysidae, Heteromysini) from a superficial marine cave in Minorca (Balearic Islands, Mediterranean Sea). *Crustaceana* **77**:769–83.

Wood, P. J., J. Gunn & J. J. Perkins. 2002. The impact of pollution on aquatic invertebrates within a subterranean ecosystem – out of sight out of mind. *Archiv für Hydrobiologie* **155**:223–37.

Woods, L. P. & R. F. Inger. 1957. The cave, spring, and swamp fishes of the Family Amblyopsidae of Central and Eastern United States. *American Midland Naturalist* **58**:232–56.

Worheide, G. 1998. The reef cave dwelling ultraconservative coralline demosponge *Astrosclera willeyana* Lister 1900 from the Indo-Pacific – micromorphology, ultrastructure, biocalcification, isotope record, taxonomy, biogeography, phylogeny. *FACIES* **38**:1–88.

Worsaae, K., W. Sterrer & T. M. Iliffe. 2004. *Longipalpa saltatrix*, a new genus and species of the meiofaunal family Nerillidae (Annelida: Polychaeta) from an anchihaline cave in Bermuda. *Proceedings of the Biological Society of Washington* **117**:346–62.

Wright, S. 1931. Evolution in Mendelian populations. *Genetics* **16**:97–159.

Wyman, J. 1843. Description of a 'Blind Fish,' from a cave in Kentucky. *American Journal of Science* **45**:94–6.

Wyman, J. 1851. [Account of dissections of the blind fishes (*Amblyopsis spelaeus*) from the Mammoth Cave, Kentucky.] *Proceedings of the Boston Society of Natural History* **3**:349, 375.

Wyman, J. 1854a. The eyes and organs of hearing in *Amblyopsis spelaeus*. *Proceedings of the Boston Society of Natural History* **4**:149–51.

Wyman, J. 1854b. On the eye and the organ of hearing in the blind fishes (*Amblyopsis spelaeus* DeKay) of the Mammoth Cave. *Proceedings of the Boston Society of Natural History* **4**:395–6.

Wyman, J. 1872. Notes and drawings of the rudimentary eye, brain, and tactile organs of *Amblyopsis spelaeus*. *American Naturalist* **6**:16–20.

Xie, Y. J. 1540. *Report on the Alu Cave*. Manuscript. (In Chinese.)

Yager, J. 1994. *Speleonectes gironensis*, new species (Remipedia, Speleonectidae), from anchialine caves in Cuba, with remarks on biogeography and ecology. *Journal of Crustacean Biology* **14**:752–62.

Yamamoto, Y. & W. Jeffery. 2000. Central role for the lens in cave fish eye degeneration. *Science* **289**:631–3.

Yeo, D. C. J. 2001. A new cavernicolous species of freshwater crab (Crustacea: Brachyura: Potamidae) from Pulau Tioman, peninsular Malaysia. *Proceedings of the Biological Society of Washington* **114**:618–23.

Yeo, D. C. J. & P. K. L. Ng. 1999. *Erebusa calobates*, new genus, new species, a troglobitic crab (Brachyura: Potamidae) from Laos. *Journal of Crustacean Biology* **19**:908–16.

Yildirimhan, H., C. Bursey & S. Goldberg. 2005. Helminth parasites of the Caucasian salamander, *Mertensiella caucasia*, from Turkey. *Comparative Parasitology* **72**:75–87.

Zacharda, M. 2000. New species of the genus *Trogloches* (Acari: Prostigmata: Rhagidiidae) from Oetztal Alps, Tyrol, with a key to the adult species of the genus. *Journal of Natural History* **34**:463–78.

Zapparoli, M. 1984. Notes on cave dwelling Lithobiomorpha from Maghreb, North Africa: Chilopoda. *Fragmenta Entomologica* **17**:181–94.

Zhang, C. 1986. On the ecological adaptation and geographical distribution of the barbine fish *Varicorhinus* (*Scaphestes*) *macrolepis*. *Acta Zoologica Sinica* **32**:266–72.

Zhang, C. G. & Y. H. Zhao. 2001. A new fish of *Sinocyclocheilus* from Guangxi, China with a comment on its some biological adaptation [sic]. *Acta Zootaxonomica Sinica* **26**:102–7.

Zheng, Z.-G. 1839. [Author to supply details; reference cited in Table 1.1.]

Index